Accolades for
"How to Build a Thriving Culture at Work"

"I LOVE THIS BOOK! The authors connect the fields of h-   motion
and organizational development in a manner *'
carefully considered and well researched   ien
mind and prepare to be challenge^   'tle.
Written by two people who have \   )n't
mince words as they leave old p.   .t
important elements of positive ps   ._ational
thinking, their new approach is som   _ field has needed
for a long time. Implement *The 7 .   *. ansformation* and you
will have a better business: an orgai...ation with a better culture and
employees with greater wellbeing."

— **Victor J. Strecher,** PhD, MPH, Professor and Director for Innovation and Social Entrepreneurship,
University of Michigan School of Public Health

"I love this book! It's a must-read in my view. Rosie & Jon's words are
timely, wise and contribute to a superior way of managing population
health. They write, 'Current approaches to employee wellbeing are not
working because: We *(those involved in workplace health promotion)* are
not addressing the aspects of wellbeing that often trump or are the causes
behind the symptoms of poor physical health.' Rosie & Jon shed a bright
light on that truth and many others."

— **Tom Emerick**, Consultant, Writer and Co-Author of trade bestseller "Cracking Health Costs,"
former VP Global Benefit Design, Wal-Mart Stores, Inc.

"A needed wake-up call for business. Ward and Robison don't just
challenge the status quo, they blow it to pieces with hard science and
experience. Leaders who want to transform their workforce into
a 21st-century powerhouse can start here."

— **Wendy D. Lynch**, PhD, Author, "Who Survives? How Benefit Costs Are Killing Your Company"

"Rosie and Jon nailed it when it comes to identifying what's wrong
in today's workplaces and providing the solutions that will allow
organizations to not just survive, but thrive in the future.
The duo is masterful in explaining the differences between the outdated,
ineffective, existing approach to workplace culture and the new, necessary
paradigm. Jon and Rosie back up their innovative ideas with hard facts
and convincing arguments. By organizing their strategy into *The 7 Points
of Transformation*, Jon and Rosie make it easy for individuals to digest
the novel concepts and put them into action. This revolutionary book
has the potential to positively shape the future of
workplace cultures everywhere."

— **Sean Slovenski**, CEO, Care Innovations - an Intel-GE Company

"Rosie Ward and Jon Robison give corporate leaders a great deal of food for thought about what it means to build organizational cultures that will withstand the tests of both time and the marketplace. It's not about workplace wellness, but about the respect for, and wellbeing of, employees. Their guide is a highly useful roadmap for creating a culture of wellbeing."

— **Al Lewis** and **Vik Khanna**, authors of "Surviving Workplace Wellness: With Your Dignity, Finances and Major Organs Intact"

"The number one issue modern executives face is creating a culture in which people can thrive, but the word culture has become a meaningless cliché... We get plenty of diagnoses, what we need is a solution... Ward and Robison show the way. Their insights are accurate; they have done the hard work of looking closely, digesting what they have seen and coming up with executable responses. I am totally impressed."

— **C. Stephen Byrum**, PhD, President and CEO, Byrum Consulting Group

"As the founder and CEO of a 32-year-old firm that has been assisting organizations large and small to transform their workplace, I applaud the data-driven work of Ward and Robison in outlining what must be done. It's not just about employee engagement, but rather designing a culture to provide the right environment for team members to be able to thrive. We've long known that the wellbeing of both employees and the organization are key, but Ward and Robison show us why, and how. Well done!"

— **Gary Kushner**, SPHR, CBP, Kushner & Company

"'How to Build a Thriving Culture at Work' is a book that had to be written. And it's long overdue. For more than 30 years, workplace wellness managers and organizational development gurus have been trying to 'fix' what's wrong with employees under the guise of health and productivity or population health management. It hasn't worked. Ward and Robison lay out the reasons in clear and compelling detail. Even more important, they describe what companies can do to achieve a thriving culture in *The 7 Points of Transformation*. For business leaders who want a sustainable wellbeing model for their organization and their employees, this is your guide."

— **Dean Witherspoon**, President and Founder, Health Enhancement Systems

"Great, great book! If you want your worksite culture to thrive, look no further. You are holding the answer here in your hands."

— **Brian Luke Seaward**, PhD, Executive Director, Paramount Wellness Institute and bestselling Author, "Stand Like Mountain, Flow Like Water"

"The newest generation in the workforce has different expectations about work and their life at work. They require employers to deliver an 'experience' through their operating work culture. They are focused on what the organization can do for their career and the experience of what it's like to be at work. Ward and Robison advise creating work cultures advocating for the wellbeing of employees. This type of organization will resonate strongly with this generation impacting their recruitment, retention and performance. Outdated cultures will not attract the best and brightest talent who we believe organizations are and will be competing for in the future. Organizations embracing *The 7 Points of Transformation* to build a thriving culture and work conditions supporting intrinsic motivation will have success retaining young professionals, as well as reap the rewards of their performance. All of us have always wanted to work in a culture supporting our wellbeing. This generation requires it... or they will move on."

— **Judy Anderson,** Emerging Advantage, Inc.

"'How To Build A Thriving Culture at Work' is a must-read for employers who want to separate the best health promotion strategies from an overwhelming amount of choices, hype and bias. Drs. Ward and Robison's *The 7 Points of Transformation* provide an actionable blueprint for improving the worksite environment."

— **Scott Foster**, President, Wellco

"This book combines everything from quantum physics to chaos theory to frame a completely new strategy for workplace health. This is a practical and inspirational guide to transforming employee wellbeing."

— **Leah Binder,** MA, MGA, President & CEO, The Leapfrog Group

"Company culture will be the business of business — Ward and Robison show you the what, why and how."

— **Josh Levine**, Co-Founder, CultureLabX

"Workplace wellness is rapidly changing from a bio-medical model to an organizational culture model. In reality, the field is returning to one of its important roots — organizational development. What better guides to this much needed approach than Rosie and Jon? These two accomplished wellness veterans have done it — read this book and see the future of worksite wellness."

— **Walter S. Elias**, PhD, President, Elias & Associates, Inc.

"Drs. Robison and Ward present a well-written and groundbreaking narrative that should be mandatory reading for every middle and upper manager who truly wants to make a difference in their organization. They present a compelling case to integrate proven behavior change science into the workplace to create a thriving, positive and healthy environment. After being in this business since the beginning of the whole wellness concept, this approach is refreshing; the key to success and long overdue."

— **Susan W. Butterworth**, PhD, MS, RHC-III, Principal, Q-consult, LLC

"A 21st-century approach to transforming the culture in your organization; this book will rock your world! Trying to teach stress management in an organization where the culture doesn't support employee wellbeing is like trying to repair a broken leg with a band aid, it just won't work. This book will show you how to change the culture first. Ward and Robison challenge old paradigms while suggesting new and better ones to take their place. I highly recommend it."

— **James E. Porter**, President, StressStop.com, and Author of "Stop Stress This Minute"

"Through humorous quotes and a plethora of research wrapped around an analogy of building a house, Rosie and Jon share real-world examples and step-by-step guidance on how to extricate your wellness program from its black hole into the light where it may flourish. This book is packed with thought-provoking opportunities to question the status quo and consider the potential for real, long-lasting transformation. Ignore this book at your peril!"

— **Michaela Conley**, MA, MCHES, CEO, Founder, HPCareer.Net, LLC

"GOOD NEWS for OD practitioners and worksite health promoters alike! Ward and Robison have amassed and made accessible the science that explains what we've long intuited and experienced — that organizational and employee wellbeing are inextricably connected and must be addressed holistically! What's more, they've gifted us a second time with a step-by-step blueprint for how we can work together to create a thriving workplace culture that supports both organizational and individual health. So what do you say? Let's join forces and do this!"

— **Kelly Putnam**, MA, ACC, OD Practitioner, Director - Culture, Change & Engagement, CHE Trinity Health

"Those of us who have been in the corporate health field longer than we would like to admit are delighted to see such industry thought leaders as Drs. Ward and Robison shed light on the science behind human behavior and behavior change. We may not like what we see, and the emperor still doesn't have clothes on, so it's time the field stopped following the next shiny new thing such as incentives from 'street-corner' vendors and examined the solid thinking on intrinsic motivation *(and put the principles to practical use in workplaces)* so fittingly presented in this book. Every health promotion practitioner should be paying attention here."

— **Sandra Wendel**, Health-e headlines, and Co-Author *(with Dr. Edward Creagan of Mayo Clinic),* "How Not to Be My Patient"

"It has been said that the truth is out there, well, Ward and Robison have found it! Prepare to have the foundation shook, the walls buckled and the roof torn off of your traditional employee wellness model. This is the first book that explores the 'truth' about worksite wellness, and offers a transforming blueprint for establishing and building a culture of wellbeing that your employees will call home."

— **Dennis Martell**, PhD, Director of Health Promotion, Michigan State University and Co-Author of the award-winning book "Effective Health Risk Messages"

"It was a pleasure reading this book. I agree completely with the philosophy, and hope companies start to shift towards this model. Understanding the value of the employee experience is key to moving organizations forward. In the 21st century, employees will flourish with autonomy and empowerment. *The 7 Points of Transformation* are the tools available for companies to make this change."

— Judith Kolish, RD, LDN, CDE, Health Care Service Corporation dba BCBS of IL, TX, OK, NM, MT

"Finally, a book that provides 'the elixir of life' for traditional wellness programs! Ward and Robison provide an intriguing and thought provoking work that is perfectly timed. This is a must-read for Human Resources professionals, CEOs and all organizational leaders. With *The 7 Points of Transformation*, they have captured the essence of where traditional wellness strategies become ineffective, and have pioneered a new way of thinking about wellbeing, that will transform and position organizations for the future."

— Bernadette Harrow, MPA, HR Management Consultant, Albony LLC

"A definitive book tackling a timely issue recently raised only in many other forms of media to date. 'How to Build a Thriving Culture at Work' asks the right questions, and provides reasoned and supported answers and suggestions that should motivate most current paradigm professionals to take action to progress workplace health/wellness promotion into a new era of development and transformation."

— Bob Boyd, OAM FACHPER LMQFHA S&LCNWI, MEnvn & ComH BHMS DipPE CWP CWPD, Director Wellness Communication Solutions and Wellness Constructs, President National Wellness Institute of Australia

"Ward and Robison have the audacity to point out what the research keeps telling us: worksite wellness in its traditional form is not working. We're not reaching enough people, we're implementing programs that produce short-term results and we're resorting to coercive measures operating under the delusion that we can 'get' people to change. Ward and Robison persuasively argue that our current paradigm is out of date and in need of a reboot. We can do better. In seven concrete steps, this book lays out a plan for building a thriving culture to foster individual wellbeing. For those who are frustrated with a business-as-usual approach to wellness, this book is a must-read."

— Laura Putnam, CEO, Motion Infusion

"From pedometers to purpose! From body fat measurement to meaning! Ward and Robison offer a revolutionary approach to individual and organizational wellbeing. This is a paradigm-shifting book that challenges the status quo and offers a refreshingly new approach to organizational health and employee wellness. The information in this book is grounded in the most up-to-date science and it provides valuable insight on what it truly takes to build an organizational culture where employees can thrive."

— Carrie Phelps, PhD, Co-Founder, Intrinsic Connection LLC, Adjunct Professor, Saybrook University School of Mind-Body Medicine

"'How to Build a Thriving Culture at Work' is an essential book for anyone interested in workplace wellbeing. Ward and Robison provide a devastating critique of outdated, traditional paradigms of health and wellness which covers extensive and fascinating scientific territory. They then provide an evidence-based, humane and ethical *The 7 Points of Transformation* plan for an entirely different approach to creating a workplace that is based on the values and principles of modern health promotion. This approach truly values employees and their integral role in enhancing organizational wellbeing."

— **Lily O'Hara**, PhD, MPH, PGD Hlth Prom, Life Member of the Australian Health Promotion Association, Health Promotion Academic and Practitioner, Assistant Professor Health and Physical Education, Emirates College for Advanced Education, Abu Dhabi, United Arab Emirates

"Ward and Robison hit a home run with this important new direction for corporate wellbeing endeavors! Their approach challenges traditional wellness and leverages deeper organizational effectiveness issues that make health matter. Without this insight, employers will miss tremendous opportunities to maximize their investments in wellbeing."

— **Brent Hartman,** MPH, MCHES, Health Risk Management Practice Leader, IMA, Inc.

"I had an 'aha!' moment reading this book. Ward and Robison make the fuzzy concept of 'healthy work culture' crystal clear, and give you specific, science-based steps to take. Anyone who wants a truly great work environment will find this a terrific guide."

— **Linda K. Riddell**, MS, Population Health Scientist, Health Economy, LLC

"Dr. Robison has been a trusted advisor and mentor for the past four years as we designed and implemented our wellbeing program. Based on my experience with Dr. Robison, it's no surprise that he and Dr. Ward have written an outstanding book that gives you the foundation to understand organizational wellbeing AND individual wellbeing in terms of where we are, where we can go and how to get to a thriving culture. We learn how typical wellness programs look at employees as a liability, rather than an asset to be respected, nurtured and inspired, and as critical to the healthy development of culture and the success of the company. Let's put an end to the coercion game and all thrive together!"

— **Human Resources Manager,** International Law Firm

"Using systematic analysis of available evidence, interspersed with compelling workplace scenarios to which we all can relate, Ward and Robison deconstruct the status quo of worksite wellness and workplace culture. They reveal common misconceptions and obfuscations. Most importantly, with *The 7 Points of Transformation*, they provide an accessible and well-tested solution for employers seeking to fulfill the potential of their organization and the people in it."

— **Bob Merberg,** The Employee Wellness Network

How to Build a
Thriving Culture at Work

Featuring
The 7 Points of Transformation

Rosie Ward & Jon Robison

How to Build a Thriving Culture at Work,
Featuring The 7 Points of Transformation

Rosie Ward, PhD, MPH, MCHES, BCC
Jon Robison, PhD, MS, MA

Publisher & Exclusive Distributor:
IHAC, Inc.
5937 West Main Street
Kalamazoo, MI 49009
269-343-0770

SalveoPartners.com

First published by IHAC, Inc.
ISBN: 978-0-9903011-0-3

Printed in the United States of America
Chelsea, MI
This book is printed on acid-free paper.

FREE Video Series

Your purchase of this book entitles you to
exclusive access to
The 7 Points of Transformation **Video Series**

These fast-paced videos, featuring Dr. Rosie Ward,
will give you an overview of each of
The 7 Points of Transformation required to build
a thriving culture at your workplace!

To access your FREE video series,
log onto: **salveopartners.com/videos**
Enter access code: **7POT**
Please enjoy with our compliments!

Contents

Introduction

et's face it: Our world is a fundamentally different place than it was just a few short years ago. With economic instability, global competition, increased demand for doing more with fewer resources, technology connecting people 24/7 and exponentially rising healthcare costs, businesses face more challenges than ever before. How organizations go about attracting and retaining great employees and energizing and engaging those employees to give their best at work is increasingly critical for survival in today's competitive marketplace. Many of the tried-and-true principles for how to build a thriving culture at work are still applicable today. However, there are gaping holes keeping organizations from achieving sustainable results, holes filled with ineffective approaches arising from outdated paradigms grounded in faulty beliefs rather than solid scientific evidence. Einstein is widely credited with defining insanity as "doing the same thing over and over and expecting a different result." It's time to reverse this insanity and create a process to build thriving workplace cultures that free, fuel and inspire people to bring their best selves to work.

This book does just that by taking a close look at organizational and employee wellbeing: what they are and what they are not, why traditional approaches to promoting them are less effective than we would like and what can be done to help improve them. We will separate fact from fiction, rhetoric from reality and provide a step-by-step blueprint for transforming workplaces into world-class cultures in which both individuals and organizations will thrive.

Although the wellbeing of organizations and the wellbeing of individual employees may seem like distinct entities, a growing body of research supports strong connections between the two. For example, in 2010, Gallup's Tom Rath and Jim Harter published their research findings from 150 countries in "Wellbeing: The Five Essential Elements." They found that the five universal elements of wellbeing *(career, social, financial, physical and community)* are not independent of one another; they are very much interdependent, with the career element playing the largest role in shaping employee wellbeing.[1]

In 2012, the Towers Watson Global Workforce Study found that focusing on employee engagement alone is no longer enough to create exceptional organizational wellbeing; high-performing organizations also need to enable and energize their employees by including support for their social, emotional and physical wellbeing.[2] Even the government is putting forth effort to address these critical interrelationships. The Centers for Disease Control and Prevention *(CDC)* and the National Institute for Occupational Safety and Health *(NIOSH)* recently partnered to develop Total Worker Health,™ which attempts to integrate occupational safety and health protection with health promotion to prevent worker injury and illness and to advance health and wellbeing.[3]

While the research clearly demonstrates the critical link between organizational and employee wellbeing, translating the research into practice continues to be a challenge. The process is hampered by a *stuckness* to long-held beliefs rooted in the aforementioned outdated paradigms. We refer to this dynamic as the clash of *Belief vs. Evidence*. This clash has emerged innumerable times throughout history in all walks of life *(to be explored in more depth in the first chapter)*. In fact, most profound learning transformations and scientific breakthroughs have been preceded by this clash. Like those who have gone before, we find ourselves at a crossroads; we must focus on the evidence and be willing to let go of these outdated beliefs to thrive and remain competitive.

Read this book if you:

- Want your organization to be the place talented and passionate people not only want to work, but are practically tearing down your doors to get into.

- Feel that the authoritative management style at your organization may be creating much of the stress that is making employees sick and disengaged.

- Wish there was a way to develop tomorrow's leaders today and to give them the tools and experience they need to be successful tomorrow.

- Believe your organization will thrive if people on the front lines can be free to use their creativity to solve the most vexing problems on their own initiative.

- Hope that your workplace could become an environment that promotes health in mind, body and spirit for all employees.

- Are concerned that wellness programs have evolved into coercive, incentive-laden clinical activities that treat employees as if they are children or lab rats.

- Think that the most healthy and sustainable growth for both organizations and employees happens from the inside out, not from the outside in.

First, the Bad News

The news about many workplace cultures is not so good. Unfortunately, efforts over the last three or four decades to improve organizational and employee wellbeing have been largely unsuccessful and, in many cases, have actually made things worse. So, we are dedicating the first six chapters of this book to exploring in detail what's wrong with current approaches. We do this because so many employees and employers alike tell us that they sense something is wrong, that the way healthy organizational cultures and healthy employees are being promoted seems shallow and "off" in some way. But most people can't seem to put their finger on what the exact problems are. We want to help you do that as a starting point for transitioning to a new way of thinking and doing — by getting *unstuck*.

The *Stuckness*: Organizational Wellbeing

For organizational wellbeing moving past the *stuckness* means challenging the paradigm of "old-school business" and redirecting the focus to the quality of the employee experience. Despite overwhelming evidence of a powerful link between effective leadership styles, positive work cultures and higher levels of organizational performance, many companies still operate with a top down, authoritarian management style, do not measure or intentionally create their desired culture, and do not effectively develop current and future leaders to maximize employee engagement and wellbeing. Too often, companies that do incorporate employee engagement surveys don't effectively do anything with the results to improve the employee experience — or at least don't do what truly makes a difference. Even organizations with an ostensibly flat organizational chart tend to be more paternalistic and authoritarian than they'll often admit. Leaders, managers and HR teams create strategies and plans for the organization and then feed them to employees who are supposed to execute them — often without any creative contribution or buy in at all. The result is widespread employee disengagement that costs U.S. businesses hundreds of billions of dollars each year.

Current approaches to organizational wellbeing are not working because:

- Employee engagement has not improved much over the past 10 years, even with increased lip service to and focus on it.

- Culture is the differentiating factor between high-performing and low-performing companies; however, most companies have not identified, articulated, measured or intentionally created their desired culture.

- Most organizations do not have a comprehensive, long-term leadership and employee development strategy. Instead, they deploy an array of training programs that do not have a clear strategy pulling everything together towards creating the desired culture.

- The majority of executive leadership teams are not operating in a truly cohesive manner, and many leaders themselves are at a point of burnout.

- What most organizations are doing to try to enhance and support employee wellbeing may actually be threatening to erode engagement and organizational wellbeing.

- Leaders and employees are being asked to do things differently but are not provided the development required for sustainable change. Changing the way we do things can only be accomplished by first developing better thinking patterns — something often bypassed in our quick-fix society.

The *Stuckness*: Employee Wellbeing

For employee wellbeing, eliminating the *stuckness* means challenging the 400-year-old outdated, biomedical, control-oriented scientific world-view that has spawned our present focus on traditional biomedical risk factors — particularly for cardiovascular disease. We measure these risk factors, quantify them and then shuttle people into workplace programs where extrinsic motivators *(carrots and sticks)* are employed to try to "get" employees to change their behaviors. The myopic focus on biomedical risk factors obscures the critical importance of workplace culture and context that only a truly holistic approach to health and wellbeing can bring. The lack of efficacy of this approach in terms of sustained change has been well documented over the past two or three decades, and yet we persist. But the bubble is about to burst. Results from The Energy Audit show that 74% of employees are experiencing a personal energy crisis.[4] They're increasingly exhausted, overwhelmed and disengaged — which is not a sustainable way of working for individuals or for organizations. As a result, many employees resist or ignore traditional wellness initiatives because they are already stressed and stretched to the breaking point and don't want to add one more thing to an already overloaded plate.

Current approaches to employee wellbeing are not working because:

- We are not addressing the aspects of wellbeing that often trump or are the causes behind the symptoms of poor physical health.

- We are stigmatizing, penalizing and ostracizing those among us who can least afford it instead of providing them with realistic, available and compassionate alternatives for healthful living.

- Vendors, consultants and business leaders often promise more than they can deliver and make claims that cannot be supported by their data or, in many cases, are not even mathematically possible.

- The measurements being used to see if workplace wellness programs are effective would be laughable if the situation were not so sad and critical.

- Many recommendations made by wellness vendors, brokers and consultants do not conform to and often directly contradict those recommended by health authorities.

- So much time, money and energy is being wasted on irrational and ineffective programs when infinitely superior strategies are readily available.

For businesses to thrive — and perhaps even survive — we simply must find a more efficient, effective and holistic way to address organizational and employee wellbeing. Based on what we know from the research on employee satisfaction, employee engagement and organizational commitment, it is highly likely that most of us can recall a time when we worked for a dysfunctional organization and/or the "boss from hell." If you have had the painful misfortune of experiencing this, chances are it caused you to be stressed out, not engaged and not producing the level and quality of work you know you're capable of doing. In addition, you likely found yourself dealing with health issues or less-than-healthful habits as your brain and body found ways to cope with your ongoing stress. Now imagine this being the experience of so many employees at the same time that their organization is attempting to deploy change strategies, and safety and wellness programs. How effective do you think any change initiative or program will be in this environment? If you guessed pretty minimal, you'd most likely be correct.

The Truth about "Healthy Work Culture"

In the business and Organizational Development *(OD)* world, Edgar Schein, PhD, is the guru and leading researcher on corporate culture. He describes culture as "the hidden force that drives most of our behavior both inside and outside organizations."[5] It goes beyond "it's the way we do things around here," the company climate and basic values. These are all manifestations of the culture. It's like looking at a river. All of the things you see on the surface, from the flow of the water to the shape of the riverbed, are manifestations of an ever-changing, powerful current beneath the surface. In terms of culture, the current that ultimately guides the strength and direction of the organization includes the unconscious, taken-for-granted beliefs, perceptions, thoughts and feelings of employees. The interaction between leaders and culture is profound and critical when considering how to transform or evolve the overall culture and subcultures within an organization.

In his seminal work, "The Advantage," world-renowned organizational consultant Patrick Lencioni writes that, to be successful, an organization must focus on two basic qualities: It must be smart, and it must be healthy. According to Lencioni, a "smart organization" is one that excels in the classic fundamentals of business — i.e., strategy, operations, finance, marketing and technology. A "healthy organization" is one in which there are minimal politics, minimal confusion, high morale, high productivity and low turnover. While being smart is only half of the equation, for most organizations, it occupies almost all of the time, energy and attention of leaders. Yet, according to Lencioni:

> *Once organizational health is properly understood and*
> *placed into the right context it will surpass all other disciplines*
> *in business as the greatest opportunity for improvement and*
> *competitive advantage. Really.*[6]

Unfortunately, in the traditional world of employee or workplace wellness, a "culture of health" or a "healthy culture" has an entirely different and considerably narrower meaning, primarily referring to the climate, or what Schein would describe as the manifestations of the culture. When most health and wellness professionals describe a "culture of health," "culture of wellness" or "healthy culture," they are referring to policies, procedures, communication practices, programs, rewards and leadership behaviors that support so-called healthy lifestyle choices and healthy behaviors. Consequently, they conceptualize a healthy organization or a healthy culture primarily as a place where employees can take an aerobics class, obtain a pedometer, get money towards a gym membership, have access to fruits and vegetables in the cafeteria and perhaps take a stress management class. Although these opportunities may provide some positive health benefits, they do not address the underlying *(nor the most important)* aspects of individual wellbeing. From an organizational perspective, the potential benefits to the company from such initiatives pale in comparison to the benefits of creating an environment where politics and confusion are minimal, relationships and open communication are cherished and employees are intrinsically motivated to come to the workplace and be involved in something larger than themselves, something that contributes meaning and purpose to their lives. Clearly, from this perspective, an organization can have a "culture of health/wellness" but still be completely dysfunctional in terms of organizational health in Lencioni's terms. Unfortunately for many workplaces, this is the consistent and unpleasant reality.

Our conceptualization of Thriving Organizational Wellbeing builds on Lencioni's definition of Organizational Health. We define Thriving Organizational Wellbeing as the term used for an organization where:

- The executive leadership team is truly a cohesive one.

- The mission, vision and values are clearly articulated, and every employee knows how he/she fits within them.

- Employees are empowered and enabled to leverage their strengths.

- Leaders and the work climate provide employees with autonomous support *(versus using incentives to drive behaviors)*.

- Clear, timely and meaningful communication is provided for employees, and employees share ideas and feedback that is actually used.

- Clear, timely and meaningful feedback is provided for employees in the spirit of ongoing growth and development *(versus simply measuring performance)*.

- The climate fosters innovation, creativity and meaningful work.

- Leaders truly value employees — and employees feel valued.

- Employees are encouraged and supported to be authentic and be themselves.

- People within the organization respect, support and care about one another as people, not just as employees there to complete certain job tasks.

- Accountability is embraced; the rules are clear and apply to everyone.
- Employees are provided the tools and resources they need to work safely and productively.
- Resources, programs, policies and the environment support employees' ability to thrive in all areas of wellbeing.
- Employees are happy and proud to work there!

"Wellness" and "Wellbeing"

You may already have noticed that we use the term "wellbeing" rather than "wellness." This is intentional. For us, wellness has become synonymous with a narrow, biomedical view primarily focused on physical health. Although earlier models of wellness were broader to include the importance of occupational, financial, emotional and spiritual health, the focus of employee wellness programs has become narrower and narrower. Consequently, "wellness" is more often than not associated with healthy lifestyle behaviors mostly related to physical health. When wellness is deployed at workplaces *(i.e., Worksite Wellness)*, it is frequently done in a manner that ignores the importance and influence of other aspects of wellbeing *(especially career wellbeing)*. When referring to the health of individual employees, we will therefore use the term "employee wellbeing," which includes the career, social, financial, community, emotional and spiritual aspects of health as well as the traditional physical aspects. Further, we will emphasize a truly holistic approach to individual wellbeing that acknowledges the numerous inextricable and complex interactions among all of these aspects. When discussing the health of organizations, we will employ the term "organizational wellbeing" and will be using Lencioni's description of a healthy organization *(minimal politics, minimal confusion, high morale, high productivity and low turnover)* as the foundation on which to build.

The *Stuckness*: "Getting" People to Change

The mantra of wellness, and particularly wellness at the workplace, has been and continues to be using extrinsic motivation *(incentives, contests, competitions, etc.)* to "get" people to change their health-related behaviors. And make no mistake about the intention, as one leader describes the reality: "Let's face it... incentives are about getting people to do things they would otherwise not do."[7] The continued reliance on controlling and coercive behavior modification techniques developed decades ago *(based on research done mostly on rats and mice)* is a pervasive *stuckness* that seriously handicaps our ability to really help the people who we serve. The effectiveness of carrots and sticks in producing long-term behavior change has been thoroughly refuted by the literature over the past 30 years, yet it continues to dominate as the modus operandi of our change efforts. The current proliferation of coercive, incentive-laden wellness programs at the workplace promoted by the wellness provisions in the Affordable Care Act has only served to intensify this *stuckness*. Ironically, this is true in spite of the fact that the claimed savings by Safeway, on which these programs are fashioned, were completely made up[8] *(we describe this in more detail in chapter 13).* In addition to decades of overwhelming research, recent discoveries in neuroscience have even elucidated some of the potential brain mechanisms that contribute to the inevitable failure of these types of approaches. Unfortunately, many health and business professionals are not aware of these scientific advances or choose to ignore the evidence in favor of hanging on to pre-existing beliefs.

Current approaches to behavior change are not working because:

- The strategies have not changed in the last 30 years, even though the evidence shows the strategies are ineffective at best and harmful at worst.

- Penalizing, prodding, coercing and preaching to people about what is wrong with them is not only ineffectual, it is unethical.

- Using incentives and punishments to "get" people to change is completely unsupported by the literature. Try it on your family, and see how well it works.[9]

- Focusing on behaviors in the first place is the wrong approach; behaviors are the outward observable actions of what is happening on the inside in terms of emotions and thinking. Sustainable change results from developing more effective thinking.[10]

- Workplace efforts to pay people to be healthy often end up penalizing the people who can least afford it.[11]

- Hundreds and hundreds of studies clearly demonstrate that intrinsic motivation is the best, and for most people the only, way to promote positive, sustainable change.

- Extrinsic motivation tends to diminish creativity, encourage cheating and lying, and reduce intrinsic motivation.

Updating the Science *(Belief vs. Evidence)*

It takes considerable time and effort to become a truly healthy organization; to have thriving organizational and employee wellbeing. Unfortunately, in a world that values immediate gratification and quick fixes, we continue to try to take shortcuts and implement cookie-cutter, one-size-fits-all approaches with, at best, mediocre results. In chapter 1 we discuss the age-old clash of *Belief vs. Evidence* and the power of paradigms that shape and often paralyze scientific progress. In fact, much of the bad news of the first six chapters has to do with a *stuckness* to outdated scientific understandings of the universe in which we live. We discuss the roots of these outdated understandings in chapter 2.

In the past hundred years, new and often startling scientific discoveries from quantum physics, psychoneuroimmunology, chaos theory and neuroscience have dramatically altered our understanding of the universe as well as our understanding of human health and illness, and the process of behavior change. Unfortunately, many of these important scientific findings have not trickled down to health and business professionals, significantly limiting the effectiveness of our workplace, community and clinical initiatives to help organizations and people thrive. In chapter 3, we summarize the important findings from quantum physics and chaos theory, which we will refer to throughout the book as we develop the blueprint for creating organizational and employee wellbeing. We share the powerful implications of psychoneuroimmunology for our understanding of human health and disease in chapter 5 and show how recent, remarkable findings in neuroscience update our understandings about organizational leadership and motivation in chapter 6.

We realize that devoting considerable time and energy to discussing the scientific foundations is highly unusual for a book on organizational and employee wellbeing, and some people will likely say, "WHY do we need to read about this stuff? Can't you just get to WHAT we need to do?" The truth is, you could perhaps skip the science stuff and go right to the "HOW to" chapters. But, because in this book we are asking business and health professionals to think about changing the way they do things — in some cases quite dramatically — we firmly believe understanding the science behind the "WHAT and HOW" is ultimately critical for successfully transforming organizational and employee wellbeing. In fact, as we explore in more detail, asking or telling people to do things differently without first involving them in the knowledge and process so they can think differently is currently a major stumbling block for traditional approaches to change for organizations and employees alike. So, in the interest of walking our talk, rather than just telling you HOW to make the changes we are suggesting, we want to explain the rationale and science behind what we are proposing by briefly addressing the following three questions:

1) What are the old scientific assumptions and why are they limited in their ability to create lasting growth and change?

2) What are the newer scientific advances that inform the proposals we are making?

3) How do these newer scientific understandings support changing the way we traditionally approach organizational and employee wellbeing?

Every profession and every organization evolves over time and reaches a point where it must transform if it is to survive. This often means having the courage to take a step back and look at the paradigms and the evidence *(or lack thereof)* that have been guiding us, and to embrace emerging paradigms, science and evidence. We recognize setting aside what is familiar isn't comfortable — even if it isn't working as well as we might like. However, for real growth and progress to happen, it is often necessary. This is the reason we spend the first six chapters examining WHY and HOW we have become *stuck* in outdated ways of thinking and doing. Our goal is to set the stage for the good news: introducing a simple yet powerful blueprint for achieving better and more sustainable results.

Now for the Good News — Really Great News!

The remaining chapters of this book contain the good news, and there is a ton of it! *The 7 Points of Transformation* will encourage you to leave behind the outdated, ineffective approaches of the last few decades and provide you with a step-by-step blueprint for improving organizational and employee wellbeing and creating a thriving culture at work. Based on a balanced fusion of the most up-to-date science, common sense and human compassion, this blueprint will help you to transform your workplace culture so both employees and the organization will thrive. Whether you consider your workplace a truly toxic environment or a good place to work that could be better, there is a starting point for you here.

The 7 Points of Transformation

We liken building a thriving culture at work that supports and enhances both organizational and employee wellbeing to building a structurally sound and aesthetically pleasing house. If you take shortcuts, skip an important step or use outdated designs or materials, the house will not withstand the test of time — including weathering the inevitable, future storms. The same holds true for organizational and employee wellbeing. We have found that when companies take shortcuts, skip important steps and base their efforts on outdated paradigms, it's like building a house on quicksand; it is not sustainable and can have dire consequences. Our step-by-step blueprint for building a thriving workplace culture avoids these pitfalls. We call it *The 7 Points of Transformation.*

- ### *Transformation Point #1: Survey the Land*
  (Data Collection and Analysis)

  As Randy Jackson said most every week on American Idol, "I'm just keepin' it real, dawg." You have to have a reality check and know what you're dealing with before you can build and deploy any strategy. In other words, you have to know about the current state of your organization and the employee experience. To accomplish that, you absolutely need to look holistically at data you likely already have as well as fill in any gaps by collecting additional data you may need to help determine your current, baseline state of wellbeing. In this chapter, we will discuss in detail:

  — What existing organizational and employee wellbeing data should be reviewed.

  — The frequency at which various data should be reviewed.

  — Additional data that may need to be collected to fill in any gaps *(and considerations to make data collection successful).*

  — How to look at the data holistically to reveal key themes and trends that will provide clues to the current state of organizational and employee wellbeing.

- ### *Transformation Point #2: Create the Blueprint*
  (Strategic and Annual Planning)

  Once you have used the data to provide feedback about the current state of wellbeing in your company, you can begin creating a thriving workplace culture. The journey begins intentionally with a vision for where you're going *(i.e., your desired culture)*. If you don't know where you're going, then starting off in any direction will do; and if you aren't clear about what you're building to get you where you want to go, the house will likely not withstand the inevitable upcoming storms. Planning needs to be approached methodically and holistically to develop and align core values and the vision for the desired culture. At this point you need to be clear about what metrics will be meaningful to evaluate how you're doing in transforming your workplace culture and to tell your wellbeing story *(to current and future employees)*. In this chapter we will discuss in detail:

— Who should be involved in the planning process.

— What questions should guide the planning process.

— How to develop effective and meaningful goals for the next 12 months based on the core values and desired culture.

— What metrics to use in each of the six areas of wellbeing to track and tell your evolving wellbeing story.

• *Transformation Point #3: Pour a Solid Foundation*
(Develop Quality Leaders)

Culture is built team-by-team, and every interaction employees have with leaders reinforces their beliefs and feelings about the culture. This is often the first place where you see cracks in your infrastructure. People quit their bosses more than they quit their company; therefore, having quality leaders is essential. Transforming your workplace culture demands leaders who can effectively navigate through adaptive challenges *(complex challenges that can't be solved using existing thinking or approaches)*. Successful 21st-century organizations radically alter how they develop leaders to effectively manage change — particularly adaptive change. Long-term sustainability requires investing in developing effective thinking patterns for leaders; ensuring the executive team is cohesive; that they take time to work *on* the business, not just in the business; and that accountability is embraced across all levels within the organization. In this chapter, we will provide a four-step framework for effective and sustainable leadership development:

— *Step One:* **Enhance Self-Awareness.** We describe the importance of self-awareness in leading adaptive change and how to facilitate the self-discovery process.

— *Step Two:* **Build Effective Thinking Skills.** We describe the importance of leaders' state of mind and quality of thinking and how to develop better thinking to lead people.

— *Step Three:* **Develop and Foster Quality Relationships so Others Can Grow.** We illustrate the importance of regarding people differently and becoming a *servant leader*.

— *Step Four:* **Grow the Organization.** We illustrate the power of leaders supporting employees in clarifying their purpose and how to leverage purpose to grow the company.

- *Transformation Point #4: Frame the House*
  (Create a Supportive Climate)

Once you have poured the foundation by effectively developing quality leaders, it's time to frame the house and create a supportive climate. Creating a supportive climate means every aspect of the business fosters living the core values and desired culture on a daily basis, which depends on communicating effectively. Communication will make or break any human interaction and is often a breakdown point for organizations. Communicating is a two-way street that requires disseminating clear, relevant information but also listening and incorporating feedback. The right approach to communication will help create the framework for organizational wellbeing and ensure that employees feel supported in their individual wellbeing. Additionally, the physical environment and policies need to align with communication and intentionally create the desired culture. When done properly, wellbeing can be positioned and leveraged to help create a thriving workplace culture that will make you an employer of choice. In this chapter we will discuss in detail:

- How to effectively position wellbeing as part of the culture and the employee experience.

- How to develop and deploy a comprehensive communication strategy that supports the desired culture.

- How to create and maintain an effective Culture and Wellbeing Team and a network of Culture and Wellbeing Ambassadors.

- Creating a climate that supports personal and professional development.

- How to embed wellbeing into the daily employee experience.

- *Transformation Point #5: Wire the House*
  (Rethink Change)

"How can I get my employees to work harder, be safer, participate, be healthier, be more innovative, etc.?" These are the wrong questions for organizations to ask. The correct question is "How can we *create the conditions* within which people can find the motivation to _____?" Creating these conditions requires thinking differently about people and change. The good news is you can accomplish this, and if you've been reliant on extrinsic motivation, you can effectively "correct" for incentives to support greater autonomy and improved intrinsic motivation. In this chapter, we will discuss in detail:

— Newer models and theories of change that better support the complexities of organizations and individuals.

— How to build upon the first four *Points of Transformation* to *create the conditions* within which employees feel autonomously supported *(versus controlled)*.

— Tips and resources that support people in getting off autopilot, becoming more self-aware and building more effective thinking.

— How to redesign existing incentive-laden wellness programs to "correct" for incentives.

• *Transformation Point #6: Decorate the House*
(Deploy QUALITY, Evidence-Based Programs and Resources)

Too often organizations start at this point, skipping or skimping on the first five *Points of Transformation*. They want to start "doing stuff." Not only can this be a significant waste of time and resources, it frequently backfires. No two organizations are exactly alike, just like no two humans are exactly alike. Just because another company deployed a program or resource that worked doesn't mean it will work for your organization. Whatever programs and resources you deploy to support all areas of wellbeing need to meet the unique needs of your organization and employees; be well-rounded in supporting total wellbeing; be effective, inclusive and supportive of positive human relationships, and be evidence-based. In this chapter we will discuss in detail:

— What to look for to know if programs and resources are quality and evidence-based *(and the red flags for what to avoid)*.

— Suggested programs and resources that support each area of wellbeing.

— How to move beyond 4P wellness programs *(pry, poke, prod and punish)* to effective, evidence-based approaches to support employee wellbeing and positively impact healthcare costs.

— How to ensure whatever programs and resources are offered have a lasting impact.

- ***Transformation Point #7: Maintain the House***
  (Continuous Quality Improvement)

  Quality, timely evaluation is a critical yet often overlooked step. If you don't know what you're trying to accomplish, what story you want to tell and what data you're going to use to guide your efforts, it becomes difficult to evaluate. Both culture and wellbeing can be difficult to measure; they are moving targets because the world and life are ever-changing. It is critical to be able to articulate where you've been, where you are currently and where you're going with organizational and employee wellbeing. Approaching wellbeing in a manner similar to Continuous Quality Improvement helps to guide efforts and provide course corrections over time to most effectively meet a moving target. In this chapter, we will discuss in detail:

  — How to create a Wellbeing Dashboard to show overall trends and support telling your ongoing wellbeing story.

  — How to communicate the state of wellbeing at your organization to employees, shareholders and customers.

  — How to effectively tweak your wellbeing strategy based on ongoing evaluation.

Returning to the concept that "Insanity is doing the same thing over and over expecting different results," we cannot keep doing what we have been doing in the name of organizational and employee wellbeing. Enough already — it's not working! We need to challenge the status quo and outdated paradigms not just to thrive, but perhaps even survive in our rapidly changing world. We have seen *The 7 Points of Transformation* in action and the difference this methodical, holistic approach makes for the organization as a whole and for the individual employee experience. We know that change is difficult and recognize that this is a dramatic paradigm shift for many people, but we believe it is needed to make a real difference. So let's start on the journey toward doing things better and creating a workplace that frees, fuels and inspires people to bring their best selves to work each and every day.

SECTION
ONE
Flawed Foundations

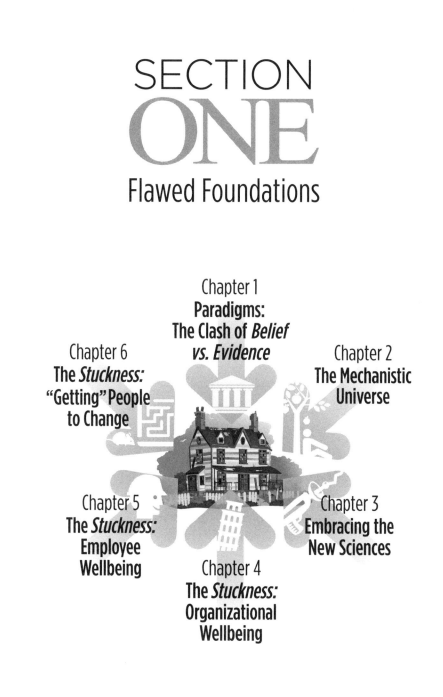

Chapter 1
**Paradigms:
The Clash of *Belief*
*vs. Evidence***

Chapter 6
**The *Stuckness:*
"Getting" People
to Change**

Chapter 2
**The Mechanistic
Universe**

Chapter 5
**The *Stuckness:*
Employee
Wellbeing**

Chapter 3
**Embracing the
New Sciences**

Chapter 4
**The *Stuckness:*
Organizational
Wellbeing**

CHAPTER I

Paradigms: The Clash of *Belief vs. Evidence*

> 66 *The proponents of competing paradigms...*
> *see different things when they look from the same point*
> *in the same direction... what cannot even be demonstrated*
> *to one group of scientists may seem*
> *intuitively obvious to another.*[1] 99

Thomas Kuhn, "The Structure of Scientific Revolutions"

You are riding home from work on the train on a still, hot August afternoon.[2] The air conditioning is broken, and the train is very full. People are crowded against one another and everyone is sweaty, sullen and cranky. To make matters worse, two young children are crying loudly, pushing and shoving each other, and bumping into people in an attempt to hang on to a man who appears to be their dad. This man, who happens to be standing next to you, is looking down at the floor and making absolutely no effort to control his children. The hotter it gets, the angrier you get. Doesn't he see what is going on? Why can't he control his children? Doesn't he realize they are annoying people in what is already an intolerable situation? Finally, you are able to contain yourself no longer. You turn to the man and say:

"Isn't there something you can do about your children?
They seem to be out of control."

After a brief pause, he looks up at you with sad, tear-filled eyes and says in a quiet voice:

"I'm sorry, you are right — it's just that we are returning from
the hospital where their mother just died unexpectedly."

Take just a minute to explore what you are feeling. What do you think would happen to your original beliefs about the situation? What would happen to your anger and rage? As a result of the newly acquired evidence, your feelings would most likely turn to sadness and remorse, perhaps even shame, and your initial assessment of the situation would change dramatically. You might even turn to the man in the next instant and say something like: "I am so sorry. Is there anything I can do to help?" What you have experienced in this encounter is a "paradigm shift." Although this may seem like a dramatic example, most of us have at one time or another experienced this kind of profound shift in thinking and feeling.

The Power of Paradigms

In our introduction, we have referred a number of times to a *stuckness* that is hampering our efforts to improve the wellbeing of employees and organizations. This *stuckness* occurs when we are so convinced that our beliefs are correct that we ignore the mounting evidence suggesting they are not. So, rather than shift our paradigm as we were able to do in the example above, we experience a *stuckness*, or what Joel Barker, in his seminal work, "Discovering the Future: The Business of Paradigms," refers to as "paradigm paralysis."[3]

A paradigm is a model or frame of reference from which we determine how we feel about and interact with our surroundings. Think of it as a set of rules and regulations that **1)** defines boundaries; and **2)** tells you what to do to succeed within those boundaries. Our overarching personal paradigm results from the total sum of our life experiences. It is, most simply, the way we look at the world, or as the late Willis Harmon, former president of the Institute of Noetic Sciences put it, "the basic way of perceiving, thinking, valuing and doing *(our beliefs)* associated with a particular vision of reality."[4] Each of us actually has "layers" of these "ways of perceiving, thinking, valuing and doing" that help create our particular vision of reality. Thus, our personal vision of reality is likely to be influenced concurrently by a human paradigm, a Western civilization paradigm, an American paradigm, a particular religious paradigm, a community paradigm, an age-specific paradigm and so on. As we have just experienced with the train story, our personal paradigms do not describe reality as it is, but merely create a picture or representation of reality as we have learned to see it.

What is most critical to understand about the role paradigms play in our lives is that they act as powerful filters of information. In essence, our paradigms actually determine what we perceive and what we believe. Something that may be perfectly obvious to a person with one paradigm may be completely invisible to a person with a different paradigm. Barker refers to this striking power of different paradigms to create different realities for different people as "the paradigm effect."[5] Here are three major characteristics of paradigms as summarized from his work:

*1) **Paradigms are common*** — They exert their powerful influences in all areas of life, from science, to politics, to organizations, to social customs, etc. In all these areas, paradigms set up rules and regulations that guide behavior and set standards for the "rules of the game."

*2) **Paradigms are functional*** — Paradigms are, in fact, necessary to help us to live in a highly complex world. They help us to continually determine what information is important and what is not and, in doing so, prevent information overload.

*3) **Paradigms too strongly held lead to "paradigm paralysis"*** — Blindly holding on to outdated paradigm thinking inhibits innovation and seriously threatens the ability to adapt to change. Barker also refers to this serious, chronic condition as "hardening of the categories."

This last point is extremely important, and it holds true for all fields of endeavor. There are countless examples in technology, business, science and culture in which individuals, businesses and institutions have paid dearly for their "paradigm paralysis." Why? Because individuals can't shake existing, outdated beliefs and incorporate newly emerging evidence that challenges the existing paradigm. In the business world, few examples are more striking than the invention of the quartz watch.

Business: A Case of "Paradigm Paralysis"

Before the invention of the quartz timepiece, Swiss watchmakers enjoyed a world market share as high as 90%.[6] With the invention of the electronic watch, that share dropped to as low as 10% in just a relatively few years. The sad but powerful irony is that this new technology was actually invented by the Swiss! That's right, the Swiss Watch Federation Research Center, the research arm of the Swiss watch manufacturers, actually presented a prototype of the first quartz watch to Swiss manufacturers in 1967. Although we don't know exactly what was said at that presentation, we can probably approximate the response of the watch manufacturers:

It doesn't tick — It looks too clumsy — It has no gears, no springs —
How can it even be considered a watch? It's too radical a change —
We just don't do things that way! —
Who do you think you are?

What we do know is that Texas Instruments and Seiko of Japan were not *stuck* in the beliefs of the Swiss Watch paradigm. They snatched up the new technology; and today, virtually all watches use quartz timing. As is so often the case, the new paradigm offering was initially met with scorn and utter rejection. This is not because the Swiss manufacturers were inherently narrow-minded or short-sighted. New paradigms, by their very nature, are anxiety producing for people. The longer they have been practicing in the existing paradigm, the more they have invested in maintaining the status quo, and the more difficult it is for them to see things any other way. As perhaps most simply and eloquently stated by Pulitzer Prize-winning author Upton Sinclair, "It is difficult to get a man to understand something, when his salary depends upon his not understanding it!"[7] Although this is certainly natural and perfectly understandable, the consequences can be devastating. In this instance, the result was the destruction of Swiss domination of the watchmaking industry and the loss of tens of thousands of jobs.

Paradigms and the Myth of Scientific Objectivity

So, why have we chosen a discussion of paradigms to introduce the material in this book? There are two reasons. First, much of the scientific basis for the approaches proposed in this book will be outside of traditional, scientific paradigms. It is, therefore, critical to understand that all science and all scientists are strongly influenced by the prevailing paradigms of their time. As with the case of the quartz watch, this is not so much a result of personal egos and narrow mindedness *(although these can certainly enter into the equation)* but more likely a result of our frequent unconscious assumptions about reality.[8] Therefore, although it may be difficult *(and perhaps painful)* to accept, the concept of an "objective" scientist defined as "uninfluenced by emotion, surmise or personal prejudice"[9] is, in reality, an illusion. This is precisely because all sciences, as well as all scientists, have paradigms that provide a framework for investigation, focusing attention and guiding inquiry in certain areas to the exclusion of others. In "The Structure of Scientific Revolutions," T.S. Kuhn describes the nature and significance of paradigms in relation to science:

> *Paradigms are constituted from the concepts, assumptions and rules that guide workers in their pursuit of knowledge and the solution of problems in a given field... Paradigms gain status to the extent that they are successful in solving problems and they lose status as paradoxes multiply.*[10]

These paradigms or models are, like our individual paradigms, made of the sum of a vast constellation of experiences that create and shape our beliefs. Like our own personal paradigms, therefore, scientific paradigms are not in fact reality, but rather a particular representation of reality subject to change as new evidence becomes available. Throughout history, scientific revolutions have been brought about when this emerging evidence demanded explanations that could not be made within existing paradigms.

Paradigms and Science: An Example from History

Before the 6th century BC, the earth was assumed to be flat. In the course of scientific inquiry, the ancient Greeks encountered numerous phenomena that could not be explained by the prevailing flat-earth paradigm:

- When they traveled from Greece, they noticed that different stars were visible from different points on the earth.

- When they watched their ships sail out to sea, the ships didn't grow smaller and smaller until vanishing as mere points in the distance, but rather disappeared while still perceptibly larger than points, always hull first with sails still visible, irrespective of the direction in which they traveled.

Through contemplating the failure of the existing flat-earth paradigm to explain these and other phenomena, the Greeks first hypothesized that the earth was not flat but spherical. This paradigm shift provided a new framework for their scientific inquiry, not only suggesting answers to these and other philosophical dilemmas of the time, but also leading ultimately to discoveries involving a more accurate understanding of the solar system.

Paradigms and Medicine — The "Tomato Effect"

By the middle of the 1500s, tomatoes had already become a staple of the continental European diet. Although they were available in America throughout the 1600s and 1700s, they were considered inedible decorative plants. In fact, it took almost 300 years for Americans to accept tomatoes as an edible food! Why? The belief was that tomatoes, like several other plants in the nightshade family *(belladonna, mandrake)*, were poisonous. Only when a brave individual provided concrete and irrefutable evidence to the contrary *(by publicly eating the dreaded fruit on the courthouse steps in Salem, New Jersey, and not dying)* did Americans begin to embrace the tomato, which is now one of our largest commercial crops.

The "tomato effect" in medicine is therefore said to occur when an effective treatment is shunned because it does not fit within the prevailing paradigm of disease mechanisms and drug action.[11] One example of the tomato effect involves using aspirin to treat rheumatoid arthritis. As far back as the late 1800s, controlled trials reported in major medical journals such as "The Journal of the American Medical Association" and "The Lancet" demonstrated the effectiveness of aspirin in treating rheumatoid arthritis. Yet, with the acceptance of the "germ theory" of disease in the early 20th century the use of aspirin to treat the infectious disease of rheumatoid arthritis made no sense. This prevailing belief was so powerful that medical textbooks of the early 1900s made no mention whatsoever of this effective treatment. In fact, it wasn't until the late 1950s that aspirin began to be recommended again by the medical establishment for this condition. As the paradigm shifted, and we gradually accepted the accumulating evidence that rheumatoid arthritis was not an infectious condition but an autoimmune disease, it made "sense" that aspirin could be an appropriate treatment.

Paradigms and Change

In the late 16th century, the Italian scientist Giordano Bruno, in direct contradiction to the prevailing belief of the time, suggested the earth might not be the center of the solar system. He was promptly burned at the stake for his scientific blasphemy. Just a few years later, Galileo expressed the same belief but went one step further and provided the supporting evidence by inventing the telescope so people could see the truth for themselves! Nevertheless, he was forced to recant and live out the rest of his life under house arrest.

So, the second important reason for exploring the paradigm concept is that it enables us to appreciate the tremendous difficulties involved in embracing paradigmatic shifts such as the ones discussed in this book. Throughout history, paradigm shifts have not only been discredited and rejected, but have often been met with violent opposition. Indeed, many of those involved in challenging prevailing beliefs have been hanged, burned at the stake, or at the very least ostracized and shunned, even when they provided the evidence to scientifically prove what they were suggesting.

We certainly don't expect any such repercussions from this book. However, because paradigms are so fundamental to our very existence, questioning them is often unsettling at a very basic level. For many readers, the critiques of contemporary approaches and the new blueprint for creating organizational and employee wellbeing proposed in this book will conflict with the beliefs we have acquired from our teachers, our parents, our health and business establishments, and our culture as a whole. The initial reaction may, therefore, include strong emotions and resistance. This is to be expected. Rather than ignore these emotions, we hope readers will examine and incorporate them into a realistic and dynamic evaluation of the evidence presented, perhaps guided by the old Buddhist saying:

Don't bite the finger, look to where it is pointing.

"Paradigm Pioneer" — An Invitation

One of the most exciting things about paradigms is that, because they deal primarily with perception and beliefs, they can be changed. People can and often do choose to look at their world through a different set of filters — they change their paradigms. Yet, moving to a new paradigm always involves risk. There is, as we have seen, the almost guaranteed and some-times extremely distasteful disapproval of existing paradigm advocates. Then there is the stress and anxiety from letting go of old beliefs and ways of doing things that carry with them significant personal investment. And, to make matters even more difficult, often only limited quantitative evidence exists to support the suggested change. So choosing to embrace a new paradigm often must be done largely on the basis of faith and intuition — from the heart and not the head, if you will. Kuhn says that individuals who choose this path must:

Have faith that the new paradigm will succeed with the many large problems that confront it knowing only that the older paradigm has failed with a few. A decision of that kind can only be made on faith.[12]

Yet, with risk comes the potential for substantial gain. Particularly in times of great stress and turmoil, like the present, those individuals most open to trying new ways of thinking and doing — the "paradigm pioneers"[13] fare the best and make the most significant contributions to their world. We invite you to consider becoming one of these pioneers!

The paradigms formed in the sciences trickle down to create the foundations for all values and institutions of our larger culture. To be "paradigm pioneers" in organizational and employee wellbeing, we first need to clearly understand the new evidence emerging in today's sciences and how it differs from the increasingly outdated beliefs associated with the old sciences. In the introduction, we referred to the ongoing struggle to overcome the influence of outdated paradigms as the clash of *Belief vs. Evidence*. Overcoming this clash by embracing the emerging scientific realities will be a central theme woven throughout this book.

We begin this process in the next chapter with a brief examination of the 17th-century scientific worldview that emerged from Newtonian physics and the Scientific Revolution. To a large degree, this view still informs all aspects of our culture, including traditional approaches to both organizational and employee wellbeing.

Summary of Paradigms
A quick summary of the importance of paradigms:

- Paradigms provide a model or frame of reference from which we determine how we feel about and interact with our surroundings.

- Paradigms too strongly held lead to "paradigm paralysis."

- Because paradigms are so fundamental to our very existence, questioning them is often unsettling at a very basic level.

- Paradigms can be (and need to be) changed to adapt to our changing world.

- Though not without risk, being a "paradigm pioneer" brings with it the potential for substantial gain.

CHAPTER 2
The Mechanistic Universe

❝*The notion of an organic, living, spiritual universe was replaced by that of the world as a machine and the world-machine became the dominant metaphor of the modern era.*[1]❞

Fritjof Capra, "The Turning Point"

In the previous chapter, we examined the power of paradigms to create the realties that we have come to believe are true. We saw that, in all walks of life, paradigms enable us to make sense of the world by helping us to filter the overwhelming amount of information coming to us at any one time, so we may focus on the most important things. We also saw that it is human nature to hold on to our paradigms in the face of contradictory information, and we saw vividly how not letting go of outdated paradigms can have devastating and often life-altering consequences.

In this chapter, we explore the scientific roots of the *stuckness* to which we have been repeatedly referring. We believe it is essential to understand the science that has brought us to this *stuckness* to effectively move beyond it. If we don't know where we've been and what got us to a place that isn't working, we'll be more likely to continue to operate under the same assumptions and repeat the same mistakes. After reviewing the major tenets of the scientific worldview that has dominated all aspects of our culture for 400 years, we will introduce newer emerging sciences that help frame the New Paradigm we propose is needed to create a thriving workplace culture in which both organizations and individuals can thrive.

If hearing "sciences" suddenly makes you cringe, have no fear. We promise to make this background information as painless, yet as meaningful as possible. We will address organizational and employee wellbeing from a broad range of perspectives, and we will include information that is rarely, if ever, included in books on these subjects. Initially you may be thinking, "What do paradigms, the Scientific Revolution, and the emerging sciences of the 20th and 21st centuries have to do with wellbeing?" We believe that they provide the all-important context for understanding the *stuckness* we describe and to fully appreciate our rationale behind the unique blueprint for creating a thriving workplace culture. Although theoretically you could skip this information and go directly to the how-to chapters of the book, we suggest that understanding the historical perspective can help to clarify what the problems and solutions really are. We invite and encourage you to bear with us for just a little bit as we take you through a brief history lesson to lay the critical groundwork for the change blueprint.

The Way We Were – The Organic Worldview

For more than 400 years, every aspect of our Western culture has been dominated by the paradigm or worldview handed down from the Scientific Revolution. In his landmark book, "The Turning Point," Fritjof Capra describes life in Europe and most of the rest of the world before the 17th-century Scientific Revolution:

People lived in small, cohesive communities and experienced nature in terms of organic relationships, characterized by the interdependence of spiritual and material phenomenon and the subordination of individual needs to those of the community. The scientific framework of this organic world view rested on two authorities — Aristotle and the Church.[2]

Indeed, medieval science, based on the reason of Aristotle and the faith of the Church, was very different from the science of today. Medieval scientists believed in an organic, living, spiritual universe. If asked, they would likely have said the purpose of science was to understand the meaning and natural order of this living cosmos to live in harmony with nature. Thus, medieval science regarded inquiry into God, spirituality, ethics and the human soul as critical to understand natural phenomena. But all of that was about to change!

The Mechanistic Universe

The 17th-century scientific paradigm or worldview developed largely as a result of revolutionary changes in physics, astronomy and mathematics emerging from the work of Galileo Galilei, René Descartes, Sir Isaac Newton, Sir Francis Bacon and others. So influential were these great thinkers that this period is referred to as the Age of the Scientific Revolution, and the description of reality they formulated is commonly called the Cartesian or Newtonian paradigm. For these men, the universe was not a living entity, but rather a great machine. Nature herself was compared to a huge clock, composed of dead, inert particles and devoid of purpose, spirituality or life. All things both living and non-living were best, and in fact only, understood as machines, some more complicated than others, but machines nevertheless. Accordingly, understanding the workings of any components of the universe, including all natural phenomena, no longer necessitated exploration of emotional, spiritual or ethical matters, but only of those things that could be measured and quantified. Though these men believed in a God of creation, they believed that God had long since left the daily functioning of the universe to the fundamental mechanical and mathematical laws he had created.

Reductionism – The Whole is Equal to the Sum of its Parts

A key concept of the mechanistic universe worldview or paradigm, "reductionism" is derived from classical Newtonian physics. The most important assumption is all complex phenomena can be understood only be reducing them to their smallest component parts. As most of us probably remember from our high school science classes, classical physics describes matter as being composed of discreet particles that can be broken down to their primary atomic and subatomic building blocks. This reductionist approach to determining the nature of reality has become the gold standard for scientific investigation in the physical sciences as well as in medicine and social sciences. In fact, in virtually every aspect of our society, the legacy of reductionism has resulted in a focus on breaking down whatever is being examined into smaller and smaller component parts, discovering how the parts relate, and then reassembling them to understand the workings of the whole. After all, if everything is just a machine, then this approach makes perfect, logical sense.

At this point, you may be thinking, who cares? On the other hand, perhaps you can already begin to see the powerful influence this 400-year-old paradigm has had on the issues we face today. As we discussed briefly in the introduction, organizations striving to remain competitive typically focus their time and energy on the classic fundamentals of business; strategy, operations, finance, marketing and technology; quantitatively measuring sales, profit margins, timing of workflow processes, etc., and adding them up to determine the health of the organization. What is often missing are the all important *(though not deemed so by the legacy of the Scientific Revolution)* qualitative realities, such as the employee experience, engagement, retention, communication and leadership effectiveness.

Many organizations tend to operate in silos rather than having truly cross-functional teams. From a reductionist perspective, it makes sense to separate people and business functions by their strengths and focus areas. However, this inevitably causes issues when communication fails, politics surface and a holistic view of problems and potential solutions is missed. Even worse, when organizations don't intentionally foster an outstanding employee experience, they typically end up focusing more on calculating the details of how to do more with less. Think of all of the business initiatives that have evolved to get more work done: Lean manufacturing, Six Sigma, automation, and 12-hour shifts, to name a few. Many of these seem like great solutions on paper; however, in too many cases, these processes actually de-humanize the workplace and do not account for the reality that humans are not machines and, unlike machines, are deeply affected by stress, fatigue, injuries and disengagement. When employees are treated like machines, not only does the workplace culture erode, but individual wellbeing and productivity suffer as well. We're not saying efforts and processes to streamline work and create efficiencies aren't important; but when they are implemented without considering the human impact, problems with organizational and employee wellbeing emerge.

The experience for individuals is analogous. To assess the wellbeing of employees, we have traditionally subjected them to filling out Health Risk Assessments and participating in biometric screenings; after which we calculate their scores and quantify their health risks based primarily on individual risk factor numbers *(e.g., cholesterol, blood pressure, blood glucose, etc.).* We rarely consider social, emotional, cultural, spiritual and work-related factors that are often the root causes of the symptoms we may have just uncovered. Then, we shuffle employees into control-oriented change programs in which they are subjected to carrot-and-stick behavior modification approaches that treat people as if they were machines, rodents or children *(more on this in chapter 6).* They may be re-ferred to a diet program in which they are likely to have a caloric intake calculated for them that will help them lose weight, as if they were a lawn mower for which calculations like this — determining how much fuel is necessary for a specific output — have some degree of accuracy. Or they may be told to join a workplace stress management program in which they will learn deep breathing exercises to reduce their stress. This, of course, is not going to be overly helpful when the source of the stress is likely the dysfunctional or even toxic environment in which employees work.

Dualism — Separating Matter from Spirit and Humanity from Nature

The concept of dualism goes hand in hand with mechanism and reductionism. Dualism divides the universe into two separate entities:

- The material universe *(anything composed of matter)* is viewed as objective, quantitative, and measurable and therefore subject to human comprehension.

- The immaterial universe, including thoughts, feelings, emotions, spirituality and human consciousness is seen as subjective, qualitative and beyond the realm of understanding.

Thus the 17th-century worldview was founded on the separation of matter from spirit and humanity from nature. Only that which could be measured and quantified was considered real. The resulting rational, mathematical, analytical approach to defining reality through science is perhaps best expressed by one of its main architects, physician and philosopher René Descartes:

All science is certain, evident knowledge… We reject all knowledge which is merely probable and judge that only those things should be believed which are perfectly known and about which there can be no doubts.[3]

The focus on the scientific method and the mathematical description of nature led to tremendous advances in physics, mathematics, chemistry, biology, astronomy and medicine as well. It is becoming more and more apparent, however, that we have also paid a significant toll for the restriction of science to studying phenomena that are measurable and quantifiable. Psychiatrist R.D. Laing describes the problem pointedly:

Out go sight, sound, taste, touch and smell, and along with them have since gone esthetic and ethical sensibility, values, quality, soul, consciousness, spirit. Experience as such is cast out of the realm of scientific discourse.[4]

After all, in a mechanistic universe inhabited by nothing but machines *(including all living things)*, these qualities do not account for much that is relevant. Yet, when we deal with organizations made of human beings, we know there is tremendous relevance and value to the experience — the experience of the employees, of the customers, and of the surrounding community that interacts with the organization. We know the importance of having strong ethics and values in business, treating people well, of having a culture and work environment full of energy and where people want to work. These experiences are important and measurable, though not easily quantifiable. As a result, they are frequently skipped over when assessing the success or health of a business.

Meanwhile, the separation of man from the rest of nature had other far-reaching implications. Searching for control over — and no longer considering himself to be a part of — nature, man was free to concentrate on scientific domination. In fact, the creators of the 17th-century worldview deemed mastery over the natural world to be the highest purpose of science. What a change from the age-old pursuit of wisdom for achieving peaceful coexistence with nature! Scientists were suddenly exhorted to take whatever steps needed to achieve this domination. For, in the words of Sir Francis Bacon, the purpose of science now was:

> *To torture nature's secrets from her so she can be forced out of her natural state and squeezed and molded.*[5]

The implications for our culture have been monumental, and we are now facing the potentially species-threatening consequences of this license to exploit the environment under the guise of scientific investigation. More specifically, as we shall soon see, the coercive, control-oriented foundation on which so many of our traditional approaches to organizational and employee wellbeing rest, as well as the language we use when we talk about and promote change, all have their roots in this outdated view of the nature of reality and the process of change.

Patriarchy — A Man's World

Throughout history, nature has always been associated with the feminine aspects of humanity. Carolyn Merchant discusses the role of this association in the organic worldview that existed prior to the Scientific Revolution:

> *Central to the organic theory was the identification of nature, especially the earth, with a nurturing mother: a kindly, beneficent female who provided for the needs of mankind in an ordered, planned universe.*[6]

However, nature as female has traditionally had an additional, opposing association. This is the image of nature as a wild, uncontrollable female producing violence and chaos through storms, droughts and other natural disasters. As the Scientific Revolution progressed, the image of the nurturing mother was gradually lost, and the association with disorder became the foundation for the call to exert control over and dominate nature.

It is therefore no mere coincidence that Sir Francis Bacon described a "feminine" nature needing to be squeezed and molded, even tortured, by a "masculine" science. The license to manipulate and exploit nature and women go hand in hand. Bacon referred to nature as a "common harlot" who "takes orders from man and works under his authority." If this seems like a stretch, it may be helpful to recall that Bacon was attorney general in England under King James I as thousands of innocent women were accused of being witches and subsequently burned to death.

Patriarchy was certainly not an invention of the Scientific Revolution. However, the belief in the natural superiority of men and masculine values over women and feminine values was scientifically reinforced and sanctioned by the emerging mechanistic, reductionist, dualistic worldview. Patriarchal cultures value the "masculine" traits of aggression, competition and control over the traditionally feminine traits of nurturing, cooperation and trust; often, in fact, devaluing the latter. Therefore, such societies are ruled by men through an elaborate hierarchy based on physical, political, and economic power and control. Similarly, most religious institutions are governed by another male hierarchy, with both hierarchies answering to an all-powerful male god. The patriarchal worldview depicts man as strong, brave and intelligent; while woman is viewed as passive, weak and lacking in intelligence. In his 1859 "On the Origin of Species," Charles Darwin provided the continued scientific validation for this underlying foundation of patriarchal culture when he wrote:

> *Man is more courageous, pugnacious, and energetic than woman,*
> *and has more inventive genius.*[7]

Of course, patriarchy still runs rampant today within organizations as well as throughout our culture as a whole. The legacy of the 17th-century worldview is clear. The path to progress revolves around wielding power to control the actions of others. For organizations, patriarchy still dominates the landscape, displayed by hierarchies of control in which the most powerful male dominates. Despite progress in the past two decades, as of 2013, women still make only 77 cents for every dollar men make. And in spite of the fact that women comprise more than 50% of the population, they currently hold only 4.4% of Fortune 500 and Fortune 100 Chief Operating Officer roles. Patriarchy's stubborn persistence has prompted the growing popularity of the Lean In movement, started in 2013 by Facebook COO Sheryl Sandberg.[8] Lean In is designed to raise awareness of gender inequalities in the workplace and challenges women to demand more in capturing leadership positions. And, of course, patriarchal values are ever present in our approaches to behavior change. Current systems constantly disregard our innate need for autonomy and focus on the modification of behavior through pressure, coercion and control. Although gender inequality in its purest form is still a source for real concern, we must also acknowlege the underlying effects of its history on the way organizations currently operate.

The mechanistic worldview or paradigm that has dominated all aspects of our culture for 400 years seems quite logical. After all, skilled surgeons need to have a solid background in anatomy to understand how the human body is put together to repair parts that no longer work; mechanics need to have a thorough understanding of how the machines they are working on fit together to repair what isn't working; computer technicians need to have a detailed understanding of how computer hardware and software interact to troubleshoot; and a business problem needs experts who have a solid history with the business and industry who can dissect the problem and determine possible solutions.

However, knowing about the pieces and parts of a person or business only allows us to go so far. Without understanding the broader context, the subtle nuances and the unseen details, we can't be truly effective in eliciting change — on an organizational or an individual level. To do that, we have to incorporate more than just the whole as a mathematical sum of its parts, more than just what we see. How often do you hear of an organization that deployed the same strategies wildly successful at another organization, only to have them fail within their company? How often do you hear, "This diet/exercise/treatment program should work for you because it worked for me"? When dealing with the complexities of human beings and organizations, machine-like predictability and controllability go out the window, and the outdated tenets of the mechanistic worldview do not help us to reach our desired outcomes.

Thankfully, the exciting scientific discoveries of the 20th and 21st centuries have made tremendous contributions to our understanding of the universe, the health of organizations and individuals, and the process of change. If we can remain open to letting go of outdated beliefs and embracing these new scientific realities, we can get *unstuck* and make the necessary adjustments to our traditional approaches to organizational and employee wellbeing; adjustments that can maximize the potential for creating world class cultures and happy, healthy employees.

Summary of Major Tenets of the Old Paradigm:
The major assumptions of the 17th-century scientific worldview:
- **Mechanism:** universe and everything in it as machines
- **Reductionism:** whole = the sum of its parts
- **Dualism:** separation of matter from spirit and humanity from nature
- **Patriarchy:** natural superiority of man and masculine values; control through power

CHAPTER 3
Embracing the New Sciences

We need to be prepared to question every single aspect of the old paradigm. Eventually we will not need to throw everything away, but before we know that we need to be willing to question everything.[1]

Fritjof Capra, "The Web of Life"

We have now seen the limits of the major tenets of the scientific worldview that has dominated all aspects of our culture for the past 400 years. In continuing on this journey of understanding the *stuckness* and what it will take to get *unstuck*, we believe it is important to introduce some newer emerging sciences that help frame the New Paradigm needed to create a workplace culture in which both organizations and individuals can thrive.

In the last 100 years, beginning with the pioneering work of Albert Einstein and continuing through the collaboration of an international group of scientists, scientific developments have changed our understanding of reality in ways nobody could have imagined possible — forcing scientists to completely rethink the foundations of classical physics as well as our assumptions about the nature of the material world. It is perhaps ironic that the major challenges to the Newtonian, Cartesian worldview now come from the very scientific discipline that spawned it — the most "scientific" and "hardest" of the sciences — physics itself! But why should those of us concerned with organizational and employee wellbeing care about these discoveries?

- Because physics has always been the "gold standard" of rational, empirical science and the measuring stick by which all other scientific disciplines are judged.

- Because discoveries in physics and in other sciences in the 20th and 21st centuries have challenged virtually all traditional assumptions of the 17th-century scientific "mechanistic universe" paradigm.

- Because this emerging scientific paradigm is having profound effects on all sciences and throughout our culture.

With that in mind, we hope you'll stay on this part of the journey for just a little bit longer. To help create a framework for getting *unstuck* from the outdated mechanistic scientific worldview, we need to examine how the new sciences of quantum physics and chaos theory are radically changing our understanding of the universe and broadening our perspectives on organizational effectiveness, health and the process of change.

Quantum Weirdness: The Double-Slit Experiment

Imagine for a moment that you are Spock, Chief Science Officer on the Starship Enterprise, and you have been asked by the Captain to help perform an experiment to test the protocol for a new technology — the "photon *(elementary particle of light)* torpedo." For this experiment, a special machine is used to project photons *(though it could be any subatomic entity)* through a piece of cardboard that has two slits in it; hence, the Double-Slit Experiment *(Figure 1)*. On the other side of the cardboard is placed a recording device that detects light. In the first part of the experiment, you close off one of the slits, turn on the machine, and start projecting the light, one photon at a time. *Figure 2* shows, not surprisingly, what you see on the recording surface. Next, you are instructed to close the opened slit and open the other slit. *Figure 3* shows, again rather unsurprisingly, what you see on the recording surface. The next step in the experiment is to open both slits. You look at the detection surface expecting to see the pattern depicted in *Figure 4*. Quite surprisingly this time, this is not what you see. As bizarre as it may seem, *Figure 5* depicts what you see on the recording surface! How can this be and why should you care? Please bear with us for just a bit as we review:

- When one slit is open and one is closed, you see a line on the detection screen indicating where the photon particles have gone through. *(Figure 2 and 3)*

- When both slits are open, you see what is called an interference pattern *(think of watching ocean waves roll onto the beach — higher at some points than others because they cancel each other out)* indicating that the photons are now acting as waves *(energy)* rather than particles *(matter)*. *(Figure 5)*

Figure 1: A beam of light is shone on a barrier in which two slits have been cut. The light that passes through the barrier is recorded on a photographic plate when either or both of the slits are open.

Adapted with permission from Greene, "The Elegant Universe"

Figure 2:
Only the right slit is open, leading to an image on the photographic plate as shown.

Figure 3:
Only the left slit is open, leading to an image on the photographic plate as shown.

Figure 4:
When both slits are open we might expect a merger of the images in Figures 2 and 3, as shown.

Figure 5:
However, this is the pattern that actually emerges when both slits are open.

It actually gets even crazier! This will take some consideration, but the sheer wonder of it can help us grasp how different the universe really is from what we have believed for so long. If you open both slits and use a device that detects particles, what you see is a line representing photon particles, as in Figures 2 and 3; however, the particles only go through one of the two open slits. But, if you keep both slits open and replace the device that detects particles with one that detects waves, you get the interference pattern *(Figure 5)* created by photon waves. But now the photons go through both slits!

As shocking as this may sound, the experiment suggests that the photon seems to "know" about and "act" upon how we are observing it (*which device we are using to measure it*). The Captain asks you, as the Chief Science Officer, to explain. You answer, of course: "Fascinating, but highly illogical."

Before you give yourself a quantum headache trying to figure out how on earth this all could possibly be, it might be helpful for you to know that, in fact, no one has a clue about how these mysterious occurrences happen. Nobel Prize-winning physicist Richard Feynman, one of the architects of quantum physics, said it best:

> *No one understands quantum mechanics. Do not keep saying to yourself, how can it be like that? Because you will go down the drain into a blind alley from which nobody has yet to escape. Nobody knows how it can be like that.*[2]

So why are we talking about quantum physics if it's so difficult to understand and perhaps even downright weird? Again, we ask for your patience and trust in this matter. The more you read, the more we believe the relevance of this information will become clear to you. Although we do not claim to understand quantum physics, and neither will you after reading this chapter, don't feel too badly about it. Einstein didn't understand it either. He describes his frustrations in the following terms:

> *All my attempts to adapt the theoretical foundation of this old physics to this knowledge failed completely. It was as if the ground had been pulled out from under one with no firm foundation to be seen anywhere.*[3]

Much of this chapter will be outside the sphere of that measurable, quantifiable "material universe" we discussed earlier. And much of it will not fit with our traditional view of physical reality. Although we may not entirely understand quantum physics, there is still much we can learn from it. Welcome to the four major tenets of the weird world of quantum physics!

Tenet #1: Complementarity — A Both/And Universe

The old, Newtonian *(Sir Isaac Newton)* view of physical reality is based on the proposed existence of tiny, solid, separate building blocks of matter that cannot be further broken down into smaller constituent parts. These particles were thought to occupy definite places in space and time that could be measured and quantified. From quantum physics, however, we now know that this understanding is incomplete and inaccurate. As we observed in the Double-Slit Experiment, photons *(and electrons, protons, neutrons and all other subatomic entities)* exist not only as particles *(like little billiard balls)* but also, and at the same time, as waves *(like electricity)*. The tenet of Complementarity teaches us that describing of any of these entities in terms of its particle nature or its wave nature is only partially correct. Both descriptions actually complement each other, and only together do they represent an accurate picture of the "things" that make up our physical reality.

What we learn from Complementarity is that we live in a "both/and" and not an "either/or" universe. Physical reality is not only about things but also about movement and process. Within one year, 90% of the atoms within our bodies are replaced, and within five years all of them are gone. Where do they go? Well, they might go to make up another person, or they might become part of a tree or a rock. So, our body is actually a work in progress — a work completely interconnected on the most basic level with the rest of the universe. Like a river constantly flowing and changing, never the same at two different points in time, we are constantly changing "shape" from our experiences and our interactions with our surroundings.

Furthermore, just as the particle and wave are not separate, but actually part of the same whole, so health and disease are not opposites, but rather both part of the bigger whole we call life. Further, contrary to Cartesian thinking, the body, spirit and mind are not separate entities but are inextricably interconnected *(we will explore this more fully in chapter 5)*. Similarly, masculine and feminine are also not opposites but part of the bigger whole. Both men and women have masculine and feminine traits. Unfortunately, in our present culture we have seen that we continue to value the masculine above the feminine, with many devastating consequences. Finally, rational science and intuition are also not mutually exclusive opposites. Many beliefs and concepts discussed in this book are based on age-old intuition. But testing these beliefs and concepts scientifically can add to our understanding of their implications.

Tenet #2: The Uncertainty Principle

Remember what Descartes said nearly 400 years ago during the Scientific Revolution: If any knowledge is limited and approximate, it is meaningless; only things known with absolute certainty and about which there are no doubts are real. Quantum science tells us quite a different story. As physicist Fritjof Capra says:

> *Twentieth-century physics has shown us very forcefully that there is no absolute truth in science, that all our concepts and theories are limited and approximate.*[4]

You might, for a moment, think back to our discussions of paradigms and how our experiences describe reality not as it is, but rather create a representation of reality as we have learned to see it. As human beings, scientists have their own paradigms that grow out of their professional and personal experiences. These together form the reality that guides their work and their life.

We learned from Complementarity that to fully understand the building blocks that make up everything in our universe, we need to be able to quantify both their particle and wave natures. As frustrating as it may seem, the second major tenet of quantum physics, the Uncertainty Principle, teaches us that although it is possible to measure the position *(particle nature)* of a sub-atomic entity and it is also possible to measure its movement *(wave nature)*, it is not possible to measure both accurately at the same time. The reasons for this are beyond the scope of this book, but a good and understandable explanation can be found in "The Elegant Universe" by Brian Greene.[5] Suffice it to say here the inability to accurately quantify matter in this way appears to be built into the universe and is not due to a lack of scientific knowledge or technique.

The Uncertainty Principle teaches us that not everything that can be counted counts and not everything that counts can be counted. So, rather than ignore those things that we can't measure, we might begin to see them as the true foundation of our being. We are often so focused on the numbers, on having something quantifiable to measure, that we miss the chance to be involved in the all-important process. The Uncertainty Principle reminds us that this obsession with measurement is an illusion. Just like unsuccessfully trying to pin down the exact location and movement of an elementary particle, we will never truly know the exact causes of most of organizational or personal health issues. That doesn't mean we should never measure anything or never look at outcomes. Rather, it means that it is an illusion to believe what we see is all, or even necessarily the most important part, of what actually is.

In fact, physicists do not even refer to sub-atomic entities as actually existing at definite places at all, but rather as showing "tendencies to exist," which they describe in mathematical probabilities. It is only possible to suggest the likelihood of an event happening. Danah Zohar discusses the significance of this in relation to our traditional conception of physical reality:

> *This essential fuzziness… replaces the Old Newtonian Determinism,*
> *where everything about physical reality was fixed, determined*
> *and measurable, with a vast 'porridge' of being where nothing is fixed*
> *or fully measurable. Here everything remains indeterminate,*
> *somewhat ghostly, and just beyond our grasp.*[6]

Tenet #3: Quantum Connectedness — A Universe of Relationships

Quantum physics also forces us to re-examine traditional views concerning cause and effect. The solid, measurable, material objects we learned about in high school are actually not things but interconnections between "things" that can only be accurately described in terms of their relationships with other "things." Physical matter is therefore a dynamic network of interconnected particles/waves that have no existence if isolated by themselves. It is through the relationship with other "things" that "things" attain their significance. In the words of the Danish physicist Niels Bohr:

> *Isolated material particles are abstractions,*
> *their properties being definable and observable only through their*
> *interaction with other systems.*[7]

The movement of electrons in an atom, which most of us studied in high school chemistry class, illustrates the new scientific understanding. Remembering the models of atoms with their electrons orbiting the nucleus, we learned that these electrons can "jump" to different energy levels *(orbits around the atom)*, either giving off or absorbing energy. We have learned from quantum physics that these movements are in large part random and spontaneous. There is no prior warning, no identifiable cause and no way to predict the outcome of events. There is no way to know exactly where the electrons are at any given point in time and no way of knowing if the electron will move to a lower or higher energy state.

Furthermore, some physicists believe that the electron may actually move in all directions simultaneously, acting as if it is "smeared out" all over space and time and is everywhere at once. Before moving, it actually puts out "feelers" in every possible direction that in essence "try out" all the possible new orbits in which it might actually settle. If this is difficult to comprehend, think about how you might solve a problem *(for example where to go on a vacation)* by examining all of the possible solutions in your mind before attempting any. Although you would eventually arrive at and act on a decision, certainly the different scenarios you investigate could have an effect on determining which course of action you finally take. In quantum physics, these feelers are called "virtual transitions," and it turns out they can have lasting effects, even though the electron eventually "makes a decision" to go only in one direction. As suggested earlier by the Double-Slit Experiment, these tiny entities that make up our universe seem to have a much richer existence than anyone could have previously imagined.

But there is more! According to traditional Newtonian thinking, the scientist as the "objective" observer stands outside of *(separate from)*, and is impartial to the measurable, material "reality" being explored. However, quantum physics defines quite a different relationship between the observer and the observed. As was suggested in the previous section on paradigms, the Cartesian idea of a purely objective scientist is an illusion because:

What is being studied is inseparable from the scientist, who devises mental constructs of his/her experiences with it as a means of characterizing his/her understanding of its properties and behavior.[8]

Remember from the Double-Slit Experiment that not only is the scientist as observer not separate from what is being observed, but in fact, the very act of observing actually alters the properties of what is being observed. Whether the photon existed and acted as a particle or a wave actually depended on how we looked at *(measured)* it at that moment. There seems to be some sort of connection between this tiny particle *(or wave)* and the scientist observing it that alters the reality of the situation. Not only is the scientist not a separate and detached observer, but the act of observation itself actually becomes part of and has a profound effect on the outcome.

We have seen how our quest for certainty and control has led us to a fascination with linear cause and effect. As we might expect, this fascination is also fundamental to our traditional understanding of the nature of organizations and of individual health as well. In the quest to have thriving organizational wellbeing, we have developed to-do lists to ensure employees are engaged and assume that, if certain actions are taken, then engagement rates will increase. Yet we know that isn't necessarily the case. In the quest for thriving employee wellbeing, we have lists of "risk factors" for most diseases and we often base much of our judgment about the degree of an individual's health on the absence or presence of these factors. This is true, even though these factors are not very good predictors of who gets and doesn't get a particular disease, who will use more healthcare, or who will be engaged and productive at work.

In addition to addressing this outdated conceptualization of cause and effect, we will talk more in the next three chapters about the effects of our current "measurement mania" and "outcome obsession" in organizations and employee wellness. But for now remember they are the logical extension of our outdated understanding of the nature of physical reality. When we are so focused on determining linear cause and effect, we miss the uncertainty, chance and chaos that appear to play a crucial role in all aspects of our physical universe.

Tenet #4: Non-Locality — Spooky Action at a Distance

The concept of the interconnectedness of all things leads to the last and perhaps the most bizarre tenet of quantum physics — Non-locality.[9] It has been suggested that the concept of Non-locality may be the single most important discovery in the history of science. It has now been proven that sub-atomic particles have some "connection" or means of "communication" between them that is instantaneous and does not diminish with distance. If two paired electrons, for example, are separated and one is taken to the other side of the room or the country *(or theoretically, the universe)*, alterations in the spin of one of the electrons will instantaneously and predictably affect the spin of the distant other! Capra sums up the striking implications of this finding:

The behavior of any part is determined by its nonlocal connections to the whole, and since we do not know those connections precisely, we have to replace the narrow classical notion of cause and effect by the wider concept of statistical causality...

27

whereas in classical mechanics the properties and behavior of the parts determine those of the whole, the situation is reversed in quantum mechanics; it is the whole that determines the behavior of the parts.[10]

Roll over, René Descartes! The overarching message from the new physics is that:

- The universe is not made up of things, but of relationships between things.

- These relationships are best understood by focusing on their connections to the whole.

- Focusing on the parts can result in misunderstanding the workings of the whole.

By the way, if you are having trouble buying into the above description of the instantaneously connected *(regardless of the distance apart)* electrons, you are in good company. Einstein actually went to his grave unable to believe what he referred to as this "spooky" action at a distance. Since his death, however, this part of quantum theory has been conclusively and repeatedly validated by experiment.

What Does Quantum Physics Have to Do With Organizational and Employee Wellbeing?

Let's think about what we have learned from quantum physics and its implications for how we view organizational and employee wellbeing. In simple terms, the understandings that have emerged from the new physics demonstrate we can benefit greatly from re-thinking many of our fundamental assumptions about how the universe is structured and how it operates. More specifically, we can:

- Learn to be comfortable with uncertainty and with the unpredictable nature of the world around us.

- Recognize that everything is interrelated and that focusing too narrowly on one or more of the "parts" often means overlooking other critical aspects, missing the big picture and increasing the likelihood of unintended consequences.

- Rethink the nature of causality and the implications for how we go about "fixing" business problems and creating individual health and wellbeing.

• Realize that the relationships we engage in as human beings are a crucial factor, if not *the* crucial factor, in determining our health and our ability to heal as well as the health and success of the organizations in which we work.

You may also be starting to see the profound implications of these suggestions and the critical importance of the fusion of organizational and employee wellbeing we discussed earlier. It becomes clear we really can't separate the two because of their profound and inextricable interconnections. The significance of the quantum revolution on the need for paradigm change related to human beings and the organizations in which they work is perhaps best summed up by world-renowned management professor and leadership consultant, Dr. Margaret Wheatley:

> *Each of us lives and works in organizations designed from Newtonian images of the universe. We manage by separating things into parts, we believe that influence occurs as a direct result of force exerted from one person to another, we engage in complex planning for a world that we keep expecting to be predictable, and we search continually for better methods of objectively measuring and perceiving the world. But the science has changed. If we are to continue to draw from science to create and manage organizations, to design research, and to formulate ideas about organizational design, planning, economics, human motivation and change processes, (the list can be much longer) then we need to at least ground our work in the science of our times. We need to stop seeking after the universe of the seventeenth century and begin to explore what has become known to us during the 20th century.*[11]

These are profound considerations, to be sure. However, this is not the end of the story. Even more recent scientific discoveries have shown us that it is not just the implications of the new understandings concerning the realities of the microscopic universe that need to be reconsidered. In fact, these sciences clearly demonstrate that the macroscopic world, the one inhabited by both humans and the organizations in which they work, is also based on very different assumptions and governed by very different rules from those that apply to the workings of machines.

Chaos and Complexity – The New Science of Change

In 1961, meteorologist Edward Lorenz was using a computer model to make a repeated weather prediction. He inadvertently entered the decimal 0.506 instead of the full 0.506127 into the computer. From this seemingly miniscule alteration, the result was a completely different weather scenario. He coined the phrase "Butterfly Effect" to suggest that a seemingly infinitesimally small occurrence, such as a butterfly flapping its wings in one corner of the globe, might create tiny changes in the atmosphere that could ultimately alter, delay or even prevent a hurricane in another part of the world.[12] Clearly, the flap of the butterfly's wings does not create the hurricane, but it is one of the numerous initial conditions that connect with a long and complex chain of events that culminates eventually in the outcome of the hurricane. Together with the other initial conditions and subsequent events, the flap of the wings leads to the hurricane; without it, no hurricane! To put it another way, you might recall the story of the straw that broke the camel's back. Although not nearly as complicated as the weather scenario, no one really knows exactly when the camel's back will give out or what could have been changed along the way to alter the final outcome.

The discovery of the Butterfly Effect has radically altered our understanding of the process of change and the nature of cause and effect in the real world. Machines are linear systems that, according to the mechanistic worldview, obey the following rules:

- Small changes to a variable will result in small changes in the system.

- Outcomes can be determined by adding the small changes.

- Fixing usually involves breaking the system down into its constituent parts and replacing or fixing those parts before putting the whole back together.

- There is usually a direct relationship between the strength of the cause and the consequential effect.

Contrary to the teachings of the mechanistic worldview, complex systems such as the weather operate under completely different assumptions. Why should we be interested in such complex, non-linear systems? Because contrary to traditional scientific wisdom, they are by their very nature both unpredictable and uncontrollable. Chaos theory and complexity science are concerned with the study of such systems. Most of us are quite aware that, even with all of our sophisticated techniques and computers, it is impossible to accurately predict the weather for more than a few days in advance. Just like the inability to accurately measure the wave and particle nature at the same time in quantum physics, chaos theory tells us that this limitation is not due to the inadequacies of our knowledge or technology, but is actually an inherent characteristic of the weather as a "complex system."

Change in complex systems like the weather occurs through myriad negative and positive feedback loops that result in nonlinear effects that twist and turn on themselves in ways impossible to measure and predict accurately. And, as we learned from the Butterfly Effect, in such nonlinear systems, there is no direct relationship between the strength of the cause and the impact of the effect — small changes in a variable can result in huge and even catastrophic alterations in the outcome. Like the myth of scientific objectivity, the old paradigm concept of linear cause and effect in such systems is an illusion. As you may have guessed by now, the same holds true for human beings and the organizations in which they work — also both examples of living, nonlinear, complex systems.

Chaos and Organizations

In her groundbreaking book, "Leadership and the New Science," Margaret Wheatley exposes how we have translated the machine imagery of the cosmos proposed by the mechanistic worldview into organizations with an overwhelming emphasis on material structure and multiple parts:

> *Responsibilities have been organized into functions. People have been organized into roles. Page after page of organizational charts depict the workings of the machine: the number of pieces, what fits where, who the most important pieces are… we've spent years moving pieces around, building elaborate models, contemplating more variables, creating more precise forms of analysis… We've created roles and accountabilities specifying lines of authority and limits to responsibilities. We have drawn boundaries around the flow of experience, fragmenting whole networks of interactions into discreet steps. We study variables as separate and well-bounded, even when we attempt to account for some of their interactions through complex statistical techniques. Information is arrayed in two-dimensional charts and graphs that chunk up the world. Charts tell us about market share, employee opinions,*

customer ratings. We have even come to think of power —
an elusive, energetic force if ever there was one as a bounded resource,
defined as 'my share of the pie.' [13]

As with all other major aspects of our culture, the relationship between science and business has its roots in the Newtonian physics of the Scientific Revolution, which gave birth to the Industrial Revolution. In the late 1800s and early 1900s, mechanistic science was forcibly interjected into the emerging field of management theory. Frederick W. Taylor, the father of "scientific management," proposed that improving the efficacy of work and the productivity of workers was basically an engineering problem. Enormous amounts of time and energy were devoted to breaking work into discreet tasks that could be performed by even the least trained workers. According to scientific management, human beings were basically seen through the lens of their work — as what they did and produced rather than who they were. Dr. C. Stephen Byrum, writing in his seminal book, "From the Neck Up: The Recovery and Sustaining of The Human Element in Modern Organizations," describes Taylor's scientific approach to management:

> *Work is understood primarily in terms of economics, the 'human being'*
> *becomes the 'economic man.' This 'economic man' then becomes a*
> *mechanical cipher driven only by satisfactions and dissatisfactions*
> *relating to money... Nowhere in Taylor's work will he be found asking*
> *a worker what he wants, what his goals are, or what would provide*
> *the greatest motivation and incentive. There is simply the assumption*
> *of the direct relationship between 'human nature' and price.* [14]

Athough some of these beliefs and the rigid, fragmented structures they created have been left behind, thinking of organizations as machines is still alive and well today. We will explore this in more detail in chapter 4.

Chaos and Employee Wellbeing

Our *stuckness* to the mechanistic worldview has had similarly profound implications for our conceptualization of human behavior. To a large degree, we continue to consider human behavior as a linear process viewed through the lens of the mechanistic reductionist paradigm. Resnicow describes this reality:

*Change is usually considered as rational and as a deterministic process
in which individuals obtain information, consider pros and cons,
make a behavioral decision, and then plan a course of action...
Consistent with this perspective, our public health statistical models
have almost exclusively assumed a linear relationship between
psychosocial predictors and behavior change; that is, greater increases
in knowledge, attitudes and intentions will lead to greater
(and proportional) changes in behavior. In other words small
inputs create small outputs.*[15]

We will discuss how recent discoveries in neuroscience invalidate these assumptions in chapter 6. The impact of the mechanistic worldview on our understanding of human behavior change is perhaps represented most vividly by the work of B.F. Skinner, whose approach, usually referred to as behavior modification or behavioral management, continues to dominate as the modus operandi for our efforts to "get" people to change. We will have more to say about the devastating legacy of this approach in chapter 6. Suffice it to say here, this approach, consistent with the assumptions of the mechanistic worldview, sees humans as basically machine-like automatons, whose every behavior is nothing more than a robotic, unthinking response to the environment. We can easily see the similarities with the view of workers expressed in the scientific management described above. In Skinner's own words:

*There is no place in the scientific analysis of behavior
for a mind or a self.*

As we have discussed, however, the new sciences tell us a very different story about chaotic, complex systems like the weather and human beings. Consistent with the teachings of chaos and complexity, Resnicow illustrates the striking similarities between these two complex systems by simply, yet ingeniously, substituting behavioral for meteorological terminology:

*The weather (BEHAVIOR CHANGE) is an example of a chaotic system.
In order to make long-term weather forecasts (PREDICTIONS OF
BEHAVIOR CHANGE) it would be necessary to take an infinite number
of measurements, which would be impossible to do. Also, because the
atmosphere (HUMAN BEHAVIOR) is chaotic, tiny uncertainties would
eventually overwhelm any calculations and defeat the accuracy of the
forecast. Even if it were possible to fill the entire atmosphere of the earth
with an enormous array of measuring instruments, e.g., thermometers,*

wind gauges and barometers (PSYCHOSOCIAL, BIOLOGIC AND ENVIRONMENTAL MEASURES) uncertainty in the initial conditions would arise from the minute variations in measured values between each set of instruments in the array. Because the atmosphere (HUMAN BEHAVIOR) is chaotic, these uncertainties, no matter how small, would eventually overwhelm any calculations and defeat the accuracy of the forecast (PREDICTION).[16]

Just as quantum physics shows we can only speak of probabilities and not certainty when it comes to what orbit within an atom any particular electron will move, chaos theory also holds true for predicting most of the real world. Quantum physics tells us that, because everything is interconnected, everything affects everything else. Chaos theory adds that it is the nature of complex, nonlinear systems, like the weather and like human beings and the organizations in which they work, to be unpredictably sensitive to small changes. Like the straw that broke the camel's back, we can never know for sure the outcome from changes *(management, leadership, wellbeing, etc.)* we introduce in a complex system. It is not possible for us to be aware of all the potential connections. Even if it were possible, we still would not accurately predict the path of such systems. Just as with sub-atomic particles, prediction and control in these systems is both impractical and impossible.

So, for business and health professionals alike, working with humans is much more like trying to predict and control the weather than it is like assembling and disassembling some predictable machine. And we all know how accurate weather prediction is! Anyone who works in these fields has experienced the lack of controllability and predictability inherent to the natural world and the human experience.

We firmly believe that these new scientific understandings will continue to illuminate the way as we develop the rationale and blueprint for transforming workplaces into world-class cultures. Now that we have a broader understanding of the paradigms, worldviews and outdated sciences that drive our *stuckness*, let's explore in more depth specifically how these play out with regards to that *stuckness*, specifically as it relates to organizational wellbeing, employee wellbeing and our approaches to change.

Summary of Key Components of the New Sciences:

The major assumptions based on the worldview informed by the updated sciences we have discussed:

• **Quantum Physics:** The building blocks that make up everything in the universe exist simultaneously as particles *(matter)* and waves *(energy)* and therefore:

  1) Everything is constantly changing and evolving.

  2) Everything is interconnected.

  3) Cause and effect is not linear, and nothing is 100% certain.

  4) The nature of the whole is always different from the mere sum of its parts.

  5) The universe is an interconnected web of relationships.

• **Chaos Theory and Complexity:** Living entities like the weather, human beings and organizations are complex systems, which by their very nature are:

  1) Not guided by the assumptions and rules that apply to machines.

  2) Nonlinear with respect to cause and effect.

  3) Extremely sensitive to initial conditions.

  4) Unpredictable.

  5) Uncontrollable.

CHAPTER 4
The *Stuckness*:
Organizational Wellbeing

❝When it comes to how we approach business, we need to rethink everything we thought we knew about management. This isn't just about a new model for measuring a business, reengineering its operations or motivating its people. This is about the nature of the world being different than we thought it was and about the need for a fundamentally different paradigm to drive the way we think and act.[1]*❞*

Charles S. Jacobs, "Management Rewired"

In case you've been wondering why we spent the past three chapters diving into paradigms, outdated worldviews and new sciences, it all starts to come together in the next three chapters in which we examine our *stuckness* with respect to organizational wellbeing, employee wellbeing and the process of behavior change. As we have discussed, in all three cases this *stuckness* traces its roots back to the scientific worldview of the 17th century. We begin in this chapter by examining *stuckness* in organizational wellbeing and how we can turn to more recent scientific understandings to get ourselves *unstuck*.

Frederick W. Taylor: "Scientific Management"— Employees as Machines

As mentioned in the previous chapter, Taylor believed it was human nature for people to "goof off" *(what he referred to as "soldiering")*. He spent his career finding ways to improve productivity and, in that regard, is responsible for the notion that our primary concern should be attending to the most efficient way of doing our work. Taylor employed the same approach to improving the efficiency of employees as he did to the machines on which they were working. He broke job tasks down to their component parts and calculated the one best way to do the job. True to the legacy of the 17th-century mechanistic, reductionist worldview, viewing men as machines and applying similar scientific methods to human work gained great popularity among managers.

Taylor believed that men were motivated purely by economic self-interest. Based on this assumption, it made sense that if employees were paid for what they produced, they would naturally and eagerly embrace any approach that would maximize their earnings. However, the pitfall of "Taylorism" was that, in true reductionist fashion, thinking was separated from doing and decision making from the work. As a result, supervisors had to micro-manage workers to ensure they didn't get away with "soldiering." Taylor assumed that working men's minds were inconsequential.[2] Dr. C. Stephen Byrum describes Taylor's view of the management/employee relationship:

> *Each man must give up his own particular way of doing things,*
> *adapt his methods to the many new standards, and grow accustomed to*
> *receiving and obeying instructions, covering details large and small,*
> *which in the past had been left to individual judgment.*
> *The workmen are to do as they are told.*[3]

It is not difficult to pick out the flaws in this mechanistic, control-oriented approach to managing employees. When we separate thinking from doing, we limit the autonomy of employees. We know that employees want autonomy, responsibility and control over their work and the ability to think and do for themselves *(we discuss the serious consequences for employee engagement when these are missing in the next chapter)*. Of course, the more power and responsibility we give to a manager, the less responsibility an employee has to accept. This is problematic — especially given that we are in a time when people are regularly discussing how the decline in personal responsibility is hurting Western civilization. However, this outdated approach to management still runs rampant in organizations today. Well-known leadership guru Peter Drucker perhaps put it best when discussing the importance of moving from telling employees what to do to embracing the importance of the knowledgeable worker:

> *The need to manage oneself is therefore creating*
> *a revolution in human affairs.*[4]

Patriarchy: Still Alive and Well in Today's Organizations

Although progress has been made in the past few decades in gender equality in this country, patriarchy is still alive and well in organizations. For example, although entrepreneurship is a critical gauge of success in modern economies, a consistent gender gap still exists. Men engage in entrepreneurial activity in the United States at almost twice the rate of women;[5] and women-led ventures have received only 7% of all available venture funds.[6] Even more concerning, a recent study conducted in collaboration with Harvard Business School, Wharton School and MIT Sloan School of Management found that, even when the pitch content is exactly the same, investors consistently prefer male-presented entrepreneurial pitches as compared to those presented by females.[7]

In 2013, Sheryl Sandberg became a household name by calling for an uprising against the patriarchal dominance in the business world. As the chief operating officer of Facebook, she is ranked on Fortune's list of the 50 Most Powerful Women in Business. In her book, "Lean In: Women, Work, and the Will to Lead," Sandberg describes the still powerful gender biases in organizations today. For example, although 50% of U.S. college graduates are women, men still hold the vast majority of leadership positions in organizations; and there has been no progress in the past 10 years in terms of women holding top executive positions within organizations.[8] Sandberg also described how women unintentionally hold themselves back in their careers. Certainly much of this phenomenon can be attributed to how boys and girls are raised differently: Ambitious boys are praised for being assertive, whereas ambitious girls are labeled as "bossy." In hopes of eliciting change, an entire Lean In movement has been started with Lean In Circles being formed throughout the country focused on women's empowerment *(LeanIn.org)*.

The damaging consequences of patriarchal workplace cultures have also been recently exposed by another highly successful woman leader, Arianna Huffington. In her new book, "Thrive," she posits that women are paying an even higher price than men for being in a work culture fueled by stress, sleep deprivation and burnout. And women, perhaps even more than their male counterparts, need to feel valued to be engaged. The problem, according to Huffington, is that most workplaces are set up according to masculine ways of succeeding:

Our current notion of success, in which we drive ourselves into the ground, if not the grave — in which working to the point of exhaustion and burnout is considered a badge of honor — was put in place by men, in a workplace culture dominated by men. But it's a model of success that's not working for women, and, really, it's not working for men, either.[9]

Huffington advocates for redefining success beyond the masculine traits of money and power to instead focus on wellbeing, wisdom and wonder. Imagine that — wellbeing as a critical factor for individual and organizational success!

The Changing Landscape Impacting Organizations

We know the rapidly changing business landscape in the United States is having a profound impact on organizations and changing what it means to conduct "business as usual":

- By 2020, the share of women in the workforce is projected to increase to 47% as more men than women retire.[10]

- By 2025, Millennials or Gen Y *(people born from early 1980s to early 2000s)* will make up the majority of the workforce. They are looking for organizations that truly value them, don't just see them as cogs in the company machine, and make a positive impact in society.[11]

- 95% of Millennials say work/life balance is important to them.[12]

- Gender bias in the workplace concerns Millennial women.[13]

With this shift in the workforce comes some important considerations for organizational and employee wellbeing. The problem is that changing an organization is really about changing people. When organizations support autonomy, allowing employees to accomplish outcomes in ways that are more natural, they see improved wellbeing and bottom-line cost savings.[14] Moving past the *stuckness* requires challenging the current paradigm of "old-school business" and redirecting the focus to the quality of the employee experience. It requires us to embrace the New Paradigm based on our understandings of quantum physics, chaos theory, psychoneuroimmunology *(which we discuss in chapter 5)* and neuroscience *(discussed in chapter 6)*. These understandings allow us to recognize organizations and their employees as thinking, evolving, complex systems capable of, and requiring self-direction, or what is commonly referred to as "the cognitive paradigm" *(discussed in chapter 6)*. We illustrate the New Paradigm in chapter 6.

Applying the New Sciences to Improve Organizational Wellbeing

Mechanism is very much alive and well in organizations today. Everywhere you look, you can see the legacy of the reductionist, control-oriented approach; from organizational charts, to organizing responsibilities into functions and people into roles, to the over-reliance on segmented data analytics to diagnose organizational problems. The machine conceptualization lends itself to creating significant bureaucracies and a focus on control. Margaret Wheatley describes the challenges of the 17th-century worldview in organizations:

> *Many organizations feel they have to defend themselves even against their employees with regulations, guidelines, time clocks, and policies and procedures for every eventuality... we are afraid of what would happen if we let these elements of the organization recombine, reconfigure or speak truthfully to one another. We are afraid that things will fall apart.*[15]

Yet, as we will see in future chapters, the more organizations aim to strictly control employees, the more it backfires. Wheatley describes the trouble we have created for ourselves in organizations by confusing control with order:

> *If people are machines, seeking to control us makes sense. But if we live with the same forces intrinsic to all other life, then seeking to impose control through rigid structures is suicide. If we believe that there is no order to human activity except that imposed by the leader, that there is no self-regulation except that dictated by policies, if we believe that responsible leaders must have their hands into everything, controlling every decision, person and moment, then we cannot hope for anything except what we already have — a treadmill of frantic efforts that end up destroying our individual and collective vitality.*[16]

Our 17th-century organizations are crumbling. Organizations need to embrace chaos and complexity and recognize that disruptions, confusion and uncertainty are actually critical conditions for awakening creativity.[17] As we start to think of organizations as living systems, we realize that organizational structures, plans, measures and values are most effectively generated by people figuring out what will work best in the situation in which they are immersed.[18] And understanding the complexity of a living system is best accomplished by tending to the relationships among its members. This means we clearly have to rethink how we deal with complexity by paying more attention to what allows people to bring their best selves to work each day.[19]

Increasingly, business leaders recognize that their companies are evolving, organic entities; what organizational expert Peter Senge describes in his seminal book, "The Fifth Discipline," as "learning organizations." Senge believes that organizations *(like all living systems)* are in a state of continuous adaptation and improvement. As we discussed previously, most change efforts face interpersonal and cultural issues that resist change; the only way to effectively promote organizational change is to create a learning organization. Learning organizations nurture new and expansive patterns of thinking and engage in what Senge refers to as "systems thinking." As we have learned from our discussions of the new sciences, the universe is at the most basic level about relationships; systems thinking focuses on how individuals interact with the system and looks at these interactions in relation to the whole, not as individual, isolated occurrences.[20]

We know it is difficult and uncomfortable to let go of old paradigms. But making the shift from relying on highly structured and controlled environments *(that treat people like machines)* to focusing on expanded thinking and the desired future vision *(which embrace the complexities of people and of systems)* will allow organizations to accomplish their purposes. Yet, we have a hard time with uncertainty. In fact, too often we rush to ease our own discomfort with having a lack of clarity or questions without easy answers by coming up with a narrow *(reductionist)* solution, ignoring everything else that isn't being dealt with at the time. We continue to be *stuck*, thinking we can control every component of the machine. However, if we step back and focus on the interrelated system as a whole, embrace the uncertainty, and move beyond the boxes that have been drawn to describe roles and relationships within organizations, we can create more viable and resilient learning and self-organizing systems able to more rapidly adapt to changing circumstances while still maintaining their identity.[21] Wheatley summarizes the new understandings:

> *As we think of organizations as living systems, we don't discard our concern for such things as standards, measures, values, organizational structures, plans, etc. But we do need to change our beliefs about where these things come from. In a living system, they are generated as people figure out what will work in the current situation. In a machine these features are designed outside and then engineered in.*[22]

The Crisis of Capacity — Threatening Organizational Wellbeing

We have discussed how organizational and individual employee wellbeing are inextricably intertwined — even more so in today's 24/7 world than in Taylor's era. Yet the legacy of Taylorism, combined with the new stressful realities of work, have resulted in employees working more hours, constantly checking e-mails on mobile devices, and having a persistent, nagging feeling that it's never enough. Intuitively, we know these types of working conditions are not sustainable — even machines will malfunction at some point if they are not allowed to rest and are not properly maintained. Yet, organizations fail to recognize the negative impact this can have on individual employees as well as organizational performance. The figure below is adapted from the work of C. Stephen Byrum, PhD, and illustrates why organizations need to care about the interrelatedness of organizational and employee wellbeing.[23]

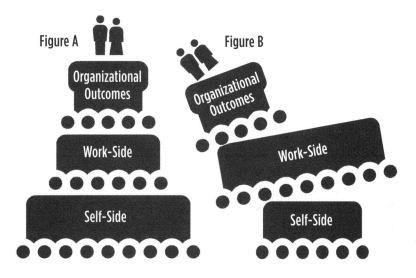

At the top of each figure are the outcomes that an organization ultimately wants to achieve. Each individual within an organization has two aspects that contribute to whether the organization achieves those desired outcomes: the self-side and the work-side. Imagine the two diagrams above each represent a three-tier wedding cake. Your mission is to get that cake in one piece to a $1 million wedding. Which cake would you ultimately want to be responsible for if you're to be successful? Most likely you answered "Figure A" because it has a much more stable base. Perhaps most importantly, you may have noticed that the supporting base is the self-side.

Byrum has been conducting research for over 40 years on the relationship between work-side, self-side and organizational performance. Based on the work of Robert S. Hartman and using his validated assessment tool *(which we will describe in more detail in chapter 6)*, Dr. Byrum has found that only 7% of the population is balanced as in Figure A. We are conditioned and feel pressured to sacrifice ourselves for the betterment of the organization, and organizations in turn reward this self-sacrifice, setting up a vicious cycle. How long do you think you could continue being imbalanced as in Figure B before your cake would topple over? And how effective do you think you're actually being at work while you are constantly trying to prevent this from happening?

Dr. Byrum's research has demonstrated that lack of work-self balance results in employees not achieving their potential at work and organizations not achieving their desired outcomes. Without good work-self balance:

- Customer service declines as a result of increased stress.

- Interpersonal communication becomes less effective.

- Workplace accidents increase.

- Turnover increases — particularly amongst top-performing employees.

- Quality decision-making is compromised.[24]

Additionally, Dr. Byrum's most recent work with Yale's Institute for Excellence has shown that having a strong self-side and work-self balance is critical to organizational sustainability.[25] This is not surprising, if we remember what the new sciences tell us about interconnectedness, relationships, and cause and effect in complex systems. Our work greatly impacts the quality of our personal lives and vice versa.

A Different Kind of Energy Crisis

Well-known business author and performance expert Tony Schwartz has been addressing work performance and the problem of employee disengagement since 2003 when he founded The Energy Project.[26] Schwartz believes burnout is one of the leading causes of performance issues and disengagement. He works with organizations to help individuals focus on managing their energy as opposed to their time. In 2010, The Energy

Project began formally collecting data to get a pulse of the world at work via their Energy Audit™. Incorporating the latest understandings about human health *(which we discuss in more detail in the next chapter)*, this diagnostic tool measures how effectively individuals manage their personal energy across four dimensions: physical, emotional, mental and spiritual.

Why should organizations care about energy? Because energy is defined as the capacity to do work. More energy available means greater capacity to do work. Schwartz's research shows that 74% of employees are experiencing a personal energy crisis. As a result, they are increasingly exhausted, overwhelmed and disengaged, which is not a sustainable way of functioning for individuals or for organizations. Schwartz also found that not taking regular breaks to replenish energy greatly contributes to this energy crisis. In fact, 62% of people who do not take regular breaks become less productive, less engaged, less efficient and less focused, which increases the likelihood of their negatively impacting organizational performance.[27]

Energy Crisis in Action: A Tale of Two Employees

Let's look a bit more closely at this employee energy crisis. Jane is the typical overachiever. Her work-life balance is similar to that of about 93% of working Americans. Her cake is about to topple over. In a typical 40-hour work week, Jane puts in ten-hour days, usually works through lunch, and does not take regular breaks. As a result, during the day, her capacity depletes so she is only working at about 60% capacity over the course of the entire day. So, although she is physically putting in 50 hours for her employer, she is only generating around 30 hours of work.

Mark, on the other hand, has better work-life balance. In a typical 40-hour work week, he puts in eight-hour days, usually takes a lunch break, and also takes micro-breaks throughout the day to replenish his energy. Mark is only human, so his capacity also depletes during the day. However, unlike Jane, Mark averages closer to 80% capacity, generating around 32 hours of work. In the same work week, although Mark is putting in 10 fewer hours than Jane, he is contributing two more hours of work for his organization. Additionally, he has those extra 10 hours available to tend to his overall wellbeing — to further support the self-side of his wedding cake, so to speak.[28]

Unfortunately, with most workers having Jane's rather than Mark's work experience, we are at a tipping point in this country. We have a capacity crisis; we take capacity for granted, and the negative consequences of the resultant stress for organizations are profound:

- In 2013, two-thirds of Americans cited work as a significant source of stress.[29]

- 64% of people frequently feel irritable, impatient and anxious at work.[30]

- 80% of workers feel stress on the job.[31]

- Workplace stress is as bad for the heart as smoking and high cholesterol.[32]

- It is estimated that 75 to 90% of all visits to primary care doctors are related to stress.[33]

It is important to note that this idea of balance does not indicate a finite end state; to view it as such is continuing the Newtonian, mechanistic perspective. Just as a gymnast on a balance beam has to make constant, subtle adjustments to move with ease and grace, businesses and individuals must do the same. And because we know from chaos and complexity that organizations are living, interdependent systems, the only way to counteract the negative impact of organizational stress and uncertainty is to focus on the quality of relationships within them. As Wheatley says:

In order to counter the negative organizational dynamics stimulated by stress and uncertainty, we must give full attention to the quality of our relationships. Nothing else works, no new tools or technical applications, no redesigned organizational chart. The solution is each other.[34]

The more organizations can recognize the critical web of interconnectedness between work life and personal life, and support a meaningful experience at work while also supporting individual wellbeing, the more effective they will ultimately be, both for the business's bottom line and employees' health.

Deadly Workplace Stress: The True Story of Mark Johnson

Mark Johnson is 46 years old and works for a city in the Midwest. He actively participated in their employee wellness program for eight years.

During that time, his focus was primarily on staying physically active and furthering his career. Mark was the picture of physical health, always the model "wellness" program participant with all of his traditional health measures *(blood pressure, weight, cholesterol and glucose)* keeping him in low-risk status for many years.

About three months ago, Mark was not feeling well at work following some physically strenuous activities. As the symptoms moved to chest pressure, a co-worker took his blood pressure. It was quite elevated, and Mark decided to go to the doctor immediately. Mark's history and good health notwithstanding, a stress test was ordered. To the surprise of all, Mark was scheduled for an angioplasty, and a stent was implanted to fix a 99% blockage of his left anterior descending artery. His reaction was, "This isn't possible. I'm only in my 40s; I exercise at least three times a week; I just passed my Air Force Fitness Assessment in November; I'm not overweight, and there is no family history of early heart disease."

Mark's health issues were not related to traditional risk factors. He was physically active and all his risk numbers were normal. What had not been accounted for was the stressful culture in Mark's work life. About one year earlier, there was a department head change that completely shifted the culture of his work environment. It went from a "family/caring" atmosphere to a "micromanaged/hierarchical" nightmare. In addition, six months prior to the event, Mark had requested assistance and information on work favoritism, believing that he was being overlooked for leadership opportunities due to a friendship between his supervisor and another employee. The culture and poor supervisory skills in the organization were obviously contributing to a great deal of unhealthy stress at work.

After his surgery, Mark came to the Human Resources office to complete FMLA paperwork. When he stopped by his department to turn in the forms following his surgery, he was met by the department head with a simple "you need to take the forms to HR." There was no acknowledgment of his situation, no concern for his wellbeing, and no mention of avenues for assistance to help with his recovery. Mark continues to work for the organization, but struggles with the culture, as do many of his co-workers.

Mark's story is all too familiar. Even Arianna Huffington *(of the Huffington Post)* has figured out the importance of organizations supporting individual wellbeing and shifting their definitions of success. She had her wake-up call in 2007 when she collapsed from exhaustion after working 18-hour days to build the Huffington Post and struggling to be a mom to two teenage daughters at the same time. Like so many, it isn't until our wedding cakes topple over *(so to speak)* that we realize how insane this lack of work-self balance is.

The dangerous levels of stress, overload and burnout in this country are very real. People simply can't take on one more thing. A company can have highly engaged employees who simply don't have any available capacity to make any extra discretionary effort. Organizations need to shift from trying to figure out how to get more out of their employees to really investing in those employees by taking care of them. Not only will this support their individual wellbeing but it will help foster greater employee engagement and all the associated benefits.

Employee Engagement — A Prime Indicator of Organizational Wellbeing

There are more than 50 identified conceptual definitions of "employee engagement." The Conference Board *(a global, independent business membership and research association working since 1916 to provide organizations with the practical knowledge they need to improve their performance and better serve society)* assembled a committee of experts in 2007 that came up with this composite definition:

Employee engagement is a heightened emotional and intellectual connection that an employee has for his/her job, organization, manager or coworkers that, in turn, influences him/her to apply additional discretionary effort to his/her work.[35]

Engagement is said to occur when employees:
- Know what is expected of them.
- Feel valued.
- Are able to leverage their strengths.
- Have quality relationships at work.
- Are cognitively stimulated.[36]

Senior leadership's actions and behaviors, and the learning and development opportunities provided in an organization play a large role in fostering engagement.[37] In addition, however, another major determinant is whether employees feel valued and supported by their direct supervisors.[38] Because leaders set the tone for the organization, increasing engagement requires a shift in thinking regarding behavior change and a new approach to learning and development *(we address this in more detail in chapters 6 and 10)*.

Engaged employees are not only satisfied, but they go above and beyond to help the organization achieve success. Disengaged employees, on the other hand, are apathetic, toxic to the work environment, can erode the culture and negatively impact productivity.[39] Engagement also has a powerful impact on individual wellbeing, affecting physical and mental health as well as workplace injuries:

- Highly engaged employees miss fewer days of work due to illness and are more resilient with respect to organizational change.[40]

- Total cholesterol and triglyceride levels significantly decrease as engagement levels increase; likewise, cholesterol and triglyceride levels increase as engagement levels decrease.[41]

- 62% of engaged employees feel their work lives positively affect their physical health and 78% believe their work lives benefit them psychologically.[42]

- 54% of actively disengaged employees feel their work lives negatively affect their physical health and 51% feel their work lives negatively affect their psychological wellbeing.[43]

- Actively disengaged employees are nearly twice as likely to be diagnosed with depression and anxiety as are engaged employees.[44]

- Individuals in workgroups in the bottom quartile of engagement average 62% more accidents than workgroups in the top quartile of engagement.[45]

These findings reinforce the need to pay attention to the critical link between organizational and employee wellbeing. Unfortunately, our typical approach to changing employee behavior does not foster, and can often inhibit, engagement. As we will discover in the next two chapters, by continuing to pursue changing behaviors through programs and mandating changes through policies and environmental interventions, we continue to miss the most important component — the people. In doing so, we set up wellness/wellbeing, safety and recognition programs as something we are doing *to* employees, rather than for them.

The Critical Role of Organizational Culture

Nothing illustrates the power of organizational culture more than this well-known scientific experiment. A group of scientists placed five monkeys in a cage and in the middle, a ladder with bananas on top. Every time a monkey went up the ladder, the scientists soaked all of the monkeys with ice water from a fire hose. This continued until eventually no monkey dared to go up the ladder — regardless of the temptation.

Then the scientists decided to substitute one of the monkeys with one that had never been in the cage. The first thing the new monkey did was to start up the ladder to get the banana. Immediately, the other monkeys beat it up. After several beatings, the new member learned not to climb the ladder even though it never knew why. A second monkey was then substituted and the same thing occurred. This time, the first replacement monkey participated in the beating of the new monkey. Eventually, all the monkeys were replaced; each time the other monkeys participated in beating the new monkey who tried to climb the ladder and get the banana.

Eventually, what was left was a group of five monkeys that were never blasted by the ice cold water yet refused to even attempt to climb the ladder to get a banana.[46] If it was possible to ask the monkeys why they beat up anyone who attempted to go up the ladder, we bet you the answer would be…

"I don't know — that's just how things are done around here."

> **Even when no evidence exists, or when conclusive evidence to the contrary does exist, we still keep doing these things because our paradigms have us *stuck* on believing they work.**

Does this sound familiar? How often do we do things that make absolutely no sense, just because it's the way things are done? This is the power of paradigms that we described in chapter 1 and the power of culture. This also describes the clash of *Belief vs. Evidence*. Even when no evidence exists, or when conclusive evidence to the contrary does exist, we still keep doing these things because our paradigms have us *stuck* on believing they work.

Organizational Culture Defined

"Culture" has become a popular buzzword when it comes to addressing employee health, safety and engagement. However, most organizations are not addressing culture; they are addressing climate and environment — and they're going about it in a way that is much less effective than it could be.

As we mentioned in the introduction, Edgar Schein, PhD, describes culture as "the hidden force that drives most of our behavior both inside and outside organizations." Schein says of culture:

- It goes beyond "it's the way we do things around here," the company climate, basic values, etc. These are all manifestations of the culture.

- The culture of an organization plays a significant role in shaping employee behavior and fostering organizational change.[47]

Culture provides the foundation and support for organizational wellbeing. Even with years of effort, employee engagement scores haven't improved much at most organizations. According to 2013 research by Gallup in 142 countries, only 13% of employees are engaged, while 63% of employees are disengaged.[48] The difference for high-performing organizations is found within their culture.

The 2012 Towers Watson Global Workforce Study found that in the highest-performing cultures, leaders not only create high levels of engagement but also create environments to support productivity and performance, and they help employees feel a greater sense of physical, emotional and social wellbeing at work — people feel energized. These high-performing cultures share the following characteristics:

- The mission and values of the company are clear.

- Standards and expectations for every employee are clear.

- Leaders work to make sure employees understand the alignment of their work and actions with the larger company purpose, vision and goals.

- Employees are well fitted to their jobs.

- Employees feel a sense of possibility and believe they will grow while working at the company *(if not by promotions then by achieving personal goals and reaching for higher levels of competency and impact)*.[49]

Additional research from Gallup shows the importance of wellbeing on traditional organizational performance metrics. People who are thriving in overall wellbeing have a 35% lower turnover rate than those who are struggling in their wellbeing.[50]

The Impact Leadership Has on Culture

The quality of leadership plays a critical role in the health of an organization's culture. Every experience of employee interaction with a leader generates a belief about workplace culture. A San Francisco healthcare system conducted a risky, real-life experiment to examine the effects its managers have on organizational performance. They classified departments in one of three categories:

- *Green* — terrific places to work *(higher than normal profitability and productivity, great employee engagement scores and better than average employee retention).*

- *Yellow* — average employee survey scores *(not bad, but not great).*

- *Red* — poor on every metric, especially turnover.

The experiment consisted of moving managers of green departments to red departments and red to green. In every case, regardless of the background or expertise of the manager, within one year the red departments became green and green departments turned red. It was the manager who made the difference![51]

Culture is learned over time and simultaneously involves behavioral, emotional and cognitive processes. The cognitive or thought processes ultimately shape the attitudes, feelings, overt behavior and values of employees. Unless these underlying processes are addressed, successful change will not be possible because organizations will eventually revert back to how they originally operated.[52]

Transforming organizational culture is not some "thing" that needs to be done; it should incorporate everything an organization does as a business — including how problems are solved and how people work together; and it starts with leadership.[53] Although it is possible for organizations to change, sustainable results will not occur unless the culture and people are fully prepared and aligned to support the changes.[54] As the saying goes, "People only support what they create." [55] Organizations need to work to foster high levels of both organizational and employee wellbeing to shift their culture and experience sustainable change. Because culture is built team-by-team, leadership development is a critical piece of this puzzle, one that is all too often overlooked. We will address leadership development in more detail in chapter 10.

Organizational Health — A Manifestation of Culture

Patrick Lencioni defines an organization as being healthy when it has integrity, "when it is whole, consistent and complete, that is, when management, operations, strategy and culture fit together and make sense." Lencioni believes that, to be successful an organization must focus on two basic qualities: It must be:

- *Smart* — excel in the classic fundamentals of business
  (i.e., strategy, operations, finance, marketing and technology).

- *Healthy* — have minimal politics, minimal confusion, high morale, high productivity and low turnover.

As mentioned in the introduction, although being smart is only half of the equation, in most organizations, it occupies almost all of the time, energy and attention of leaders. Futhermore, an organization can have a "culture of health/wellness" but still be completely dysfunctional in terms of organizational health in Lencioni's terms. Unfortunately for many workplaces, this is the consistent and unpleasant reality. Writing in "The Art of Health Promotion" in 2012, longtime workplace wellness guru Dr. Dee Edington hit the nail right on the head:

Behavior change is really the mantra of wellness,
but if a person achieves a lifestyle behavior change,
only to return to the same unhealthy environment,
what can we expect will happen? We set up wellness for failure
if we don't work on improving the environment and culture
before we work on individual behavior change.[57]

Thriving Organizational Wellbeing

A May 2013 Harvard Business Review article examined what it means to have an authentic, thriving organization. The authors identified six common imperatives that allow organizations to operate at their fullest potential by providing people the opportunity to do their best work; the authors actually refer to it as "the organization of your dreams":[58]

1) *Let People Be Themselves.* The ideal organization is keenly aware of dominant currents in its culture and nurtures individuality. It doesn't resort to conventional performance appraisal systems and instead focuses on self-determination with support from management.

2) *Unleash the Flow of Information.* Ideal organizations don't spin information, and they respect their employees' need to know what's really going on; they strive for radical honesty and transparency whenever possible.

3) *Magnify People's Strengths.* Ideal organizations support their best employees in becoming even better with great training and development.

4) *Stand for More Than Shareholder Value.* People want to be part of something bigger than themselves; there needs to be shared meaning and purpose. This becomes even more important with the demographic shift in the workforce. A 2014 Deloitte Touche survey found that Millennial employees want to make a difference and expect businesses to care.[59]

5) *Show How the Daily Work Makes Sense.* Leaders go out of their way for job enrichment and deliberately consider the tasks each employee performs to see if they make sense.

6) *Have Rules People Can Believe In.* The dream organization provides compelling reasons to embrace necessary structures that support the organization's purpose.

Perhaps you are thinking this sounds like an unachievable utopia, but we think there's tremendous merit in considering and working towards creating a truly authentic organization. There is an old saying that when we go to work, we need to leave our car windows cracked so our real selves can breathe while we're there. We hope to help make that no longer necessary! Our conceptualization of Thriving Organizational Wellbeing *(see Figure C on the following page)* keeps both perspectives of culture and the ideal authentic organization in mind while building on Lencioni's definition of Organizational Health.

Figure C
Thriving Organizational Wellbeing:

- The executive leadership team is truly a cohesive one.

- The mission, vision and values are clearly articulated and every employee knows how she/he fits within them.

- Employees are empowered and enabled to leverage their strengths.

- Leaders and the work climate provide employees with autonomous support *(versus using incentives to drive behaviors)*.

- Clear, timely and meaningful communication is provided for employees, and employees share feedback and ideas that are actually used.

- Clear, timely and meaningful feedback is provided for employees in the spirit of ongoing growth and development *(versus simply measuring performance)*.

- The climate fosters innovation, creativity and meaningful work.

- Leaders truly value employees — and employees feel valued.

- Employees are encouraged and supported to be authentic and be themselves.

- People within the organization respect, support and care about one another as people, not just as employees there to complete certain job tasks.

- Accountability is embraced; the rules are clear and apply to everyone.

- Employees are provided the tools and resources they need to work safely and productively.

- Resources, programs, policies and the environment support employees' ability to thrive in all areas of wellbeing.

- Employees are happy and proud to work there!

Or it can be easily boiled down to one company's mission with regards to the employee experience:

We make it so Monday mornings don't SUCK!

Building a Thriving Workplace Culture

"Culture eats strategy for breakfast, operational excellence for lunch, and everything else for dinner!"

— Peter Drucker

Organizational cultures, like all living systems, are dynamic. They are constantly adapting to external and internal conditions. So, trying to assess organizational culture is complicated by the reality that we are trying to pin down a moving target. But it also raises the possibility that culture change can be managed as a continuous process rather than through big shifts *(often in response to crises)*. As Senge says in "The Fifth Discipline":

A corporation cannot be 'excellent' in the sense of having arrived at a permanent excellence; it is always in the state of practicing the disciplines of learning, of becoming better or worse. [60]

Thus, a stable "destination" may never — and perhaps even should never — be reached. As is the case with all living systems, organizational culture change and employee wellbeing are ongoing journeys, not just a series of events or programs. The culture of the organization should always be learning and evolving.

The problem is that too often organizations try to create a culture of engagement and empowerment by mandating policy changes or applying a one-size-fits-all approach to their employees. However, empowering employees and increasing motivation cannot be accomplished through the use of force; it has to be elicited from within by helping employees to shift how they think about their choices *(we will address this in more detail in chapter 6)*.

As important as it is to define the desired behaviors and manifestations of the thriving culture we are trying to create, it is also critical to define those that indicate dysfunction, so we can address them before they get out of hand. Here is a short checklist of some of the most prevalent manifestations of a dysfunctional culture:

- Your best employees are leaving the organization.
- Stress levels are high.
- There's a lack of trust and great apprehension with any new initiative or change management tries to implement.

- People have stopped bringing forward ideas.

- Collaboration is not great; people tend to operate in silos.

- Innovation has slowed or halted.

- Participation in company events is low.

- You have a wellness program or healthy options in the workplace but people either don't participate or are just going through the motions.

- You have an increase in strains, sprains and low back injuries.

- You have an increase in behavioral health issues, GI, headache and back-pain claims and an increase in anti-anxiety and anti-depressant medication use.

If you find you have a slightly or even a significantly dysfunctional culture, it needs to be tended to ASAP! Not only is it critical for your survival and future growth, but it is an indispensable prerequisite to successfully deploying any change initiative. According to research conducted by Jeffrey Pfeffer, a professor of organizational behavior at Stanford University's Graduate School of Business, unhealthy workplaces can cause up to 125,000 employee deaths each year and add up to $130 billion in excess annual company costs. Pfeffer states:

Many of the individual behaviors you are focusing on in your health and wellness programs (such as) stop smoking, eat better, exercise more, are in fact the consequences of the environments in which they (employees) are working. If you work people to death, of course they are going to smoke more, drink more and eat worse.[61]

If your culture is dysfunctional, you can pretty much guarantee traditional wellness program focused on behavior change will fail, especially if the program includes incentives, which can have unintended consequences as well *(we will discuss this more fully in chapter 6)*. Your best bet is to refocus efforts on creating thriving organizational wellbeing.

A Case Study of Jones Corp.

The true life events at a company we'll call Jones Corp. provide a good example of the importance of paying attention to signs of a dysfunctional workplace culture as well as what can go awry when organizational well-being plummets. Jones Corp. had a history of winning awards and being a great place to work. However, with growth and a dynamic marketplace, things began to change. The executive team held onto its outdated identity far too long and was in denial about any conflicting information it received via employee feedback surveys and exit interviews. They were out of touch with what was happening within the organization. It got to the point that the norm amongst employees was to not be fully honest on surveys because people knew nothing would change. In fact, people learned not to provide critical comments as management would likely retaliate.

As stress levels rose, top quality employees started leaving the company. Yet leadership found excuses each time and provided a "spin" on each departure. Interestingly, in spite of this, there were still many highly engaged employees. The employee experience varied greatly depending on the department in which people worked; the manager or leader made all of the difference. One department in particular had a very effective leader:

- He was a great advocate for his employees. He supported them in finding meaningful work, helped them feel valued and pushed innovation.

- His employees felt like they were in a "protective bubble," so to speak, from the craziness in the rest of the company. As long as they were treated well, they were engaged.

- The employees in this department were a highly energized, cohesive team.

Eventually, however, this all changed. Morale plummeted and highly-skilled, top-performing employees started leaving this department as well. And many other employees in this department were actively seeking other employment and praying to get out of the situation. What happened? When we asked the people who left and those who were seeking other employment, they all had the same answers:

- "Our boss changed; we don't understand it, but he's not the same anymore."

- They reported feeling micro-managed and not empowered with the necessary autonomy to do what was right by the customer.

- They reported being frustrated with inconsistencies in how the manager treated people and how he applied discrepant standards without valid explanations.

- They said their boss had become "nit-picky" and they couldn't remember the last time he had said something positive; and finally

- Not surprisingly, the increase in turnover started to raise concerns among the customers.

What happened with Jones Corp. is not that uncommon. Unfortunately, companies frequently fail to recognize the damage that this type of culture can have on the employee experience and employee wellbeing. For instance, as this shift at Jones Corp. was occurring with top-quality employees leaving and morale plummeting, here is what happened to one employee who we will call Robin.

- She began to feel the stress that her colleagues had experienced before they ultimately left the company.

- She shifted from being highly engaged to having her wellbeing erode. Where she once felt her boss had her back and supported her, she now ended up walking on eggshells.

- She was reprimanded for doing the things to innovate and grow that were once supported. As a survival instinct, she started to withdraw; after all, who wants to go to social functions and pretend when you feel betrayed and don't know who to trust?

- She described feeling like she was being put into a dark, tiny box and then reprimanded for not being outgoing and withdrawing.

- And the tipping point: She had a death in the family and never received any human acknowledgment from her boss; no "I'm sorry for your loss" or any token statement you'd expect from a complete stranger.

• She started not sleeping; her gastrointestinal *(GI)* system was severely compromised; she was having chronic headaches and back aches; and she was an emotional wreck, which her child sensed and responded to by acting out in school.

Watching previously outgoing, engaged employees withdraw should have been an immediate red flag for Jones Corp. However, rather than examining why this shift was happening with Robin and her co-workers, leadership instead created excuses and blamed the individual employees for having "performance issues."

Even when a traumatized employee from an unhealthy culture begins to work in a new, healthier culture with a truly thriving workplace and a phenomenal boss, the lingering effects often last. People like Robin report continuing to walk on eggshells, still worrying about pissing off the new boss. The employees continue to be concerned about whether they're doing a good job or whether they will be reprimanded for staying home with a sick child or other concerns, which have nothing to do with the new boss but which linger from the traumatic experiences with their previous boss.

Unfortunately, what happened at Jones Corp. and with Robin happens all too often. But our hope is that such stories become less common as organizations begin to realize the importance of intentionally fostering a culture of thriving organizational wellbeing and the critical connection it has to employee wellbeing *(which we will be addressing in the next chapter)*.

Summary of the Shift In Organizational Wellbeing:

Old Paradigm — Profit/Productivity Focus:

- **Taylorism** — Pay employees for what they produce and they will inherently find more efficient ways to do things; engineer thinking out of jobs; managers prescribe and control job tasks.

- **Patriarchy** — Masculine definition of success *(money and power)* with accolades given for long work hours, stress and burnout.

- Focus on having individual employees improve their behaviors.

New Paradigm — Employee Experience Focus:

- Support wellbeing, especially work-life balance as a primary means to improve organizational performance.

- Develop authentic and transformational leaders to foster employee engagement and create desired workplace culture.

- Focus on organizational culture and interrelatedness of organization and individual wellbeing.

CHAPTER 5
The *Stuckness*:
Employee Wellbeing

> ❝*The biomedical model, like an X-ray,*
> *is ultimately a representation, one so powerful and pervasive*
> *that we often mistake it for fact.*[1]❞

David Morris, "Illness and Culture in the Postmodern Age"

J ust as was the case with Organizational Wellbeing, our *stuckness* with respect to employee wellbeing traces its roots back to the scientific worldview of the 17th century. And just as was the case then, it is to more recent scientific advances that we turn to get *unstuck*. We believe that some historical context will be helpful both in understanding the *stuckness* and illuminating the path for getting *unstuck*.

René Descartes: Separating the Mind and Spirit from the Body

Of all the great thinkers of the Scientific Revolution, probably none has had a greater impact on Western medicine than René Descartes. Descartes took the concept of the mechanistic universe and applied it directly to all living things, including, of course, human beings:

> *I do not recognize any differences between the machines made by craftsman and the various bodies that nature alone composes.*

> *I consider the body as a machine… my thought… compares a sick man and an ill-made clock with my idea of a healthy man and a well-made clock.*[2]

Descartes also extended the reductionist, dualistic concept of separation of material and immaterial phenomenon to include the belief that the human mind and the body were separate entities:

> *There is nothing included in the concept of the body that belongs to the mind; and nothing in that of the mind that belongs to the body.*

In fact, Descartes used this argument to convince the Catholic Church to permit the first dissection of human cadavers in medical school. The reigning Pope was adamantly opposed to this proposition but finally relented when Descartes argued that, since the spirit or soul was housed in the mind, no harm would come to them from such procedures performed on the body. As the story goes, in return for the Pope's blessing, Descartes promised that medicine would leave all matters of the soul and spirit to the church, concerning itself only with the body. Although a victory for the training of physicians, this agreement unfortunately set the tone for Western medical science for centuries to come, dividing the human experience into distinct and separate spheres that could never overlap. So, following the prevailing reductionist dogma of the day, the "human machine" was essentially divided into three disconnected parts: care of the soul or spirit was given to the church, care of the body was given to medical science, and care of the dispirited mind eventually became the domain of psychiatry.

A 17th-Century Understanding of Health and Disease

The Old Paradigm, 17th-century worldview in essence created the biomedical model that remains to this day as the foundation of Western approaches to health and disease. Following in this tradition *(often referred to as "Cartesian" in honor of the contributions of Descartes)*, biomedicine views human beings basically as sophisticated machines that can be analyzed in terms of their parts. Sickness and disease are considered to be "malfunctions" of the biological "mechanisms" of the machine. The role of the doctor as repairman is to find the underlying cellular or molecular malfunctions and/or causative organisms and to "fix" the machine. Issues related to the mind or spirit are separate from and irrelevant to health concerns. After all, machines have neither minds nor spirits! The underlying foundation of the biomedical model is summarized below:

> Human beings = *machine*
> Disease = *malfunction of the machine*
> Doctor = *repairman*
> Focus = *physical determinants of disease*

Also consistent with the basic tenets of the Old Paradigm, biomedicine has been characterized by a historic neglect of women's health issues.[3] It is no coincidence that the doctor is presented as the repairman. From menopause to autoimmune diseases to breast cancer, mainstream medicine has historically failed to adequately invest in and research issues that affect women's health, and women have been routinely excluded as research participants in many important areas of study.

Determining Cause and Effect: The "Germ Theory of Disease"

By the time the 19th century arrived, this mechanistic, reductionist, scientific approach to medicine had become firmly entrenched in society. Almost all of the basic structures of the human body had been discovered, and great progress had been made in the understanding of the body's physiological processes. With the work of Louis Pasteur and Robert Koch, the "germ theory" in which bacteria were seen as the single cause of all disease became widely accepted. While this may seem unreasonable given our knowledge today, the idea of a disease being caused by a single factor *(linear causality)* fit perfectly into the existing Cartesian paradigm, the human body as machine whose breakdown can be traced back to the malfunctioning of a single part or mechanism that can be replaced or repaired.

Strengths and Weaknesses of Biomedicine

Although traditional approaches based on the biomedical model have resulted in great advances in our understanding of health and disease, we will see that the underlying mechanistic, reductionist view of reality has also placed significant limitations on this understanding. As we learned in chapter 3, as in many other areas of scientific endeavor:

> *When scientists reduce an integral whole to fundamental*
> *building blocks — whether they are cells, genes*
> *or elementary particles — and try to explain all phenomena*
> *in terms of these elements, they lose the ability to understand*
> *the coordinating activities of the whole.*[4]

For contemporary Western medicine, the problem is that 85% of healthcare costs in the United States today result from chronic medical conditions related to our psychosocial environment and our associated lifestyles.

For many of these conditions, including cancers, heart disease, depression, chronic fatigue syndrome and osteoporosis; and particularly for behaviorally-oriented issues related to alcoholism, smoking, sedentary lifestyle, eating/nutrition-related issues, etc., traditional biomedical approaches are much less effective. This is because more than ever before, these problems necessitate understanding human beings not as machines that can be reduced to their constituent parts, but rather as complex systems like the weather; that is, dynamic, integrated wholes, including not only the physical, but also the emotional, social and spiritual components of our experience. These are precisely those factors that have been for so long ignored, and even belittled, by the 17th-century worldview and the biomedical model.

Clearly, for the vast majority of these complex illnesses, the germ, single cause theory of disease simply does not apply. Even when germs are involved, they are usually only one of many potential contributing causes. The end result is that rather than being helpful, the mechanistic, reductionist, dualistic orientation often interferes with our understanding of health and illness by blocking our vision of the whole person and the bigger picture.

The Limitations and Pitfalls of Biomedicine: Heart Disease

To illustrate, let us use coronary heart disease as an example. We know a tremendous amount about the pathophysiology of this disease. Almost everyone is aware of the major biomedical, lifestyle "risk factors" linked with this disease. Yet, it is common medical knowledge that all of these risk factors *(smoking, high blood pressure, high cholesterol, diabetes, etc.)* combined with genetics explain only about half of who gets the disease.[5] The question, of course, is: What explains the other half?

Our knowledge of risk factors for disease comes mostly from epidemiological studies, in which large groups of people are followed over a period of years to determine the existence of relationships between lifestyle risk factors and causes of death. For example, we gained much of our original understanding of the biomedical risk factors for heart disease from the Coronary Pooling Project, research that combined and analyzed results from the first six big epidemiological studies of coronary heart disease. Scientists looked at the relationship between mortality and the three major risk factors; cigarette smoking, high blood pressure and high cholesterol levels in a total group of about 7,300 men, followed for almost 10 years *(note that the first six big studies to examine the epidemiology of heart disease included only men)*. What researchers found was surprising. Fully 80% of the men with all three risk factors and 90% of the men with two risk factors did not have heart attacks during the period. In fact, most of the men who had heart attacks did not have any of these risk factors![6]

Furthermore, even for the most well-known of the traditional biomedical risk factors, actual causes are often anything but clear. High blood pressure is a good example. It is well known that upwards of 90% of the high blood pressure seen in the physician's office is of the "essential" type. This means that there is no known physiological cause for the condition. Cholesterol is another example. We hear so much about the relationship of exercise and, especially, diet in controlling cholesterol levels and ratios. Yet, substantial evidence shows stress may play as large, if not a larger, role in determining levels of cholesterol in the blood. In one study, the average cholesterol levels of medical students increased over 100 points during the course of studying for and taking an important exam.[7] What exercise program or dietary intervention can provide that kind of a change?

Furthermore, as often happens when people's health is reduced to a focus on their numbers, there is growing evidence that we have overemphasized the importance of cholesterol as a predictor of who will and will not have a heart attack.[8] It is indeed a testament to the profound, ongoing influence of the 17th-century legacy of the mind/body separation that, as recently as 20 years ago, a review of the hundreds of identified risk factors for coronary heart disease in "The Journal of The American Medical Association" included absolutely no mention of emotional, social or spiritual factors.[9]

This is not to suggest that people should not be aware of their blood pressure, cholesterol and other traditional biomedical risk factors for heart disease. What it does suggest is that these risk factors are actually not very accurate predictors of who will and will not get a particular disease; they cannot function as the "specific etiology" described by the germ theory of disease. In fact *(as we will discuss in more detail)*, it is becoming evident that these "biomedical risk factors" are often more likely to be "symptoms" of underlying emotional and or psychosocial issues that are the true, although extremely complex and difficult to quantify, causes of many of today's common illnesses.

Our inability to look beyond the measurable physical risk factors of Descartes' material universe has caused us to ignore a rapidly growing body of evidence that suggests that unlike machines, human beings have personalities, thoughts, feelings and emotions, all of which appear to contribute significantly to our resistance to illness and our ability to heal ourselves. And unfortunately, this *stuckness* has to a great degree informed the faulty approaches to workplace wellness programs that are not producing the desired results businesses seek. As you might guess, these new understandings about the complexities of human beings and health and wellbeing have emerged from newer scientific discoveries — in this case in the middle part of the 20th century and a science called Psychoneuroimmunology.

Psychoneuroimmunology *(PNI)* — The Physiology of Attitudes, Beliefs and Emotions

You may be thinking, "What in the world are you talking about now *(why do scientists have to use such ridiculously long names),* and what does this have to do with organizational wellbeing?" We learned in chapter 3 from quantum physics and chaos theory that everything is interrelated — the wellbeing of individual employees impacts the wellbeing of an organization and vice versa. We covered examples of this in chapter 4. When we refer to the "wellbeing" of employees, we are referring to a holistic perspective, which, contrary to the agreement between the Pope and Descartes and the resulting biomedical model, does include an interconnected mind, body and spirit. The new science of PNI is providing us with a large and growing body of research that demonstrates how attitudes, beliefs and emotions can profoundly impact our health. The term psychoneuroimmunology can be better understood by breaking it down into its constituent parts *(being careful to remember that the whole is, in reality, always greater than the sum of its parts!).*

- Psycho → *the mind and the emotions*
- Neuro → *the nervous system*
- Immuno → *the immune system*

PNI has shown us most conclusively that these three systems are inextricably intertwined and interconnected. Although going into detail on this complicated science is beyond the scope of this book, a brief overview of what we have learned from PNI is important because it has profound ramifications for the way we view health and illness and for what we do to positively impact organizational and employee wellbeing.

The "Electrical" and "Chemical" Brains[10]

Many of us remember being taught that the brain and central nervous system are primarily an elaborate telephone complex *(back when telephones had wires, of course)*. Electric charges *(action potentials)* travel along trillions of miles of wires *(axons and dendrites)* and cause cells to release substances *(neurotransmitters)* that travel across spaces between cells *(synapses)*. Depending on the type and number of these substances, the electronic message either continues on or stops at the neighboring cell, signaling feelings, emotions, thoughts, etc.

While this type of "electrical" communication is certainly part of brain activity, the latest research supports the existence of an older and more widespread communication system often referred to as the "chemical brain." In this system, nerve cells release various neuropeptide chemicals *(serotonin, dopamine and endorphins are just some of these chemicals that may be familiar)*, which then travel to different parts of the brain through the extra-cellular spaces. All cells in the brain contain receptors that are especially designed to recognize and grab on to these chemicals. Once grabbed, the neuropeptides are incorporated into the new cell where they set in motion a chain of biochemical events that cause all sorts of changes to occur within the cell. It now appears that this is how most messages resulting in thoughts, feelings and emotions manifest in the brain.

Up until a few years ago, it was commonly believed that this "chemical" communication took place only within the brain; after all that is where the thinking, feeling and emoting happen, isn't it? Thanks to pioneering work in PNI however, we now know that cells producing and having receptors for these chemicals are found throughout the body — suggesting that thoughts, feelings and emotions do not just occur within the brain. Although this may be a difficult concept to grasp given 400 years of training to the contrary, it is actually one that has been understood on an intuitive level for some time. It is well known that the center of emotions in the brain is located in an area called the limbic system. This area is loaded with neuropeptides and their receptors. We now know that these same neuropeptides and receptors are also found in large numbers throughout the lining of the gut as well as in other areas of the body. So when we say, "I'm having a gut feeling," that's exactly what we are having. And when we say somebody is a "pain in the neck," it's very likely to be the case as well!

Over the past 30 years or so, the evidence for this mind/body link has been steadily growing. Hundreds of studies have changed the way we understand the interrelationships between the mind, body and spirit. Here are just a few examples of what we have learned:

- Positive expectations about treatment *(placebo effect)* can significantly improve outcomes for a wide variety of medical conditions *(this is even true when people are told beforehand that the treatment is a placebo!)*.[11]

- Negative expectations about treatment *(nocebo effect)* can diminish outcomes.[12]

- How people feel about their health *(perceived health)* is one of the most accurate predictors of how long people will live.[13]

- People who look at the world in a pessimistic way tend to have suppressed immune function and more medical problems.[14]

- People who are optimistic have less illness, fewer doctors' visits, improved survival following heart attack and increased survival time with breast cancer.[15]

- The more stressed you are, the more likely you are to catch a cold, the more severe it is likely to be, and the more slowly you will heal.[16]

- The body's immune functions can be enhanced with relaxation, meditation and even humor.[17]

- Different forms of meditation and relaxation have been shown to be effective for treating anxiety, panic disorders, and various types of pain and even perhaps reducing the risk of heart attack and stroke.[18]

So, we see that PNI negates the reductionist framework of the biomedical model, in which the body, mind and spirit are seen as separate and non-interacting. In his typically eloquent manner, Dr. Deepak Chopra sums up these eye-opening findings saying:

Sad or depressing thoughts produce changes in brain chemistry
that have a detrimental effect on the body's physiology,
and likewise, happy thoughts, loving thoughts of peace and tranquility
of compassion, friendliness, kindness, generosity, affection, warmth
and intimacy... each produce a corresponding state of physiology
via the flux of neurotransmitters and hormones
in the central nervous system.[19]

PNI and Employee Wellbeing

Let's think about this for a moment. If you have an organization in which people are stressed and pessimistic *(for the kinds of reasons we explored in the previous chapter)*, not only are those people more likely to get sick and injured, and recover at a slower rate from illness and injury *(thus hindering productivity, customer service and more)*, but the physical illnesses, mental states and attitudes can be contagious. We can all likely think of people who brighten the room when they **leave**. Similarly, people's pessimistic attitudes can spread like a bad cold; next thing you know, you have a workplace full of negative people who are not only more likely to get sick and injured but are creating a disengaged and toxic work environment. By not addressing the real roots of the stress, every program and "solution" becomes merely a weak and temporary bandage. If employees are unhappy, it is essential to understand why. That could mean addressing workloads, firing or retraining ineffective managers, improving communication, and working hard to rebuild the culture. Yet, all too often current approaches focus on trying to modify individual employees' behaviors that our *stuckness* dictates must be the major determinants leading to their compromised health.

As a specific example, let's take a look at low back pain and back injuries, a common cost-driver for organizations. Consider these three questions: **1)** Would you describe your work as monotonous?, **2)** How satisfied are you with your job?, and **3)** How tense or anxious have you been in the past week? When asked what these questions are assessing, most people think it must be stress or job satisfaction. In fact, these questions are part of a comprehensive back-pain assessment used by doctors in New Zealand to predict, with 83% accuracy, who will be out of work more than 30 days due to low back pain.[20] Of course, traditional medical questions are also part of the assessment, but these doctors understand the critical role organizational wellbeing plays in employee health. In fact, a primary reason for why someone with low back pain will choose to go out on disability is dissatisfaction with a supervisor or work situation.[21] And, not surprisingly, many organizations have seen an increase in recent years in either medical or Workers' Compensation claims related to low back issues. When we are working with organizations that are experiencing back issues, our first question is not, "Do you have good ergonomics and safe lifting programs in place?" Sure, those are important, but they focus on the individual and are often a bandage to underlying organizational wellbeing issues. Instead, we first ask how morale has been, what relationships are like between management and employees, and how the organization has been doing with stress.

As our paradigm shifts from a biomedical view of health and illness to a holistic perspective, the overall philosophy and the underlying assumptions about why people get sick and how they heal also shift. We outline these underlying assumptions below. Although they may conflict with more traditional scientific explanations, these assumptions are very much in tune with the most recent scientific understandings of the nature of the universe and the realities of the human experience.

> **Assumption One** — The potential for health or illness in humans *(as complex systems)* is the result of an extremely complicated interaction among many variables:
>
> • *Genetics.* Genetics play an important role in determining the ways in which we are likely to be either resilient against or vulnerable to illness. Whether these strengths and weaknesses get expressed depends on a complex interaction between many aspects of a person's life experience.[22] For example, a person with a genetic predisposition to cancer who grows up in a family that discourages emotions, who ends up living in social isolation, and who has been exposed to industrial toxins in his or her geographic location, may develop cancer. Another person with the same genetic propensity for cancer, but experiencing different emotional/social/environmental circumstances, may not develop the disease.
>
> • *Personality.* PNI has taught us that thoughts, attitudes and beliefs can boost or deplete the function of our immune system and create positive or negative changes in the physical body. We also know that a person's ability to experience emotions and express emotions to others influences health. Both suppression

and overexpression of feelings appear to diminish immune function and make us more vulnerable to disease. Furthermore, the specific types of illnesses we get may be, at least in part, a reflection of our personality and emotional style. People who are chronically angry and hostile suffer more heart attacks and greater coronary artery blockage.[23] Research also points to relationships between personality and other diseases, including cancer and rheumatoid arthritis.[24]

- *Environment.* The types of organizations and communities we live and work in daily have an ongoing impact on each of us. Ideal environments provide access to safe, clean living and working spaces free from violence. They also offer supportive and diverse social/spiritual interactions, economic resources, intellectual stimulation, contact with nature, an abundant variety of foods, and opportunities for rest, movement, pleasure and play. When access to any of these important factors is absent, the resulting imbalance can lead to physical and/or emotional illness.

- *Social and Spiritual Influences.* Close relationships at home, at work and in the community are very important determinants of health. People with many social contacts live longer and have better health than people who have few social ties.[25] Social connection through membership in community and religious groups, as well as pursuing a sense of spirituality through individual meditation or prayer, also impacts health and mortality. In fact, whether people participate in organized religion or explore spirituality in their own context *(for example, through a connection to nature)*, research shows individuals who report a deep sense of spiritual values also report less frequent use of medical services, fewer minor illness and more complete recovery from minor illness than the national average.[26]

- *Lifestyle Choices.* This aspect of health has been the primary focus of workplace wellness efforts for the past three decades. Following the biomedical model, the prevailing belief has been that illness can be prevented and health can be created primarily by adopting certain lifestyle-related behaviors: low-fat *(now low-carb)* eating, aerobic exercise, smoking cessation, stress management and control of blood pressure and cholesterol.

Although the holistic approach supports the idea that individual lifestyle choices impact health, it views this as only one part of the complex "equation" *(a decidedly nonlinear one!)* that determines a person's health experience. A holistic philosophy takes a systems perspective in emphasizing that the "lifestyle choices" people make must be understood in the context of their genetic preferences, personality, relationships and the social and physical environment in which they live.[27]

• *Chaos and Chance.* Last, but certainly not least, we have learned from the new science of chaos that, as complex systems, human beings are always to an important degree unpredictable and subject to random and sometimes dramatic change. Although we know that all of the above mentioned factors influence our state of health at any one time, it is frequently not possible to accurately predict why one person gets sick while another does not, or why one heals while another does not. Therefore, blaming people for their illness because they did not exercise enough, because they ate the wrong foods, or because they did not think positively is not only unethical, but also unscientific. Chaos teaches us to be both humble and compassionate in the face of the complex and "wonder-full" universe in which we live.[28]

Assumption Two — There is meaning embedded in health problems, injuries and behavioral struggles:

Pain, illness, behavioral struggles and injuries don't always "just happen." They are often at least partly a reflection of life imbalances: physical manifestations of our emotional/spiritual struggles. We can learn valuable information about ourselves and our lives by paying close attention to when we get sick and even sometimes where in our body our sickness manifests. It is also important to ask ourselves what the illness, pain, injury or behavioral struggle forces us to do differently. Significant health struggles can propel us to take risks and change our lives in ways we may have been too timid to attempt before. We all know people whose jobs have essentially made them sick.

Twice in my life *(Rosie)*, I have had the unfortunate experience of working in a toxic culture, resulting in poor leadership, poor employee morale, high levels of disengagement, lack of trust and employees feeling devalued. In both instances, my physical and emotional wellbeing were essentially sucked out of me. I found myself not sleeping well and getting colds and illnesses at every turn. My GI system acted up. My skin produced strange rashes and hives. I was more accident-prone. I got frequent headaches and eye twitches, had increased neck and back pain, overate, and became more irritable, absent-minded and impatient. Yet, within days of being removed from these work environments, my physical and emotional health quickly and steadily improved. It is certainly no wonder many employers find anti-anxiety and antidepressant medications as the top one or two category of drugs on their prescription drug reports!

Assumption Three — Each of us is inherently good, and we all have a deep internal wisdom to guide us on a natural process toward health and healing:

The holistic perspective views people as naturally good; always striving to improve themselves and their health. Whenever it appears we are not doing so, it is not because we are "undisciplined" or don't care about our health... it is because we are overwhelmed with distress that leaves us unable to take care of ourselves or treat others in a respectful way. Distress that leads to unhealthy behaviors and illness often results from hurtful or oppressive experiences in our lives.[29]

Hopefully, as you read through these updated assumptions, you are beginning to get a feel for the tremendous differences between a biomedical and a truly holistic approach to health. The dominance of the mechanistic, reductionist worldview and the biomedical model has directed those of us concerned with employee wellbeing to focus our efforts on a narrow swath of the complex array of the health determinants. The overwhelming majority of workplace programs continue to focus on eliminating risk factors by attempting to modify individual health behaviors — with, as most people are keenly aware, less than desired success. *(Chapter 6 will elaborate on how ineffective and potentially damaging our stuckness to the Old Paradigm in relation to behavior change has been and continues to be.)*

Perhaps you have also noticed the underlying theme that runs deeply throughout these assumptions. All of the issues that impact our health are

75

intimately tied in with the bigger picture — the social and environmental context in which they exist. In fact, a large body of research over the past three or four decades strongly demonstrates that if we really want to make the most impactful difference in the health of individual humans, the focus simply must shift to also addressing the social context out of which those issues arise. Let us see how and why this is so.

The Social Determinants of Health

It is widely acknowledged that poverty is the single biggest risk factor for poor health. It is easy to see how people living in abject poverty, without the basic essentials, suffer immensely in both mortality and morbidity. But there is much more to this story than initially meets the eye, and it has powerful implications for how we address employee wellbeing. The causes of disease and premature mortality for people in abject poverty are easily identified and very different from the reality in developed countries such as the United States. Without adequate nutrition, sanitation and shelter, millions of people in underdeveloped nations are afflicted with and die from starvation, dysentery and malaria. For most people living in countries such as ours, these consequences of abject poverty have all but been eliminated. But this does not mean that social and environmental factors have therefore been erased or even minimized as underlying causes of morbidity and mortality. In his masterful work, "The Status Syndrome: How Social Standing Affects Our Health and Longevity," physician and epidemiologist Dr. Michael Marmot, the world's leading expert on the social determinants of health, explains:

> *We are dealing with the diseases people get when the society is rich enough to have dealt with malnutrition and poor sanitation: heart disease, diabetes, mental illness. These used to be labeled wrongly rich people's diseases.*[30]

Our *stuckness* to the mechanistic, reductionist, biomedical, linear cause-and-effect conceptualization of health has caused us to miss the forest for the trees. Consider the following sobering findings that Marmot presents from his and others' research:

- • For each mile traveled on the subway from downtown Washington D.C. to Montgomery County, Maryland, life expectancy rises about a year and a half *(20-year difference from first to last stop)*.

- Despite considerable westernization of diet and lifestyle, continued widespread cigarette smoking, and increasing blood cholesterol levels, in Japan, rates of heart disease are low and going down, not up.

- Whether they are rich *(Japan)* or relatively poor *(province of Kerala in India and Costa Rica)*, societies that are socially inclusive have good health.

- People whose jobs involve high demands and low control have a much greater risk of heart disease and depressive symptoms than those in jobs with more control.

- The lower the social position, the higher the risk of heart disease, stroke, lung diseases, diseases of the digestive tract, kidney diseases, HIV-related disease, tuberculosis, suicide and other "accidental" and violent deaths, even after traditional risk factors are taken into account.

- Traditional biomedical risk factors such as smoking, cholesterol, blood pressure, blood sugar, etc., account for less than one-third of the social gradient in mortality from heart disease.

While a holistic perspective on health does not ignore traditional biomedical and behavioral risk factors, the picture this research clearly paints demonstrates that, in many situations, these factors may not be the actual underlying causes of illnesses but rather the consequences of those causes. Decades of studies from all over the globe consistently show what Marmot refers to as a "social gradient" in health. The final report of the World Health Organization *(WHO)* Commission on Social Determinants of Health, published in 2008, of which Marmot was the chair, presented the conclusions this way:

The Commission takes a holistic view of the social determinants of health. The poor health of the poor, the social gradient in health within countries, and the marked health inequities between countries are caused by the unequal distribution of power, income, goods and services, globally and nationally, the consequent unfairness in the immediate, visible circumstances of people's lives — their access to health care, schools and education, their conditions of work and leisure, their homes, communities, towns or cities — and their chances of leading a flourishing life. Together, the structural determinants and conditions of daily life constitute the social determinants of health and are responsible for a major part of the health inequities between and within countries.[31]

If you take a moment to look again at the research findings listed above, you will discover that this social gradient — what Marmot refers to as "The Status Syndrome" — clearly operates independently of traditional risk factors and absolute levels of wealth; within and between countries; and across gender, age and racial lines. Our physical and mental health are deeply affected by the context of our lives and specifically by how we compare to those around us in our social connectedness and our ability to take part fully in the society in which we live. Although the diseases that people suffer and die from in underdeveloped nations differ from those in wealthier nations, the process has more in common than it might seem at first blush. We know that with infectious disease, anything that weakens the host increases the likelihood of getting sick. So, too, it seems with the diseases that plague more affluent, developed nations. As Marmot summarizes the research findings:

The circumstances in which we live — that foster autonomy and control over life, love, happiness, social connectedness, riches that are not measured by money — affect illness. It is precisely because these benefits of life are doled out unequally in society that we have inequalities in health and death. Life and death are not opposites; they are intimately related... These social inequities in health — the social gradient — are not a footnote to the 'real causes' of ill health in countries that are no longer poor; they are the heart of the matter.[32]

As we start to see the enormous implications of PNI and the research on the social determinants of health, we can begin to understand fully how interrelated organizational and employee wellbeing really are. If organizations only focus on the "smart" aspects of business, they may be doing more to contribute to the rapid decline of not only the performance of their organization, but the health and wellbeing of their employees as well — and it becomes a vicious cycle. Likewise, if organizations find employees seem to be declining in their health and wellbeing, they might do better to look at how the society in general and the organization specifically might be contributing to the employee experience rather than automatically concluding behavior change programs that attempt to pay, prod and coerce employees into being healthy are needed. Clearly, it is time for us to rethink our conceptualization of health.

Rethinking Health

Imagine for a moment you are attending a health-related conference, sitting in a large room with many hundreds of people, listening to the keynote presentation. The speaker begins her presentation by asking, "Do you consider yourself to be healthy?" She pauses briefly and continues, "Please raise your hand if you think you are healthy." What did you think about before you decided whether to raise your hand ? What does it mean to you to be healthy? What if you looked at the people sitting next to you? Could you determine whether you were more or less healthy than they? How would you go about deciding that? Maybe by surmising if they are older, younger, taller, shorter, fatter or thinner, or if they have more or less hair than you, or are dressed more or less well?

If you could ask the people around you three questions to help you determine who was healthier, what would you ask? Maybe how much do they exercise, drink or smoke? What are their diets like? How about blood pressure, cholesterol and body mass index? What does it mean to be healthy?

I *(Jon)* have been keenly interested in this question for 25 years or so, as I studied exercise physiology, nutrition and health education in college. Over the past quarter century, I have had the great fortune to work with people in many walks of life to help these individuals improve the quality of their lives. I have also had the considerably less than good fortune over the same time period to be diagnosed with multiple sclerosis and to have learned about health from an altogether different perspective. Before my attack, I ran marathons, participated in triathlons and played competitive racquetball. After the attack, I was forced to teach myself how to walk all over again, and now I need assistance climbing stairs and stepping over curbs. What I have discovered through this journey is that, although everyone seems to be talking about health, there is actually very little agreement and lots of confusion about what it really is — much of it, perhaps by now not surprisingly, based on the outdated scientific understandings we have been discussing. Let me show you what I mean. Here is the most popular and often cited definition of health, from the WHO:

> *Health is a state of complete physical, mental and social well-being and not merely the absence of disease or infirmity.*

How does this definition feel for you? Is it a good description of what health is all about? Well, for the past decade or so, when I am the presenter at these conferences, I have been conducting an informal experiment about this with my audiences. After showing this definition, to which most people *(including health professionals)* respond fairly positively, I ask everyone to please stand. I tell them that in a moment I am going to ask only those people who have the complete absence of disease and infirmity *(from the WHO definition above)* to remain standing. Before we do that, however, I suggest that we probably should consult the dictionary — everyone likely knows if they have a disease or not, but the concept of "infirmity" may be a little more difficult. So, according to the dictionary, infirmity is:

1) A bodily ailment or weakness especially one brought on by old age; and/or

2) A failing or defect in a person's character

After the laughter subsides, I ask everyone who has the "complete lack of disease and infirmity" to remain standing and everyone else to please sit down. Usually, out of a group of a few hundred, this leaves 20 or 30 people still standing. Next, again following the definition, I ask everyone who has "complete physical, mental and social wellbeing" to please remain standing. Usually, only a very few people *(three to five)* are still standing. At this point I remind those who are still standing that telling the truth is a sign of mental health — everyone laughs and the remaining people sit down.

To complicate and confuse the matter even more, even when health is defined as more than just the absence or opposite of disease, it is still most often envisioned as some "optimal" or "perfect state" that can be achieved if we just try hard enough. In a recent webinar I *(Jon)* attended, one of the leading authorities in the workplace wellness industry called for a re-definition of health and then showed a graphic similar to this one *(fonts have been altered to protect the innocent)* to demonstrate what this "new" conceptualization might look like in relation to physical health:

Physical Health

- High Energy
- High Capacity for Performance

• Absence of Illness • At Risk • Chronic Disease • End of Life

According to the speaker, the people on the far left of the continuum *(who were referred to as "outliers")* had reached some extraordinary level of health. The suggestion was that the focus of our efforts should be dedicated to studying what these people had "done" to achieve this state and then proceeding to convince others to emulate their behaviors.

Hopefully, our discussions so far will help you begin to understand how misleading and *stuck* in Old Paradigm thinking this conceptualization is. See if you can identify some of the issues first without looking at, and then by considering, the following questions as you review the graphic:

1) Can only people without illness or risk have high energy and capacity for performance? Can't people at risk or with chronic disease have high energy and capacity for performance?

2) What does it mean to be at risk? For what? Who is not at risk?

3) Given what we have learned about cause and effect in complex systems, what is the likelihood that we can determine exactly or even nearly why some people ended up with a chronic disease or became "outliers," while others did not?

4) Again, given what we have learned from chaos and complexity, if the "outliers" created their optimal state of health, does that mean anyone with illness or at risk caused their respective health problems?

5) Given what we have learned from the research on the social determinants of health, how much of the "outliers" good health can be determined by examining their individual behaviors anyway?

Shifting from Wellness to Wellbeing

The traditional way organizations and much of the health establishment view health and wellness *(and therefore try to improve it via flawed wellness programs)* is clearly a linear, reductionist approach to conceptualizing health. The problem is, of course, that as human beings, we all live with varying amounts of physical, emotional and spiritual baggage. Look how many people even got close to the definition of health in our earlier exercise. How many people have ever known anyone who has come close to being in "optimal health" — no risks, no illness and no chronic disease? As medical writer David B. Morris suggests:

Complete well-being is a fantasy. Health, whatever else it might be is something that happens not so much in the absence of illness as in its presence.[33]

The WHO definition is not a bad one; it, like so many of our understandings, is just *stuck* in an outdated scientific worldview. Is there a definition that better fits the realities of the human experience as we have been describing them? In his often cited 1975 article, "Medical Nemesis," physician and philosopher Ivan Illich hit the nail on the head:

Health is not freedom from the inevitability of death, disease, unhappiness and stress, but rather the ability to cope with them in a competent way.[34]

Perhaps another way of saying this is that health is about what we do with what we are given. Isn't this so much more like the actual reality of the human experience? Clearly, all human beings have their health challenges, so defining health as the absence of these struggles makes little sense. Certainly people can be healthy *(and have the capacity and energy for performance)* even if they have high blood pressure, cancer, multiple sclerosis, dyslexia or depression.

In the final analysis, living skillfully and compassionately with our inevitable struggles, rather than perpetually searching for the latest "holy grail" of "optimal health," may come closer to what it truly means to be healthy. Furthermore *(as we will discuss more fully in chapters 13 and 15)*, the constant pressure to strive for this unreachable perfection; the quest for the perfect body, the perfect diet, the perfect exercise program, the perfect risk factors, behaviors, etc., makes us all a little crazy and sets us up for almost inevitable frustration and failure.

As we mentioned in the introduction, we intentionally use the term "wellbeing." Although earlier models of wellness were broader, and recognized and included the importance of occupational, financial, emotional and spiritual health, operationally, the focus of employee wellness programs has become narrower and narrower — *stuck* in the legacy of the outdated 17th-century reductionist worldview. Consequently, "wellness" is more often than not associated with the biomedical model, focusing on lifestyle behaviors mostly related to physical health.

However, according to research from the Gallup Organization, employee wellbeing is comprised of five essential elements:

- *Career Wellbeing* — how you occupy your time, liking what you do every day, having meaning and purpose in your work and your life.

- *Social Wellbeing* — having strong relationships and love in your life.

- *Financial Wellbeing* — effectively managing your economic life.

- *Physical Wellbeing* — having good health, and enough physical and mental energy to get important things done each day.

- *Community Wellbeing* — sense of engagement you have with the area where you live.[35]

Just as we learned from complexity and chaos theory, Gallup found none of these elements is independent of any other. They are highly interdependent. If we focus too much in one area but ignore other areas, we will not reach a high level of wellbeing. Even more telling, Gallup found that career wellbeing is the most important of the five essential elements, the one that has the greatest impact on our overall wellbeing and quality of life. This clearly demonstrates the critical need for leaders and organizations to think more consciously about the impact they have on employee wellbeing. And as we saw in the previous chapter, there is a powerful relationship between organizational and individual employee wellbeing. Therefore, organizations need to focus on creating a culture and environment that will support all elements of wellbeing, not just the physical.

> Career wellbeing is the most important of the five essential elements, the one that has the greatest impact on our overall wellbeing and quality of life.

The Food for Thought Pyramid — How To Really Enhance Your Health

My (*Jon*) friend and colleague Laura McKibbin has developed an amazingly creative graphic to display what a comprehensive and holistic description of health might look like. The "Food For Thought" Pyramid is structured like the food pyramid used to be, with the most important foundations of health at the bottom of the pyramid.[36]

The "Food for Thought" Pyramid
How to REALLY enhance your health — Laura McKibbin, LICSW

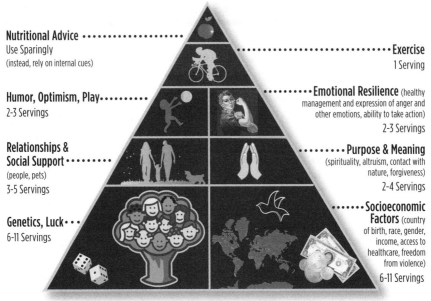

Nutritional Advice
Use Sparingly
(instead, rely on internal cues)

Exercise
1 Serving

Humor, Optimism, Play
2-3 Servings

Emotional Resilience (healthy management and expression of anger and other emotions, ability to take action)
2-3 Servings

Relationships & Social Support
(people, pets)
3-5 Servings

Purpose & Meaning
(spirituality, altruism, contact with nature, forgiveness)
2-4 Servings

Genetics, Luck
6-11 Servings

Socioeconomic Factors (country of birth, race, gender, income, access to healthcare, freedom from violence)
6-11 Servings

Sources: *Dean Ornish, Jon Kabat-Zinn, Bernie Siegel, The Buddha, Gloria Steinem, Viktor Frankl, Glenn Gaesser, Mother Teresa, Martin Seligman, Jesus of Nazareth, Jon Robison, Larry Dossey, Jean Baker-Miller, the World Health Organization, my Mom, your gut intuition.*

As you can see, the base of the pyramid has little to do with personal strivings for biometric or behavioral perfection and everything to do with the context of our existence and the circumstances we have been dealt. Without the life-sustaining foundation represented by the bottom of the pyramid, fruits and vegetables, exercise and low cholesterol will likely have minimal impact on personal health. Genetics, luck and a range of social and cultural factors provide the critical platform on which a healthful existence is built and remind us about the complexities and importance of context to understanding the true meaning of human health. And while there is certainly a place for individual behaviors like nutrition and exercise, they are always considered most effectively in the context of the social environment in which they exist.

So, how do we leave this updated understanding of what health is really all about? One of our favorite commentaries on the subject comes from a wonderful book called "Healthy Pleasures" in which the authors, one a physician and one a psychologist, say this:

Many of us increasingly view ourselves as fragile and vulnerable, ready to develop cancer, heart disease or some other dreaded disease at the slightest provocation. In the name of health we give up many of our enjoyments. The point is that worrying too much about anything — be it calories, salt, cancer, or cholesterol — is bad for you, and that living optimistically, with pleasure, zest, and commitment, is good. Medical terrorism shouldn't attack life's pleasures. [37]

We hope you have been able to grasp how incorporating the remarkable findings from PNI with the burgeoning research on the social determinants of health creates a very different understanding of what human health or wellbeing is all about. Next, in the final *stuckness* chapter, we turn our attention to the difficult and controversial topic of motivation.

Summary of the Paradigm Shift in Employee Wellbeing:

Old Paradigm — Employee Wellness *(biomedical):*

- **Focus** — *Disease.* The main objective is to identify and eliminate risk factors for disease.

- **Emphasis** — *"Unhealthy" Behaviors.* These are the primary determinants of health status.

- **Motivation** — *Fear.* The reason for change is to prevent disease and premature mortality.

- **Human Nature** — *"Bad."* Left to their own devices, people naturally gravitate towards unhealthy behaviors.

- **Organization's Role** — *Expert.* Main job is to uncover unhealthy behaviors and recommend alternatives.

- **Change Process** — *Next Chapter*

New Paradigm — Employee Experience *(holistic):*

- **Focus** — *Wellbeing.* The main objective is to address the complex web of factors that influence health.

- **Emphasis** — *Relationships.* Meaning in life and supportive social environments are the primary determinants of health status.

- **Motivation** — *Happiness.* The reason for change is primarily to enhance purpose and joy in life.

- **Human Nature** — *"Good."* People have a natural wisdom, ability and desire to seek health.

- **Organization's Role** — *Ally.* Main job is to facilitate people's connection with their internal wisdom.

- **Change Process** — *Next Chapter*

CHAPTER 6
The *Stuckness*: "Getting" People to Change

❝ There's a time to admire the grace and persuasive power of an influential idea and there's a time to fear its hold over us. The time to worry is when the idea is so widely shared that we no longer even notice it. When objections are not even raised we are not in control. We do not have the idea... it has us.[1] ❞

Alfie Kohn, "Punished By Rewards"

So far, we have examined our science, culture and health from the perspective of the dominant worldview of the last 400 years, what we are calling the Old Paradigm. Looking at a summary of this information in Table 1, what is most important to note is the vertical categories flow logically and naturally from each other. Thus, a mechanistic worldview naturally informs a reductionist science *(machines are best understood and fixed by attending to their constituent parts)*. Similarly,

Table 1: The Old Paradigm

Worldview
Mechanistic

Science
Reductionist
(whole = sum of its parts)

Culture
Control oriented
(hierarchical, patriarchal)

Health
Biomedical
(fix the machine)

Traditional Approaches to Change
Extrinsic *(controlled)* Motivation
(carrots and sticks)

a reductionist science that emphasizes separation from and control of nature leads logically to a control-oriented, hierarchical, patriarchal culture. Combined with a reductionist science, such a culture naturally creates a medical model focused on "fixing" and controlling the human "machine" by altering measurable physical factors seen as the specific determinants of poor health. We believe looking at the big picture in this way is critically important for helping to put into perspective the changes to promoting both organizational and employee wellbeing that we propose in the remaining chapters of this book.

The final entry at the bottom of this table is the topic for this last chapter before we get to *The 7 Points of Transformation* for creating thriving workplace cultures. Again, we propose it makes perfect sense that the traditional approaches for addressing organizational and individual employee change are exactly what they are. In fact, it is hard to imagine how any other approach could have followed given the paradigm out of which they historically emerged. Unfortunately, as was the case in the previous two chapters, these outdated approaches have been rendered relatively obsolete due to new scientific understandings of the nature of change in complex systems, as well as by recent discoveries in neuroscience.

Motivation Matters

Change is hard — for both organizations and individuals alike. We have learned a great deal about motivation and human behavior over the last 50 years. Yet, you wouldn't know it by looking at how most organizations approach change.

Since the early 1990s, business and leadership researchers have definitively demonstrated that the key to organizational effectiveness is having committed employees who are empowered and intrinsically motivated.[2] Yet, as we saw in chapter 4, the 17th-century mechanistic approach to business is still prevalent today and unfortunately, it does anything but empower employees. For example, it is often said in business that "what gets measured gets managed." We believe metrics are important *(and will address data and metrics in chapter 8)*; however, as Margaret Wheatley puts it:

The search for measures has taken over the world as the primary means to control systems and people. We depend on numbers to know how we're doing for virtually everything... the work of modern managers is to interpret and manipulate these numerical views of reality.[3]

> **People can't be paid or punished into these behaviors; they contribute or withhold their best efforts depending on how connected they feel to the organization, manager or team.**

The problem is that most managers choose measurement as a primary path to achieving greater accountability, focus, teamwork, innovation and quality and then spend inordinate amounts of time and energy trying to find the right reward to tie to the right measure — thinking this will produce more of their desired results.[4] But it doesn't work. People can't be paid or punished into these behaviors; they contribute or withhold their best efforts depending on how connected they feel to the organization, manager or team. People are motivated by work when they understand how it contributes to something beyond themselves — work that provides them with autonomy, growth, meaning and purpose.[5]

Motivation also matters when it comes to the complexities surrounding health and wellbeing, yet organizations and the health establishment have been going about trying to "get" people to change in the wrong ways based on the same flawed Old Paradigm assumptions *(depicted in Figure 1)*. In this chapter, we will explore how current approaches to fostering successful behavior change are not working.

Over the past three decades, a wealth of scientific research has clearly demonstrated that intrinsic motivation is the best, and for most people the only way to promote positive, sustainable change.[9] This is another one of those situations we described previously where we find ourselves at a crossroads. As is so often the case, the choice is between remaining *stuck* in our Old Paradigm beliefs regarding motivation and evolving to a better understanding by embracing the latest research, thereby helping us to better foster and support sustainable change. To get a better feel for where we are and where we can go, we describe the evolution from Motivation 1.0 to Motivation 4.0.

Motivation 1.0 — Knowledge Leads to Change

If you remember from our discussion in chapter 5, the legacy of the scientific worldview of the 17th century depicts man as a sophisticated machine and behavior change as a linear process. From this perspective it logically flows that if you give people knowledge, they will change their attitudes and beliefs and then change their behavior. As Resnicow describes in his insightful article on the implications of the new sciences for health promotion and human behavior:

> *Change is conceptualized as a linear, deterministic process where individuals weigh pros and cons and at the point at which the benefits outweigh the costs, 'decisional balance' tips them toward change...*[10]

So, educate people more and that will automatically lead to change, right? Of course, especially given what we have learned about cause and effect in complex systems, it is clear that this assumption is, at best, overly simplified and, in practice, relatively ineffective. In fact, most people know what behaviors are good for them and what are harmful, and yet many do not change those behaviors accordingly. How many people do you know who have made any sustainable change because they were nagged or scared to death and told they should? The *stuckness* of seeing people as information-processing machines as opposed to meaning-generating beings *(living systems)* greatly inhibits our ability to help promote change. As Wheatley puts it:

> *We never succeed in directing or telling people they must change.*
> *We don't succeed by handing them a plan, or pestering them with our interpretations or relentlessly pressing forward with our agenda, believing that volume and intensity will convince them to see it our way. You can scream and holler as much as you want, but if people don't regard what you're saying as important they'll just ignore you and go on with their life. (In this way all people behave like teenagers).*[11]

Motivation 2.0 — Incent People to Change

So, if knowledge is not enough to create behavior change, what are we to do? The answer for the past 60-plus years, of course, has been behavior modification — offering people rewards *(carrots)* and/or applying penalties *(sticks)* to get them to do what we want them to do. It would, in fact, be difficult to overstate the extent to which this approach *(generally referred to as extrinsic motivation)* has saturated our culture. From enticing children to behave by offering them extra TV time, desserts and toys; to inducing students to learn with stickers, gold stars and grades; to rewarding employees with parking places, bonuses and vacations; the "carrot and stick" approach to motivation, based largely on the work of B.F. Skinner, is rarely questioned.

In keeping with the scientific management theories of "Taylorism," incentives have also been used for decades to attempt to increase employee productivity and engagement. However, the problem with traditional reward and recognition programs is not only that they fail to motivate people, it's that motivating people is not really the issue. What matters is having intrinsically motivated, committed and engaged employees who exhibit high levels of discretionary effort to support the mission and vision of the organization.[12]

When it comes to workplace wellness programs, the use of incentives to promote behavior change has increased exponentially due to the wellness provisions in The Affordable Care Act *(more about this in chapter 13)*. Amazingly, there is scant evidence that these types of extrinsic motivation effectively achieve any of the health outcomes targeted in typical workplace wellness programs. Furthermore, substantial research suggests their use may have significant adverse consequences. Because this method of motivation is so widespread, we want to spend a bit of time exploring where it comes from and why it fails.

Behavior Modification: The Legacy of Skinner

B.F. Skinner developed his theory of human behavior, most accurately described as Behaviorism, in the 1950s. At that time, Freudian psychology, which depicted all human problems as emanating from deep, unconscious urges, was the dominant theory of human behavior. Skinner developed a much simpler view. He believed all human actions could be explained by the principle of "reinforcement." This is closely akin to what we commonly think of as reward. Skinner's theory states most basically that behaviors followed by rewards *(positive consequences)* are likely to be repeated. So, for instance, when the phone rings, we pick it up. The reason we pick it up is because we know someone will be there to talk with us.

If every time the phone rings we pick it up and nobody is there, we will eventually stop picking up the phone. Thus, the behavior of answering the phone is reinforced by the consequence of human contact on the other end.

Although this example certainly seems reasonable, Skinner believed that ALL human actions resulted from this same process. He concluded that human beings have essentially no free will; all of our actions are merely mindless "repertoires of behavior" that can be fully explained by the environmental consequences that follow them. It is not difficult to see the link between this theory of human behavior and the mechanistic, Cartesian worldview we spoke of earlier in the book. Skinner was perhaps the "ultimate Cartesian," for he took the concept of mind/body separation one step further than did Descartes, believing, as he put it:

There is no place in the scientific analysis of behavior
for a mind or self. [13]

Skinner was so confident in this theory of human behavior he felt it explained even the most complicated human experiences. In his own words, he described the evolution of love between two people:

One of them is nice to the other and predisposes the other to be
nice to him and that makes him even more likely to be nice.
It goes back and forth and it may reach the point at which they are
very highly disposed to do nice things to the other and not to hurt
and I suppose this is what would be called being in love. [14]

Hardly something you would choose to say to a loved one over a candle-light dinner! Note that Skinner did all of his experimental work on animals — rats, mice and pigeons — and then extrapolated the results to humans. This was not a problem for Skinner and other behaviorists. In true Cartesian fashion, they believed humans were just more sophisticated machines than pigeons — but machines nevertheless. Luckily, for our purposes, rather than having to rely on belief to determine whether Skinner's extrapolations have merit for humans, we have a wealth of research that we can turn to for evidence. As a quick summary, before examining the research, remember there are basically two main types of motivation:

- *Extrinsic/Controlled Motivation* is being driven to do something due to pressure or tangible rewards rather than for the fun or interest of it. Essentially, extrinsic or controlled motivation involves carrot and/or stick approaches in which people do something because someone else is trying to get them to do it.[15]

- *Intrinsic/Autonomous Motivation* is doing an activity because it is interesting and the activity itself provides spontaneous satisfaction. Intrinsic or autonomous motivation is when people do something because they want to do it.[16]

Extensive research spanning the last three decades consistently demonstrates that change efforts fail in the long term when based on carrot-and-stick approaches.[17] In a 2012 TED Talk, Edward Deci, PhD, one of the world's most respected authorities on motivation, summarized the relevant literature:

There are literally hundreds and hundreds and hundreds now of scientific investigations that have shown when you're autonomously motivated your behavior will be more creative, you'll be a better problem solver, when you encounter obstacles you'll be able to think outside the box and figure out what to do about them, your performance will be better particularly at heuristic activities, and your emotions will be much more positive. And very importantly, autonomous motivation is associated with both physical and psychological health.

In the context of a business environment, the principles of Skinner's behavior modification *(no place for a mind or a self)* don't work precisely because people need to use their minds.

People are complex beings filled with thoughts, feelings, attitudes, personalities, skills, experiences and goals whose work is typically complex and requires higher-order cognitive skills including problem solving and decision-making. [18]

Skinner's experiments on lab animals are far too simplistic to explain the complexities of human motivation. Focusing on short-term fixes through the use of carrots and sticks may result in short-term behavioral compliance that could temporarily help the organization financially. However, in the long run, the literature is clear: The negative consequences greatly outweigh any potential short-term benefits. Aside from failing to produce long-term behavior change, extrinsic motivation often:

- Diminishes performance and creativity.
- Fosters short-term thinking.
- Encourages cheating and lying.
- Becomes habit forming.
- Reduces or extinguishes intrinsic motivation.[19]

The more organizations try to cultivate desired behaviors through measurement and reward, the more organizations damage the quality of the relationships within the organization and the more they obscure and trivialize the meaning of work. As a result, people become less, not more, engaged.[20] The measurements take over defining what is meaningful; the focus narrows; and people become more disconnected from any larger purpose or greater meaning of their work, becoming increasingly obsessed with meeting the specific requirements being measured. And as increasing numbers of organizations come to rely on Motivation 2.0, employees get better and better at playing "the numbers game" and lose real motivation to do their best work.[21]

The same holds true for individual health behavior change. Consider behavior change and the fear of death. Dr. Dean Ornish conducted research on heart patients who had double or quadruple bypass operations. These patients had a simple choice: make drastic lifestyle changes *(i.e., eat healthy foods, stop smoking, reduce stress, exercise)* or die. Even with the ultimate "motivator" of avoiding death, only 10% made sustainable lifestyle changes two years post operation. As a result, Dr. Ornish re-designed his program with a different purpose; heart patients were taught to appreciate life rather than fear death. The program included yoga, meditation, healthy diet and stress counseling — all focused on finding purpose and having them enjoy life more fully. Two years post operation 70% of the patients had made sustainable lifestyle changes. The difference was in the approach. When people looked forward and built on what they had and what they wanted rather than simply trying to win a prize or avoid a negative consequence, they had much better success with long-term change.[22]

Some of the lack of effectiveness of incentives can be explained by the Principal-Agent Model. This model demonstrates that when an organization or an individual *(i.e., the Principal)* tries to get other people *(i.e., the Agent)* to do something by offering a reward *("do this and you'll get that")* or punishment *("don't do this and you'll get that,")* the Agents start weighing the consequences to determine if the reward *(the carrot)* or the punishment *(the stick)* is really worth it: the focus shifts to being purely transactional. Often, offering an incentive to try to get someone to change behaviors has the opposite effect because it sends a message that "this new behavior must SUCK or you wouldn't need to bribe me to do it."[23]

The bottom line is that although extrinsic motivation *(carrots and sticks)* can lead to short-term compliance, it rarely leads to long-term commitment and contributes to unwanted consequences. Behavior change is not as simple as finding a magic trick to motivate people or accessing the right pressure point to get them to behave differently. Behavior change requires a fundamental shift in how people think about their lives and their choices — a shift to foster intrinsic motivation.

> **The bottom line is that although extrinsic motivation *(carrots and sticks)* can lead to short-term compliance, it rarely leads to long-term commitment and contributes to unwanted consequences.**

Motivation 3.0 – "Get" People to be Intrinsically Motivated

Quite a bit of lip service has been paid lately to the importance of intrinsic/autonomous motivation. Yet, even when the critical importance of intrinsic motivation is acknowledged, efforts to elicit it are often fundamentally flawed — especially when it comes to workplace wellness. The common belief is incentives are needed to get initial participation and that somehow, "magically," people will then become intrinsically motivated. However, the data do not support this, especially with regards to monetary rewards. The literature is clear that monetary rewards undermine people's intrinsic motivation.[24]

In spite of this, the field of Behavioral Economics continues to invest significant resources trying to determine what level of extrinsic incentives will produce a specific behavior change — thinking that some formula of incentives will produce intrinsic motivation and lasting change. Interestingly, when it comes to health behavior change at the workplace, even Behavioral Economists find it difficult to come up with research that supports the efficacy of using incentives for long-term behavior change. For example, with respect to the use of carrots and sticks promoted by the wellness provisions in the Affordable Care Act, in a recent article in "The New England Journal of Medicine," behavioral economists Kevin Volpp and colleagues concluded:

> *Although it may seem obvious that charging higher premiums for*
> *smoking (body mass index, cholesterol or blood pressure)*
> *would encourage people to modify their habits to*
> *lower their premiums, evidence that differential premiums change*
> *health-related behavior is scant. Indeed, we're unaware of any*
> *insurance data that convincingly demonstrates such effects.*[25]

In spite of this dismal conclusion, these same researchers continue to investigate every conceivable combination of behavioral techniques *(gimmicks)* to try to nudge, pressure, coerce and pay people to change their health-related behaviors. Unfortunately, contrary to what they often claim, what always ends up happening is precisely what the literature since Skinner documents. When the incentives are gone, the behaviors rebound. A 2013 study serves as a perfect example.[26] This study involved a weight loss intervention for employees of a children's hospital. More than 100 employees who were overweight or obese by medical standards were randomly assigned to one of three groups for 24 weeks:

1) ***Control group*** — participated in monthly weigh-ins only.

2) ***Individual incentive group*** — received incentive of $100 per month for meeting weight loss goals.

3) ***Group incentive*** — *(five people in each group)* received incentive of $500 per month per group for meeting weight loss goals.

Participants also received $20 for each monthly weigh-in, $50 for completing the 24-week weigh-in, and $50 for completing the 36-week weigh-in. In case you might be scratching your head at this point, the total resource allocation for incentives for the 100 employees comes to a whopping $56,000! There were all kinds of twists and turns as far as how the incentives were actually applied for the different groups. You can read about them in the article if you really want to know what they were. Suffice it to say, it isn't necessary to know all those details to understand the realities of what happened.

Here are the weight loss results of the two experimental groups *(the control group basically stayed the same)*:

Individual Incentive Condition:
- Average weight loss at 24 weeks = 3.7 pounds
- Average weight loss at 36 weeks = 1.8 pounds

Group Incentive Condition:
- Average weight loss at 24 weeks = 10.6 pounds
- Average weight loss at 36 weeks = 7.5 pounds

You don't need to be a rocket scientist *(or even a statistician)* to see what happened. In fact, it is exactly what you would expect and what every other study in the previous few decades confirms. Pay *(incentivize)* people and they will lose some weight in the short term. When the program is over, they will regain the weight. The group with the individual incentive condition gained back more than half their lost weight between week 24 and week 36. Even in the condition that had the most complicated incentive setup, participants gained almost 30% of their lost weight back in just those three months. As usual, the researchers' conclusions ignore the obvious:

A group-based financial incentive was more effective than an individual incentive and monthly weigh-ins at promoting weight loss among obese employees at 24 weeks.[27]

This savvy spin on the results would make any political party proud. It is true that the group condition resulted in a greater initial weight loss and a slower regain. Of course, there are hundreds of studies showing short-term weight loss and variable, but steady, regain with all matters of incentivized conditions. Clearly, this is exactly what happened here: relatively small amounts of weight lost that were steadily regained once the incentives were discontinued. But there is more! Listen carefully to the researchers' claims:

The difference in weight loss between the group incentives and the control group was sustained 12 weeks after the incentive intervention ended... our study is the only randomized trial to compare the effects of

*group-based and individual incentives or demonstrate a statistically
significant difference in weight loss between incentive and control groups
after incentives ended.* [28]

Did you catch the misleading *(invalid)* component of this conclusion? Here
is a hint — they repeated it twice. If you remember, although weight loss
was not specifically incentivized during weeks 24-36, people were still paid
$50 to come in at 36 weeks and get weighed. Clearly the extrinsic motiva-
tion was still in place at this time, and yet they still gained back
almost a third of their lost weight. We will have lots more to say about the
chicanery that abounds in weight loss research in chapters 13 and 15. For
now, however, the point is that Behavioral Economics notwithstanding, the
literature to this point remains quite consistent about the lack of efficacy of
extrinsic motivation to produce sustainable health-behavior change.

We appreciate that asking organizations built around this unfounded belief
about incentives to embrace the New Paradigm *(even if it is an evidence-
based one)* is unsettling. But last time we checked, we are in the 21st
century, not the 17th, and not even the 20th. We need to stop treating people
like non-thinking machines or rodents if we want to promote lasting change
and growth.

Even those attempting to let go of this addiction to Motivation 2.0 and
move to Motivation 3.0 to try to embrace intrinsic motivation don't fully
understand how to foster it. Although the leading approach in workplace
wellness, despite all contrary evidence, is that getting participation will
eventually lead to intrinsic motivation, we've heard many other flawed
suggestions for "getting" people to be intrinsically motivated. See if you
can identify the flawed, mechanistic paradigm guiding these tactics:

- Share powerful success stories — *If people were predictable
  like machines, sharing someone else's success should "get"
  them to be motivated themselves.*

- Create a "culture of health" and make sure leaders model
  healthy behaviors — *If people were controllable and predictable like machines, they would take advantage of healthy lifestyle programs and want to please their managers by being like
  them; however, we already discussed the flaws of this approach
  in chapter 4.*

- Have a good branding and marketing strategy — *Motivation
  1.0 — if you communicate the message correctly, people will act.*

- Make sure programs are fun and easy to do — *If you can get people to comply and complete a program, they should keep doing the program even after it ends; and we know how often that actually happens.*

- Develop environmental policies to elicit desired behavior — *Humans aren't thinking beings, so let's control their environment; somehow subconsciously they will create new habits to comply with the policies and then be intrinsically motivated.*

Sadly, we could continue for several more pages — each approach being fundamentally flawed because it's based on a mechanistic assumption that people can be controlled; yet, ironically, all are done thinking the result will be intrinsic motivation. The question that is traditionally asked in Motivation 3.0 usually goes something like this, "If I don't use incentives, how do I motivate my employees to _____?" *(work harder, be safer, be healthier, participate in programs, etc.)*

This is simply the wrong question to ask, because motivation is not something that can be "done to" someone. You can't "get" someone else to be intrinsically motivated. The proper question that needs to be asked is:

> *"How can we create the conditions within which others will motivate themselves?"* [29]

First and foremost, creating these conditions starts with fostering thriving organizational wellbeing. In his book, "Management Rewired," Charles Jacobs put it perfectly when he wrote:

> *All we need to do is shape the culture that shapes the thinking.* [30]

> **People have to first gain clarity about what matters to them, considering their whole life, and tap into better thinking.**

Shaping the thinking means embracing the "cognitive paradigm," recognizing the importance of the cognitive process over the behavior itself. The nuances of our behavior communicate what we are thinking; therefore, change initiatives only work when we change the way we think. [31] In other words, lasting change needs to come from within and be inside out. People have to first gain clarity about what matters to them, considering their whole life, and tap into better thinking.

Think about it: Most people you know who have made some sort of profound change started by having some sort of "awakening" or new thinking about what truly matters to them. So we need to think less about motivation and more about *creating the conditions* to support better thinking; only then can we continue with *creating the conditions* for individual change *(which we will discuss in more detail in chapter 12)*.

As Paul Marciano states in his book, "Carrots and Sticks Don't Work,"

At the end of the day, successful organizations don't motivate employees; they engage them. Motivating employees and engaging them are entirely distinct concepts.[32]

Motivation 4.0 – Support better THINKING

The research clearly demonstrates that engagement and sustainable change require supporting intrinsic or autonomous motivation. However, at the heart of intrinsic motivation are an individual's values and thoughts; therefore, fostering intrinsic motivation requires moving a little further upstream to understand and shift how we think. In the now famous words of Albert Einstein:

*The world we have made as a result of the
level of thinking we have done thus far
creates problems we cannot solve at the same level
of thinking at which we created them.*

Research over the past two decades has conclusively demonstrated the importance of fostering self-leadership within organizations so that people are influencing themselves *(as opposed to waiting to be told what to do)* and emphasizing the intrinsic value of tasks *(finding meaning and enjoyment in their work)*. Higher degrees of intrinsic motivation are associated with greater job satisfaction, employee engagement and commitment to the organization.[33] At the heart of intrinsic motivation and self-leadership are an individual's values and thoughts. The underlying premise is that people can use specific cognitive strategies to influence or control their own thoughts, ultimately impacting both individual and organizational performance.[34] Managing this so-called "thought self-leadership" involves strategies that replace dysfunctional thought patterns with more constructive ones. In organizations, the challenge is to create an environment that fosters developing and maintaining such constructive thinking.[35]

Lessons from Neuroscience

The last decade has seen an explosion in research on the functioning of what is by far our most complex and poorly understood organ: the brain. According to the neuroscientists involved:

- 98% of everything we know about the brain has been discovered in the last eight years!

- 80% of what scientists thought was true about the brain before 1995 has been found to be false, or misleading.[36]

Even though we are just cracking the surface of understanding what is going on in this marvelous organ, the research is already helping us to understand more about the way humans function. For the purposes of how this relates to organizational and employee wellbeing, we want to provide you with a brief overview of how what we are learning contributes to our understanding of human motivation for behavior change. The graphic below depicts four areas of the brain we know play a critical role in change.

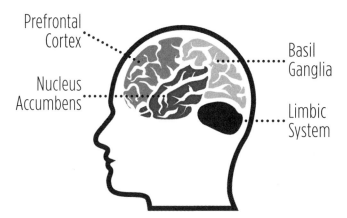

- The **prefrontal cortex** of the brain is a "holding area" where our working memory is stored. This is where we first compare ideas and perceptions to other information. It is a highly energetic part of the brain that supports higher intellectual functions *(creativity, innovation, decision making)* and is frequently engaged when we encounter something new; however, it can only store a small amount of information at any one time and fatigues easily.

- The **basal ganglia** are deeper in the core of the brain. They are stimulated by routine, familiar activities, and they form and store long-standing habits. The typical way people behave is rooted in the basal ganglia. In routine activity, the basal ganglia can function extremely well without conscious thought *(e.g., riding a bike).*[37]

- The **limbic system** is traditionally thought of as the "seat of emotions." It is loaded with those cells we discussed earlier that are responsible for our feelings and emotions, and our "flight or fight" response to stressful situations.

- The **nucleus accumbens** is sometimes referred to as the pleasure center of the brain. It is involved in releasing dopamine in response to pleasurable experiences, including sex, love, food, music and many different types of mood-altering chemicals.

What we have learned from neuroscience research in the past decade firmly supports what we have been saying about motivation. First, let us look at what happens in the brain in response to extrinsic motivation. When we are told what to do *("do this or you'll get that")*, the prefrontal cortex immediately sends a message to the basal ganglia saying, in essence, "hey, this request *(or demand)* is unfamiliar." The basal ganglia respond with, "no way — that is not how we do things around here — danger!" The limbic system is then stimulated and the fight-or-flight response ensues. At the same time, information flow to the prefrontal cortex is minimized; this is no time for thinking and creativity — it is time to run or fight!

Now let's see what the brain's response is to intrinsic motivation. When we are doing something because we want to, because the act of doing it brings its own reward, a special group of cells called mirror neurons are activated. These mirror neurons send a calming signal to the basal ganglia and the limbic system as if to say, "Everything is fine; nothing to concern yourself with here." At the same time, the prefrontal cortex is stimulated, so critical thinking and creativity are enhanced. As an additional bonus, the nucleus accumbens is stimulated, leading to a generalized pleasurable feeling that "all is well."

The more we operate from a 17th-century mechanistic perspective and try to "get" individuals to change or try to "fix" them, the more the brain sends out powerful signals that something is wrong. These signals stimulate our fear and anger responses, and draw energy from the prefrontal region. In addition, the brain has a keen ability to detect the difference between authentic inquiry *(i.e., I'm asking you a question for no other reason than I'm genuinely curious about you and interested in you)* and persuasion *(i.e., I'm asking you a question to try to "get" you to somewhere I think you should be — or I'm incenting you to do something I think you should do)*.[38] The brain has an innate desire to solve its own problems and create novel connections. When people work out their own solutions, the brain rewards them with pleasure. In "Management Rewired," Charles Jacobs explains that the real rewards we reap from what we do actually arise intrinsically:

> *The nucleus accumbens releases its dopamine when*
> *we're engaged in the work that leads to the accomplishment*
> *of our goals, not when we accomplish the goals.*
> *It's the work itself that is rewarding.*[39]

The Critical Role of Intrinsic Thinking

In addition to our greater understanding of how the brain functions in the change process, we have learned how various patterns of thinking influence us. Robert S. Hartman was a well-respected philosopher and the father of axiology *(the science of value)*. He believed our value system defines who we are. It is the lens through which we view the world, formulate choices and make decisions. It evolves over time and manifests in how we assess, evaluate and size up situations, solve problems and take action. In other words, values are in the judgments we make; judgment is a primary manifestation of values. Here are a few important highlights from Hartman's work measuring thinking patterns:

- In the 1960s, collaborating with colleagues at MIT, Hartman created the Hartman Value Profile *(HVP)* to measure the hierarchy of values that underlie how people think and how they translate their thinking into the choices they make.

- The HVP is not a psychological assessment. Hartman was a sophisticated mathematician and used predicate calculus to help create and score the HVP. It's essentially a quantitative assessment of thinking patterns. *(We will discuss the importance of not just measuring thinking patterns but being able to develop and activate better thinking in chapter 10.)*

103

- The HVP has been validated in at least eight countries and is used in the Harvard School of Management, at the Pentagon, and in hundreds of workplaces.[40] Hartman's work was nominated for a Nobel Prize in 1973, just months before he died.[41] His work is carried on today through the Robert S. Hartman Institute at the University of Tennessee at Knoxville.[42]

- The HVP allows people to have a fuller experience of themselves by helping them to understand how they habitually think.

- The HVP is also used in organizations to help both leaders and employees understand their stress and resiliency, and support efforts to improve team cohesiveness.

Now that we know we can measure thinking patterns, let's examine what these thinking patterns are and how they can be used to help guide our choices.

Intrinsic, Extrinsic and Systemic Thinking: A Closer Look

Hartman identified three dimensions of our valuing or thinking that guide our choices: Intrinsic (I), Extrinsic (E) and Systemic (S). We view ourselves and the world around us in terms of our I, E and S valuing/thinking.

Systemic *(S)* thinking values abstract concepts and ideas. Based on our own concepts and ideas, we make sense of the world around us and ourselves. Systemic thinking allows us to see things at a 30,000-foot level, or "the forest through the trees." Although Hartman's definition of systemic thinking has some similarity to our earlier discussions, it is particularly different when it comes to people. Essentially, as Hartman defines it, Systemic thinking is like a puzzle — looking for a match to our pre-existing ideas and beliefs. If something or someone matches our ideas, we give it value; if not, we are dismissive.

When Systemic thinking dominates, what we learn about people is VERY information-poor and limited because it assumes our ideas about these people are all there is to know. It manifests as black/white and either/or thinking, and is associated with "shoulds":

- "It should be this way."

- "You should do XYZ."
- "I really should do ABC."

Systemic thinking is deeply rooted in the habit center of our brain and typically involves the first thoughts that come to mind. But we know that our first thoughts about people are not always our BEST thinking. In fact, our initial assumptions or judgments about people are often wrong, because we only ever know a sliver of the total reality of someone else. So when organizations deploy programs based on limited ideas of who people are and how they "should" be, it's no wonder programs fail.

See how well you react the next time someone tells you that you should do something or behave differently. Chances are, thoughts like, "Yeah, but you don't have a clue about my life," "Easy for you to say," or "Screw you!" might come to mind. When workplace initiatives are presented to employees this way, it's no wonder they're not jumping up and down with excitement and saying, "Thank you."

Extrinsic *(E)* thinking values function and shows up as what we do. When we view people and the world through this lens, we tend to focus more on their functionality. In other words, we pay attention to labels, categories, achievements and what they do. As a result, we treat people more like things, as if people were replicable and predictable, clearly harkening back to the legacy of the mechanistic worldview.

Consequently, we spend significant energy using our thinking and expertise to get people to do what we think they should *(i.e., "If I say or do XYZ, then it should get Mary to do ABC.")*. This is where the unfortunately ubiquitous use of incentives comes into the picture. If people were lab rats or robots, it would make sense that they would do what we want *(at least in the short term)* if we simply find the right or large enough incentive; but as we have seen, not only is this approach rarely effective, it can actually make things worse.

Intrinsic *(I)* thinking values the inherent uniqueness in people. When we view people and the world through this lens:

— We recognize there is far more going on than what we can see.

105

— We understand that people have inherent value simply because they exist *(independent of titles, roles, achievements, accomplishments or health status)*.

— We allow a space for more than what is merely apparent to us on the surface.

By now you can probably see the imprint of the new sciences on these assumptions. Intrinsic thinking is the most information-rich and mathematically correct thinking about people. Intrinsic thinking values not just what is seen and our ideas about what we see, but what is unseen and as new thinking that stems from activating our prefrontal cortex[43] *(we will discuss this more in chapter 10)*.

Intrinsic thinking opens us up to the tremendous learning possibilities that emerge when we embrace the complexity and uncertainty all around us. Consequently, Intrinsic thinking tends to take a few seconds longer to access than Systemic thinking. Systemic thinking is our first thought, and acting on it doesn't create a space or opportunity for new, information-rich Intrinsic thinking. Therefore, Intrinsic thinking is typically the weakest, least developed of all three dimensions and generally unsupported in our very Systemic-dominant world.[44] Unless we increase awareness of our thinking and disable the Systemic-thinking dominance, Intrinsic thinking *(and motivation)* doesn't have a chance.

Hartman's research clearly demonstrates that, although all three dimensions of valuing/thinking are necessary, the optimal hierarchy is I>E>S. In simple terms, this means people are valued more than things, and things are valued more than mere ideas of things or people.[45] The research shows if people have an inverted hierarchy of thinking *(i.e., S>E>I)*, they will not effectively cope with life's circumstances.[46] Let's look at a quick example:

• As is so often the case, Systemic thinking *(S>E>I)* dominates when Mary thinks about herself — especially when it comes to her health and wellbeing. She has all kinds of ideas *(S)* of how she should look and what she should be doing; ideas constantly reinforced by her employer's wellness program. These ideas of who she should be guide what she does *(E)* to try to meet that ideal.

- So Mary will work really hard at a program, diet, etc., trying to achieve her Systemic ideal. And she will seek out programs that provide her with the Extrinsic motivation *(E)* she is often told she needs. The problem: Life throws her curve balls, and the programs don't meet her unique needs. Mary then either starts beating up on herself *(e.g., "Why isn't this working?" "Why can't I just stay motivated?")* or working even harder and trying a plethora of other programs.

- And the vicious S/E loop continues like a gerbil on a wheel, creating stress and unnecessary struggle but never getting anywhere because S>E>I aims for perfection *(which we all know doesn't exist, but we keep striving for it anyway)*.

- If Mary could view herself via I>E>S, instead of focusing on what she should do or who she should be, she could better accept who she is in this moment and gain greater clarity about what she wants for herself. Based on that clarity, she could have flexibility to course-correct when something isn't working without beating up on herself. I>E>S allows for ongoing growth and development rather than constantly striving for an unreachable perfection.

You may be thinking, "Of course I recognize the uniqueness of people." However, conceptually recognizing that the Intrinsic *(i.e., valuing the inherent uniqueness in others)* is important and having the awareness and skills to create a space for it and activate it are very different. In fact, research using the Hartman Value Profile shows that our culture generally does not support I>E>S. As a result, the Intrinsic dimension of thinking is typically weak, and the skills needed to activate the Intrinsic dimension are even weaker.

What Happens When Intrinsic Thinking is Weak or Missing

When people lead with their E and S domains of thinking about others, people are limited in what is possible because they are only working with what they can see, as if that is all there is:

- How often do we see others in terms of a label we've created for them?

- When we see someone and automatically think, "He/she is lazy will never be a top-performing worker" or view a person as if she/he is a disease or condition, we minimize the contributions that person can bring to the outcome.

• When we only work with what is apparent to us and what our ideas are about a person *(E and S thinking)*, that person can never be anything other than our ideas about him/her. The result is judgment, impatience, frustration and jumping to conclusions.

There is a line in the movie, *Avatar*. "I SEE You." The Avatar species use this phrase to indicate they see the WHOLE person *(i.e., I>E>S)*. However, the humans *(operating from an S>E>I perspective)* see the Avatars as things that have no value and are expendable. And we saw the destruction that resulted from this limited, information-poor thinking. The hierarchy of best thinking *(mathematically correct thinking)* about people is:[47]

Intrinsic *(I)* > Extrinsic *(E)* > Systemic *(S)*

This means we truly value the inherent uniqueness of people first, more than their function, roles, health risks, etc., and more than our limited ideas of who we think they are or should be.

When you think of what we do in organizations in terms of employee engagement, and particularly in workplace wellness efforts, it makes sense why efforts fail. Our approach is backward, it's S>E>I. Leaders often overvalue the function of employees *(E)* and focus on their behaviors. Yet employees are essentially screaming they really want to feel valued as people *(I)*. Similarly, traditional approaches to employee wellness identify a health standard *(S)* and then create actions and programs *(E)* employees are suposed to do that should work *(if they were predictable like machines or rodents)*. When the programs and actions don't work, the

> **The hierarchy of best thinking *(mathematically correct thinking)* about people is:**
> Intrinsic>Extrinsic>Systemic

carrot becomes the stick, and a vicious cycle ensues. Desired outcomes for individuals and organizations will continue to be limited as long as Intrinsic thinking is weak.

For example, take typical feedback and performance appraisal systems in organizations. A landmark study at General Electric found that the company's performance appraisal system didn't work, and it actually backfired by producing results opposite of what was intended, with the areas being criticized showing the least improvement. This is because most performance management systems stem from S>E>I thinking.

- The Systemic *(S)* is the "ideal" rating an employee should have or how she/he ideally should have performed her/his job *("ideal" stemming from "Taylorism," assuming there is one right way to do things).*

- When managers criticize an employee or provide negative feedback, it is usually either met with dread and dismissed or negatively impacts that employee's self-image.[48] Think about how you feel when someone offers to provide you with feedback on your performance. Your typical response is not, "Yay! I'm so excited to have an opportunity to improve."

- And even when managers praise an employee, they are essentially saying that employee only has value by matching the manager's ideas about how things should be. So employees spend their time trying to figure out how to please the manager to receive recognition or feel valued rather than feeling truly valued for their unique gifts and contributions to the organization. At GE, the extrinsic reward of praise during performance reviews didn't motivate any higher level of performance because people were already doing the best they could.[49]

It is also important to recognize that, contrary to what we are increasingly hearing from health and business professionals, there is simply no evidence that you can bring about Intrinsic change via Systemic means. In other words, unlike the faulty thinking in Motivation 3.0, you can't "get" someone to be intrinsically motivated. We will discuss more details on how to elicit Intrinsic thinking in chapter 10.

To summarize what we have learned so far about the power of Intrinsic thinking:

- Extrinsic strategies cannot be used to "get" intrinsic motivation.

- Being able to activate Intrinsic thinking is critical to success for businesses and individuals, but it takes time and effort to develop and strengthen our Intrinsic thinking. Without it, we will continue to regard others as things — and they will know it, and the lack of outcomes will show it.

- Research shows it is possible to increase and strengthen Intrinsic thinking; and increasing it even a little can have profound results and help move us to the most beneficial hierarchy of thinking: I>E>S.[50]

Punished By Rewards

Because the carrot approach to incentives has not worked, many in health promotion/wellness are shifting to the stick approach, particularly in light of the wellness provisions in the Affordable Care Act. Why do people think that strong-arming people and instilling fear of punishment will work? Again, a wealth of evidence shows it does not. We will address this more fully when we discuss the implications of the wellness provisions in chapter 13.

We have clearly spent a good deal of time and energy exploring this fascinating phenomenon we call motivation. After all, understanding how and why people do what they do and don't do what they don't do is truly central for those of us who hope to really help organizations and individuals to better care for themselves. Furthermore, because of the ubiquitous cultural acceptance of the Skinnerian doctrine, motivation is also one of the most difficult areas in which to affect real change. Regardless of how often we discuss this information with colleagues, the question, "But do incentives work?" always seems to linger. In his groundbreaking work, "Punished by Rewards," Alfie Kohn gives us the most scientifically and ethically accurate answer to this important question:

If your objective is to get people to obey an order, show up on time and do what they are told, then bribing or threatening them may be sensible strategies. But if your objective is to get long term quality in the work place, to help students become more careful thinkers and self-directed learners, or to support children in developing good values, then rewards, like punishments, are absolutely useless.[51]

We leave this section by adapting our previous Table 1 to reflect the new scientific understandings we have gained about our universe, our health and the process of change — and how they lead to sustainable, thriving organizational and employee wellbeing. Again, please note as was the case with Table 1 (on page 85) the vertical categories in Table 2 flow logically from the paradigms above them. And in good standing with what we have learned from our exploration of the new sciences, it depicts an approach that is a work in progress. We clearly have a long way to go to surrender our outdated beliefs and embrace the exciting approaches informed by these new understandings.

Table 2: The New Paradigm

Worldview
Organic-Living

Science
Holistic
(whole > the sum of its parts)

Culture
Relationship oriented
(equalitarian)

Health
Bio-psycho-social-spiritual
(holistic)

Sustainable Approaches to Change
Intrinsic (autonomous) motivation
I>E>S Thinking in action

So, with that, we come to the end of our first six chapters in which we have examined and critically compared the Old Paradigm scientific assumptions and approaches with those informed by more recent scientific discoveries. We realize there is a lot to digest in these chapters. But we feel it's critical for understanding the need to shift the paradigm, and we hope it helps provide a common sense, evidence-based approach for understanding the blueprint for creating thriving organizational and employee wellbeing we are about to present. The remaining chapters provide that blueprint and will help you to put the new sciences and New Paradigm into action in your organization.

The Evolution of Motivation

SECTION
TWO

The Seven Points of Transformation

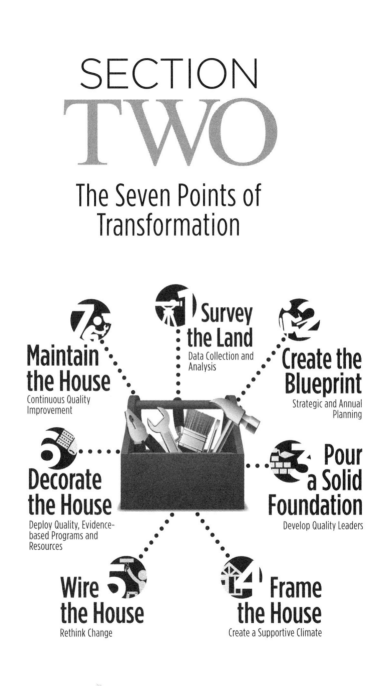

Survey the Land
Data Collection and Analysis

Create the Blueprint
Strategic and Annual Planning

Pour a Solid Foundation
Develop Quality Leaders

Frame the House
Create a Supportive Climate

Wire the House
Rethink Change

Decorate the House
Deploy Quality, Evidence-based Programs and Resources

Maintain the House
Continuous Quality Improvement

CHAPTER 7
An Overview

*❝ Too many organizations — not just companies,
but governments and nonprofits as well — still operate from assumptions
about human potential and individual performance that are outdated,
unexamined and rooted more in folklore than in science.[1] ❞*

Daniel H. Pink, "Drive"

N
ow that we have laid the foundation for WHY we have been *stuck* when it comes to organizational and employee wellbeing, it is time for the WHAT and the HOW. WHAT do we do differently? HOW do we leave the ineffective approaches of the last few decades behind and begin a more effective, sustainable journey? Using lessons learned from the new sciences, emerging research on neuroscience and motivation, the changing workplace landscape, and decades of experience and common sense, we have created a step-by-step blueprint for transforming your workplace culture so both employees and the organization will thrive. We call this approach *The 7 Points of Transformation*, and we will be detailing each step in the remaining chapters of the book.

We are not expecting business and organizational development professionals reading this book to suddenly become experts in employee wellbeing; however, it is important to understand the fundamentals to break free from misguided vendors and consultants deploying outdated wellness programs and strategies. Likewise, we do not expect health and wellness professionals reading this book to become organizational development experts; however, it is important to understand the basics to shift your approach and the value proposition of employee wellbeing within your organization or your client organizations. We are hoping that, regardless of your expertise, you will see things in a new, more holistic way. Following *The 7 Points of Transformation* is not meant to be a solo journey; remember that organizational change requires involving many people *(ideally all employees)* and leveraging quality relationships. We hope the insights you gain will allow you to better align, partner with, and learn from talented people who all bring valuable perspectives and expertise to create a thriving workplace culture.

Whether you consider your workplace a truly toxic environment or a good place to work that could be better, there is a starting point for you here. But before we get into the step-by-step blueprint, we want to briefly address two macro-level considerations that tee up *The 7 Points of Transformation*: changing workplace culture and the power of language.

Critical Considerations Regarding Workplace Culture

As we discussed in chapter 4, workplace culture is essentially the mindset of the organization. It is the collective story employees tell themselves and influences the way they perceive the world and therefore how they act.[2] Although a few years ago it wasn't even on the radar of CEOs and executive leaders, workplace culture is now a top 10 issue that greatly concerns them.[3] Culture can no longer be viewed as some "other" thing that is done. It has to incorporate everything that an organization does as a business, including how problems are solved and how people work together. The culture should be linked to everything that is done within the operations of the organization to provide common goals, a common language and a common way of doing business.[4] Culture is the best way to build your company brand. Ultimately, organizations should hire, develop, manage performance and fire based on cultural fit. As simply put by Tony Hsieh *(CEO of Zappos)*, "For organizations, culture is destiny." [5]

Senior leaders report that up to 75% of their change projects do not yield the promised results.[6] Why? We would argue this is because organizations do not fully understand what it takes to transform their culture and subcultures in a sustainable way and that they are basing their change efforts in the Old Paradigm and the associated outdated sciences. Creating a culture in which both organizational and employee wellbeing thrive requires thinking differently about strategic direction and change. How can we expect great change results when we continue to treat organizations like machines and the people within them like rodents, cattle or small children?

Culture can be a major hindrance for established organizations that wish to develop a new strategic direction. Too often, organizations focus on changing the strategy without addressing the culture; so even though the strategy and direction changes, the culture doesn't necessarily change with it.[7] Imagine a group of toddlers who are busy playing with toys. You now decide it's time for them to clean up and get ready for dinner. Do you think the toddlers will readily stop what they're doing and happily go along with the new direction?

Likely not. Instead, you'll probably be faced with a few tantrums and challenges in shifting their focus. Now imagine shifting direction for what is considered *(and perhaps has been for years or even decades)* "normal" business operations for an organization. Even though new strategies and directions may make sense conceptually, they often fail at implementation due to being too far out of line with the organization's prior underlying assumptions — the heart of the culture. So unless the underlying assumptions are addressed, and conscious effort is made to shape the cultural story, successful change will not be possible because the organization will eventually revert to how it originally operated.[8]

Herein lies the challenge. Although organizational transformation usually involves changing the culture, the worst way to change the culture is by focusing on changing the culture. The best way to proceed is to *create the conditions* that foster the desired thinking, assumptions and behaviors.[9] Starting any strategic change requires having energized and empowered people and the tremendous cooperation of numerous individuals. Organizations that skip steps may create the illusion of speed but do not produce satisfactory results. In addition, critical mistakes made in any phase of the change process can have detrimental results.[10] In our quick-fix society, it's natural to jump to deploying solutions that seem like a magic bullet; yet we know this doesn't work. Perhaps Margaret Wheatley states it best:

Our ideas and sensibilities about change come from the world of Newton. We treat a problematic organization as if it was a machine that had broken down.
We use reductionism to diagnose the problem; we expect to find a simple, singular cause for our woes. We sift through all the possible causes of failure, searching for that one broken part — a bad manager, a dysfunctional team, a poor business unit. To repair the organization, all we need to do is replace the faulty part and gear back up to operate at predetermined performance levels.[11]

Nothing from Newtonian logic has prepared us to work with the behavior of living networks; and in organizations, we are working with networks of people and relationships, not billiard balls.[12] These living networks create the culture, and any organizational change involves altering the culture.[13] This can be a daunting task, because organizations as a whole can have an overall culture but also have many subcultures.[14] So how do we *create the conditions* in each subculture that support thriving organizational and employee well-being? Embrace the new sciences and the New Paradigm.

As we unfold the New Paradigm and explore each of *The 7 Points of Transformation* in detail, keep in mind two critical, yet often overlooked, underlying assumptions:

1) Transforming workplace culture is a *journey*, not a destination. We used an analogy in the introduction likening culture to a river that is constantly flowing and changing with the underlying current guiding the waters. Cultures are dynamic; they shift incrementally and constantly responding to both internal and external changes. Transforming culture is working with a moving target; it requires resiliency and flexibility to adapt and course-correct as our world, the environment and people change. With this understanding, it makes sense that a stable "destination" will likely never be reached, and in fact shouldn't be.

> **Transforming workplace culture is a *journey*, not a destination.**

Even if you've achieved a great culture with thriving organizational and employee wellbeing, the work is not done. Just as a garden will become overgrown with weeds if not properly cared for, culture needs to be tended to so it can thrive. Even great cultures can quickly turn toxic if ignored. Like individual wellbeing, culture change is really an ongoing journey; it is not an operational process, event or program. It is a long-term shift in how the company and its people think and work. Given this, metrics and strategy take on markedly different meanings.

2) Transforming workplace culture requires changing from the *inside out*, not from the outside in. Culture simultaneously involves behavioral, emotional and cognitive processes. The deepest level of culture is cognitive — the shared language, perceptions and thought processes that ultimately shape the attitudes, feelings, overt behavior and espoused values of employees.[15] In chapter 6, we explored how focusing on outwardly observable behaviors keeps us *stuck* with regard to

> **Transforming workplace culture requires changing from the *inside out*, not from the outside in.**

supporting sustainable change, and we discussed the need to develop and support better thinking. The same understanding holds true for organizational change. To have sustainable change, we have to address the underlying thinking habits that guide behavior.

> Outside-in approaches don't work because the *underlying thinking* has not changed. Although an outside-in program can shift behaviors for a period of time, once the program ends, people revert to old behaviors because individuals haven't truly changed their thinking patterns.

The challenge is that most approaches to organizational change take an outside-in approach by focusing on the environment and behaviors and using communication strategies and programs to try to foster change. However, this approach doesn't work. Jim Hart, CEO of Senn Delaney *(a consulting firm known for its work with oganizational culture change)* states that outside-in approaches don't work because the *underlying thinking* has not changed. Although an outside-in program can shift behaviors for a period of time, once the program ends, people revert to old behaviors because individuals haven't truly changed their thinking patterns.[16] We have to move from a mechanistic, billiard-ball approach to change. We have to stop dealing with mass and instead work with energy and the dynamics of living systems.[17] Therefore, creating your desired cultural story starts with determining what kind of thinking is necessary to frame the behaviors to implement its strategy.[18] Then, you must commit to hiring and firing based on your culture and whether employees live your culture and core values.

The Power of Language

With a vastly different scientific lens through which to view organizational and employee wellbeing, you would expect just about everything that follows to differ significantly from the status quo. Instead of mechanistic, reductionist, dualistic, patriarchal, biomedical underpinnings, we have quantum, chaos and complexity, PNI and neuroscience as the foundations for everything we suggest. You will notice, for instance, as we move through *The 7 Points of Transformation*, we deliberately omit certain words and terms commonly used with organizational and employee wellbeing. We do this to better align our language with the updated scientific understandings we have introduced. Words have an amazing power to impact the way people think and feel. As the great writer/storyteller Rudyard Kipling put it:

> *Words are the most powerful drugs used by mankind.*
> *Not only do words infect, egotize, narcotize and paralyze,*
> *but they enter into and colour the minutest cells of the brain.*[19]

Given that, we want to briefly review the terms we are *not* using, and in some cases, what we will replace them with, to better reflect the realities of our non-linear, non-mechanistic, holistic world.

- **"Getting" People to** *(change, exercise, lose weight, partici- pate, increase their productivity, etc.)* — This term clearly originates from a control-oriented, Skinnerian conceptualiza- tion of change and unfortunately is one of the most common phrases uttered by business and wellness professionals. Instead we will talk about *creating the conditions* for and *supporting* desired outcomes.

- **Driving** *(participation, engagement, performance, etc.)* — More throwback to the 17th-century focus on controlling the natural world. When the early American settlers needed to get cattle to the market to be slaughtered for meat, these early set- tlers did so with a cattle drive. Although we may be OK driving cattle, and perhaps our cars, driving people just doesn't make sense. Instead, we will talk about *eliciting better thinking, fostering engagement* and *supporting people* to grow and thrive, acknowledging their humanity and the non-linear, complex nature of change.

- **Motivating People** — Motivation is not something you can do to another person; to try to motivate others is again to view them as controllable machines or rodents. The literature is con- clusive that the most effective motivation comes from within people. Therefore, we again will refer to *creating the conditions* and *supporting* people to grow and thrive and *fostering* and *eliciting* better thinking.

- **Human Resources, Human Capital** — Both terms harken back to the conceptualization of humans as inanimate objects to be used and manipulated as you would any other natural resource As one young CEO put it:

  My dad's generation views human beings as human resources.
  They're the two-by-fours you need to build your house.
  For me, it's a partnership between me and my employees.
  They're not resources. They're partners.[20]

And unlike resources or capital, *human partners* have a need for autonomy, a need to direct their own lives. Given that, you will see us talking about *partners*, *people* and *employees* — viewing them as whole, self-directing human beings. In fact, progressive companies such as Whole Foods, Target and others refer to their employees as "team members" or "crew members."

- **Healthy Work Culture** — Unlike much of the workplace wellness industry, we do not view healthy cultures as those that subsidize gym memberships, offer fresh produce in their cafeterias, and have other policies, programs and practices focused on trying to promote healthy lifestyle behaviors. Instead, we use the phrase *thriving workplace culture* to describe organizations in which there are minimal politics, confusion and turnover and high morale, productivity and overall wellbeing.

- **Participation vs. Engagement** — Although business and health professionals often use these terms interchangeably they really have very different meanings. *Participation* simply refers to taking part in something, or even completing some program or task. *Engagement* deals with how employees feel about their work, as Ringleb and Rock write in a fascinating article entitled "Neuroleadership in 2009":

  When a person is engaged, they are attracted to, inspired by, committed to and even fascinated by their work or their input to the work relationship.[21]

The workplace wellness world has been over-using *engagement* to describe program completion rates and participation; however, it is possible to have high participation in wellness programs, company events, employee surveys, etc., and not have engagement. Likewise, it is possible to have people highly engaged in their work and in their own personal wellbeing who do not participate in programs. We suggest that engagement — true engagement — is what matters. Too often participation in programs is driven by coercion. The appropriate term to describe what is going on in these cases is really *compliance* and we don't believe compliance has much of a role in organizational or employee wellbeing.

- **Wellness** — As discussed in a previous chapter, we believe wellness has become overly linked to the biomedical conceptualization of human health. The vast majority of workplace programs focus on identifying physiological risk factors and targeting personal behaviors related to exercise, nutrition and smoking. Instead, we use the term *wellbeing* to encompass the holistic nature of the human experience.

- **Personal Responsibility** — Traditional approaches to helping people improve health at the workplace have focused on individual health behaviors as the major determinants of health status. As a result, personal responsibility is widely discussed and used as a rationale for outcome-based incentive programs aimed at improving health. We are not saying people have no role in their own health and wellbeing; however, as we have discussed, the literature is clear that the social determinants of health are far and away the most impactful. Taking lessons we have learned from complexity and chaos theory, whether it be stress at home or at the workplace or work-life balance itself, it is critical to address larger contexts if we hope to have any chance of long-term success. So, for example, teaching people stress management techniques may be potentially helpful but will not negate the toxic health effects of a dysfunctional work environment. Therefore, rather than talk about personal responsibility we instead refer to the complexity, interconnectedness and the relationships involved with both organizational and employee wellbeing.

- **Weight Loss Programs** — Weight loss programs, contests and competitions *(one of the mainstays of traditional workplace wellness initiatives)* have little chance of actually helping people to lose weight or be healthier long term. These programs may make things worse for many people. We will address these issues and alternatives in chapter 15, but for now, Dr. Dee Edington's words ring loud and clear:

  Weight loss money is money down the toilet.[22]

Introducing The 7 Points of Transformation

As mentioned in the introduction, we liken building a thriving culture at work that supports and enhances both organizational and employee wellbeing to building a structurally sound and aesthetically pleasing house. If you take shortcuts, skip an important step or use outdated designs or materials, the house will not withstand the test of time — including weathering the inevitable future storms. The same holds true for organizational and employee wellbeing. We have found when companies take shortcuts, skip important steps and base their efforts on outdated paradigms, it's like building a house on quicksand; it is not sustainable and can have dire consequences.

It also takes an additional level of commitment to transform a house into a home — a home where people feel safe, feel valued and want to spend their time. Do your employees see your organization as a place where they can learn, grow, have meaningful work, build strong social connections, make a difference, feel energized and valued, and be supported in their wellbeing? Or do they view your organization as temporary housing — somewhere to land until they can find the organization that will foster their growth and support them? In his bestselling book, "Delivering Happiness," Zappos CEO Tony Hsieh captures the concept perfectly:

> *Our goal at Zappos is for our employees to think of their work not as a job or career, but as a calling.*[23]

Our step-by-step blueprint for building a thriving workplace culture, *The 7 Points of Transformation*, not only guides you in building the house but also in turning that house into a home where people are practically knocking down the doors to get in to be a part of something extraordinary. The following chapters will detail important considerations and the WHAT and HOW for following each of *The 7 Points of Transformation* to build a thriving workplace culture. Again, we cannot emphasize this enough, transforming your workplace culture is a journey, and you cannot take shortcuts, skip steps and expect the best results.

> **Transforming your workplace culture is a journey, and you cannot take shortcuts, skip steps and expect the best results.**

And now that you hopefully have a better understanding of WHY we are *stuck* and need a new paradigm for organizational and employee wellbeing, we are excited to bring *The 7 Points of Transformation* to you! We have witnessed them in action and have seen time and time again the difference this methodical, holistic approach makes for the organization as a whole and for the individual employee experience. We know change is hard and recognize this is a dramatic paradigm shift for many people, but we believe it is necessary to make a real difference. So let's start taking a closer look at how to create a workplace that frees, fuels and inspires people to bring their best selves to work each and every day.

CHAPTER 8
Transformation Point #1:
Survey the Land
(Data Collection and Analysis)

*Counting sounds easy until we actually attempt it,
and then we quickly discover that often we cannot recognize
what we ought to count. Numbers are no substitute for clear definitions,
and not everything that can be counted counts.*[1]

William Bruce Cameron, "NEA (National Education Association) Journal," 1958

Before embarking upon the journey to plan and build a new house, you first have to survey the land. You have to know what you're dealing with before you can build and deploy any strategy. In other words, you have to know the current state of your organization and the employee experience. Understanding the current state allows for having a more thoughtful, holistic view of what is and isn't working in your organization and how that relates to the desired culture you want to foster to support thriving organizational and employee wellbeing. Keep in mind that you don't want to collect and analyze data just to have more data; the point is to understand what feedback is meaningful to your organization and what will allow the organization and the employees to grow and thrive. And because culture is a "moving target" and an ongoing journey, there needs to be flexibility to determine what measures are right for your organization.

Organizations' systems for capturing, monitoring and sharing performance information are often flawed. Paul Niven, author of "Balanced Scorecard," describes this issue with organizations:

Although the methods of modern business have transformed dramatically over the decades, our systems of measurement have remained firmly mired in the past. At the root of our measurement misery is an almost exclusive reliance on financial measures of performance. These systems may have been perfectly suited to the machinelike, physical asset-based nature of early industrial endeavors, but they are ill-equipped to capture the value-creating mechanisms of today's modern business organization. Intangible assets such as employee knowledge, customer and supplier relationships, and innovative cultures are the key to producing value in today's economy.[2]

That said, it is critical we broaden our perspective on how we use data. For a learning organization, it is essential to differentiate between dynamic and detail complexity.[3] Too often, management is addicted to numbers and measuring activity. Management over-surveys employees *(and many times does nothing with the results),* runs monthly and quarterly reports, conducts annual evaluations and relies on monthly progress checks to let employees know how they're doing. The focus on trying to analyze every part of the system to look for the weak areas to "fix" is clearly a throwback to the reductionist perspective of the 17th century.[4] Yet, we know that building on strengths provides far better results.[5]

What is needed is an entirely different mindset, paradigm and skill set to embrace dynamic complexity. This means not looking at data in silos, but instead looking holistically for emerging patterns, considering qualitative data and shifting how we view data in the first place. Understanding interrelationships and patterns of change creates clarity by helping to uncover what lies beneath the details.[6] It also means not relying on measurement to define what is meaningful and instead using data as a helpful servant to provide feedback that supports employees in being empowered to learn and grow to better themselves and the organization.[7] Although measurement is traditionally viewed as a one-way street, where the data provides the direction for what should or shouldn't be done, feedback is a much broader concept. From a systems perspective, feedback represents a reciprocal flow of influence, recognizing nothing is ever influenced in just one direction.[8] Unlike the typical, reductionist approach, data is most effectively used to provide meaningful feedback for understanding, and guiding organizations as living systems. The following chart provides a summary comparison for understanding this shift in approaching data.[9]

Shifting Our Approach to Data Collection and Analysis

New Paradigm **Feedback** *(Organization as a Living System)*	Old Paradigm **Measurement** *(Organization as Machine)*
• Context-dependent	• One size fits all
• Self-determined *(the system chooses what to notice)*	• Imposed *(the criteria are established externally)*
• Information accepted from everywhere	• Information is put in fixed categories
• The system creates its own meaning	• Meaning is pre-determined
• Newness and surprise are essential	• Prediction and routine are valued
• The focus is on adaptability and growth	• The focus is on stability and control
• Meaning evolves	• Meaning remains static
• System co-adapts with its environment	• System adapts to the measures

Shifting the paradigm also requires thinking differently about who is involved with collecting and reviewing the data. Typically, management reviews data and then decides on organizational strategy and operations based on the data. However, when organizations include a broader array of data and more people, they will better understand what is happening and what needs to be done. Margaret Wheatley states:

> *We need a constantly expanding array of data, views and interpretations if we are to make wise sense of the world. We need to include more and more eyes. We need to be constantly asking: 'Who else should be here? Who else should be looking at this?*[10]

Once you've reviewed existing data in a holistic way, it will become clearer what gaps you may need to fill by collecting additional information to help you determine the current, baseline state of organizational and employee wellbeing, and how you might start identifying and moving towards your desired workplace culture. Although they are profoundly intertwined *(as all aspects of complex systems always are)*, we will address the various data based on whether the information provided is used more to determine the state of organizational wellbeing or employee wellbeing. So let's start with organizational wellbeing.

Organizational Wellbeing Data

Determining what data to collect and review can seem like a daunting task. However, if you start by keeping the "end" in mind *(realizing, of course, that there is no real end when it comes to wellbeing but rather an ongoing journey)*, it becomes a little clearer what data will actually be meaningful for your organization. That said, before we address the data, let's revisit our conceptualization of Thriving Organizational Wellbeing.

Thriving Organizational Wellbeing

• The executive leadership team is truly a cohesive one.

• The mission, vision and values are clearly articulated and every employee knows how she/he fits within them.

• Employees are empowered and enabled to leverage their strengths.

• Leaders and the work climate provide employees with autonomous support *(versus using incentives to drive behaviors)*.

• Clear, timely and meaningful communication is provided for employees, and employees share feedback and ideas that are actually used.

• Clear, timely and meaningful feedback is provided for employees in the spirit of ongoing growth and development *(versus simply measuring performance)*.

• The climate fosters innovation, creativity and meaningful work.

• Leaders truly value employees — and employees feel valued.

• Employees are encouraged and supported to be authentic and be themselves.

• People within the organization respect, support and care about one another as people, not just as employees there to complete certain job tasks.

• Accountability is embraced; the rules are clear and apply to everyone.

• Employees are provided the tools and resources they need to work safely and productively.

• Resources, programs, policies and the environment support employees' ability to thrive in all areas of wellbeing.

• Employees are happy and proud to work there!

Using this conceptualization to provide direction toward fostering thriving organizational wellbeing, let's discuss the metrics that will likely be helpful for guiding that journey.

Organizational Culture

Highly successful companies have distinct and clearly identifiable organizational cultures. However, many people are not aware of their culture.[11] One of the first questions we ask when working with organizations is, "How would you describe your organization's culture?" It's always interesting to see how that question stumps people. More often than not, they can't clearly answer it. In fact, it's amazing how many different answers we get from people within the same organization. And most of the answers we receive tend to describe working relationships, aspired values and other manifestations of culture. But then when we ask if people have ever measured their culture, most reply "no" and have no idea of what their culture really is *(remember that Schein defines culture as "the hidden force that drives most of our behavior both inside and outside organizations.")* and how to leverage it for strategic change.[12]

Organizational culture is the best way to build your company's brand for the long term and has to be intentionally managed. At Zappos, the belief is that if they get the culture right, most other things *(e.g., building a great long-term brand, outstanding customer service, and passionate employees and customers)* will happen naturally on their own.[13] And this belief has translated into great success. Zappos has become one of the world's largest online shoe and clothing retailers since it was founded in 1999. Just 10 years after it began, the company was sold to Amazon in 2009 for an estimated $1.2 billion. Zappos is known for providing exceptional customer service and building customer loyalty while consistently being listed on "Fortune" magazine's list of "100 Best Companies to Work For" — even after being acquired by Amazon.

No strategic organizational change will succeed if it is not aligned with culture. Therefore, we firmly believe it is essential to:

- Understand your current organizational culture.
- Define your preferred or desired culture.
- Intentionally reduce any disconnect between your current and preferred culture.
- Foster aspects of your culture where there is no disconnect.

You can't expect to improve organizational or employee wellbeing without transforming your workplace culture — period!

> You can't expect to improve organizational or employee wellbeing without transforming your workplace culture — period!

The good news is organizational culture can be measured. One highly validated tool is the Organizational Culture Assessment Instrument *(OCAI)*.[4] It is based on the Competing Values Framework developed from research conducted on the major indicators of effective organizations. The OCAI allows for identifying:

- Which of four main culture types are dominant in your organization.
- Core attributes that reflect the culture.
- The strength and congruence of your culture.

In other words, the OCAI allows you to see what your current culture is, what your preferred culture is, and how aligned or disconnected your current and preferred state are. Any disconnect should immediately indicate the need for change because it means your preferred culture is not the current reality. If you want to learn more about the OCAI, how it is scored and how to implement it, we recommend reading "Diagnosing and Changing Organizational Culture" by Kim Cameron and Robert Quinn.

Although the OCAI is a useful tool, even Cameron and Quinn state that there is no one best way to assess culture. The OCAI provides significant value in assessing dominant characteristics, leadership style, employee cohesiveness, and what gets rewarded and celebrated *(or what matters in determining success)*. However, with all we have learned in recent years about the critical connectedness between organizational culture and employee wellbeing, a pitfall of the OCAI is it misses measuring the employee experience of feeling valued and connected to the vision, and the norms of how the organization supports employee wellbeing. Several instruments exist in the world of employee wellness that claim to measure healthy cultures. However, as we addressed in previous chapters, every current tool really measures climate and whether organizations support healthy lifestyle behaviors, with the questions and recommendations largely from a 17th-century reductionist, biomedical perspective on health.

In light of our continued frustration regarding the lack of fusion of organizational development and employee wellbeing — including assessing culture — we opted to draw from the research and develop our own tool that bridges this gap: the Thriving Workplace Culture Survey *(TWCS)*. We tested the questions with numerous organizations and then enhanced and revised the TWCS until we found the most useful tool to guide culture transformation efforts and the journey toward thriving organizational well-being. The TWCS is designed to be deployed as an all-employee survey; after all, how can you expect to truly understand your workplace culture without asking every employee? The free Workplace Culture Audit at the beginning of this book provides you with a broad overview of what the TWCS measures. Obviously, we are biased toward our holistic tool, but regardless of whether you use our tool, we hope you will keep in mind these important guidelines as you search for a tool that works for your organization.

Survey Considerations

At this point, we want to address a couple of critical considerations to implementing culture surveys — and really any employee survey.

- *Surveys should be provided by a third party.* There are many surveys you can do internally; however, if you want your employees to provide honest feedback about management and leadership, the work environment and the culture *(especially if there are already any trust issues with management and leadership)*, we suggest partnering with a qualified expert who understands what you want to measure and can provide you with meaningful guidance in using the results. This can help reduce concerns about confidentiality. If trust is really low, you may want to have your survey partner specifically address how data is collected, analyzed and reported to help alleviate some concerns *(keeping in mind some employees may inherently never trust surveys, no matter who provides them)*.

- *Be careful of how survey comments are provided to you.* Presuming you use a third party to implement the survey, do your homework regarding how the third party handles survey comments. We have seen countless survey providers who sell packages in which leaders can purchase the comments. When the comments are provided, they are provided exactly as written by employees. This becomes especially risky if the results are broken down by smaller departments or divisions. We can't tell you how many times we have heard managers say, "I think I know who said XYZ comment" or they try to figure out which employee wrote the comment based on the way it was written. This is a recipe for disaster and can cause problems for any subsequent surveys you may want to deploy. If comments are provided, they should be provided as a synthesis of common themes and should not be the actual words of individual employees.

• *When implementing the survey, leadership has to communicate in a way that is inclusive of employees and allows them to feel part of the process.* Employees need to feel that completing the survey allows them to be part of creating the future of the organization. Every leader within the organization should understand why the survey is being deployed and how it relates to strategic objectives and change efforts. And each leader has the responsibility to communicate clearly to employees, with passion and optimism, to maximize survey response rates and the likelihood that people will provide honest feedback.

• *Do NOT incent employees to complete the survey.* If you have to coerce your employees to give you feedback, be suspect of the feedback and consider that, by not participating, your employees may be telling you something important about your culture. If you have a high trust, thriving culture where employees feel valued, you wouldn't have to drag them kicking and screaming to provide feedback.

• *Do NOT deploy a survey if you don't plan to both communicate the results and DO something productive with the results.* Trust is eroded quickly when organizations ask employees for their feedback and then don't do anything with the results. The 2011 global engagement research from BlessingWhite found that deploying engagement surveys without visible follow-up actions actually decreases employee engagement.[15] You have to be willing to look at the good, bad and ugly, and do something meaningful with the feedback or it will backfire.

• *If you have a history of deploying surveys without visibly using the results, you have to eat crow.* If you're one of the many organizations we have come across that is obsessed with surveys but has a history of not broadly communicating results and not visibly using results to improve, you can not just deploy another survey and expect employees to jump up and down with excitement to waste their time providing you with more feedback that won't be used. Just as in any relationship, when we've messed up, we have to own up to it before trust can be restored. In this case, the most senior leader would ideally communicate in-person to employees. If you're a very large organization, then a combination of in-person and recorded videos can suffice, but the message can't be done via e-mail or other written communication. Of course the communication will vary from organization to organization, but the apology will likely be something like:

> *"I know we haven't handled employee surveys well in the past, but I want to assure you we recognize that failure and that this time will be different. We are all in this together; we want you all to be actively involved in helping us to create a workplace where we all want to be and can thrive. We will communicate the results to everyone and involve you all in developing strategies to address the results and help us improve."*

Yes, this means the CEO or president needs to acknowledge being human, admit failure and check her/his ego at the door. Believe it or not, these admissions and actions alone can do wonders to set the stage for creating a thriving workplace culture.

• *Explicitly link any change and improvement efforts to survey feedback.* Don't assume employees will associate organizational changes or any new policies, programs and resources as having resulted from their feedback. It will go a long way toward building trust if you explicitly communicate that these changes are being made based on employees' feedback and thank them for helping to transform the organization.

• *Don't over-survey employees.* Surveys can be useful for gathering information on the current state of organizational and employee wellbeing and evaluating efforts over time. However, as we've already established, too often management is obsessed with measurement and surveys. If you survey employees too frequently, they will suffer from survey fatigue.

You shouldn't survey employees again — about anything — unless you've shown you actually listened to and did something with the feedback they provided. We suggest twice per year for any survey is probably plenty and that other methods *(which we describe in this chapter)* can also be used to gather data.

It is always informative when we implement culture surveys in organizations. When leaders encounter the data, it forces them to face the reality of the current state of their organization, the preferred culture employees desire and how big the disconnect between the two really is. Many times, survey results confirm *(good or bad)* what leadership suspects is happening in their organization, but there are often valuable surprises that offer new understanding and insights. Sometimes we have received push-back from leaders who say, "We already know things aren't great in our organization, and doing a culture survey will just add fuel to the fire." Here's a little tip: Just because you don't ask employees about the current state doesn't mean it doesn't exist and won't fuel their discontent. The longer leadership ignores problems, the worse the culture actually gets. However, when communicated and implemented appropriately, a culture survey can help start the journey of healing because employees will see leadership is no longer ignoring their concerns.

Employee Engagement

We already discussed the important relationship between employee engagement and various measures of organizational wellbeing and performance as well as individual employee wellbeing. A Deloitte "Global Human Capital Trends 2014" survey found 79% of businesses are worried about engagement and retention. In fact, it is their No. 2 issue after leadership.[16] If your organization has data from a good quality employee engagement survey, those results can also help in understanding one piece of a complex puzzle that impacts organizational wellbeing.

If you don't already have results from an employee engagement survey, you may want to think twice before implementing one. Consider using a survey to assess culture and finding other ways to determine engagement. We are not against quality employee engagement surveys; however, as we mentioned, over-surveying employees can backfire. And surveys may not be as useful as once thought for measuring employee engagement. Although several well-respected organizations provide validated surveys and bench-marking tools to assess engagement, the survey approach is not keeping up with today's rapidly changing workplace.[17] Assessing engagement levels via an annual survey doesn't necessarily help organizations understand the real day-to-day issues or the passion and soul of employees.[18] Ultimately, engagement can really be considered one manifestation of the culture — of the company brand as it relates to the employee experience. So using a survey to measure culture and then using other timely and relevant measures to determine engagement may be more meaningful. And some-times the survey results may not be as useful as you'd like to think.

Unintended Consequences from an Employee Engagement Survey

A couple of years ago, I *(Rosie)* was chatting with a manager in a large healthcare organization, and he was describing what happens each year when the organization deploys the engagement survey. This organization partners directly with Gallup, yet the results are still questionable. This manager told me employees (himself included) in his area train all new em-ployees to fill out the survey with "all 4s and 5s — no matter what." I asked him why. He replied, "Because otherwise our leader will 'have the talk' with us and make our lives annoying for several months, yet nothing will change or be done to improve the results. So we've learned it's better to just avoid the nonsense altogether and make sure any new employee understands how things work when survey time comes."

Don't get us wrong, we are advocates for having good data and believe a quality culture survey is part of an evidence-based, metric driven strategy to support a thriving workplace culture. However, be aware of the potential pitfalls that can occur with surveys *(like the situation just described)*. And even if a survey is valid, employees complete the survey honestly, and management uses the results to improve the employee expe-rience, surveys can only be done periodically to avoid "survey fatigue" *(which becomes even more problematic in a toxic work culture or in organizations that over-survey employees yet don't do anything meaningful with the results)*.

135

Beyond Engagement — Measuring and Fostering Happiness

You may be now wondering, what do we measure if we don't measure employee engagement via an annual survey? We suggest data from engagement surveys may sometimes be almost too late; such data may provide lagging indicators of organizational wellbeing. And, although engagement is certainly important for business performance, it is not the whole story. In an April 2014 article written for Forbes.com, Josh Bersin suggests that using the word "engagement" limits our thinking because most businesses consider engagement to mean that employees are going the extra mile or giving more discretionary effort. In light of this common use of "engagement" in the business world, Bersin states,

> *We aren't just looking to get people 'engaged.'*
> *we want them to be 'married.' That is, fully committed.*[19]

So what is a leading indicator of organizational wellbeing? More recent research indicates employee happiness is an important predictor of business performance. In addition to being more engaged, happy employees produce more than unhappy ones over the long term.[20] And when happiness is combined with being engaged and highly energized *(yet knowing how to avoid burnout)*, employees are considered to be thriving. And the benefits to organizations of having thriving employees is profound. Thriving employees:

- Across industries and job types, demonstrate 16% better overall performance *(reported by their managers)* and 125% less burnout *(self-reported)* than their peers.
- Are 32% more committed to their organization.
- Are 46% more satisfied with their jobs.
- Miss less work.
- Report significantly fewer doctor visits.[21]

On the other end of the spectrum of happy, thriving employees are people who dislike or even hate their jobs and employers. These employees do just enough to avoid being fired, which is even more problematic for organizations trying to embark upon the journey for strategic change. Because happiness is a variable that can change practically every hour, it is important to frequently take the pulse on employee happiness levels to identify and address any problems early. Some companies are serious enough about employee happiness that they assess it more formally using a web and mobile application that provides managers a daily dashboard. Other organizations do something as simple as asking employees to drop a red, yellow or green marble or chip in a container at the end of the day to indicate how they felt about the day or week at work.[22] Regardless of how it is assessed, happiness matters to organizational wellbeing and performance.

Quality of Leadership

We know every experience employees have when interacting with a leader generates a belief about the workplace culture.[23] Given that, it is critical to clearly understand the effectiveness and quality of your leaders:

- Do you know how effective your leaders are?
- How do employees view company leaders?
- How are leaders supporting or hindering organizational and employee wellbeing?
- Is your executive team truly a cohesive one?

You can gather much of the feedback and understanding about the quality of your leaders via the culture survey or any past engagement or perception surveys. Exit interview results also can sometimes provide insight into the quality of leaders. Another helpful way to find out how effective your leaders are is to look at their teams. Are their teams full of happy, engaged and energized employees? Or are they just collecting a paycheck; or worse, getting sick, injured or leaving the organization? Don't underestimate the value of simply asking employees — either individually or via focus groups — to better understand employee experience and how leaders impact employee wellbeing. We will more fully address HOW to develop quality leaders in chapter 10. At this point, the critical goal is to have a good baseline understanding of the effectiveness of your leadership team.

Other Metrics

The following list includes other metrics that may be meaningful in helping you better understand the current state of your organizational wellbeing:

- *Turnover.* Turnover is very telling of your current state of organizational wellbeing. If your best, talented employees are leaving, it should be a red flag you have greater issues to address.

However, low turnover doesn't necessarily by itself mean organizational wellbeing is thriving. It could mean the job market in your industry or geographic location isn't great or is very competitive, and you have people who are merely biding their time. Given that, turnover, like every other metric, should always be viewed within the larger context of what the totality of the data indicates.

• *Employee Referrals.* If your organization is hiring, whether current employees are or are not referring people to apply and interview for open positions may, in part, reflect your organizational wellbeing.

• *CAHPS – Consumer Assessment of Healthcare Providers and Systems (For Hospitals, Health Plans and Medical Clinics).* Healthcare organizations have another set of metrics collected via an annual national survey of patients. It includes their ratings of provider quality, patient adherence to recommended treatments, patient experience and malpractice lawsuits. Healthcare organizations with good CAHPS scores can receive significant financial benefit.[24] There is also a specific rating just for hospitals *(HCAHPS)*. Not surprisingly, Gallup found that as employee engagement scores increase, patient complaints decrease and the HCAHPS rating increases.[25] In other words, improving organizational wellbeing at healthcare organizations can very likely improve the quality of healthcare in our country — imagine that!

• *Demographics.* It can also help to pay attention to the demographic makeup of your employee workforce. If you already have a significant and growing population of Millennials for example, it is even more imperative for your organization to immediately begin to foster thriving organizational wellbeing and autonomous motivation. These are essential for what this segment of the incoming workforce wants in an employer. This means having even a greater sense of urgency for shifting organizational strategy regarding leadership development, hiring and onboarding. [26]

Employee Wellbeing Data

Obviously, there is significant overlap of organizational wellbeing and employee wellbeing data — particularly when it comes to engagement and happiness. We will now address some metrics we believe are most helpful when assessing employee wellbeing.

Stress/Burnout:

Findings from the Deloitte "Global Human Capital Trends 2014" survey found two-thirds of business leaders citing "the overwhelmed employee" as a top business challenge.[27] And they should be concerned. We know that 74% of employees are experiencing a personal energy crisis and are feeling overwhelmed.[28] Furthermore, dangerously stressful work environments are actually pushing many workers to seek alternative employment. In a 2014 international Monster poll, almost 7,000 employees responded to the question, "Has stress from work ever driven you to change a job?" The following is a summary of the responses from workers in the United States:

- 57% experience very stressful work lives.
- 42% have purposefully changed jobs due to a stressful work environment.
- 35% have thought about changing jobs due to a stressful work environment.[29]

Being overwhelmed can be a leading contributor to disengagement. Additionally, employees can be engaged, but if their work-life balance is not serving them well, they won't have the capacity to give any extra discretionary effort. Here are some possible sources to provide you with information on employee stress:

- **Employee surveys** *(again, this will depend on how you have been recently using surveys)*. Some engagement and perception surveys include questions related to stress; our Thriving Workplace Culture Survey includes questions to assess stress.

- **Hartman Value Profile** *(HVP)*. Remember the wedding-cake analogy from chapter 4? The HVP we discussed in Chapter 6 includes metrics that quantify stress and resiliency in your personal life and at work. On an individual or group level, reports can help determine how out of balance people are and if addressing stress needs to be a starting point for any developmental efforts.[30]

• **Talk to and LISTEN to your employees!** It is pretty easy to tell if employees are stressed and burned out if you just pay attention. You don't need a formal tool to get a sense of stress levels. When you see and hear employees are on overload, it's time to pay attention.

Medical, Workers' Compensation and Disability Claims Data

There is value in examining data for all types of claims. It can help in seeing trends and provide insights into employee wellbeing. However, because claims data are historical in nature, use the numbers with caution. Unlike machines, human beings are not predictable. Past claims are not necessarily a good predictor for future claims, and data alone do not help in determining what contributed to the claims. That said, here are some of the indicators to look for when reviewing claims data that can help fill in a piece of the wellbeing puzzle:

Medical Claims:
It can be overwhelming to review medical claims data. Looking at overall costs is not typically very useful because costs in general continue to rise. Additionally, many annual claims summary reports do not factor out any high-cost claims that may skew the data. Keeping that in mind, we have listed some details to notice with medical claims that can help contribute to a greater understanding of employee wellbeing.

   • *Percentage of Lifestyle-Related Claims.* This is not to start treating employees like machines to "fix" behaviors presumed to result in lifestyle claims. This is simply to understand year-to-year if the percentage is increasing or decreasing. Depending on the size of your organization and how you structure your healthcare benefits, some lifestyle claim diagnosis data can be helpful. For example, we know several organizations that have waived copays and deductibles for diabetes medication to better meet their employees' needs *(based on claim reports).*

   • *Prescription Drug Reports.* Many organizations find anti-anxiety and antidepressant medications are the top two prescriptions for both quantity and cost. If this is true for your organization, consider the state of your organizational wellbeing may be a prime contributor to both the stress overload and possible toxic work culture.

- *Mental Health Claims.* Once again, we know the important relationship between mental/emotional wellbeing and organizational wellbeing. If mental health claims are increasing, it's time to take notice and examine what role the organization may be playing in declining employee wellbeing.

- *Musculoskeletal Claims.* Musculoskeletal claims *(i.e., strains, sprains, headaches and back pain)* certainly have a component related to physical health and fitness. However, there is also a strong association with stress manifesting itself in these types of physical issues. If you see an increase in these claims, look at what is happening with Workers' Compensation and disability *(addressed next)* and look at how the organization may be contributing to this less-than-favorable trend.

- *Emergency-Room Use.* Most health plans or insurance brokers can provide more detailed data regarding emergency-room visits. With some simple data organizing, you can see what conditions people are seeking treatment for in the emergency room and use the data to support education and resources to help employees to make informed, effective healthcare decisions. We will address healthcare consumerism in more detail in chapter 13.

Workers' Compensation Claims:

When examining Workers' Compensation claims, review the diagnoses, the day of the week the incident occurred and in which department the employees work. Realize that nearly three times as many workers suffer nonfatal injuries outside of work as they do at work.[31] So caring for the whole person, whether he/she is physically at work or not, matters.

There are many diagnoses of Workers' Compensation claims that could indicate organizational wellbeing issues, but back injuries and musculoskeletal injuries *(i.e., strains and sprains)* should raise concern that a larger workplace culture issue may be a culprit. As we mentioned in chapter 4, we have seen an increase in claims due to back pain over the past several years. Our first question to leaders is not, "Do you have a safe lifting/ergonomics program in place?" Of course safety and ergonomics are important, but we know there is often more to it. Instead we ask leaders:

- "How has morale been lately?"

- "What are the relationships like these days between management and employees?"
- "Are your employees engaged... are they happy?"

In every single case, the leaders indicate larger organizational wellbeing issues are occurring.

The day of the week claims are filed and in what department or area people who are filing them work can also be very telling of the state of organizational wellbeing. For example, if many of the claims are reported on Mondays *(and also Fridays)*, it should raise a red flag. If employees are not happy at work *(especially if they had a musculoskeletal injury over the weekend)*, they may decide to file a Workers' Compensation claim on Monday. Or they may decide to lengthen their weekend by filing a claim on Friday. We aren't saying every claim occurring on a Monday or Friday is suspect, but if this becomes a trend, it should be identified as a potential red flag. If many claims show up in one area *(especially if they are musculoskeletal claims)*, you may want to look at the leader*(s)* in that area and further investigate happiness, morale and engagement.

Disability Claims

We already discussed considerations with back pain, stress and depression with organizational wellbeing in chapter 4. So it's probably not surprising to know that back pain and mental illness are among the fastest growing causes of disability. Back pain and other musculoskeletal problems accounted for nearly 34% of all new disability claims in 2011, with mental illness accounting for 19% of all new claims.[32] When disability claims are due to stress, anxiety, depression, back pain and musculoskeletal problems, it should signal a need to take a critical look at organizational wellbeing data to see if/how the organization may be contributing to employee disability.

The Pendulum of Claim Costs – Riverdale School District

We met with a school district, we'll call Riverdale School District, that was doing really well with reducing their Workers' Compensation and disability claims and saving money. A few years ago, the district implemented a return-to-work program *(designed to get employees back to work quicker after injury or disability)*, started aggressively managing claims and implemented very progressive safety initiatives. However, at the same time, district leaders described concerns they had for employees regarding very high stress, low levels of trust, decreased morale and disengagement.

In listening to district leaders, we were curious if their concerns about organizational wellbeing might be manifesting elsewhere, so we asked to see their medical claims reports. Just as we suspected, there was a significant increase in musculoskeletal claims *(especially back injuries)*. In fact, musculoskeletal claims were the district's second top major diagnostic category for medical issues. The district's medical claims report also indicated other possible physical manifestations of stress, including gastrointestinal issues, headaches, and prescriptions for anxiety, depression and other possible conditions. Riverdale was swinging on the pendulum of claims costs, trading off improved Workers' Compensation and disability claims for worsening medical claims.

Riverdale is not unique with experiencing the pendulum of claims costs. We have met with other organizations that are doing well with regards to their medical claims experience and costs; yet these organizations also describe increased stress and workloads, morale issues and more. In these cases, the claims pendulum swings to the other side, where Workers' Compensation and disability claims increase — especially if the medical plan has increased the deductible and out-of-pocket expenses. Unless you examine your data comprehensively and incorporate the critical impact organizational wellbeing may be having on claims, it will be easy to fall into the trap of using a bandage approach rather than addressing the underlying issues. Regardless of the industry, this same trend of disengagement, stress and other indicators of poor organizational wellbeing manifesting in increased claims appears quite often.

Perceived Wellbeing Status

Do you know how employees perceive their overall wellbeing? Do you know if they even would appreciate additional support and resources for various aspects of their wellbeing? One simple way to capture a baseline of wellbeing is to ask employees. Either insert the following two questions into an already existing survey you plan to deploy, or have employees provide feedback on these questions separately in another survey.

Please indicate how satisfied you are with each area of wellbeing in your life.

	Very Satisfied	Somewhat Satisfied	Neither Satisfied nor Dissatisfied	Somewhat Dissatisfied	Very Dissatisfied
Career Wellbeing / Purpose *(liking what you do every day at work)*					
Social Wellbeing *(having strong, connected relationships and love in your life)*					
Financial Wellbeing *(managing your economic life well)*					
Physical Wellbeing *(having good health and enough energy to get things done each day that are important to you)*					
Emotional Wellbeing *(having enough mental energy to get things done each day that are important to you)*					
Community Wellbeing *(feeling connected to the community where you live)*					

If you annually ask employees about their satisfaction with each area of wellbeing, you can start to see if overall perceived wellbeing is improving or declining and how employees feel about their individual areas of wellbeing *(we will discuss building a Wellbeing Dashboard in more detail in chapter 14).*

How important it is for our company to develop more programs and resources to better support you in each area of wellbeing?

	Extremely Important	Important	Undecided	Not at all Important
Career Wellbeing / Purpose				
Social Wellbeing				
Financial Wellbeing				
Physical Wellbeing				
Emotional Wellbeing				
Community Wellbeing				

If you ask employees how important it is to have resources to support their needs, you can tailor how you support them and *create the conditions* for thriving wellbeing in a meaningful way. Because all areas of wellbeing are interrelated, your employees and your organization will receive much greater benefit from providing resources that matter. This allows everyone to be part of creating meaning and honoring the living systems rather than incenting employees to try to "get" participation in programs that do not interest them.

Perhaps you have noticed what is missing in our recommendations for data to help determine the state of employee wellbeing — the two most common sources of data in traditional workplace wellness programs:

- Health Risk Assessment *(HRA)* Data
- Biometric Screening Data

We've already established the *stuckness* of focusing on the biomedical model in chapter 5. We aren't saying that knowing your blood pressure, cholesterol, glucose and triglyceride levels doesn't have value on an individual basis. However, as an employer, what value does spending time and money to collect this data provide? What will it tell you about the state of your employee wellbeing? We can tell you what most HRA and screening data will tell you: "Your employees need to lose weight, eat more fruits and vegetables, exercise more, quit smoking and perhaps reduce stress." There — we just saved you thousands of dollars. In addition, these interventions are fraught with the potential for increasing costs and negatively impacting health in the form of overdiagnosis and overtreatment. We will have more to say about the lack of evidence base for and the pitfalls of these interventions in chapter 13.

If the employer's role is to *create the conditions* within which people can thrive in their wellbeing, medicalizing the workplace no longer makes sense. You will learn a lot more about the state of employee wellbeing by looking at stress, employee engagement and happiness rather than biomedical health risk factors. And instead of trying to play doctor, employers can spend the time and money providing quality tools and resources to help employees better partner with their healthcare providers for prevention and to meet their specific healthcare needs. We will also discuss more about providing quality, evidence-based programs and resources in chapter 13.

Analyzing/Addressing the Data

Too often data is reviewed in silos: This includes having different people reviewing the data *(and then not discussing what they have found)* and having the same person responsible for different data but not looking at metrics together. Examining data holistically will also reduce the tendency to feel you need to survey employees for every little thing and allow for better designed surveys *(if surveys are one source of information you use)*.

Therefore, it is critically important to look for patterns in the data. If you take a step back, you can gain perspective:

- What shows up more than once?
- Have you seen something similar before?
- Knowing the interrelatedness of organizational and employee wellbeing, what is standing out to you?
- What might the data be telling you about the employee experience, engagement, morale and happiness?

Using the data to provide meaningful feedback means viewing the inter-relationships and patterns of change rather than seeing things as static snap-shots. To do so requires slowing down and taking a more thoughtful and reflective approach. Peter Senge describes one of the "learning disabilities" organizations have with "the parable of the boiled frog." If you put a frog in a pot of boiling water the frog will instantly scramble and try to escape. If you put it in a pot of room temperature water, it will stay put. Then, as you gradually increase water temperature, the frog will adjust until it becomes increasingly groggy, won't be able to climb out of the pot, and eventually dies. The frog is hard-wired to sense threats to its survival based on sudden changes, not slow, gradual ones. In that respect, businesses are like frogs; they often don't pay attention to slow, gradual processes and feedback and instead wait until they are in hot water.[33] This frequently results in making rash decisions and wasting resources on hopeful "quick fix" solutions that almost never work and frequently backfire *(enter the recent push for outcome-based wellness incentive programs to address the "sudden emergency" of rising healthcare costs, which we will address in more detail in chapter 13)*. Organizations need to learn to slow down and pay attention to the subtle as well as the dramatic feedback.[34]

In addition to slowing down, one of the critical competencies for organizations is to *create the conditions* that generate new knowledge and help it to be freely shared.[35] For this to happen, the data collected and how it is reviewed need to emerge from a deeper understanding of the importance of people coming together and aligning towards a greater purpose and more meaningful work.[36] Freely sharing information, both within and outside of the organization, requires moving beyond fear and hoarding data to develop trusting relationships.

In order to really walk this talk, Zappos created a unique "Culture Book." This was originally an opportunity for all employees to contribute a short paragraph to answer the following question: "What does Zappos culture mean to you?" The book was then made available to all employees, without censorship to the entries and with those entries anonymous if the writer so desired. If you are thinking this sounds a bit scary, in the words of CEO Tony Hsieh:

> *For Zappos, it was a risk worth taking. If the company was truly*
> *going to stand behind its culture and core values,*
> *there couldn't be a better way to see if Zappos was doing it right.*

Eventually the opportunity was opened up to all stakeholders, including customers. Again, from the CEO:

> *Would you be comfortable printing everything your employees,*
> *customers and partners have to say about your culture?*
> *What would it take to get you there? No culture book is worth much*
> *unless it reflects culture and values that are already in place.*

Using Feedback to Begin Your Thriving Wellbeing Journey

Keeping in mind that building and transforming organizational culture is a journey, what is your current state telling you about the strength of your culture and where you are on that journey? What is your current state telling you about your brand?

- Is your culture already great and just needs to be tended to and supported?
- Is your culture OK but not great?
- Is your culture riding on the train to "dysfunction junction?"

Regardless of your current culture state, starting the process for strategic change requires having energized, empowered people and real cooperation.[37] Sustainable results will not occur unless the culture and people are fully prepared and aligned to support change.[38] Therefore, if your culture is anything less than great, and if people don't have visible passion and purpose for your organization's vision and values, eliciting sustainable change will be an uphill battle. Zappos views passion as essential fuel that propels the company forward, and they value determination — seeing both as being contagious when it comes to influencing attitudes.[39] Here are some questions you can ask yourself and your employees to get a sense for how ready you are to begin strategic change and how much work needs to be done first to *create the conditions* for employees to be energized and empowered to embrace and guide the change:

- Does your organization have a clear purpose and passion that aligns employees? Do they believe in what you do and where you are headed?
- Do YOU believe in what the organization does and where it's headed?
- Do your employees view their work as a job, a career or a calling?

- Are YOU passionate about the company? About your work?
- Are your employees happy? Are YOU happy?

If you answered "yes" to most of these questions, you are building on solid ground. If you answered "no" to several of these questions, you are not building on solid ground; in fact, you may be trying to build a house on quicksand.

Once you have brought together a broad group of people to examine the data and help you determine your current organizational and employee wellbeing states, you can determine how aligned you are with your desired culture and your core values, and start creating plans to transform your organization — which we will address in the next chapter.

Summary of Transformation Point #1
Data to Collect and Holistically Examine

Data to Collect / Analyze	Frequency of Collection / Analysis	Key Themes to Look For

Organizational Wellbeing Data

Data to Collect / Analyze	Frequency of Collection / Analysis	Key Themes to Look For
Workplace Culture Survey	Every 2 years	Disconnect between current and preferred state of organizational wellbeing
Employee Happiness	Daily / Weekly	If there's a downward shift in happiness, tend to it ASAP; if it's increased, what can you learn about what may have contributed it *(and keep doing it)*?
Turnover / Exit Interviews	Quarterly	Are departing employees top performers? Are there trends with exit interview feedback? Are there areas losing more employees than others?
Employee Referrals	Quarterly *(depends on hiring needs/frequency)*	Are employee referrals increasing or decreasing?

Employee Wellbeing Data

Data to Collect / Analyze	Frequency of Collection / Analysis	Key Themes to Look For
Workers' Compensation and Disability Claims	Quarterly	Are there red-flag claims *(Mon. morning or Fri. claims)*? Any increase or decrease in back and musculoskeletal claims?
Medical Claims	Annually	Claims that reflect poor organizational wellbeing; possible trade-off for Workers' Compensation claims; trends in emergency-room claims; lifestyle claims
Wellbeing Satisfaction	Annually	Is overall wellbeing satisfaction improving or not? Are there specific areas of wellbeing improving or worsening?
Stress / Burnout	Depends on how data is collected	Are stress levels increasing more in one area than others? Do you see stress relating to other feedback from organizational wellbeing data?

CHAPTER 9
Transformation Point #2:
Create the Blueprint
(Strategic and Annual Planning)

> 66 *If you don't know where you're going, you might not get there.* 99
> Yogi Berra

In his bestselling book, "The 7 Habits of Highly Effective People," Stephen R. Covey's first three habits — **1)** Be proactive, **2)** Begin with the end in mind, and **3)** Put first things first[1] — could easily describe an effective approach to creating the blueprint for transforming your workplace culture so organizational and employee wellbeing can thrive. Once you have used the data described in *Transformation Point #1* to provide feedback about the current wellbeing state in your company, you can begin the journey of creating a thriving workplace culture. The journey begins intentionally with a vision for where you're going *(i.e., your desired culture)*. Of course, just as the new sciences inform a new way of thinking about data and measurement, they also inform a new way of thinking about and approaching strategy and planning.

In his book, "The New Strategic Thinking," Michel Robert uses 25 years of working with over 500 CEOs to reframe how businesses approach strategic planning:

> *It's not about writing a strategic plan and instructing the troops to 'make it happen.' It is about a fundamental shift in the way senior management, and the people they rely upon, look at the company and its environment.*[2]

He continues by stating, "one must achieve supremacy of thinking before one can achieve supremacy of strategy." Robert is not alone in believing this perspective. The entire field of strategic planning has shifted; former advocates for planning are now calling for strategic thinking. It makes sense — especially because most existing planning processes are derived from Newtonian beliefs.[3]

Think about it, a typical strategic plan contains a lengthy, detailed description of current industry conditions, examines how to increase market share or reduce costs, states countless overwhelming goals and initiatives and houses a detailed budget. The plan is usually created by executives and then handed down to managers to execute. Consequently, instead of thinking creatively, managers spend considerable time running numbers and trying to figure out how to meet the objectives they have been assigned.[4] Peter Senge described this fixation on events as another one of the learning disabilities that cripples organizations:

> *Conversations in organizations are dominated by concern with events: last month's sales, the new budget cuts, last quarter's earnings, who just got promoted or fired, the new product our competitors just announced, the delay that was just announced in our new product, and so on.*[5]

When people's thinking is dominated by short-term events, generative learning cannot be sustained within organizations. Strategic thinking requires focusing on the big picture rather than being immersed in the numbers and operational details.[6] Strategic thinking also requires new skills for being acutely aware of what is happening now.[7]

When new thinking and skills are brought to the strategic planning process, the likelihood of meeting the needs of the constantly changing world increases. Strategic planning needs to evolve to be more about building collective wisdom. Margaret Wheatley describes this shift:

> *I want to use the time formerly spent on detailed planning and analysis to create the organizational conditions for people to set a clear intent, to agree on how they are going to work together, and then practice to become better observers, learners and colleagues as they co-create with their environment.*[8]

In making this shift from an Old Paradigm approach to strategic planning to a New Paradigm approach, you start by exploring who to involve in the process to leverage the collective wisdom to support transforming your workplace culture so both organizational and employee wellbeing thrive.

Who to Include in Wellbeing Planning

Effective strategic planning involves a lengthy, thoughtful process that ideally involves multiple stakeholders within the organization.[9] The best way to create ownership is to have the people responsible for implementing the plan be part of developing it:

> *No one is successful if they merely present a plan in finished form to others… it simply doesn't work to ask people to sign on when they haven't been involved in the planning process.*[10]

Ideally, everyone in the organization would be involved somehow in the planning process. We know organizations that have essentially shut down for a half or full day to allow all employees to participate in developing a new strategic plan for the organization. Leaders assign employees to groups that intentionally bring together people from varying departments and locations who do not normally interact on a regular basis. Then, the groups begin examining what is and isn't working *(from their perspective)* and what they think the company should focus on in the next three to five years. Once the smaller groups have completed their work, all of the groups come together and present a summary of their discussions. When companies do this, it's always fascinating how many common themes emerge in a very visible way for everyone to see. Furthermore, the employees are usually highly engaged from playing a critical role in the change process. If your organization is very large and spread out, an alternative is to use this process at each location and then funnel all of the summary input to a centralized document to capture the feedback. Don't underestimate the power of having as many employees as possible participate in the planning process!

If you already have an organizational strategic plan, and embarking upon a new planning process seems overwhelming or just doesn't make sense at this point in time, we recommend creating an addendum to the overall plan to specifically include organizational and employee wellbeing. If wellbeing planning is separate, then it is critical to include a broad cross-section of the organization so employees are well represented. The employee experience will vary greatly by location, department, shift, job classification, manager and more. Therefore, the more people you can include when planning to support wellbeing, the greater the likelihood you will determine how to best *create the conditions* within which wellbeing can thrive.

Long-Term/Strategic Planning

Once you have your planning team(s) created, start creating your future-vision. In addition to using the feedback provided by holistically examining the data to determine what is and is not working well, strategic planning should include a creative component.[11] It's like having a blank canvas on which you get to paint the new future for your organization. In their book, "Blue Ocean Strategy," W. Chan Kim and Renee Mauborgne studied 150 strategic moves made by companies varying greatly in size and industry. The authors found that how companies approached strategy consistently separated winners from losers in creating an unknown market space *(a.k.a. "blue ocean")* that resulted in sustainable growth for the organization. Instead of focusing on beating the competition, these successful organizations focused on making the competition irrelevant by significantly increasing value for customers and the company *(which, in turn, opens up new market space).*[12] We have seen organizations flourish by shifting how they approach strategy and focusing on fostering both organizational and employee wellbeing. In doing so, they are unmatched by competitors because these strategic-minded companies *created the conditions* in which employees can thrive.

Clarifying Core Values

For organizational and employee wellbeing to be firmly embedded in your culture, it is essential that they be included as a core part of organizational strategy and change. Everyone in the organization needs to be clear on the organization's vision and core values, and how wellbeing aligns with where the company is headed. Lencioni describes the second discipline for building organizational health, creating clarity:

> *Within the context of making an organization healthy, alignment is about creating so much clarity that there is as little room as possible for confusion, disorder and infighting to set in. Of course, the responsibility for creating that clarity lies squarely with the leadership team.*[13]

Does every employee in your organization have clarity about the company vision and values? We don't mean just memorizing words on a wall but truly understanding what the vision and values are and how they guide strategy and operations. Do all employees know how they fit in and contribute to achieving the future vision of the company? Knowing that organizations are living systems that change and evolve, is it time to revisit your core values and vision?

In "The Advantage," Lencioni outlines six issues that leaders must completely agree upon to provide clarity for employees. One of these requires identifying core values that guide how everyone behaves in the organization.[14] Core values are the two or three behavioral traits inherent in your organization and lie at the heart of the organization's identity; they can almost be viewed as your cultural brand.

However, most organizations have not done the work to truly identify their core values. The values they have listed on their website, walls and marketing materials are usually "Permission-to-Play" values that reflect the minimum behavioral standards required in the organization and are usually not unique. Permission-to-Play values often include words like *honesty, integrity* and *respect for others*. Although these values are important to use for hiring, they do not set your organization apart and uniquely define it. Unless you can claim that your organization is more committed to these values than 99% of your competitors, these are not your core values.[15]

Core values can be identified by looking at the inherent organizational traits that have existed for a long time.[16] One of the best ways to do this is to notice the qualities of employees who already embody what is best about the company. What is it that makes them admired by the leadership team and others? You may also want to reflect on employees who were not a good fit and have benefited the organization by leaving. What made them a distraction or problem? Once you have successfully identified and described your core values, they need to be protected. Every policy, activity, employee hired, employee let go, and strategy should reflect the core values.[17] Zappos understands the power of core values in creating clarity and intentionally building culture:

> *We believe that it's really important to come up with core values that you can commit to. And by commit, we mean that you're willing to hire and fire based on them. If you're willing to do that, then you're well on your way to building a company culture that is in line with the brand you want to build.*[18]

With what we now know about the critical importance of wellbeing for workplace culture, your organization may want to revisit its values to ensure core values have been identified, communicated and aligned with your company identity and brand while also supporting wellbeing. Having clarity about what you want your organization to become is imperative. Recognizing that organizations are living systems, no companies or individuals can effectively co-create their environment without first having that clarity of their desired future state.[19] In his book, "The Five Dysfunctions of a Team," Patrick Lencioni credited a friend who built a $1 billion business as saying,

If you could get all the people in an organization rowing in the same direction, you could dominate any industry, in any market, against any competition, at any time.[20]

We agree and would add that, when everyone is rowing with the underlying current of the water *(i.e., the culture)*, it's a much smoother journey than rowing upstream. Once you have clarity of where you are headed, you are ready to develop a long-term strategy to support you on your journey.

Franklin Industries — An Example of Alignment in Action

One of our clients, we'll call Franklin Industries, wanted to *create the conditions* for employees to truly embrace and align with the company values and vision. Feedback from employees via culture surveys indicated that employees did not have clarity of the company vision nor how they fit into the big picture. So we worked with the executive team to revisit the company's core values. Once executives had clearly articulated their core values, they wanted to ensure every employee truly embraced the values and vision, so they launched a transformative process for the company and all employees.

The president held an all-company meeting. At that meeting, he revisited some culture survey results and described the work the executive team had done to clarify the core values. He then painted a vibrant picture for the employees by describing how the core values and vision fit together and where Franklin Industries was headed. He gave employees an opportunity to share their thoughts on the core values and how they will know if, collectively, the company is living those values.

After the all-company meeting, each department held special clarity meetings. At these meetings, the departments spent time creating their own departmental mission and vision statements as well as answering the following questions:

- What do we want others within the company to know about what we do in our department?

- What do others within the company think we do?

- What are some things we do in our department that might surprise people?

- How does our department contribute to the vision of Franklin Industries?

- How does our department contribute to Franklin Industries living its core values?

- How can we best collaborate with other departments to ensure our vision and values are central to our daily work?

Once the employees in each department answered these questions, employees were given the task of finding their own creative way to educate the rest of the company. Over the course of several months, departments presented their overview to the entire company at monthly company-wide clarity meetings. These presentations were also recorded to benefit those who were absent and future employees. Some departments used great creativity and created skits and songs, while others turned their presentations into a Jeopardy-like game. Not only were the employees in each department engaged in the process, but the confusion and frustration among departments eased as people better understood how each area functioned and how they could best work together.

Once there was clarity for how each department aligned with the core values and vision, it was time to support employees in clarifying how they, as individuals, fit into the big picture. Employees were given a short exercise during which they were asked to reflect on the following:

- How they see themselves living the vision and core values on a daily basis.

- What gifts and talents they have that can help the company achieve its vision.

- What they want their manager to know about them to best support them.

Employees reviewed their reflections with their managers during scheduled one-on-one meetings. *(This also helped open communication in departments where managers had been neglecting having regular meetings with their employees.)* This discussion then became a standard topic revisited during annual individual goal setting and development plan discussions. Not surprisingly, Franklin Industries saw dramatic improvement in culture survey results. The company also experienced greater collaboration among departments and could see happiness and engagement increase among employees.

Many of our clients have taken an approach similar to Franklin Industries. Each time, we are impressed at how impactful it is to set the stage for a thriving workplace culture. Embarking upon any transformation journey is easier when all employees are clear about core company values, know where the company is headed and understand how each employee fits into the big picture.

Developing a Long-Term Wellbeing Strategy

If you are at a point where you can embed a long-term strategy for wellbeing in your organization's overall strategic plan, we recommend including wellbeing as an initial consideration for determining your company's future direction. If you are approaching wellbeing, for now, as an additional planning process, we recommend convening a team of no more than 15 people who represent a broad cross-section of your organization. These individuals will act almost like elected officials, bringing employees' input into the planning discussions. This way you can include as representative a range of views as possible while still having a small enough group to be effective. In either case, we usually give people involved in wellbeing planning some work to prepare for the meeting to make the best use of the time. For example, we might give planning team members the following questions and ask them to come prepared to offer feedback on behalf of the employees they are representing:

> **1)** Fast-forward to five years from now. If our organization has a thriving culture in which people love coming to work, feel valued and supported in all areas of wellbeing, and the organization is strong and growing, how might life look different on a daily basis?

2) What will tell us that we have created a culture in which both organizational and employee wellbeing can thrive?

3) What behaviors will we see that are consistent with the company values?

4) What behaviors will we see that are consistent with our desired culture?

5) What behaviors might we see that will hurt our desired culture?

6) What practices do we need to keep doing to allow people to be their best?

7) What practices do we need to stop doing to allow people to be their best?

8) How do we want to hold one another accountable for intentionally fostering our desired culture?

9) How will we know we're moving in the right direction?

It is critical that employees participate in setting the vision and clarifying how a thriving workplace culture will be manifested in terms of behaviors, communication practices, training and development, and resources provided. By being part of the process, employees will better understand how they fit into the picture. According to Wheatley,

The work of any team or organization needs to start with a clear sense of what they are trying to accomplish and how they want to behave together... once this clarity is established, people will use it as their lens to interpret information, surprises, experiences. They will be able to figure out what and how to do their work.[21]

Humans are far more emotional than logical when rallying behind a vision or cause. Therefore, the future vision must be inspirational and take people beyond themselves while still having an immediate experiential appeal. The story of the Ski Resort is a great example of this.

The Ski Resort

In his groundbreaking book "Management Rewired," Charles Jacobs tells the story of a ski resort on the edge of a small New England town whose new owners wanted to build vacation condominiums to increase the viability of the resort and save it from being closed. The developers called a town meeting to introduce the project to the townspeople who needed to vote to make needed zoning changes for the condo project. As Jacobs tells the story, the developers were quite thorough and well prepared to present to the community:

Nicely bound handouts with the details of their proposal were stacked on the table in front of them, and attractive architectural drawings of the housing development were prominently displayed on easels on both sides of the stage. The condominiums were cleverly designed and landscaped to blend in with the surrounding woodlands... Dressed in ties and jackets, they spoke persuasively and with compelling logic about how important the resort was to the economy of the town and what would happen should it go bankrupt... Detailed financial statements established both the necessity of the development for the economic health of the resort and the huge benefit it would bring to the town.

The community residents who opposed the project felt overwhelmed by the time the developers' proposal was finished. The project opponents were afraid the town would change for the worse because of the project, but they had neither the resources nor the experience to combat the thorough, professional presentation the developers made. When rebuttal time came, the audience was quiet, and the developers sensed that they had won the day. Just then, an Old Yankee in a faded plaid shirt and corduroy pants stood and spoke deliberately:

"I don't understand much about all these numbers," he said, "and you fellas seem like nice people. But your argument for the condominiums reminds me of the man that just had to have a pickle to eat with his sandwich. He would take a bite of the sandwich and then take a bite of the pickle. Another bite of the sandwich and then another bite of the pickle followed. His lunch was the sandwich and that should have been enough for him, but it wasn't. He always had to have that pickle to make what he called a 'complete' meal. Gentlemen, you're asking for one hell of a big pickle."

The man sat down, and after a short period of nervous silence, laughter spread gradually throughout the room. Although the man had done absolutely nothing to counter the details of the developers' arguments, he had tapped into the community's emotional sentiments. The money saving investment that might save the resort suddenly turned into a "hell of a pickle" that nobody really wanted. The condominiums were voted down, and the resort closed a few years later. A metaphor had defeated the developers' polished, formidable presentation.[22]

When embarking upon wellbeing planning, tap into employees' emotional sentiments and create a vision that inspires people. During the initial wellbeing planning session, we facilitate a discussion based on the questions we provided to *create the conditions* for the group to fashion an inspirational vision of the future. When needed, we prompt the group to ask about leadership, communication, interpersonal relationships, work load, stress and any other areas we know are critical to both organizational and employee wellbeing. We then use the feedback provided at the planning meeting to create a three-to-five year timeline — beginning with the end in mind and then backing up from there to determine a starting point and to inform the annual planning and goal setting. *(We will talk more about a New Paradigm approach to goal setting later in this chapter.)* While the desired future culture may or may not change dramatically, the approaches used to transform the culture may change. For example, you may have clearly articulated what a thriving workplace culture looks like for your organization; however, as the world and your employees change, exactly how you go about living that vision may change. Therefore, we always remind organizations to view the plan as a living, fluid guideline that shapes their transformational journey. We also encourage revisiting the plan on a regular basis to discover what tweaks might need to be made along the way.

Determining Metrics to Guide the Wellbeing Strategy

Once you clarify and articulate the long-term vision and strategy, pay attention to how you will know if you are headed in the right direction. With that in mind, planning and examining the data we described in the previous chapter go hand-in-hand. Use data and metrics to provide holistic feedback and to guide strategic thinking and planning. When you begin with the end in mind *(recognizing, of course, there really is no final end or destination)*, you can better determine what types of data and measurements will be most useful in evaluating how you're doing on the journey of transforming your workplace culture. According to Wheatley:

- The most meaningful measures are those generated by people doing the work because people support what they create. So part of strategic planning needs to include determining who creates the measures.

- It is important to determine how you will know when measures have become obsolete or are producing unintended consequences.

- Organizations need to ensure they are inviting uncertainty, newness and surprise with their measures and are challenging people to look at things in new and different ways.

- When determining what information to gather from the measures, pay attention to those that will help your organization, teams and individuals grow in the right direction.

- Determine what measures will be informative about essential behaviors *(accountability, learning, teamwork, quality and innovation)*.[23]

Remember that *Transformation Point #1* is the starting point — holistically examining existing data and filling in any gaps to inform you about the current state of organizational and employee wellbeing. It is common during the planning phase to identify new and different measures that will be meaningful, especially once core values have been clarified. We encourage organizations to think about what metrics they need to be able to understand and use to tell their wellbeing story. Stories are powerful. The human mind works through stories, and people embrace stories to make sense of their experiences. In the cognitive world in which we live and work, stories are far more powerful than logic.[24]

I *(Rosie)* also have found that stories work much better than logic and numbers when creating a *burning platform* for leaders for why they need to care about burnout and employee wellbeing. I can stand in front of a room full of leaders and present slide after slide with data from chapters 4 and 5 to create an argument for why leaders need to care about wellbeing, or I can cut to the chase and speak to their hearts. I put up one simple slide with a picture of my son when he was 8 months old *(who doesn't melt by seeing a cute, smiling baby?)*. I then proceed to tell my story of how inextricably connected organizational and employee wellbeing are and why they should care.

Meet Peyton

This is my son, Peyton, when he was about 8 months old. He was the happiest, fun-loving baby. When he was around 5 or 6 months old, he started getting unexplained fevers — wickedly high fevers that lasted for five days. His fevers started coming almost like clockwork every 30 days or so, never with an explanation. Yet, in between these fever episodes, you'd never know anything was wrong. Now imagine him at 9 months old, sick with another fever, suddenly going limp, lifeless and unresponsive. Imagine this happening numerous more times in the upcoming months; being in and out of specialists with no one able to tell you what is wrong with your son.

Now imagine, while all of this is going on, what happens in your work life. I tried to not schedule major travel or client appointments in anticipation of episodes. Both my husband and I were on the verge of having negative balances in our paid time off accounts for work. We were stressed beyond belief waiting for the next episode. During each fever episode, we didn't sleep; we stayed up watching him like a hawk, freaking out if his breathing changed, and scared he would die while we slept. So we were stressed all of the time and sleep deprived one week out of every month — yet both in very demanding jobs and trying to continue to do good and meaningful work. Several times, my husband and I looked at each other and said, "This is how people end up losing their jobs." Here is my question to you: If I were your employee, what would you do?

Well, what my employer at the time did made all the difference in the world. My employer fully supported me. Every time Peyton had another fever, I received text messages from my boss asking how my husband and I were doing and how Peyton was doing. The company rallied behind me so I didn't have to worry or feel guilty about work. The company wanted to make sure I was also taking care of my own wellbeing. My employer created the conditions in which I felt secure in my employment, valued as a person and could tend to my family. In return, when I was at work, I gave more than 150% of myself and hung up the phone on recruiters who called me wanting to present other employment opportunities. Nothing was worth more than the support I received from my employer. And with all of this going on, I was still able to lead my area in having profound growth — because I was supported in tending to the self-side of my wedding cake.

That one simple, personal story has a much greater impact in helping people "see the light" for how important both organizational and employee wellbeing are. So how does this fit with planning? When you think about it, stories are really about planning. The beginning is your current state; the end is your desired future. The middle is your transformational journey. So when you frame planning in terms of telling your wellbeing story, the approach you take and the metrics you use will hopefully become clearer. This is not an invitation to go backward to Newtonian views and become obsessed with measuring every little thing; you do not want to collect tons of data for no reason. This is an opportunity to be forward-thinking and determine what two or three metrics in each wellbeing area will be most meaningful to understand the current and evolving state of wellbeing at your company and whether you are moving in the right direction. The following are some common measures our clients have used to assess the six aspects of employee wellbeing at the organizational level:

- *Career Wellbeing/Purpose:* Whatever metrics you use in this area should best reflect if people like what they do at work each day and if they have a sense of purpose. The metrics should be reflective of thriving organizational wellbeing. Some examples include:
  — Culture survey results
  — Engagement survey results
  — Turnover
  — Employee referrals
  — Percentage of employees taking advantage of training and development opportunities
  — Job mobility within the company *(percentage of employees being promoted or moving laterally to new positions)*
  — Self-report satisfaction via employee survey *(using the sample questions we provided in the previous chapter)*

- *Social Wellbeing:* This area of wellbeing refers to the quality of relationships people have in their lives — their entire lives. It can be a little trickier for organizations to determine what metrics will give them a sense of their employees' social wellbeing; however, here are some examples that might be useful:

— Forfeited or unused paid time off balances at the end of the year

— Self-report satisfaction via employee survey *(using the sample questions we provided in the previous chapter)*

— Participation at company-sponsored events and activities

• *Financial Wellbeing:* Financial wellbeing has more to do with feeling financially secure than making a lot of money. Here are some examples of metrics commonly used by organizations to get a sense of financial wellbeing:

— Percentage of employees contributing to retirement plans

— Average percentage of pay employees contribute to their retirement plans

— Number of loans or early withdrawals against the plan

— Self-report satisfaction via employee survey *(using the sample questions we provided in the previous chapter)*

• *Physical Wellbeing:* Metrics used here should reflect some of what contributes to good physical health and having enough physical energy to get important things done each day. Here are some examples commonly used:

— Lifestyle-related medical claims

— Musculoskeletal-related Workers' Compensation claims

— Average sick days *(if sick time is tracked separately from vacation time)*

— Self-report satisfaction via employee survey *(using the sample questions we provided in the previous chapter)*

Notice once again what we did NOT include here: biometric screening and HRA results. As we mentioned in the previous chapter, we think there are much better ways for organizations to spend their resources; additionally, depending on how they are implemented (especially if there is a large incentive attached to achieving specific outcomes), we would be suspect of the results (more about this in chapter 13).

• *Emotional Wellbeing:* Metrics used here should reflect a good sense of resiliency and work-life balance and having enough mental energy to get important things done each day.
— Mental health-related medical and disability claims
— Antidepressant and anti-anxiety prescriptions
— Self-report satisfaction via employee survey *(using the sample questions we provided in the previous chapter)*
— Stress and burnout

• *Community Wellbeing:* This area of wellbeing considers how connected people feel to the community in which they live. The more connected they are, the better they are doing in this wellbeing area. Some possible metrics that could be useful for organizations include:
— Percentage of employees taking advantage of volunteer time-off benefits
— Percentage of employees participating in charitable giving campaigns offered by the organization
— Self-report satisfaction via employee survey *(using the sample questions we provided in the previous chapter)*

Once you have decided what metrics will be meaningful for helping you understand the state of wellbeing at your company and for telling your wellbeing story, determine how you will collect that information and how often. We suggest creating a data collection/evaluation repository to house all relevant metrics and develop a Wellbeing Dashboard. This can be as simple as an Excel spreadsheet or more elaborate using a database. Having all relevant metrics in one place allows for greater ease in providing feedback on the current wellbeing state and the evolution of your wellbeing story. You can use the Wellbeing Dashboard to run analyses and create meaningful reports and communication for current employees, future employees and customers. *(We will revisit this in more detail in chapter 14.)*

Short-Term/Annual Planning

When the core values, vision and the desired culture have been clearly articulated and you have determined what metrics to use to tell your wellbeing story, you can establish goals, objectives and timelines for how to best start your journey. Embracing the New Paradigm means thinking differently about annual planning. Most annual operating plans are overly detailed, outlining tasks that need to be completed to achieve stated goals. It's not that determining tasks has no value, but people can become so narrowly focused on the task that they aren't aware of the process and the course corrections that may be necessary along the way. Embracing the New Paradigm means learning how to facilitate the process of change, and how to foster relationships and nurture growth and development.[25] It is important to approach annual planning with the intent to ensure your collective actions align with your long-term vision and goals. This includes checking yourself against the future vision and challenging conventional wisdom so you can consistently reinvent the business to keep abreast of change.[26]

With that being said, we want to briefly address how to shift goal setting from an Old Paradigm to a New Paradigm approach. In a 2009 research article titled "Goals Gone Wild: The Systematic Side Effects of Over-Prescribing Goal Setting," the researchers argue that goal setting has become over-prescribed in organizations, resulting in powerful and predictable side effects. Using examples ranging from unintended consequences with sales goals to fiascos with the Ford Pinto and Enron, the researchers illustrate how the use of goal setting in organizations can result in:

- Reduced employee performance.
- Shifts in focus away from important but non-specific goals.
- Harm to interpersonal relationships.
- Eroding workplace culture.
- Fostering of risky and unethical behaviors.[27]

The researchers' findings are actually not surprising, given what we already addressed in chapter 6 regarding motivation and change. When goals are too specific, employees narrow their focus to meeting the measurable outcomes. This intense focus can essentially blind employees to other important aspects of the task and engender a wide variety of risks *(including safety, ethical issues, alienating colleagues or customers and more)*.

It can also cause people to ignore important aspects of performance not specified in the stated goal.[28] Using a Newtonian approach to goal setting ignores the non-linear, unpredictable, complex nature of our world and the process of change. Consequently, goal setting can end up causing unwanted consequences. Furthermore, as we described in chapter 6, using incentives tied to meeting goals and "getting" people to change can result in even more disastrous problems.

Rethinking goal setting requires shifting the focus to value the process and the journey, not just the end result. This new approach requires using strategic thinking to be flexible and adjusting the strategy and plan as needed to allow the strategic vision to become the reality. Just as we described in the previous chapter, rethinking goal setting also requires thinking differently about how we use data to provide real-time feedback and inform the plan and the process. After all, the goal is not about getting to some concrete end state, but rather guiding the organization on its evolving, ongoing journey.

What to Include in an Annual Wellbeing Plan

The purpose of an effective annual plan is to translate the strategic vision into actionable steps to guide organizational change. However, this cannot occur in a bubble. What steps are taken will depend on your starting point, your desired future state and the current realities of other competing priorities within your organization and the competitive marketplace. That said, a good place to start is to answer the following questions:

- Given what we know about the current state of our organization and where we ultimately want to be, what will be the most meaningful changes to make over the next 12 months to start us on that journey?

- How will we know we are headed in the right direction?

- In what areas of wellbeing are our employees most wanting support and resources? *(based on feedback via employee survey, using the sample questions we provided in the previous chapter)*

Your answers to these questions will help you set goals that allow you to focus on the transformation process and what makes sense to meet the unique needs of your organization.

If you're still not sure where to start, we suggest looking at the three critical building blocks of successful change: improving trust, quality communication and developing effective leaders. We have found that even good organizations have opportunities to improve their organizational wellbeing — especially as it relates to the executive team being truly cohesive, having a comprehensive leadership development strategy and reducing silos within the organization. We explore leadership development in detail in the next chapter. For now, recognize that, though it takes time to develop an environment in which people feel safe, creating this environment is critical for lasting change.[29] So if there are any issues around having a safe, trusting environment, these need to be tended to first.

Getting Started with Planning for Strategic Change

It can sometimes feel overwhelming to embark on the journey of strategic organizational change. From the information provided so far, you may be beginning to understand the critical importance of embracing the New Paradigm as you are aligning organizational and employee wellbeing. But, without handing this book to everyone on your leadership teams and within your organization, how do you gain support for challenging the status quo? This is likely best done by appealing to the emotional aspects of people's brains, and creating focus and a sense of urgency — a *burning platform* for why change is necessary. If you are not the CEO, you can create this *burning platform* for him/her, then expand to create this platform for all employees.

To create this *burning platform* for all employees, leadership can bring everyone together at a meeting or event to rethink business as usual and begin to believe that work life will be truly different moving forward. The message delivered can be framed as an opportunity for employees to participate in creating a new future for the company — and for themselves.[30] Imagine if you worked for a company and your CEO called an all-employee meeting called "Envision the Future: Starting the Journey toward Extraordinary" *(or something along those lines)*. At that meeting, she/he stands before employees and says something like this:

> *"I'm so glad you are all here today and am honored to*
> *be with all of you! First, I want you to know how much I truly*
> *value each and every one of you as unique, talented individuals.*
> *I also want you to know how excited I am for what I truly*

*believe is a phenomenal time for our company and for each one of us.
We have a lot of great things going for us, but we also have things that
are not as good as they could be — and I fully recognize that.
We are all works in progress.*

*We've had some challenging times, and I'm sure we will face other
challenging times — after all, that is the ever-changing nature of life.
But I wanted us all to be together today because we have a tremendous
opportunity before us to come together and collectively create
our future — the future of our organization and our individual futures.
I know this may be a lofty goal, but my hope is that together, we can
transform our company so none of us come to work feeling like this is a
job, or even a career, for that matter. I want every single one of you to
feel passionate about what you do each day.*

*With that, I know how important having a thriving workplace culture is
to your day-to-day experience, to our customers and to our company.
I also know what a critical role a thriving culture plays in your
individual wellbeing. We can't have an extraordinary company if we
are sucking the energy and wellbeing out of you. So today is the first
day of a new journey for us, and I'm hoping you all are and will be as
excited as I am for the possibilities of what lies ahead.*

*I want every person in this organization, all of your loved ones,
and all current and future customers to know that our company is truly
something extraordinary; that, above everything, we support our
employees so they can thrive in all areas of their lives. This is the
cornerstone for our success. So I'm asking each and every one of you to
join me in creating a collective vision and strategy that will transform
our daily work experience and bring wellbeing
to the forefront of all that we do."*

Imagine how you would feel if you were an employee listening to this
message from your CEO. Our guess is that, even if you had a rocky history
with the company and were skeptical, you would probably be at least
a little inspired, curious and hopeful. And notice in this example the CEO
didn't mention efficiency, cutting costs, being healthier, increasing sales,
etc. People will always come together in support of a cause they believe
in; it doesn't require cumbersome control structures and systems.[31]

Once you have your blueprints ready and have created your strategic
and annual plan, you can start building your house by pouring a solid
foundation. The quality of your leaders determines the strength of your

foundation. We will address developing quality leaders in the next chapter.

Summary of Transformation Point #2
The New Paradigm Approach to Strategic and Annual Planning

Components of the Plan	Key Considerations
Strategic Planning *(3-5 years)* Organization's Core Values	Ensure all employees have clarity on the core values and know how their behaviors support or clash with the core values and how employees individually fit into the company vision.
Focus More on Strategic Thinking than Planning	Focus on the big picture while also paying attention to the present. What shifts need to be made to ensure alignment with the future vision?
Create a *Burning Platform* for Why Organizational Change is Needed	Hold a special event to inspire employees to be involved in the process and embrace wellbeing as part of the future of the company.
Develop Long-Term Organizational and Employee Wellbeing Plan	Include as many employees as possible and create a vision for wellbeing that supports the company in living into its desired future vision.
Determine Additional Wellbeing Metrics/Tell Your Wellbeing story	Determine what is meaningful at an organizational level to tell your employee wellbeing story.
Annual Planning Determine What is Most Meaningful for the Next 12 Months	Starting point will likely be improving trust, quality communication and developing effective leaders.
Establish Metrics to Guide the Plan	What will tell you that you're headed in the right direction?
Holistic Support for Wellbeing	Emphasize wellbeing areas of most interest for employees to have more resources and support while not completely ignoring the other areas.

CHAPTER 10
Transformation Point #3:
Pour a Solid Foundation
(Develop Quality Leaders)

The bottom line for leaders is that if they do not become conscious of the cultures in which they are embedded, those cultures will manage them. Cultural understanding is desirable for all of us, but it is essential if leaders are to lead.[1]

Edgar Schein

When watching a comic movie about the workplace, we all laugh about how ridiculous and over-the-top bosses can be and how they negatively impact the main characters; it's good movie-making. We've watched movies like this more than once and laughed just as hard with each viewing. However, in real life, what makes bosses so difficult is often a bit less explicit and not so funny. In many cases, managers and leaders *think* they are doing a decent job and don't realize the negative impact they are having on the people they are supposed to be supporting. They aren't intentionally being horrible; but their lack of self-awareness, skill, clarity of direction, ability to deal with change and stress, and their own impaired personal wellbeing impact their effectiveness.

There are two main types of challenges organizations face: technical and adaptive. Each requires a different leadership approach. Technical challenges are those challenges for which existing knowledge can be applied to bridge the gap between the organization's current reality and where it aspires to be. With technical challenges, leaders can draw on existing knowledge and experience to solve problems.[2] For example, perhaps your organization is preparing to move locations or install a new computer system. If you've gone through similar changes before, you can look back at the processes and steps taken, what did and didn't work, what vendors you used, etc., and then start the fairly predictable change process.

Adaptive challenges, on the other hand, are more complex. With these types of challenges, the gap between an organization's current state and where it

> **The majority of challenges organizations face, including changing their culture, require adaptive work.**

aspires to be cannot be closed using existing approaches; it can only be closed by people reframing how they think and operate. Adaptive work is hard because it challenges our deeply held beliefs, and the values that made us successful may become less relevant.[3] Adaptive change involves experiencing loss in letting go of certain elements of the past — loss of a way of doing things, loss of loyalty to the way things have always been done, loss of feelings of competence, loss of authority and reporting relationships and more.[4] The majority of challenges organizations face, including changing their culture, require adaptive work.

Ronald Heifetz, whose research and work with Harvard University has focused on helping organizations and leaders build capacity for adaptive change, defines leadership as "the activity of mobilizing people to do adaptive work."[5] This is critical when we view organizations as complex living systems that are inherently uncontrollable.[6] We fully recognize that transforming your workplace culture to one in which both organizational and employee wellbeing thrive is asking you to take on an adaptive challenge. This can, and often does, promote considerable discomfort. However, as Heifetz states:

> *Followers want comfort, stability and solutions from their leaders. But that's babysitting. Real leaders ask hard questions and knock people out of their comfort zones. Then they manage the resulting distress.*[7]

Leading through adaptive change requires shifting from providing leadership in the form of solutions to having the locus of responsibility lie in the collective intelligence of employees at all levels.[8] It also means shifting from viewing leaders as heroes to viewing them as hosts, to stop assuming that:

- They have the answers and know what to do.
- People will do what they're told if they're given good plans and instructions.
- More complex and challenging situations require more control and power from the top down.[9]

Leaders who journey from hero to host recognize that you can't expect people to "buy-in" to plans created for them. As we described in the previous chapter, people will much more willingly support those things they've played a part in creating. Today's leaders know that hosting others to engage in meaningful conversations and contribute their insights is the only way to solve complex problems; it is the only way to lead through adaptive change. Consequently, hosting leaders can benefit greatly if they:

- *Create the conditions* for people to work well together.
- Provide the scarce resource of time.
- Guide people and the system to learn from experience.
- Ensure people know leaders support them.
- Minimize politics and bureaucracy.
- Provide meaningful feedback for others to guide the transformation journey.
- Collaborate with people to develop meaningful measures of progress.
- Are willing to stand up to other leaders who want to revert to old command and control models.[10]

Strong leadership is required for organizations to successfully cope with change in today's competitive business world.[11] Ultimately, the success of organizational transformation efforts depends on leadership effectiveness.[12] To effectively lead through adaptive change, leaders can transform their mindset and skill sets to move from hero to host — to become in essence *servant leaders*. Coined by Robert K. Greenleaf in 1970, the term describes leaders who focus primarily on the growth and wellbeing of the people and the communities within their organization; they share power, put others' needs first, and help people develop and perform as highly as possible.[13]

A Framework for Effective Leadership Development

Despite all we have learned, many organizations still take a Newtonian view when it comes to leadership — especially regarding employee wellbeing and behavior change. They look at the pieces and parts of what competencies and skills make up a good leader and aim to "fix" weak areas rather than viewing leaders as whole and part of the living system. So it is not surprising that lack of quality leaders is the first place where you see cracks in your infrastructure. The quality of leadership is EVERYTHING! It determines the health of the organization, the employee experience of the culture on a daily basis, and ultimately employee wellbeing — particularly physical and emotional wellbeing. In fact, a 2013 study published in the "Journal of Occupational and Environmental Medicine" found that having leaders with a transformational leadership style, which builds trust and conveys a sense of meaningfulness while individually challenging and developing employees, is associated with increased employee wellbeing.[14]

Consequently, quality leadership development is a critical cornerstone of any high-performing organization and thriving workplace culture and a pre-requisite for any successful employee wellbeing initiative. Successful 21st-century organizations reconsider how to develop leaders to effectively manage change — particularly adaptive change. Effective leaders *create the conditions* to allow others to be empowered toward achieving goals and obtaining results.[15] Therefore, strategic organizational change not only considers the underlying culture, but also the relationship between leaders and their employees. In fact, it is the relationship between a leader and those being led that can best energize an organization.[16]

We recognize there are countless books on leadership development, so trying to boil it down to one chapter doesn't do justice to this hugely important matter. Keeping this in mind, we focus on what the new sciences and emerging research tell us about what leaders of our complex, ever-changing workforce need to be effective and to support thriving organizational and employee wellbeing. In this chapter, we provide a four-step framework for effective, sustainable leadership development:

1) Enhance Self-Awareness

2) Build Effective Thinking Skills

3) Develop and Foster Quality Relationships so
Others Can Grow

4) Grow the Organization

Within each step are unique considerations for three main levels of leadership within your organization:

• Executive / Senior Leaders

• Mid-Level Leaders/Managers

• Informal Leaders

As we explore our leadership development framework, we keep in mind that EVERYONE in the organization is a leader — whether formally or informally. Embarking upon an adaptive change journey to transform your workplace culture requires everyone to embody good thought self-leadership *(which we described in chapter 6)*. So whether you are reading this book as a formal leader in your organization, are responsible for leadership development, or are a self-leader trying to promote change without having a formal leadership role, we think you'll find our approach insightful and helpful.

Step One: Enhance Self-Awareness

Organizations can only learn through individuals who learn.[17] Or, as renowned psychologist Carl Jung is credited with saying, "Who looks outside dreams; who looks inside awakens." This sentiment has been echoed by numerous leadership experts. In his bestselling book, "Leadership from the Inside Out," Kevin Cashman states that the ability to grow as a leader is based on the ability to grow as a person and to have a personal awakening.[18] In his latest book, "The Pause Principle: Step Back to Lead Forward," Cashman defines the critical importance of the Pause Principle as:

> *The conscious, intentional process of stepping back, within ourselves and outside of ourselves, to lead forward with greater authenticity, purpose and contribution.*[19]

He continues to describe how too often we allow ourselves to be overcome by our busyness. We are unhealthily attached to our smartphones, and too caught up and distracted to take the necessary time to sift through complexity and find purpose. The more we rush, the more we end up going everywhere but being nowhere. If we want to lead with "transformative significance," we need to step back first.[20] Joseph Jaworski writes in his book, "Synchronicity: The Inner Path of Leadership," that:

> *True leadership is about creating a domain in which we continually learn and become more capable of participating in our unfolding future.*[21]

So it is probably not surprising that self-awareness is now one of the fastest growing competencies in leadership development programs.[22]

To lead adaptive change, to go somewhere you haven't been before, you need to take time to transform yourself, which starts with becoming more self-aware by asking yourself:

- Who are you at the core of your being?
- What are you wanting for yourself — as a person? as a leader?
- What do you need to feel like your role at this company is your purpose or your calling?
- Do other people see you as being the person you want to be?
- How do you know when your thinking is and isn't serving you well?
- What do you need to protect your individual wellbeing — so your "wedding cake" doesn't topple over?

These are just some reflective questions people at all levels of leadership can start to ponder as they pause to look within themselves. Some people can gain great insight and self-awareness by simply reflecting on and journaling about these questions. Others do well with the support of a coach and working through home exercises that deepen their self-awareness. We typically have leaders complete various assessment tools to support their journey to greater self-awareness. We have found that having people take the Hartman Value Profile *(HVP)* and even completing a Life Balance Wheel helps deepen their understanding of themselves and starts their journey toward thriving in their individual wellbeing. We also engage people in interactive, experiential activities that allow them to be more aware of their thinking and the profound difference it makes when their thinking is serving them well versus when they are not leading with their best thinking.

The Story of Olivia Stephens

Olivia Stephens entered the small conference room where we were holding the first in a series of leadership workshops. She was glued to her smartphone and clearly irritated that she was being asked to take time out to "work on herself." Her department had the highest growth in the past two years, and her team was full of top-performing employees. Olivia knew she was a good leader and didn't see the point in spending time on "soft skills." Then we started to review the results of the HVP all of the leaders took prior to the workshop, and things changed for Olivia.

As she reviewed her HVP results, Olivia was faced with the quantitative data that revealed her habitual thinking patterns about herself and the world around her, including how she shows up at work. Olivia prided herself in being a "doer" and getting things done. This was reflected by very strong Extrinsic scores. However, her scores related to stress, being a perfectionist, resiliency and work-self balance were weaker. Knowing that when people are stressed, their habitual thinking patterns will become even more prominent, we noted that, although being productive is certainly positive, productivity can also have unintended consequences. As we explored various score patterns, Olivia began to see how she values the uniqueness of people *(Intrinsic)* even less when she is stressed, and she started to wonder if her employees felt dismissed by her.

As we continued exploring the self-side HVP scores, Olivia started to see how her perfectionism was actually hurting her own wellbeing. Then we walked the team through some exercises to help them be more aware of when their thinking is and isn't serving them. Olivia had to leave the room because she became very emotional. By completing these assessments and exercises, she had hit the pause button and realized how little she had actually been present in her life — at home and at work. Olivia truly cared about people; however, her habitual tendencies to focus on tasks were taking over in her stress-filled world.

In that moment, Olivia shifted from a stressed, task-driven leader to an open, vulnerable person. She knew she wanted a different experience for herself and for people with whom she interacted, but she didn't know how to get it and didn't want to sacrifice the things that had made her so successful. Once her eyes were opened and Olivia had greater self-awareness, we were able to support her in moving forward on her developmental journey, and it just took a few hours of hitting the pause button and creating a space for her to look within herself.

Just as was the case with Olivia Stephens, increasing self-awareness inherently promotes individual wellbeing. Becoming more self-aware and gaining clarity of what matters can help leaders of all levels avoid burnout and better handle the stresses that come with adaptive change by diverting them from autopilot toward making more thoughtful choices. This is a critical starting point because stress essentially shuts down the prefrontal cortex and higher level brain functioning and allows the more primitive parts of our brain to take over. When this happens, we are pulled more toward immediate gratification and less toward creativity and innovation, even when it undermines our long-term wellbeing. The remedy is to rely more on our prefrontal cortex by gaining more control of our attention and then learning to better regulate our emotions.[23]

Step Two: Build Effective Thinking Skills

Once leaders have greater self-awareness of their purpose, what matters to them, their wellbeing, and when their thinking is and isn't serving them well, they have a solid foundation on which to build effective thinking skills. We established in chapter 6 that behaviors are merely observable manifestations of thinking. Therefore, according to neuroscience, management is really about changing minds.[24] Or, in the words of Jaworski:

We need to be open to fundamental shifts of mind. We have very deep mental models of how the world works, deeper than we can know. To think that the world can ever change without changes in our mental models is folly… it's about a shift from seeing a world made up of things to seeing a world that's open and primarily made up of relationships… a deeper level of reality exists beyond anything we can articulate… When we start to accept this fundamental shift of mind, we begin to see ourselves as part of the unfolding. We also see that it's actually impossible for our lives not to have meaning.[25]

Leaders' states of mind and quality of thinking are critical to organizational wellbeing and performance. Results from the Organizational Performance Study™ *(a study performed by the organizational culture consulting firm Senn Delaney)* found that having leaders in a State of Thriving is critical to having a high-performing organization and involves a balance of three psychological states of mind:

> **1)** *Vitality* refers to having a sense of being energized, feeling alive, being present in the moment, having a high sense of wellbeing and being engaged. When people have Vitality, they are also more optimistic and confident, and have a high level of trust of others in the organization.

2) *Learning Mindset* refers to having a sense of growth and development, wanting to improve, being curious and having a thirst for knowledge and creativity. When people have a Learning Mindset, they see their jobs as part of their source for ongoing learning.

3) *Purpose and Direction* refers to having clarity, alignment and a personal vision. When people have a strong sense of Purpose and Direction, they can see beyond just the company mission to the larger community or global vision.[26]

The researchers also found that a person's State of Thriving predicted individual performance:

- When leaders integrate and balance all three aspects of the State of Thriving, the likelihood of having sustained high organizational performance is greater than 70%.

- When leaders also score high in all three aspects, it is an 80% predictor of high organizational performance.[27]

- When people are Thriving in their work, they are living at their best and are energized and enriched. In other words, work is not something that depletes them; instead, it enables their Thriving to be sustained.[28]

Additional results from the Senn Delaney Thriving Global Leadership Survey™ show leaders operating in a high-thriving state of mind do better during crisis and feel more positive about the future.[29] So now that we know how important state of mind is, let's explore how to develop a Thriving mindset, or best thinking.

"Cracking Open the Intrinsic" via Intrinsic Coaching®

In chapter 6, we introduced the work of Robert S. Hartman on identifying thinking patterns. Although Hartman is credited with identifying and measuring Intrinsic **(I)**, Extrinsic **(E)** and Systemic **(S)** domains of thinking *(i.e., the inherent capacity a person has)*, acquiring the capacity and ability to activate intrinsic thinking is a very different story. Christina Marshall, founder of Intrinsic Solutions, International — I>E>S applied — is credited with "cracking open the intrinsic" and figuring out how to activate I>E>S via a methodology she developed called Intrinsic Coaching®.[30] Intrinsic

Coaching® is unlike "quick fix" approaches that promote the idea that we can have meaningful change by cramming information into a one- or two-day training. The training builds on axiological science and Marshall's own research and is based on what neuroscience teaches us is needed to lay down new myelin — experiential learning and development that builds both awareness and skills. Participants meet via phone two hours per week for approximately six to seven months *(50 hours total)*. They are presented with material and then engaged to put what they are learning into practice — starting with increasing awareness about their own thinking. Each week as awareness increases, participants build additional skills to learn how to temporarily disable the dominance of their Systemic thinking and create a space for Intrinsic thinking.

Intrinsic Coaching® has been systematically validated.[31] To date, it is the only methodology substantiated in the literature to be consistently effective in increasing intrinsic capacity and shifting thinking patterns so people can activate I>E>S.[32] People who learn Intrinsic Coaching® increase and activate their Intrinsic dimension of thinking — allowing them to fundamentally shift how they regard others and get better results. These people report improved communication — including listening better and interrupting people less frequently; recognizing that what they see is only a sliver of what is happening for another person and, therefore, holding back in dispensing advice; and not being as frustrated with people. As a result, they are less stressed, their relationships improve, they are able to bring forward greater creativity and they get more done with less time.[33] As Marshall herself says:

> *It isn't knowledge about thinking that is lacking. It isn't a lack of things to think about that is the main problem. It is awareness-in-progress of our processes of thinking, and making awareness of the process in progress more important than awareness of the content. That is the beginning of the shift from habitual S>E>I to the choice of I>E>S. It is the beginning of intrinsic intelligence, which begins the end of turmoil and suffering that doesn't need to be.[34]*

Think about the process of babies learning to walk. Babies take in incredible amounts of stimuli from their environment and run it through a filter as if to think, "Hmm, what is this telling me about what I want and what I will try next?" As they become more and more aware of their own bodies and their environment, babies start figuring out how to coordinate movements. Each time they fall down, they receive new stimuli to process and inform their next attempt. They keep falling down and trying again — practicing over and over until eventually it all comes together and they are walking. Each time babies take in stimuli, pause to reflect and be more self-aware, and then put what they're learning and noticing into practice, they lay down more myelin in the brain until the behavior of walking emerges and becomes a habit — a habit that is very hard to change. *(Have you ever known a runner who worked with a coach to try to change her/his gait? It's nearly impossible because the habits for how we walk and run are deeply set in the basal ganglia.)* Unless people suffer an injury or illness that impacts the basal ganglia, they don't have to think about walking; it's automatic.

You would laugh at parents who think they could send their child to a two-day intensive workshop to learn how to walk. You would also probably laugh at people who think they could read a book about how to be a great golfer, how to dance, or how to ride a bike and then be skillful at that activity. Until you fumble and bumble, practice, become keenly aware of yourself and then make fine-tuned adjustments, you can't do any of these things really well. But when you invest the time to learn and practice — all along becoming more self-aware — eventually you do these things with less effort; it becomes more automatic. Why then do we think shifting how we think and regard others can be done by reading a book or going to a two-day intensive workshop? In our ongoing quest for "quick fixes" and immediate gratification, we miss the opportunity for transformative, sustainable change.

> **In our ongoing quest for "quick fixes" and immediate gratification, we miss the opportunity for transformative, sustainable change.**

I *(Rosie)* can't tell you how many leadership teams I have worked with who tell of spending thousands of dollars on consultants providing one- to three-day workshops. They frequently say the same thing — that they used the concepts for a while but then went back to their old ways of doing things. Why? Because our brains are designed to form habits and be efficient. When a habit emerges, the brain stops fully participating in decision-making and diverts focus to other tasks; it becomes more efficient.[35] The challenge is that these habits never really go away; all we can do is recognize them and create new habits by developing new thinking patterns. Much like a read/write CD, we can essentially write over old scripts in our brains with new ones. If we don't write new scripts, our habitual patterns will unfold automatically. So it makes sense that most approaches to improve leadership effectiveness don't work because they are still primarily about conveying more information and do not involve developing new and better thinking.

Consequently, I *(Rosie)* have been using Intrinsic Coaching® as a cornerstone for leadership development, culture improvement and employee well-being efforts for many years, and the benefits are truly profound. When you start from a framework of better thinking, a sustainable foundation is built on which other training and programs can be successful, because the primary consideration is how people are regarded and whether they feel valued.

Examples of I>E>S in Action

What does best thinking *(i.e., I>E>S applied)* look like? In a nutshell, it is reflected in better listening, greater resilience and truly valuing the Intrinsic when it comes to people. Here is how some people have described the difference being able to activate I>E>S in thinking has made in their lives:

- *"My stress is lower because I realize it's not my job to fix my people; it's my job to tap into their good thinking and help them fix themselves, and this is a fabulous tool to start on that path."*

- *"I now have a greater ability to put myself in someone else's shoes and a better way to handle life's challenges — personally and professionally."*

- *"I now have more compassion and a better ability to really listen. I thought I was a good listener before, but I was wrong."*

- *"I'm a better manager, parent, spouse and friend."*

- *"I am finally finding balance in my life again through gaining greater clarity of what matters and what I'm wanting in my life."*

We can't move past the Old Paradigm and support others in embracing organizational change and finding empowerment to lead their own individual change until we have first changed our thinking. Trying to "do" differently without thinking differently is doomed to fail because we will fall back on deeply rooted habits — period!

> **Trying to "do" differently without thinking differently is doomed to fail because we will fall back on deeply rooted habits — period!**

Step Three: Develop and Foster Quality Relationships So Others Can Grow

Maya Angelou is credited with saying, "I've learned that people will forget what you said, people will forget what you did, but people will never forget how you made them feel." Shifting how we regard others is critical to success. In "Leadership and Self-Deception," the authors illustrate how our thinking about people influences how others perceive our behaviors:

- If we regard people as people, rather than things, the outcome will be different — even if the behavior is the same. For example, two people may have the exact same role within your organization; both may be avoiding a particular customer. If their manager views them as things *(or values what they do more than who they are)*, both may be scolded for the same behavior. However, if they are viewed as unique people, their manager may ask the employees about their experiences with this particular customer and learn that one employee avoids the customer because he is verbally abusive, whereas the other employee is just avoiding work.

- We can always tell when we're being coped with, manipulated or outsmarted, and we typically resent it.

- It doesn't matter if someone is using a skill he or she learned in order to be more effective; what we'll know and respond to is how that person is regarding us when doing those things.

- People do not respond to what we do; they respond to how we're *being*.[36]

Great leaders are both transformational and servant leaders. They truly care about the people they are privileged to lead.[37] Without the awareness and ability to activate I>E>S in our own thinking so we can regard people as unique and *be* differently with them, others find it very difficult to feel truly valued. You can't shift who you're being until you shift how you think.

In one of many Dilbert comic strips mocking ineffective leadership, Dilbert's boss asks, "What's the newest management jargon I need to pretend to understand?" After briefly interacting with an employee, Dilbert's boss determines he needs to fake having passion and fake caring. He comes upon an employee who tells him "My uncle died."

Dilbert's boss replies, "Woot! What was his name?!" with a fist pump in the air. Again, it's not what we do; it's who we're *being*. You can't fake caring or being authentic. Luckily, when people learn the skills to activate I>E>S in their thinking, they can authentically care and value others as unique individuals.

We explored in chapter 4 how the relationship people have with their immediate supervisor profoundly influences their level of engagement and their wellbeing. This also extends to the home. A 2011 study found that children's sense of wellbeing is affected more by the mood of their parents when they get home than by their parents working long hours. Therefore, how we feel at work can negatively impact our children.[38] So if leaders don't support employee wellbeing, they may not just be harming employees, but their children as well. In the world of employee wellness programs, we frequently hear concerns for how to reach the home *(usually within the context of trying to control the healthcare costs of dependents)* that often result in ineffective communication campaigns. If you want to reach the home, ensure you have quality leaders that value employees.

Once leaders activate best thinking, they are much more effective in leading adaptive change by developing and fostering quality relationships. Without the ability to activate I>E>S, leaders will remain transactional. Not only do transformational leaders consistently outperform transactional leaders *(like those depicted in the Dilbert cartoons)*, it is not even possible for transactional leaders to foster adaptive or transformational change.[39] Zappos recognizes that their managers need to be servant leaders; they *create the conditions* for their leaders to remove obstacles and enable their employees to succeed.[40] In fact, research has shown that managers will plateau in their careers if they can't develop and transition from expertise and control to authenticity and shared purpose.[41] This evolution not only requires pausing to build self-awareness but also to foster team collaboration and increase strategic innovation.

When leaders authentically value others as unique individuals, people feel it. And when people feel valued and trusted, they are better able to stretch themselves, embrace adaptive change and grow. Only when leaders foster collaborative relationships are they able to grow the organization and move towards the desired future culture. So all developmental programs and resources provided in this step should allow leaders to apply I>E>S thinking to embrace and foster their own wellbeing, effectively handle difficult conversations and conflict, lead strategic planning discussions, *create the conditions* for employees to use their strengths and talents each day, and support employees in embracing the pause themselves — to slow down and see the big picture.[42]

Step Four: Grow the Organization

In a world of chaos and complexity, we need leaders. But we don't really need bosses. Growing the organization requires leaders who can help the organization look at itself — to be reflective and learn from its activities and decisions. The leaders' job isn't to make sure people know exactly what to do and when to do it. The leaders' job is to ensure there is strong and evolving clarity about what the organization is and where it's headed. Great leaders help employees clarify their purpose and find meaning in their work.[43] THIS will provide the maximum benefit for employee wellbeing, much more so than whether your leaders visibly participate in wellness programs and support healthy lifestyles:

- Who cares if your leaders are role models for "healthy behaviors" if they treat their employees like mindless machines or small children?

- Who cares if your leaders help communicate messages about wellness programs if employees don't trust them?

- Who cares if your workplace has healthy food, an onsite fitness center and other traditional wellness initiatives that make up what many people refer to as a "healthy culture" if employees are stressed or miserable because of their relationship with their manager?

- Who cares about employee wellness when your boss and your work are essentially making you sick?

A couple of years ago, there was a GE Healthcare commercial that, using the power of story, showed the benefit of *creating the conditions* within which employees can connect to the company vision and a greater purpose. The commercial featured employees working in a manufacturing plant that builds machines to detect cancer. These employees had the opportunity to meet cancer survivors — people who benefited from the machines they built. The cancer survivors wanted to thank the people who built the machines that saved their lives, and the employees got to experience the purpose and benefit of their work. Can you imagine what that meeting did for employees in terms of how they worked together and how they felt about their work? The employees in the commercial said that day changed their lives. That's how powerful connecting employees with a greater company purpose can be!

Leading adaptive change and fostering the desired organizational culture in which both organizational and employee wellbeing can thrive is much more effective when people can activate their best thinking, recognize the organization as a living system, and tend to the importance of developing and maintaining good relationships. Leaders can no longer ignore wellbeing as if it is beyond the scope of their jobs. People who agree their manager cares about them as individuals:

- Are more likely to be top performers
- Produce higher quality work
- Are less likely to be sick
- Are less likely to change jobs
- Are less likely to get injured on the job[44]

We will provide specific examples for how leadership can actively support employee wellbeing in the next chapter. For now, recognize that, because transforming your workplace culture is an adaptive change, it can be uncomfortable and unsettling. Growing the organization requires leaders to help develop clear identity in the midst of confusion.[45] If people in your organization have been historically stifled by autocratic leadership, keep in mind that it can take 12 to 18 months for employees to actually believe this time things will be different — that leadership is sincere in truly wanting them to contribute. When leaders can rely on everyone's creativity, commitment and generosity, they will successfully guide adaptive change.[46]

Developing and Implementing a Comprehensive Leadership Development Strategy

Determining the best approach for developing leaders within your organization necessitates having a clearly defined vision to guide the strategy. Frequently we meet with organizations that simply offer a one-hour or half-day training once per year on communication and performance management, or they have leaders complete online modules; then they wonder why their culture, the employee experience, and wellbeing are not improving. We also have met with organizations that invest in growing their employees and leaders, but there's no clear rhyme or reason for what these companies offer and no consistency with how development opportunities are provided. There is no overarching strategy guiding development plans. In keeping with our house analogy, this approach to developing leaders is like jumping in at *Transformation Point #6* to decorate the house without having completed the steps to ensure the house will be structurally sound. Because the quality of your leaders is so closely intertwined with successful organizational change, the employee experience, and both organizational and employee wellbeing, we suggest embedding your leadership development strategy in your planning so you intentionally grow leaders to meet your needs today and in the future. Include in your plans a three- to five-year leadership development strategy that also prepares you for succession planning and any changes in the demographic makeup of your workforce. And, of course, include the leaders in the planning process so they are part of creating their own journey. We now examine some considerations for each level of leadership within your organization.

Executive/Senior Leaders

A Harvard Medical School study found that 96% of leaders report feeling burned out.[47] If you or your executive leaders burnout, how effective do you think your organization will be in navigating adaptive change? Therefore, taking time to tend to individual wellbeing and build resiliency is critical for executive leaders. This is usually the starting point for any executive team development and will trump any other work because ignoring it will interfere with fostering quality relationships. Exactly what tending to individual wellbeing looks like varies with the organization and the leader involved. Some experts advocate for meditation, while others simply call for taking time to pause and reflect. We have found that leaders will ultimately do what works best and is most meaningful for them. Lencioni describes four disciplines that build organizational health:

1) Build a cohesive leadership team
2) Create clarity
3) Over-communicate clarity
4) Reinforce clarity[48]

Building a cohesive executive leadership team first requires building trust among the leaders. This makes sense because any trust issues can make it challenging to communicate effectively, handle conflict and set the vision for the company. Lencioni states that when successfully accomplished, this approach is foolproof:

When an organization's leaders are cohesive, when they are unambiguously aligned around a common set of answers to a few critical questions, when they communicate those answers again and again and again, and when they put effective processes in place to reinforce those answers, they create an environment in which success is almost impossible to prevent. Really.

However, "If an organization is led by a team that is not behaviorally unified, there is no chance that it will become healthy." [49] Even in reasonably functional cultures, we have found that many executive teams are not operating as a truly cohesive unit. Once we work to help build the team's cohesiveness, it makes a huge difference and fuels other initiatives.

We use Lencioni's four disciplines as a guide when working with executive leaders, and the impact the disciplines have is profound. When working with organizations to help them develop a comprehensive leadership development strategy, we always start with the executive leaders because they set the tone for the rest of the organization. If they are not a cohesive team, all bets are off for transforming workplace culture and having thriving wellbeing. How quickly the leadership development plan unfolds depends on what it takes for leaders to become a cohesive team. For really dysfunctional teams, it can take one to two years before the executive group is truly a team; for teams that are starting from a good place, it may not take as long. If you follow this approach, we recommend setting the expectation that the goal is, first and foremost, to ensure that the executive team is a cohesive one and to make it clear that how long that takes depends on the leaders on the team. Here is a typical approach we use with executive teams:

1) **Two-Day Offsite Workshop** *(Enhance Self-Awareness).*
    We often hear from leaders that they don't have time for reflection, self-awareness and strategic thinking because they are too frequently sucked into the business rather than being able to work on the business. Yet the purpose of the executive

team is to guide the strategic direction of the company, so helping leaders to get away is important. At this initial workshop, we focus solely on starting the journey to help the leaders be a cohesive team. We assess trust and how much dysfunction they see in the organization, review their individual and team Hartman Value Profile *(HVP)* results to promote self-awareness, facilitate exercises to help leaders see how their thinking isn't always serving them well, discuss stress and burnout, provide individual coaching and start rebuilding or enhancing trust and communication. We also help leaders see the vision for their development journey and include them in providing input into next steps.

2) **Intrinsic Coaching® Development** *(Build Effective Thinking Skills).* We have all leaders spend the next seven months becoming more self-aware and developing the skills to activate and apply best thinking (I>E>S) with one another, with their teams and in their lives. One important consideration involves which leaders can be in the same series learning Intrinsic Coaching® and which leaders need to be in separate series. If any lingering trust issues exist, we recommend the leaders not all be in the same series. When people are worried about looking good to their boss or colleagues, or have strong Systemic (S>E>I) thinking about any fellow leader, it will interfere with their learning. We also provide individual coaching for leaders when needed.

3) **Two-Day Offsite Workshop** *(Develop and Foster Quality Relationships).* Once the leaders are able to activate and apply best thinking, we reconvene and continue to complete any additional needed work for them to be a cohesive team. We usually see great breakthroughs at this point because the leaders are coming together and interacting from a different framework of self-awareness and thinking; and they all have a common language they can use to support one another and move into the other disciplines to create organizational health. It's amazing how much more productive strategy and planning discussions are once the leadership team brings forward better thinking!

4) Ongoing Support *(Grow the Organization).* We continue
with a combination of quarterly off-site workshops, individual
coaching and additional support to guide executive leaders as
they build the health of their organization, collaborating with
other partners when and where needed to ensure the leaders
are receiving the best support possible. Nothing is prescriptive
*(that would be applying Newtonian logic to developing lead-
ers).* We meet leadership teams where they are so they can
fully embrace the New Paradigm to *create the conditions* for
organizational and employee wellbeing to thrive.

Mid-Level Leaders/Managers

The approach we take with mid-level leaders and managers is similar to
the executive team. We focus on enhancing self-awareness and supporting the management team in being cohesive. It has been said that "managers assert drive and control to get things done; leaders pause
to discover new ways of being and achieving."[50] Furthermore, successful
leadership depends on the quality of the attention and the intention leaders
bring to any situation.[51] Mid-level managers are typically on overload,
trying to carry out the organizational plans and tend to employee relationships. We frequently hear from them, "I just don't have time and can't take
on one more thing." We have found that when mid-level managers are
supported to take the time to become more self-aware and do this work,
they are better leaders, and more effective in prioritizing their work and
guiding employees through adaptive changes.

We typically start by facilitating workshops with mid-level managers to
help them be aware of their own stress and wellbeing, when their thinking
is and isn't serving them well and how important employee wellbeing is to
transforming their culture. Some organizations will have their mid-level
managers also complete Intrinsic Coaching® development the first year;
others wait until year two due to timing and budgetary considerations.
When organizations wait until year two to have managers complete
Intrinsic Coaching® development, we tend to facilitate more frequent
workshops with the mid-level leaders/managers during the first year and
also provide access to their own individual coach so they can continue
increasing self-awareness and tap into better thinking for themselves. We
then create a developmental strategy that provides opportunities to develop
any tactical skills these people need to effectively lead their functional area.

In the world of workplace wellness, we frequently hear complaints about "getting" mid-level managers on board to actively support employee wellness efforts. The common approach is to try to dictate strategy to managers and give them scripted messages to communicate. But we've already learned the critical importance of involving people in the planning and strategy creation process. We have found that embedding personal wellbeing work into leadership development does wonders for managers and leaders in their ability to recognize the importance of wellbeing and to *create the conditions* within which employee wellbeing can thrive.

Informal Leaders

Lack of opportunity is one of the biggest reasons people leave companies.[52] Research examining 175 teams *(representing 10 different companies)* measured what influences organizational commitment. The study found that career development had the highest impact on team commitment levels *(compared to leadership, manager and pay)*. And when poor ratings for managers were combined with poor ratings for development, commitment levels were the lowest.[53] When organizations significantly invest in training, career development and mobility, they outperform their peers in almost every industry. When people are given opportunities to grow, they stay excited, the business becomes more innovative and agile, and top-performing employees want to stay.[54]

> When organizations significantly invest in training, career development and mobility, they outperform their peers in almost every industry.

Therefore, pouring a solid foundation is not just about developing current leaders or future leaders; not every employee wants to move into management. However, all employees have the capacity to be self-leaders. Organizations need to support individuals to learn and grow in order to learn and grow themselves as a living system. When people have a high level of personal mastery, they have a special sense of purpose and are in a continual learning mode. And people with high levels of personal mastery are more committed to their organizations and take more initiative.[55] Having a sense of purpose starts with self-awareness. The power of starting here for any employee wellbeing initiative is profound. Transforming workplace culture involves everyone. If employees burnout and cannot bring their best selves forward, change will be difficult. Don't underestimate the power of supporting people in knowing themselves better and clarifying their purpose. One of the most popular classes Google offers employees is "Search Inside Yourself," which includes three parts: attention training, self-knowledge and building useful mental habits.[56] We have found personal self-growth workshops focused on developing better thinking, clarifying life purpose and building resiliency to be well-attended — without needing to use incentives to coerce employees. As we will see next, the result is that providing training and development to enhance and learn new professional skills, improve communication and more will have a greater likelihood of succeeding for the long term.

A Case Study of Cooper Engineering

One organization we have worked with for years we'll call Cooper Engineering. We started their comprehensive leadership development strategy by using year one to lay a foundation for sustainability. This began with facilitating a two-day offsite workshop focused on supporting the executive leaders in becoming a truly cohesive team. Prior to that workshop, each leader completed the Hartman Value Profile *(HVP)* assessment. On day one of the workshop, we focused on self and team awareness. We conducted an initial assessment of trust within the team and the degree of dysfunction members saw in their team and their organization. This created a baseline understanding of their starting point. Using the power of story and tapping into their emotions, we built the business case to help the leaders see why they were embarking upon this developmental journey and created the vision of how their journey might unfold. Then we spent time on self-awareness, reviewing the HVP results to help the leaders have a better experience of themselves — their habitual thinking patterns, their stress and degree of work-life imbalance, and insights into how their strengths might be contributing to frustrations within their leadership team, the teams they lead and the organization as a whole. We concluded day one with individual coaching sessions with each leader and gave all leaders some take-home exercises to reflect on what they were noticing and what was opening up for them based on the assessment and the work done on day one. The leaders were asked to explore what they were wanting for themselves, their leadership team, the teams they lead, their employees and the organization.

Day two began with a discussion and planning session based on day one experiences and homework, and then progressed to exercises to improve their team cohesiveness and set the future direction. Over the next seven months, the executive team started its developmental journey by completing Intrinsic Coaching® development. This had a dramatic impact on shifting the leaders' thinking about themselves and others, and on how they interacted with one another and their teams. Once the executive team could activate better thinking, we resumed the offsite workshops to continue building organizational health *(which included clarifying their core values and helping employees connect to the company vision)*, supporting leaders in tending to their own wellbeing and supporting wellbeing for employees. Once that foundation was laid, we could address the executive team's needs to lead organizational growth and change.

We started with the executive leaders for Cooper Engineering because, based on their dynamics, the skeptical executive team needed to embrace the leadership development journey before they could lead and support the managers on their journey. Our focus for the managers during year one was first on self-awareness of their own wellbeing and burnout, and then on some short-term competencies they needed. For the employees, the focus was primarily on supporting wellbeing with programs and resources, but also included self-awareness and support in shifting thinking by providing a six-week series to support healthy thinking and access to Intrinsic Coaching® services. Seeing the shift in the executive leadership team, the managers and employees became more engaged and supportive of the development strategy. In year two, the managers completed the HVP and Intrinsic Coaching® development, and participated in workshops and coaching to become a more cohesive team, learn to embrace accountability and support them in more effectively developing their employees.

Employees who were not formal leaders were asked to participate in creating mission statements for their departments, and come up with individual goals and development plans for how they could best support the company's vision and strategic direction. Additionally, individuals identified as potential future leaders were offered the opportunity to complete Intrinsic Coaching® development.

One Leader's Developmental Journey — In His Own Words

One of Cooper Engineering's executive leaders was profoundly impacted by becoming more self-aware of his own thinking and then using what he learned via his Intrinsic Coaching® development to activate better thinking. Here is how this one leader, who we will call Matt Green, described his experience.

My journey started with what I now see is extremely dominant systemic thinking. As a degreed engineer in a business management role, I have plenty of opportunities to successfully apply my analytical skills to develop new business opportunities and execute plans for growth. As a leader I have been able to successfully inspire others to meet project objectives, and I provided as many opportunities as I thought I could to help employees achieve their own objectives.

What happened for me was a difficult yet profound experience. The executive leadership team was in the process of creating a significant shift in business strategy; we tended to be very reactive, yet were trying to develop and implement a more proactive growth model. As we attempted to develop this proactive growth model, I offered ideas based on what I was hearing from the team in terms of desired objectives. But I was met with resistance at every turn.

I quickly became frustrated toward the process and my peers; I was offering solutions to all of the things they were asking for, yet none of them wanted it. I recognized that people were more concerned about how this would affect their positions in the company. I assumed that my intentions were being recognized as selfless; however, this was not the case at all.

I grew so frustrated that I quit; and I learned the hard way how much my thinking had harmed my position in the company. I received several well-wishes from my direct reports and others, but not a single peer said anything to me for over two days. In looking back, although I didn't have the language for it yet, I think I realized that my systemic thinking had become so overwhelming that I had alienated myself from the executive team. I shared my realization with my fellow leaders a few days later and that I recognized there was more going on with the team; fortunately, I was reinstated, but some damage had been done.

We started to address this and other issues at an initial two-day offsite workshop. And then we began participating in Intrinsic Coaching® development; it was positioned as a way to promote better communication among our leadership team and to improve communication to the rest of the company. We often hear that the key to being a good communicator is being a good listener, but no one tells you HOW to be a better listener. The Intrinsic Coaching® development taught me to be aware of my thinking in a conversation and determine if I am valuing my thinking more or valuing the person across from me. It also taught me to pay more attention to what is happening in the moment with other people and not assume that what I say is taken at face-value.

I recently had the opportunity to activate better thinking in handling a difficult situation with one of my direct reports. Karen used to report to the CEO but, after a reorganization, she now reports to me. Prior to this, we had worked very well together on several projects. Things went well for the first couple of months she reported to me; but, as time went by, I noticed she was not adhering to some of our company policies. These weren't serious, but Cooper Engineering had some recent history with this that hurt our culture, so I was very sensitive to this.

Long story short, I was now faced with someone who was deeply entrenched in her own systemic thinking. Everything I said or did was viewed by Karen as having malicious intent and that I was out to get her. And when I attempted to show her how some of her behaviors might be detrimental to the current culture and her ability to work within it, it only made matters worse. Then I remembered to lean on my Intrinsic Coaching® training and shifted my approach. Once I realized Karen's systemic thinking was dominating, I knew the only way we could have a productive discussion was for me to meet her there and provide some relief for her systemic thinking. I reassured her that I truly wanted what was best for her. By repeating that I was very interested in her wellbeing and growth, I was able to create a space for Karen to start opening her thinking about what I was wanting for her so she could better articulate what she was really wanting for herself. What was truly profound for me is that I started to see that by being aware of my thinking and managing my habitual, systemic thinking, I was able to shift our relationship and am now witnessing her growth. What's even better is that, as part of Karen's development plan, she is now in the midst of completing Intrinsic Coaching® development. And I am seeing her start to be more aware of her thinking and shifting how she interacts — with me and others. Who knew being aware of your thinking and being able to activate better thinking would be the missing ingredient for success?!

Matt's experience is not uncommon. We frequently are met with initial skepticism from leadership teams when we inform them that part of their developmental journey includes spending 50 hours investing in being fully aware of their own thinking and then building the skills to activate best thinking. We get it: People still want a "quick fix" or think they're already a good listener and effective leader — and many leaders we work with are very good at what they do. But, as Matt learned, it's not about what you do, it's about who you're *being*. And you can't be differently until you think differently.

We know there is much more to be said in more detail on how to develop quality leaders. However, we hope you have a better sense of what it takes to approach leadership development in a comprehensive and sustainable way, giving you a solid foundation that can withstand any storm. We also hope you are seeing what relationships and partnerships you may need to create to approach leadership development differently — so that you are pouring the foundation to support both organizational and employee wellbeing. When you have quality leaders, you can then frame the house and create a supportive climate, which we address in the next chapter.

Summary for Developing Quality Leaders

3 Levels of Leadership to Include in Development:

1) Executive/Senior Leaders
2) Mid-Level Leaders/Managers
3) Informal Leaders

2 Building Effective Thinking Skills

3 Developing and Fostering Quality Relationships So Others Can Grow

1 Enhancing Self-Awareness

4 Growing the Organization

4 Steps for Development

CHAPTER 11

Transformation Point #4:
Frame the House
(Create a Supportive Climate)

66 *Open, honest communication is the best foundation for any relationship, but remember that at the end of the day it's not what you say or what you do, but how you make people feel that matters the most. In order for someone to feel good about a relationship, they must know that the other person truly cares about them, both personally and professionally.*[1] 99

Tony Hsieh, "Delivering Happiness"

O nce you have poured a solid foundation and are effectively developing quality leaders in your organization, it is time to frame the house and create a supportive climate. We have already established that climate is a manifestation of your workplace culture — the underlying attitudes, values and assumptions that guide your organization. Changing workplace culture is an ongoing journey. So it is important that your climate supports a culture in which both organizational and employee wellbeing can thrive. We cannot emphasize this enough: you can't create a supportive climate without first knowing where you're headed and without having a solid foundation to get you there!

Creating a supportive climate means every aspect of the business fosters living its core values and desired culture on a daily basis. This starts with the hiring process. Companies with thriving organizational and employee wellbeing understand the importance of protecting their culture and use cultural fit as the most important factor in the hiring process, even above background and skills. If you hire people who have great skills but don't embody your core values your culture can erode as quickly as a pile of sand in a storm.

Zappos is committed to hiring only people who fit with their culture. After being hired based on cultural fit, all employees complete a four-week training — regardless of their position. During this time, they learn about the importance of customer service, the long-term company vision and the philosophy of the company culture. Then, everyone spends two weeks taking phone calls from the customers so they truly understand the core of their business. At the end of the training program, Zappos offers everyone the option of accepting $2,000 to quit. They want to make sure employees are not just there for a paycheck. Consequently, everyone at Zappos lives the culture and values of the company.[2]

Sure, Zappos' hiring process may sound extreme, but it certainly speaks volumes about the importance of culture! Once people are hired in your organization, the training, the on-boarding process, and everything that acclimates new employees to the company needs to reinforce the core company values and desired culture, and *create the conditions* so employees truly feel valued. If you've done the work we suggested in *Transformation Point #2* and have included as many people as possible in the planning process, it will be easier to *create the conditions* for both organizational and employee wellbeing to thrive, because everyone will have been part of creating the vision for their desired culture.

If your workplace culture is currently far from thriving, doing the work in the first three *Points of Transformation* will set you well on your way and will provide you with a road map for how to start putting culture first. Once you've identified your desired culture, evaluate your current climate to determine how to move forward. Consider the following questions:

- What behaviors do/will we see that tell us we are living our core values and desired culture?
- What behaviors do/will we see that might sabotage our core values and desired culture?
- If/when we see behaviors that are not aligned with our core values and desired culture, how do we want to address them?

Human beings are not perfect. We all have days when we do not bring our best selves forward to work. Embracing accountability — so all employees view it as part of their role to *create the conditions* for and protect a thriving workplace culture — is critical to long-term success. Many of our clients keep workplace culture as a standing agenda item for all department and one-to-one meetings. This creates a consistent framework for discussing how people see that they are and/or are not living the core values and culture, and how that ultimately impacts organizational and employee wellbeing.

Addressing Employee Performance Issues

Even in companies that are diligent about tending to their culture, perform-ance issues with employees do arise. When this happens, we suggest that the direction for coaching and course-correction with employee behavior should stem from whether what the employees are doing is aligned with and fostering the culture and values or inhibiting them. For example, let's say your organization has determined that teamwork is a critical aspect that tells you the core values and desired culture are being embodied. One employee, Mary, is struggling to meet objectives and deadlines set for her area. Mary's supervisor has open dialogue with her to try to determine what conditions are not present for her to succeed. It is determined that the likely culprit of Mary's issues is that she is not asking for support and is not tapping into her team. She is trying to do everything herself, but it isn't working. Mary's supervisor revisits the values and agreed upon behaviors, and lets her know that teamwork is an important expectation. Perhaps Mary's previous employers did not support teamwork; however, by her supervisor reinforcing the need to be accountable to the culture including the importance of teamwork, Mary will hopefully see it is OK to lean on her team and will ultimately acclimate to being successful in her environ-ment. However, if Mary is provided appropriate coaching and development but continues to struggle with being successful and meeting expectations, then her supervisor may eventually decide to start managing her out of the organization. Organizations that put culture first and recognize its impor-tance not only hire, coach and support performance based on cultural fit, they also fire based on lack of cultural fit because of the impact it can have on the other employees and the organization as a whole.

How Mendelsohn Partners, LLC Protects its Culture

One of our clients, we'll call Mendelsohn Partners, has done a tremendous amount of work over the past few years to transform its culture. About five years ago, Mendelsohn was at a critical juncture. Several high-performing employees had left the organization, sales were dropping and morale was in the toilet. Executive leaders knew if they didn't do something fast, their company very likely wouldn't be around in a few years. True to the hard-wiring of being human and wanting a quick-fix, Mendelsohn's leaders wanted a partner to help them perform a miracle turnaround for their company. However, after we met with them and helped them see for themselves how so much of what they were doing was just simply being *stuck* in an outdated paradigm, the leaders became a little more open to doing things differently and managing their impatience for wanting things fixed immediately. They realized it had taken them years to get to their current state, and it would take considerable, diligent effort to change employees' perceptions and to rebuild trust. With that, we began to guide them through *The 7 Points of Transformation.*

What stands out today when we talk to Mendelsohn's employees is that they consistently state, "This is one of the best places to work!" Obviously, a lot has changed for the better over the past few years. Now that things have started to improve, the key to Mendelsohn continuing to *create the conditions* for thriving organizational and employee wellbeing is that they put as much effort into leveraging their strengths, supporting what is working well, and protecting their desired culture as they do in strategy and operations. In the process of transforming their culture, several employees were also ultimately managed out of the organization for no longer fitting into the culture Mendelsohn was working so hard to create. Here are some additional examples of how Mendelsohn is protecting its transformed culture:

- Every manager seeks ways to support and provide opportunities for employees to find greater meaning in their work.

- Every manager regularly meets with employees to discuss work load and work-life balance and to ensure they are not pushing themselves to the point where their personal wellbeing might suffer.

- Programs and resources are provided that support employees in all areas of wellbeing so they have a solid foundation from which to bring forward their best selves to work.

- All employees participate in quarterly interactive culture workshops where employees reflect on how they see themselves and others behaving in ways that are or are not consistent with the core values and desired culture so that issues can be addressed early — before too much damage occurs.

- Employee recognition is now based on how people are living the core values and contributing to a thriving workplace culture.

Obviously, Mendelsohn has put forth profound effort to transform its culture; so it is no surprise leaders are very focused on ensuring the company's climate is supportive and protecting their culture. However, when things are going well, it can be easy to become complacent and take for granted that the workplace culture is thriving. Sometimes we hear people say, "Things are really good here at our organization; why are we spending so much time talking about culture?" Certainly, there is not as much work that has to be done in terms of repair, but because culture is a moving target, it can get away from you quickly and put you in repair mode if you don't intentionally live it and protect it.

Creating a Climate that Supports Employee Development

One of the best predictors of employee happiness and engagement is whether employees are able to leverage their strengths at work each day.[3] Given this, it makes sense that *creating the conditions* for continued growth and development is essential to having thriving organizational and employee wellbeing. Does your workplace culture and climate support and value taking risks and trying new things? Or has fear of failure crippled innovation? When employees are supported and challenged to bring all of their talents to work, regardless of whether those talents fit in a formal job description, they will be more creative and ultimately happier.[4]

Supporting employee wellbeing by fostering personal development can also have a profound impact on organizational wellbeing and performance. In his book, "The Dream Manager," Matthew Kelly uses a business parable to illustrate how supporting employees in personal development can transform an organization.[5] Kelly describes a complete turnaround for a janitorial company by recognizing that the company's success depends on the employees becoming the best versions of themselves. This company hired a "Dream Manager" who was available to work with employees to help them realize their dreams and purpose in life. Initially, the "Dream Manager" was a financial planner *(because most of the employees had low incomes)*, but eventually another "Dream Manager" was hired who was more akin to a life coach. More employees started gaining clarity about their dreams and purpose. These employees started thriving at work and recognizing their job as a significant contributor to having the things they ultimately wanted in life, helping them to realize their dreams. Turnover improved so much that the company had to devise a plan to start developing employees for their next job and outplacement, because they didn't want people to be *stuck*. Essentially, every aspect of the company improved; and it all started by taking a risk to bring in someone who could work with employees to become more connected to what they wanted for themselves.

Granted, Kelly is describing a fictitious company. However, this parable provides a powerful example of the benefits of investing in wellbeing and supporting employees in clarifying their purpose and how it aligns with their role in the organization. Furthermore, it illustrates that, for people who may not find the nature of the work itself very fulfilling, being provided opportunities to find meaning and connection to their work with what is important in their personal lives can have as much of an impact on happiness and engagement as fostering professional strengths.

Deliberately Developmental Organizations

In their book, "Immunity to Change: How to Overcome It and Unlock the Potential in Yourself and Your Organization," Robert Kegan and Lisa Laskow Lahey explore how our individual beliefs and the collective mindsets in organizations combine to create a powerful immunity to change. They suggest that what will distinguish leaders *(and ultimately organizations)* from others is their ability to develop themselves, their employees and their teams:

> *Leaders who ask themselves, '**What can I do to make my setting the most fertile ground in the world for the growth of talent?**' put themselves in the best position to succeed.*[6]

Kegan and Lahey's work supports people in identifying the thinking that holds them back and then provides a framework for doing the difficult adaptive change work needed to move past their limiting thinking.[7] We established in the previous chapter that adaptive challenges cannot be solved with existing thinking and resources. The reason adaptive challenges are so difficult is because of our "blind spot" — where we don't recognize our own *stuckness* and try to continue using faulty thinking and strategies. Therefore, adaptive change work involves some recognition of and correcting for our own blindness. Adaptive change work in this context recognizes the overlap between our work and our personal selves, and the importance of organizations investing in support for both.[8]

Kegan and colleagues have continued this work in identifying what they believe is the cornerstone for a high potential culture — a Deliberately Developmental Organization *(DDO)* that supports people in turning personal struggles into growth opportunities.[9] They view the construct of work and life as being separate to be a false one:[10]

> *To an extent that we ourselves are only beginning to appreciate, most people at work, even in high-performing organizations, divert considerable energy every day to a second job that no one has hired them to do: preserving their reputations, putting their best selves forward, and hiding their inadequacies from others and themselves. We believe this is the single biggest cause of wasted resources in nearly every company today.[11]*

DDOs view work as an essential context for personal growth.[12] They are organized around the conviction that organizations prosper best when they are deeply aligned with people's strong, innate motive to grow:

> *Deep alignment with people's motive to grow **means fashioning an organizational culture in which support to people's ongoing development** is woven into the daily fabric of working life, visible in the company's regular operations, day-to-day routines and conversations.[13]*

These organizations represent serious departures from typical, business-as-usual principles and practices.[14] In DDOs, people are expected to work on identifying and overcoming patterns of thinking and behavior as part of doing their job well. The root causes of these patterns are usually about "unwarranted and unexamined assumptions and habitual ways of behaving."[15] In other words, people are supported and expected to do significant adaptive change work.

DDOs create a culture in which people embrace their vulnerabilities as prime opportunities for personal growth. DDOs are committed to developing every single person by weaving personal growth into daily work. **They operate on the assumption that personal growth of employees and the bottom line are interdependent.** The personal growth work that is the key to a DDO is profound adaptive change work in which people are challenged and supported via coaching to recognize and transcend their blind spots and the thinking that has them resisting change. But people don't do this work in a bubble in DDOs; they reveal their inadequacies at work. This re-quires the organization to create a high-trust culture and climate to make it safe to show vulnerability, which takes time and patience.[16]

DDOs view their core values as their "North Star" for guiding what they do and believe personal growth is essential to living those values. Conse-quently, people working in DDOs can clearly describe the shared set of principles that guide them because the core values are a living part of the system, not just words on a wall.[17] DDOs go beyond simply accepting employees' inadequacies; they cultivate them as part of the journey towards organizational transformation. In DDOs, employees feel valuable even when they're messing up because they can see their limitations as their "growing edge" on a path to the next performance level rather than as fail-ures. The focus is on the thinking that led to the issues or poor decisions. With that, DDOs create a climate and community that make employees feel safe and promote accountability, transparency and support for doing self-work that many may otherwise find uncomfortable, because this work is basically about adaptive change.[18]

Identifying and creating DDOs is relatively new but stems from years of work by Kegan and colleagues. After three years of searching, they have only identified a small handful of companies to date. Two that have been operating as a DDO for over 10 years, and seeing great success, are Bridge-water Associates *(an East Coast investment firm)* and Decurion Corporation *(a California real estate company)*. Bridgewater is recognized as a top-performing money manager and has won more than 40 industry awards just in the past five years. It also has been consistently ranked as the largest and best performing hedge fund manager in the world. Decurion's portfolio of companies have won numerous awards while benefiting from consistent, profound growth over the past few years. Kegan and colleagues will be publishing a book in 2015 on their DDO work.

Effective Communication: The Cornerstone for a Supportive Climate

Perhaps becoming a DDO is beyond where your company is right now. However, *creating the conditions* to recognize the interrelatedness and complexities of work and personal lives is important if you want to have a thriving workplace culture. A supportive climate is essential to ensure your workplace culture is truly being manifested in a way that both organizational and employee wellbeing can thrive. If you want to protect your culture and foster employee growth and development, you must start with effective communication. Communication will make or break any human interaction and is often a point of breakdown for organizations. Therefore, it is not surprising that we view effective communication as a cornerstone for integrating and aligning all of the components that make up a supportive climate.

Communicating is a two-way street that requires disseminating clear, relevant information but also listening and incorporating feedback from employees. The right approach to communication will help create the framework for organizational wellbeing and ensure that employees feel supported in their individual wellbeing. When it comes to aligning organizational and employee wellbeing, we provide three main components of a communication strategy that can help create a supportive climate.

1) Provide clear leadership communication
2) Embed employee wellbeing into culture change efforts
3) Develop and implement a holistic communication strategy

Step One: Provide Clear Leadership Communication

Gandhi is credited with saying, "Be the change you wish to see." In the previous chapter, we established how leaders set the tone for the organization and the employee experience of the workplace culture. Because changing workplace culture starts from the inside out with changing thinking, leaders cannot grow the organization until they first do some work developing themselves. No one in your organization will believe any change message unless the CEO and executive leaders become the change they want to see in the organization. So what does it mean for leaders to "be the change" in culture transformation efforts? They have to walk the talk. This includes doing their own self-development work and intentionally living the core values and desired culture. Leaders with integrity know they have no choice but to walk their talk. There are terrible, disabling consequences in organizations when leaders do not practice what they preach.[19]

One organization we work with we'll call Pearson Properties. After receiving feedback from employee surveys that the executive team was out of touch with employees and didn't listen to or incorporate feedback, the CEO decided it was time to start the company's change journey toward better communication. The company executives began their own self-development work and communicated they were doing so to employees to be transparent about leadership's faults. Executives started being more visible by getting out of their offices and intentionally making time to talk to employees *(and actually listen to them)*. Leaders made a point to give public credit to employees when their ideas were implemented. Certainly employees didn't trust them at first, but as Pearson executives consistently were being the change they wanted to see, the employees gradually opened up and embraced the new two-way flow of communication.

In addition to walking the talk, leaders must clearly articulate the talk so people know the direction in which the company is headed and how they align with the culture change journey. Without clear communication, there is usually great stress and confusion. Additionally, people end up suffering from "MSU *(making stuff up)* Syndrome."[20] The first step in ensuring leaders can both walk the talk and communicate it effectively is to implement Lencioni's four disciplines that build organizational health *(described in the previous chapter)*:

1) Build a cohesive leadership team
2) Create clarity
3) Over-communicate clarity
4) Reinforce clarity[21]

Leaders cannot clearly communicate about culture change, provide clarity of purpose and support employees' understanding of how they align with the company vision if they are not part of a cohesive team with clarity of direction.

We also want to make an important distinction and clarification regarding having leaders walk the talk and communicate the vision. We are referring to leaders *creating the conditions* that show employees they are valued as people. This is very different from how people usually describe a "wellness culture/climate." Typically, "walking the talk" with regards to a culture of health/wellness refers to leaders promoting the wellness vision and modeling healthy behaviors. We can, unfortunately, name leaders in various organizations who walk the talk in living a healthy lifestyle, but every action and communication sends a message to employees that they are anything but valued. We also know leaders who are personally challenged by their physical wellbeing, yet are doing profound work in other areas of wellbeing and are leading thriving workplace cultures. Trying to create a supportive climate for healthy lifestyle without first supporting a thriving workplace culture will typically backfire.

Step Two: Embed Employee Wellbeing into Culture Change Efforts

Once the purpose and direction for culture change are clear, and the daily work practices support a thriving culture, employee wellbeing efforts can better align with organizational wellbeing efforts. This starts by moving away from employee wellness programs based on the Old Paradigm and toward embracing the New Paradigm. For starters, we suggest eliminating the term "program" when referring to employee wellbeing. Certainly, part of creating a thriving workplace culture will include implementing various programs and resources *(we will discuss these in more depth in chapter 13)*; however, reducing the importance of employee wellbeing to a "program" sets it up for failure. "Program" implies it is something temporary — with a start and stopping point — and something extra on employees' already overloaded plates. Instead, we suggest embedding employee wellbeing into your culture by positioning it in one of two ways:

1) Create an overarching employee wellbeing benefit of employment; or

2) Position employee wellbeing as part of your culture brand and a platform for who you are as a company in terms of how you value and support your employees and the employee experience.

In either case, employee wellbeing is now continuous and positioned in a way that it is part of the organization's culture. It sends a message that employee wellbeing is critical to the success of organizational wellbeing *(and vice versa)*. Repositioning employee wellbeing becomes less about "doing stuff" to employees and trying to change narrow health behaviors and more about a way of communicating and aligning resources to support the whole person. If you have a traditional wellness program, some additional communication will be required in the first three *Points of Transformation* so

> **Employee wellbeing is critical to the success of organizational wellbeing *(and vice versa).***

employees truly see that the paradigm is shifting. We usually recommend that the executive leaders communicate the shift and expansion as part of collectively involving employees in the strategic planning process. A message might sound something like the following:

"At XYZ Company, we have had a wellness program in place now for three years. I know some of you really have appreciated some aspects of the program and some have not. In any case, we have been primarily focused on only one aspect of your overall wellbeing. And we recognize there is so much more than just physical health — even though it is important. We also know how important your total wellbeing is to the wellbeing of our organization. So, as part of our journey to transform our culture and become an organization in which you are proud to work and are happy to be a part of, we will be relaunching the wellness program and expanding it to be a wellbeing benefit and part of our brand identity, showing how we value and support you. Just like the rest of this culture change journey, this is about YOU; so the new employee wellbeing benefit will be a platform created by you, for you. We will be asking you to help name and brand our new benefit and determine what types of programs and resources to offer that would be most meaningful to support you all in your own wellbeing."

If you haven't yet gone down the path of offering a traditional wellness program, then there will still need to be some communication about the importance of employee wellbeing as part of the culture change journey; but you hopefully won't have to overcome the over-focus on health risks. In either case, the point is to set the stage so people see that this isn't a program and isn't something temporary or extra; it is part of the company identity.

Once you've communicated that employee wellbeing is an overarching benefit or platform, you can start to create a structure to bring that to life as part of daily operations. This begins with establishing two main teams to guide the employee wellbeing aspect of the culture change journey:

- Culture and Wellbeing Team
- Culture and Wellbeing Ambassadors

Culture and Wellbeing Team

Although you ideally want every employee to be part of the planning process for transforming the culture and supporting employee wellbeing, logistically, there needs to be a small team of people to lead and guide the change journey and represent their fellow colleagues. Keeping in mind the important relationship between organizational and employee wellbeing, we suggest creating a Culture and Wellbeing Team of five to 12 people. The purpose of this team is to guide living and implementing the strategic and annual plan, and ensure the organization is *creating the conditions* for organizational and employee wellbeing to thrive. Who should you include on this team? We suggest considering how your organization functions operationally in terms of culture change and communication and include people from the functional areas who will have a practical perspective to take into account. Some common examples include people working in the following areas:

- IT
- HR *(one person usually will suffice)*
- Marketing/Communications
- Union *(if applicable)*
- Production *(if a manufacturing type of business)*
- Faculty and Staff *(if an educational institution)*
- Training and Development
- Safety/Risk Management
- Facilities/Building Maintenance
- Senior Leadership Team Member
- Mid-Level Management
- Administration, Doctors, Nurses and Staff
  (if a hospital or clinic)

If you work in an organization that has been *stuck* in the Old Paradigm with wellness programs and has a wellness committee, we usually recommend revisiting that committee to determine who should be on the team with the broader scope and who no longer makes sense to have on the team. It can be helpful to create a short job description that includes the purpose of the team, the time commitment *(the typical time commitment includes monthly meetings with some assignments outside of the meetings)*, and the length of time you want people on the team. Ideally, the strategic and annual plans you created in *Transformation Point #2* will guide each meeting agenda to ensure the plans are evolving into a living reality.

Culture and Wellbeing Ambassadors

To have a functioning team, the Culture and Wellbeing Team needs to be small. However, creating a broad reaching network of Culture and Wellbeing Ambassadors can help to ensure that employee feedback and work done to create the plans are actually implemented. The ambassadors help create a two-way communication and feedback channel to ensure employees are included in the workplace culture change journey. Ideally, you would have an official Culture and Wellbeing Ambassador representing every location, department and shift; and the more, the merrier! In Utopia, everyone in the organization would be an ambassador and supporting people in living the core values and desired culture every day. But we know that is not practical. Instead, the ambassadors serve as a conduit between the Culture and Wellbeing Team and the rest of the employees. The ambassadors provide ideas and feedback from the employees to the team to be considered as the employee wellbeing plans unfold during the year. The ambassadors also serve to reinforce and communicate messages from the team to help support accountability for everyone living the desired culture. Again, this network of ambassadors is much different from the "wellness champions" that many organizations have.

Organizations *stuck* in the Old Paradigm that are running wellness programs often have "wellness champions"; however, their role tends to be much more myopic — running around communicating healthy lifestyle messages and encouraging people to participate in wellness programs.

Other organizations have much greater involvement from their Culture and Wellbeing Ambassadors *(especially those who are spread out over multiple locations)*. When ambassadors are involved more than as a conduit for communication, they frequently have an "inspiration guide" to provide ideas for how to best rally employees, and champion wellbeing and the culture change journey. Regardless of the ambassadors' level of involvement we recommend the Culture and Wellbeing Team meet with them. During this meeting the Culture and Wellbeing Team shares the vision and ideas created for how to best leverage the network of ambassadors, but then lets them design and create their own involvement. You may find out you have some ambassadors who want to be more involved, and have gifts and talents that can help intentionally create a thriving workplace culture.

Physical Environment, Policies and Procedures to Support Wellbeing

Another aspect of embedding wellbeing into your culture involves the physical environment as well as the policies and procedures that guide daily operations. Keep in mind that just because the physical environment supports wellbeing does not mean the underlying culture does. We frequently hear from employees who work at companies where the physical environment and policies support wellbeing; they have an onsite fitness center, a relaxation room, onsite programs, flexible work arrangements and more. Yet, the underlying cultural norm is that your life will be unpleasant if you take the time to utilize such resources; there is a mismatch between the culture and the climate. Even if your organization is communicating regularly, the quality may be lacking and the message may not be clear or relevant to your employees.

The physical environment can include everything from the layout of your workspace *(e.g., If your desired culture is one of openness, does the physical environment support collaboration? Does the physical environment support good ergonomics?)* to whether the environment is conducive to tending to your own personal wellbeing during the day *(e.g., inviting areas for taking breaks or socializing, sit-to-stand workstations, quiet areas for self-reflection, etc.).* Any program or resource you may want to deploy should align with the physical environment as well as with any operational policies and practices. We discuss in detail programs and resources to support wellbeing in chapter 13.

Ideally, if your culture truly supports wellbeing, your organization won't need formal policies and procedures on that front. However, taking the step to formalize processes to explicitly support wellbeing can also aid in protecting the company's core values and desired culture. That said, it is important to recognize that simply having the physical environment, policies and procedures to support wellbeing does not necessarily translate into an employee experience in which they feel valued and know that their wellbeing matters.

Step Three: Develop and Implement a Holistic Communication Strategy

The final component of creating a supportive climate involves developing an annual comprehensive communication plan that aligns company-wide and organizational wellbeing communication with messages that support and reinforce employee wellbeing. Many times, embedding wellbeing into the culture also becomes more about a well designed and implemented communication strategy than about "doing stuff." Having a comprehensive communication strategy can help align the things you are likely already doing to support the various areas of wellbeing so employees see and appreciate the holistic nature of how the company values their wellbeing. The components of a holistic communication strategy include:

- Wellbeing Communication Plan
- Employee Wellbeing Brand
- Employee Wellbeing Overview
- Employee Wellbeing Leaders' Guide

Wellbeing Communication Plan

One of the biggest complaints many organizations receive from people is that leaders don't communicate enough or that there is frequent miscommunication. Even if your organization is communicating regularly, the quality may be lacking and the message may not be clear or relevant to your employees. Meaningful communication supports employees in having clarity of vision about how they fit into the bigger picture and how they can tend to their own wellbeing. Before you can create and implement a communication plan, consider the following questions:

- Do you know how your employees want to receive communication?
- Do you know what types of organizational and employee wellbeing information employees find to be the most meaningful?
- Are you communicating some messages too much, so that people ignore the message, and they essentially become "white noise"?
- Does your communication support employees in having autonomy, mastery and purpose?

Communication works best when it supports and reinforces the culture change journey that people have already been part of creating. When working with leaders, we are often surprised at how many underestimate the importance of communicating basic information about the state of the business to employees. Likewise, we are often surprised by the 17th-century, mechanistic mindset when it comes to employee wellbeing. Frequently we see employee wellbeing messaging based solely on National Health Observances or topics of risk identified via medical claims or biomedical-focused assessment results, such as HRAs or biometric screenings. Instead of being integrated, there is a mismatch and separation of organizational and employee wellbeing communication.

Because we live in an age of information overload, you need to mindfully plan for all proactive company communication so it best meets everyone's needs. We suggest creating an annual plan, broken down by month, that includes what organization-wide communication needs to be conveyed and how, and doing the same with employee wellbeing communication. Mapping out the communication strategy in a plan allows for determining if there is communication overload some months or perhaps not enough communication in other months. It also helps create a framework for ensuring you are regularly reinforcing important messages and promoting resources available for employees. The following is an example of part of an annual communication plan:

Month	Culture Reinforcement Messaging	Organizational Wellbeing Communication	Employee Wellbeing Communication
Jan.	**Core Values** *How are YOU living our core values?* • CEO asks at quarterly all-employee meeting • Formal message about core values in quarterly newsletter • Department meeting and 1:1 agenda item	**Culture Survey Results** • Overview of results by CEO at all-staff meeting • Summary in quarterly newsletter • Agenda item for department meetings • Elicit employee feedback on how they see the results guiding the culture journey	**ALL Areas of WB** • Newsletter article on importance of balance and total wellbeing • E-mail and intranet reminder of "Anti-New Year's Resolution" workshop on 1/14 • Fliers posted to reinforce EAP services that support life balance
Feb.	**Living our Culture** *How are YOU behaving that contributes to us living our desired culture?* • Bi-monthly e-mail from CEO asks employees to reflect on their contribution to the culture • Periodic "ads" throughout the month on home page of intranet with this question • Department meeting and 1:1 agenda item	**Annual Purpose/Goal Setting** • Reminder in all meetings for doing final prep work for discussing purpose and goals with manager • SurveyMonkey® short quiz on departmental function; surprise recognition to all who "pass" • Collective collage created on intranet from everyone's purpose statements; promoted via e-mail	**Career WB** • Redistribute professional strengths inventory to employees with reflective questions *(e-mail)* • Promote new round of mentoring program *(e-mail, intranet, HR guest at department meetings)* • Reminder of upcoming training and development workshops *(department meeting agenda, intranet)* • Reinforce company's employee development framework *(managers in 1:1 meetings)*
March	**Protecting our Culture** *How are YOU behaving that might be sabotaging us in living our desired culture?* • CEO asks at annual all-employee meeting • Employee workshops facilitated for brainstorming how to hold one another accountable when sabotaging behaviors surface • Department meeting and 1:1 agenda item	**State of Business Update** • Annual all-employee meeting; annual report distributed to all employees and reviewed at meeting • Follow-up town hall meetings at each location with CEO • Q&A agenda item in all department meetings	**Financial WB** • E-tip and fliers posted on creating a personal financial vision • Reminder of the in-person and live webinar options for the financial planning workshop • Reinforce examining retirement plan contributions and allocations • Reinforce healthcare consumerism resources • Reminder of employee emergency loan fund

217

Notice that the plan aligns and links together all messaging. For example, in March, the focus is on the financial aspect of both organizational and employee wellbeing. The messaging and any additional programs, resources or initiatives planned align with that month's focus. It may not always be possible to totally align all communication, but the more you can thoughtfully plan to ensure a holistic and integrated approach to communication, the more effective your communication strategy will be in helping employees see everything is interconnected. Creating an integrated communication plan also further supports the idea that creating a thriving workplace culture is a collaborative effort. The only way to create such a communication plan is via collaboration within the organization.

Employee Wellbeing Brand

Highlighting employee wellbeing as an important part of the company identity and the employee experience can be helpful. In the interest of having employees be part of creating the culture, we usually suggest including employees in the process to name and brand the employee wellbeing benefit or platform. This can be done in a number of ways. Sometimes the culture and wellbeing team will meet and brainstorm names to call the "umbrella" for employee wellbeing support and then have the employees vote. Other times, organizations will ask their employees to submit ideas and then have people vote. Either way, the process works best when people are included in creating the employee wellbeing brand. Once a name has been selected, a logo can be created and used in communications to highlight the organization's support of employee wellbeing *(e.g., including all employee wellbeing messaging in the annual communication plan)*.

Employee Wellbeing Overview

Once employee wellbeing has a formal brand with a name and logo, we suggest creating a summary document that ties together all of the organization's programs and resources to support employee wellbeing. As a starting point for creating an overview, we usually suggest listing each wellbeing area and then all company benefits, programs and resources that support that area *(recognizing, of course, that many things inherently support more than one area of wellbeing)*. Here are some examples of what some companies choose to highlight:

- **Career Wellbeing** — mentoring programs, training and development opportunities, employees participating in strategic and annual planning, employee recognition, strengths-based career planning

- **Social Wellbeing** — adoption assistance, effective communication classes, paid time off, new baby leave for women and men, company-wide social events, Employee Assistance Program, nursing mothers' room

- **Financial Wellbeing** — retirement plans, company-paid disability plans, financial budgeting programs and resources, bonus opportunities

- **Physical Wellbeing** — wider variety of healthful food options available, standing and walking meetings, 100% coverage for preventive care, workshops on intuitive eating and positive body image

- **Emotional Wellbeing** — life purpose and resiliency workshops, relaxation areas, Employee Assistance Program, quarterly "let loose" days

- **Community Wellbeing** — paid time off for volunteering benefit, company-sponsored charitable events, environmental/green initiatives, company-sponsored community help initiatives

Many times when beginning this process, organizations start to realize how much they actually do that supports employee wellbeing. They just weren't thinking of wellbeing and weren't communicating it in that manner. So, instead of having employee wellbeing viewed as an extra program or initiative, it becomes more about repackaging what the company already provides and creating alignment within the organization.

Once you have created a comprehensive list of all the ways the company supports employee wellbeing, select a handful of benefits in each wellbeing area that are the most meaningful and really reflect how the company values its employees. Use those to create an Employee Wellbeing Overview. This can be simple and created in-house using basic software packages, or it can be elaborate, using an outside design firm. What's most important is bringing your employee wellbeing brand to life and creating an appealing communication piece to provide all current and future employees. The following is an example of a simple Employee Wellbeing Overview:

Employee Wellbeing Overview

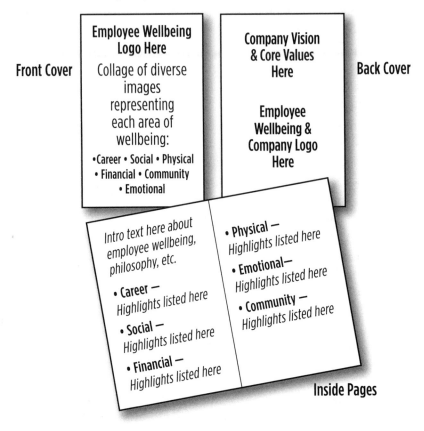

Most of our clients use a color-coding system as part of the employee wellbeing branding; whatever colors are used in the Employee Wellbeing Overview are also used on subsequent communications. For example, if the color chosen for career wellbeing is blue, all flyers, e-mail templates and messaging related to career wellbeing would include shades of blue. And if the color chosen for community wellbeing is purple, all corresponding messaging would include shades of purple. Over time, people start to look for the color(s) that represent(s) the programs and resources they are most interested in to support their wellbeing.

Besides using color, wellbeing is explicitly communicated in messaging, so people start to feel that it truly is embedded in the culture. Here are some examples of messages you might use in e-mails, fliers, newsletter articles and in person that convey the wellbeing language:

- "In ongoing support of your career wellbeing, we will be having an informational session next week on our new mentoring program."

- "To continue supporting your community wellbeing, we are implementing a volunteer benefit that gives you paid time off to help charitable organizations."

- "In support of your financial wellbeing, financial planners will be available to you free of charge during the next month for one-to-one appointments."

- "To support your physical and social wellbeing, we will be forming teams for *(a local walk/run or fitness event)* and would love to have you and your family participate."

When the employee wellbeing brand and language is consistently used by all leaders, marketing, human resources and other employees, it starts the process of embedding wellbeing into your culture. If the only person using the wellbeing branding and language is the person typically responsible for employee wellness, the branding and language won't have the same effect. The branding needs to come to life in daily communication practices.

Employee Wellbeing Leaders' Guide

Intentionally speaking to employee wellbeing in communication is not natural, nor will it likely be at the top of mind for most leaders. However, if you're following the framework for leadership development we described in the previous chapter, expecting leaders to more overtly communicate and support employee wellbeing shouldn't be too much of a stretch. By including personal wellbeing as part of your comprehensive leadership development strategy, all leaders in the organization typically have a greater appreciation for the importance of individual wellbeing — making it more natural to *create the conditions* to support it. That said, we usually include one related workshop as part of any leadership development effort. This session provides an initial framework and guide for how to intentionally support employee wellbeing. We give leaders a basic guidebook and then engage them to tweak and expand the framework to best meet their needs *(knowing they are much more likely to support what they have helped to create)*. Here are some common components of a leaders' guide for providing inspiration to effectively support employee wellbeing:

- **Why Wellbeing Matters** — includes sample messaging and talking points to support leaders in conveying the message to their teams of why the organization cares about individual wellbeing.

- **Thriving in Your Personal Wellbeing** — includes personal reflection exercises *(that support the other development work they are hopefully doing)* to support leaders in fostering their own wellbeing, along with suggestions for how they can convey their own personal wellbeing journey to their teams to create a safe space for doing self-work.

- **Communicating and Reinforcing Wellbeing** — includes activities and resources to support leaders in being change agents, sample language to use to promote wellbeing, sample team meeting agendas for including dialogue on culture and wellbeing, and sample dialogue for meeting with individual employees.

Creating the Conditions for Thriving Organizational and Employee Wellbeing

Creating a climate that supports a thriving workplace culture starts with quality leaders who walk the talk to support both organizational and employee wellbeing. It also includes aligning your communication, policies, environment and daily business practices with your desired culture so that people truly feel valued, are supported to stretch themselves, can grow personally as well as professionally, and know wellbeing really matters. Organizations that put this all together are likely to become great places to work and employers of choice.

Summary of Transformation Point #4
Frame the House: Create a Supportive Climate

Organizational Wellbeing	Employee Wellbeing
• Leaders clearly articulate the culture change vision and expectations for living the culture	• Embed wellbeing as part of the culture change journey; reposition wellbeing as a benefit or platform for how the organization supports employees and the employee experience
• Identify behaviors consistent with desired culture and those that might sabotage the desired culture	• Create a Culture and Wellbeing Team and network of Ambassadors
• Hire, develop people and *(if necessary)* fire based on culture fit first	• Develop an integrated wellbeing communication plan
• *Create the conditions* for employees to leverage their strengths and talents each day	• Engage employees in developing an employee wellbeing brand
• Support and encourage innovation and taking risks	• Create an Employee Wellbeing Overview
• Provide opportunities for profound personal and professional development	• Provide leaders with a guide for how to intentionally support wellbeing and engage them to determine how they can best *create the conditions* for support
• Leaders truly walk the talk in terms of employees feeling valued and knowing their wellbeing matters	• Ensure physical environment, policies and practices support thriving wellbeing and are aligned with the culture

CHAPTER 12
Transformation Point #5:
Wire the House
(Rethink Change)

We have to accept two simple truths:
We can't force anybody to change, and no two people see the world the
same way. We can only engage people in the change process from the
beginning and see what's possible. If the issue is meaningful to them,
they will become enthusiastic and bright advocates. If we want people's
intelligence and support, we must welcome them as co-creators.
People only support what they create.[1]

Margaret Wheatley, "Finding Our Way"

As we explored in previous chapters, having the ability to activate I>E>S in our own thinking allows us to create a space for others to have their own insights and guide their own change. One of the stories that always resonates with us involves a nurse, Karen, who was brought in to assist with a situation involving a man we'll call Bruce. By "stubbornly refusing" to put his mother into hospice care, Bruce was prolonging her suffering and depriving someone else of the long-term care bed. The other nurses had already labeled Bruce as "difficult" because they could not change his mind; now it was Karen's turn to work with him.

As Karen began talking to Bruce, she put into practice the fundamental elements she had learned in her Intrinsic Coaching® training to see more than what was merely apparent *(i.e., to be able to value and see the Intrinsic)* and disable the dominance of her Systemic *(S)* thinking. She asked him, "What are you wanting that is important to you regarding your mother's care?" That question *(and her ability to listen more fully and not interrupt him)* brought out a story no one had previously heard — because no one had asked the question. Bruce's mother had adopted him from an orphanage when he was little. He felt she saved him and he owed her his life. Now a team of healthcare professionals was asking him to give up on the woman who had never given up on him; he just couldn't do it. Now that Karen had this new insight into Bruce, she shifted her approach.

- Karen's internal dialogue *(her Systemic thinking)* gave her the impulse to try to convince Bruce that he wouldn't be giving up on his mother. However, she recognized the impulse for what it was — her trying to get him to replace his thoughts with hers and then judging him for refusing, which is what everyone else had already done. With that recognition, she was able to stay quiet and listen.

- She told Bruce she was going to change his mother's dressings and asked him if he wanted to stay and see the extent of her condition; he said he did. Before he had always been asked to leave, and now he had been asked to be a part of the process. As they talked, Bruce asked Karen questions, and she answered them and also asked him again what he wanted for his mother's care based on what he was experiencing now.

- Karen realized how limited she would have been by not leading with her Intrinsic thinking with Bruce. By activating I>E>S in her own thinking, she created a space for him to have new thinking and clarity about what he wanted for himself and his mother. His mother had dedicated everything she had to protecting him from pain and surrounding him with all the comfort she, as a loving mother, could provide. Now it was his turn to do the same for her — to protect her from pain and surround her with comfort, as only her loving son could do. Bruce realized on his own that a hospice environment could give his mother all that he wanted for her.

- By tapping into her Intrinsic thinking *(as a result of having increased intrinsic capacity)*, Karen provided a completely different experience for herself, her patient and Bruce. The other nurses were amazed she was able to "get through" to Bruce, but Karen knew her shift in thinking was what made all the difference.

Create Moments of Insight

Even with a solid foundation and a well-framed house with a supportive climate, individuals and organizations do not change easily. People are complex beings, and organizational change is really about changing people — which involves leading through adaptive challenges and asking people to think instead of being on "autopilot." It is not surprising that even when people change in organizations, these individuals often return to previous behaviors unless a new equilibrium is established where the change becomes a cultural norm.[2]

Effectively leading change is not about forcing it on people; instead, it requires deliberately *creating the conditions* for innovation. It starts with shifting the locus of responsibility for problem solving from the executive suite to the collective intelligence of employees at all levels.[3] This makes sense, as we have already established what happens in the brain when we are told what to do; we automatically push back like we're two years old. But when we solve problems ourselves, the brain releases neurotransmitters that provide an adrenaline-like rush while creating a complex set of new connections to enhance our mental resources and overcome the brain's resistance to change. Consequently, facilitating change starts by cultivating moments of insight for people.[4] These insights need to be generated from within, not given to people as conclusions and directions to follow. If we want to support people's efforts to change the way they think or behave, the best way is to learn to recognize, encourage and deepen their insights.[5] So asking powerful questions and providing the support and the conditions for employees to have new insights and thinking and to find their own solutions is the best way to "wire the house," so to speak.

When people are more aware of their thinking and elevate the value of the Intrinsic dimension, activating I>E>S for themselves and others, they get better results in life. People describe being less frustrated with others, having less job-related stress and feeling higher levels of job satisfaction.[6] Thriving organizational and employee wellbeing requires rethinking change to build on a different foundation than we currently use; it requires moving away from controlling behaviors and focusing on "quick fixes" to developing better thinking — including activating I>E>S thinking when it comes to people. Before we explore "wiring the house" in a way that *creates the conditions* for thriving organizational and employee wellbeing, we want to look at the evidence as it relates to current theories and models of change.

Overview of Theories and Models of Change

In chapter 6, we explored the Evolution of Motivation and how the 17th-century mechanistic, reductionist worldview, along with its outdated science, has kept us *stuck* when it comes to change. We also explored new understandings from science and research that are shaping a more effective way to support and foster sustainable change. Because we are ultimately talking about changing people, we must understand the evidence regarding how people change. So bear with us for just a moment while we briefly examine how the evolution of theories and models of change are shaping how we think about individual change.

Transtheoretical Model/Stages of Change

The Transtheoretical Model of Behavior Change *(TTM)* is also frequently referred to as Stages of Change and is the dominant model used in trying to change health behaviors. Developed by Dr. James Prochaska and colleagues, TTM assesses an individual's readiness to act on a new, healthier behavior and provides strategies, or processes of change, to guide the individual through the proposed stages of change. In general, TTM states for people to progress through the stages, they need:

- to see the pros of changing outweighing the cons *(decision balance)*
- confidence they can maintain changes in situations that will challenge them to revert to old behaviors *(self-efficacy)*
- strategies and processes to help them maintain the change[7]

There are five stages of change in TTM:

- **Stage One:** *Precontemplation.* People at this stage are not ready to change and have no intention of changing within six months. According to TTM, encouraging people to be more conscious of the benefits of changing their behavior can help at this stage. A typical approach at this stage is to give people the facts about the risks and benefits of their behavior in the hopes they will become more aware of needing to change.

- **Stage Two:** *Contemplation.* People at this stage are said to be thinking about changing within the next six months. According

228

to TTM, encouraging people to work at reducing the cons of changing their behavior can help. A typical approach at this stage might be to ask you to visualize yourself practicing healthier behaviors or to pick a role model who might inspire you.

- **Stage Three:** *Preparation.* People at this stage are ready to start taking action within the next 30 days. According to TTM, this is where people get things ready to change and create a support structure. A typical recommendation at this stage might be to encourage you to set a behavior change goal, tell people who can support you, and plan for how to replace the unhealthy behaviors you are trying to change.

- **Stage Four:** *Action.* People at this stage have already made changes in their health behaviors within the past six months and are working towards making the changes permanent. A typical recommendation at this stage might be to give yourself rewards along the way as you meet certain milestones towards your health behavior goal.

- **Stage Five:** *Maintenance.* People at this stage changed their behaviors more than six months ago, so the focus is on maintenance and not slipping back to old unhealthy behaviors during stressful times. A typical recommendation at this stage might be to remove any temptation *(e.g., unhealthy foods)* from your house so you don't make it easy to fall back into old unhealthy habits.

TTM recognizes that progression through the stages of change can be non-linear. However, even with this recognition that change can take a long time, some of TTM's recommendations, and the way they are often applied, mirror the 17th-century mechanistic worldview. The assumption is that people are predictable and can be controlled and manipulated. TTM usually narrowly focuses on one health behavior at a time, not accounting for the complexities of being human. We can't tell you how many wellness vendors report success by how many people progressed through the various stages of change. They will say something like, "15% of employees moved from precontemplation to contemplation" and so on — as if movement through a stage makes a difference; and as if once they are there, they will move on to the next stage and not regress to an earlier one.

Around the time that TTM was becoming so popular, I *(Jon)* had a discussion about it with one of the leaders in the health promotion field who was extolling its virtues. He said, "What I like about TTM is that it makes things simple for practitioners in the field." I responded that what I ***didn't*** like about TTM was that it made things simple for practitioners in the field. Promoting change "in the field," or anywhere else for that matter, is anything but simple, as others have pointed out.[8] Furthermore, if you do a literature review of the studies using TTM, you will find that the overwhelming majority apply TTM to addictive behaviors *(e.g., smoking, alcohol and drug use)* — which are arguably quite different from other lifestyle behaviors and certainly different than trying to promote change on an organizational level. In fact, the appropriateness and efficacy of TTM for more complicated health behaviors, like those involved with most workplace wellness programs, has been challenged by numerous researchers.[9] Also note that, particularly in the action stage, the approaches to change fall back on the Skinnerian carrot-and-stick techniques with the many associated pitfalls and dangers we previously discussed.

Intentional Change Theory

Just as we evolved with our understanding of human behavior and motivation from Skinner, our understanding of change has evolved since Prochaska. The idea of change being smooth, continuous, predictable and relatively simple does not fit with the experiences of most people. True to what we know from complexity and chaos theory, change is a complex process, both on an individual and an organizational level. Change involves all the complexities surrounding the relationship between individuals and the collectivism of corporate or societal cultures.[10]

The Intentional Change Theory *(ICT)* evolved out of management and organizational studies in 2006. The theory claims that "there is more to the self than what organizations have recognized, let alone leveraged toward employee productivity and satisfaction."[11] ICT describes the change process as being non-linear and discontinuous and is often experienced as a set of discoveries or epiphanies. The process begins with someone having a desire to change, whether it is conscious or through a moment or event that awakens him or her. Then, the change process involves a sequence of discoveries that function as an iterative cycle to produce sustainable change at an individual level that looks something like this:

- **Identifying my ideal self and personal vision** *(not to be confused with who I think I should be; but rather, my greater purpose and who I want to be in life)*; activating my ideal self serves a motivational function to guide all my actions and decisions toward deeper self-satisfaction. Once I am clear about my desired future state, I am emotionally fueled by hope and self-efficacy.[12]

- **Having a greater understanding of my current real self** *(and then comparing where I am today to my ideal self to assess my strengths and weaknesses).*

- **Creating my learning agenda and plan to move towards my ideal self.**

- **Experimenting and practicing with my new thoughts,** feelings, perceptions and behaviors; and when things don't work, using that feedback to inform myself and make adjustments to my plan and my journey.

- **Having trusting relationships** that enable me to process and experience each discovery in the process.[13]

If organizations want to foster intentional change, they will benefit greatly from supporting this path of self-discovery with employees so they can ultimately guide adaptive changes as they emerge. This approach to change seems to align much better with the new sciences and what we know about the power of connectedness and relationships, feedback loops, and ultimately finding meaning in our lives and working toward a greater purpose.

Theory U

At the same time that ICT was emerging, Theory U surfaced as a framework and method for leading profound change via connecting to the more authentic, higher aspects of our selves. C. Otto Scharmer suggests that in a time of profound institutional failures, collectively creating results no one wants, we need a new consciousness and collective leadership capacity to meet challenges in a more intentional, strategic way. Theory U suggests that:

The success of our actions as change-makers does not depend on What we do or How we do it, but on the Inner Place from which we operate.[14]

Essentially, this framework recognizes that we can't transform the behavior of systems unless we transform the quality of awareness and attention that people apply to their actions within these systems, both individually and collectively. Like what we know from chaos theory,

> **The success of our actions as change-makers does not depend on What we do or How we do it, but on the Inner Place from which we operate.**

the proposition of Theory U is that instead of learning from the past, we need to learn from the emerging future.

At the core of Theory U is *presencing (sensing + presence)*. If you imagine a big "U," we move down one side of the U that connects us to our habitual thinking and to the outside world, to the bottom of the U that connects us to the world that emerges from within us. At this place, we have to let go of old thinking, our old ego and self, and start to connect to our future possible self — which requires slowing down, pausing and having a different level of listening. This is much like the process we describe in *Transformation Point #2* for understanding the current state of your culture

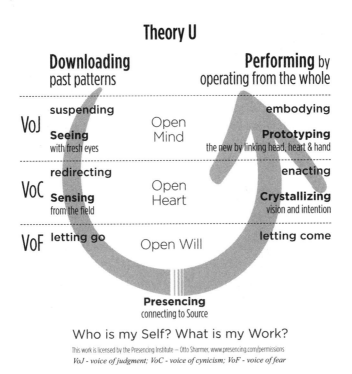

Theory U

Downloading past patterns

Performing by operating from the whole

VoJ — suspending / **Seeing** with fresh eyes

Open Mind

embodying / **Prototyping** the new by linking head, heart & hand

VoC — redirecting / **Sensing** from the field

Open Heart

enacting / **Crystallizing** vision and intention

VoF — letting go

Open Will

letting come

Presencing connecting to Source

Who is my Self? What is my Work?

This work is licensed by the Presencing Institute — Otto Sharmer, www.presencing.com/permissions

VoJ - voice of judgment; VoC - voice of cynicism; VoF - voice of fear

and where you desire to be. Once our current and our best future selves meet and begin to resonate with each other, we move up the other side of the U, bringing forward the new thinking into the world. This process can happen on an individual or an organizational level.[15]

Susan's Journey to *Presencing*

Like many leaders, Susan was experiencing the overload of trying to do it all — lead her team at work, respond to pressures and responsibilities from senior management, be a good mom and cultivate personal relationships — while trying to find the time to care for her own wellbeing. Her fellow leaders were also experiencing a sense of overload; consequently, they were *stuck* and unable to come up with inspiring strategies for expanding their organization's product and service offerings. They were becoming very task-focused and ineffective in communicating with one another. Susan and her colleagues were *stuck*. They knew what they should be doing but were unable to figure out how to actually do it! They kept reverting back to typical task-focused goal setting and action plans. They held planning meetings to brainstorm new products and services, and continued to focus on what more they could do — adding to their overloaded plates rather than looking at what and how they could approach work differently. They were also encouraged to set personal action plans for exercising and trying to take care of their health — adding even more onto their overloaded plates. Like her fellow leaders, Susan continued to look to her past for answers for how to handle her current and future challenges but wasn't really getting anywhere; it was a vicious cycle of *doing* more and *being* less.

Susan's boss was known for taking risks and experimenting. This time his experiment paid off; he hired a well-respected leadership coach, Steven, to work with Susan and the other leaders for eight months. Initially, Susan was annoyed; she didn't have time to sit and have conversations with a coach about the things she needed to change. But Susan decided to be open to the process. Steven created a space for Susan to start to focus her attention inward rather than on people and situations outside of herself. As Susan's focus turned inward, she started to see how much she was looking to her past for solutions to her current challenges. She felt lost and uncomfortable. But as she learned to set aside her old self and old thinking, she found a place of stillness in her mind — a place where she started to gain greater clarity about who she was at her core, what mattered to her and what she wanted for herself based on where she was now; Susan experienced *presencing*.

Once Susan had greater clarity about what she wanted for herself, Steven supported her in using that clarity to create a vision for turning what she was wanting into a reality. Susan slowly learned to become keenly aware of her habitual self and to let it go so she could encourage her best future self to emerge and guide her. She was able to let go of much of her self-judgment and worries and learned to communicate in a different way, thereby creating the support structure she needed to allow her to have more of the things she wanted. At the end of their time working with Steven, Susan and her fellow leaders met with one another and shared what they learned about themselves and what they all needed so they could support one another. This created a great sense of community among the leaders. They used their new way of thinking and ability to find *presencing* to redesign how they were going about business strategy and operations — so they could lead from the emerging future rather than from the past. They phased out some products, services and operations that didn't really make sense anymore and were able to better engage their employees to help create the future. Not only did Susan's engagement at work increase, but so did that of her colleagues and their employees. The employees could sense a difference in the leaders and responded positively.

Susan was also able to find *presencing* as it related to her personal life. She started to let go of beating herself up because she wasn't able to meal plan, exercise and tend to her friendships like she once did. In learning from the emerging future, Susan looked at the realities of her life today and rethought how she wanted her relationships, her health and her overall well-being to be to support her in bringing forward her best self. And as life continues to change, Susan is better able to find stillness in her mind and *presencing* to guide her journey. Susan has learned that it's not about being perfect, but about being true to herself and flexible, to honor what matters to her most within the context of the challenges life throws her way.

Adaptive Solution Dynamic

Susan's initial story is not unique; she was looking to the past and trying to apply technical solutions when what she was facing was adaptive change. It is no wonder that most attempts for individual change fail, and most employee wellness programs don't work for improving individual wellbeing. We've already established the complexities of being human and of wellbeing. Changing thinking and behaviors requires adaptive change; however, our typical approach is to apply technical solutions to adaptive challenges.

The Adaptive Solution Dynamic *(ASD)* was developed by Dr. Barbara Daiker to describe the three interrelated components that occur when a leader is supporting an organization in finding solutions to an adaptive challenge:

- **Rational Tools** — includes the data typically used to support the technical aspects of change *(forecasting, profit-and-loss analysis, etc.)*.

- **Relationship Commitment** — both internal and external relationships are critical and need to be productive in order to align everyone with the strategy and vision for change.

- **Achievement Drive** — refers to the determination and effort of leadership to continue moving towards a positive direction, regardless of barriers or frustrations along the way.[16]

ASD recognizes the complexities of organizations embarking upon adaptive change. No one component is effective by itself. However, in relationship with one another, and with clear vision and strategy at the center guiding change efforts, organizations can effectively grow through adaptive challenges.

The approaches suggested by ICT, Theory U, and ASD align well with the New Paradigm, recognizing that the whole is greater than the sum of its parts and that sustainable change emerges within a culture that fosters supportive relationships. Now that we are a little more familiar with change models that better align with the new sciences, let's explore how we apply the models to support organizational and employee wellbeing.

Better Thinking to Support Organizational Wellbeing

In workplace cultures where organizational and employee wellbeing thrive, change is embraced and encouraged. After all, we know the only certainty in this life besides death and taxes is change. How do your organization and your employees view change? Is it embraced or dreaded?

Here are some questions you may want to ponder regarding the role of change in your culture:

- How do you plan and prepare for change?
- Do you view new challenges as opportunities for growth?
- Do you encourage and support change?
- Do your employees lead change? In other words, do you specifically encourage and support change from the bottom up as much as from the top down?

When it comes to change, leaders need to think of running businesses with human beings who don't like being controlled and who identify best with small groups.[17] If organizations want to have engaged and intrinsically motivated employees who can face adaptive challenges, companies need to *create the conditions* for:

- Autonomy *(people being able to think and do for themselves)*
- Mastery *(people having opportunities to learn and grow, and become highly skilled)*
- Purpose *(people to feel their work is meaningful and connected to a greater purpose and vision)*[18]

The more employees can work together to guide the change process, the greater the likelihood that it will be successful.[19] At Zappos, employees are encouraged never to accept or be comfortable with the status quo because not responding quickly and adapting to change can be devastating. So Zappos employees are encouraged, supported and recognized for bringing forward new ideas *(autonomy)*. Employees are provided constant opportunities for growth and development *(mastery)*, and the leaders ensure that all employees have great clarity on the culture and vision, and how they fit into the picture *(purpose)*.[20]

Leaders also must recognize the power of the human need for immediate gratification and that conscious reasoning isn't what directs our actions. Therefore, to support people in acting in accordance with longer-term goals, it is essential to keep in mind the vision of the future you're working toward while also being willing to challenge conventional wisdom so you can completely reinvent the business.[21] In his book, "Management Rewired," Charles Jacobs states that what most managers typically do fails in practice; he suggests that they need to ***stop doing*** most of what they're doing today, including:

- Rewarding good performance as often as possible
- Punishing poor performance
- Giving timely feedback on performance problems
- Prescribing corrective action for performance problems
- Setting measurable objectives
- Making an effort to closely supervise employees[22]

A growing body of research suggests that old-fashioned performance appraisals often create fear, reduce performance and generate stress.[23] Additionally, the more responsibility managers hold, the less responsibility employees have to accept. Instead of closely managing performance, Jacobs suggests managers should turn the tables upside down and put as much responsibility on the employees as possible, so that:

- Rather than telling employees what to do, the manager should ask them what they think needs to be done.
- Rather than handing objectives to the employee, the manager should ask the employee to set them.
- Rather than giving employees feedback on their performance, the manager should ask them how they think they are doing.
- Rather than telling employees how to fix a problem, the manager should ask them what they think they should do to fix it.[24]

We definitely have come a long way since the scientific management of Taylorism of a century ago! Certainly, this is a more complicated way to manage; in principle it seems quicker and easier to give direct feedback and exert direct control. But as we learned in chapter 6, what seems quicker, easier and more direct actually is not as effective and can end up causing more unintended consequences than if you take the time to engage employees to think for themselves. The solution is to provide clarity of vision and support, and then give employees autonomy to create their own change process; in other words, treat them like adults.

Better Thinking to Support Employee Wellbeing

We've already discussed the importance of addressing the complexities of the human experience and seeing people as holistic, thinking beings. In doing so, it no longer makes sense to try to control behaviors with carrots and sticks. It also doesn't make sense to invest a lot of time and resources toward narrow biomedical risk factors. If you want to support employees' wellbeing and help them embark upon a meaningful, sustainable change journey, *create the conditions* to support employees and then let them be the authors of their own journey.

> **If you want to support employees' wellbeing and help them embark upon a meaningful, sustainable change journey, *create the conditions* to support them and then let them be the authors of their own journey.**

Supporting better thinking for employees naturally lends itself to coaching. However, not all coaching is equal. For the purposes of this discussion, we want to make a very important distinction between coaching applied in the Old Paradigm way, to try to "get" people to be intrinsically motivated *(i.e., Motivation 3.0)* and coaching applied in the New Paradigm way, to elicit better thinking *(i.e., Motivation 4.0).*

Why Health Coaching via Motivation 3.0 Doesn't Work

Health coaching as a means to facilitate behavior change continues to increase in popularity. Unfortunately, often the faulty assumption is that using incentives to get employees to complete a coaching program will result in sustained change. Most health coaching provided by wellness vendors, healthcare providers and insurance companies is based on Motivational Interviewing *(MI)*. MI is focused on trying to elicit motivation within a person and resolve ambivalence regarding changing a particular health behavior. However, how MI has been applied in employee wellness has often veered far from its original intent. For starters, the training is not consistent; MI is supposed to be taught in an initial two-day workshop with suggestions for ongoing practice and feedback that can take years to result in proficiency. However, in our "quick fix" society, people can attend a two-day workshop to be "certified" and can then use MI in coaching. Yet we've already established how this short-term approach to learning doesn't work or make sense. Unfortunately, quality control in MI practice and training has been non-existent.[25]

Even with quality training and application, we question whether MI actually shifts thinking for the coach or the recipient. I *(Rosie)* have had countless discussions with physicians, psychologists, health educators and others who have had MI-based coaching training. In each case, even for those who have been training and practicing for years, it is evident the people are approaching supporting change from an S>E>I framework — trying to use MI as a tool in the toolbox to "motivate" others to change or to "get" them to be intrinsically motivated. In reality, the Intrinsic is often missing altogether; I>E>S is not activated in the thinking of the coach or the client. If it were, it would be reasonable to presume that MI could overcome the pitfalls of incentives and improve health. However, a 2012 study looked at the impact of financial incentives on completing health coaching-based behavior change programs *(using MI techniques)* and subsequent risk reduction. The researchers found that offering financial incentives for completing the program was associated with higher program completion rates but not with changes in health risks or improved health.[26] How do we explain this?

Let's look at how most health coaching *(particularly coaching based in MI)* addresses behavior change. The approach is "simple." The health coach tries to assess where a person is in terms of Stages of Change and then asks fairly scripted questions intended to "get" the person to move along the change continuum, closer to taking action. For example, the health coach might say something like:

- *"On a scale of 1 to 10, how motivated are you right now to engage in ABC behavior?"*
- *"On a scale of 1 to 10, how confident are you in your ability to engage in ABC behavior?"*
- *"Tell me all the reasons why exercising is important to you."*
- *"What benefits would you gain from losing weight?"*
- *"What is the downside of NOT doing XYZ health behavior?"*

The problem here, of course, is that this approach stems from a mechanistic, simple, cause-and-effect worldview that assumes people are predictable and can be manipulated if we just ask the right questions. If the coach just asks these questions, it should "get" employees to see why that health behavior is important and then they'll be motivated to make changes, right?! Yet, we know the process is much more complex than this.

Although perhaps an improvement over Skinner's carrots and sticks, this is clearly still an outside-in approach that puts people in a passive role. Health coaches sit in the driver's seat — supposedly knowing what's best for their clients and asking questions with a motive to try to "get" individuals to change specific health behaviors that the coach, their doctor or some HRA decided they needed to change. Furthermore, in most typical conversations like the above examples, the clients are put in a defensive role to explain why they rated themselves a certain way; then the coach jumps right to strategies trying to "get" the clients to come up with ways to move to a higher number and take action. The clients are essentially being asked to tap into old, Systemic thinking to apply a technical solution to an adaptive challenge. Trying to "get" people to be intrinsically motivated doesn't make sense.

These typical health coaching conversations are also almost always reductionist — narrowly focused on one or two specific, isolated health behaviors. Yet we know we cannot separate and isolate aspects of our wellbeing. Rarely in these conversations is there silence and *pausing* encouraged, and rarely are people invited to look at their greater purpose and what they want for themselves. Sustainability doesn't come from people recalling a memory of an answer a health coach gave them; it comes from tapping into best thinking in moments of decision. So how do you create a culture that supports better thinking?

- **Ensure Transformation Points 1-4 are in place.** Effective thinking stems from trusting, safe relationships. If organizational wellbeing is suffering, it will be impossible to *create the conditions* for individual employees to find their best thinking and to create meaningful change.

- **Incorporate I>E>S in meetings, training programs and workshops.** This means valuing employees' thinking about situations and information more than the information itself. Embrace and support space for pause and reflection; then engage employees to think, and make it safe for them to do so.

- **Provide access to highly skilled Certified Intrinsic Coach®️ coaches.** Instead of providing typical health coaches taking an S>E>I approach and failing to truly engage employees to change lifestyle behaviors, provide access to coaches who can activate I>E>S in their own thinking and support employees as whole beings to find better thinking about whatever matters to them and their wellbeing.

"Correcting" for or Minimizing Damage from Incentives

We know from the research that once an incentive is in place, you have to keep it *(and regularly increase it)* to produce the same temporary behavior change and compliance. We regularly hear people say, "But our organization is already well down the path of using incentives. Is there a way we can move away from incentives without it blowing up in our face?" The really good news is yes, you can. Let's explore an example of what one company did to "correct" for incentives and shift their Old Paradigm employee wellness program.

Redesigning Employee Wellbeing at Piper Associates

One client we'll call Piper Associates is a light manufacturing firm with about 350 employees. The company had a traditional wellness program in place for five years that was focused on lifestyle behaviors and biomedical risk factor reduction. Piper hired a vendor who conducted required annual biometric screenings and HRAs for employees, and facilitated some four-to-six week wellness challenges throughout the year. If employees participated in the program, they received a reduction in their health insurance premiums.

Although the annual vendor reports showed projected costs savings due to risk reduction *(we will discuss the problems with these kinds of claims in the next chapter),* Piper still experienced annual increases in healthcare costs. The leadership team was concerned that employees were just "going through the motions" with the wellness program and was considering moving toward requiring employees to meet specific health outcomes to receive the reduced insurance premium. Piper had also acquired two new locations within the past three years and was having lots of issues with morale and engagement at those newer locations.

We worked with Piper to go back to the drawing board and fill in the gaps needed to better support organizational wellbeing while also redesigning its wellness program.

- Piper took a break from HRAs and screenings, and redeployed that money to provide programs and resources that better supported all areas of wellbeing;

- Piper moved away from having a wellness program to launching a wellbeing benefit. Employees were engaged by leadership to help create and brand the new wellbeing benefit;

- Wellbeing was incorporated into leadership development curriculum and communication started linking wellbeing, to be more a part of daily business operations *(just like employee safety)*; and

- They redesigned their incentive program.

Piper's leaders didn't feel they could just get rid of the incentive program, but they did let us help them redesign it. Their previous program had a point-based structure; after employees completed the required HRA and biometric screening, they had to earn 200 points from various activities. We changed the required activity to completing a culture survey and a healthcare consumerism workshop *(more on that in the next chapter)*. Then we created a new option for earning points; employees could earn 150 of the 200 required points by intentionally working on their own wellbeing with the support of a coach.

We were very deliberate in our language and did not want to say "set a goal" or something that would lend itself to more S>E>I. Employees earned their points by completing five sessions with a Certified Intrinsic Coach® and completing a short reflection at the end of their coaching experience. Employees initially saw this as an easy way to earn points; 90% of the program participants signed up for this criterion. The burden was on the coaches to create a space for employees to become more self-aware and have better thinking — knowing that most of the employees didn't really want to be there and were hoping to just go through the motions. By having skilled coaches who could activate I>E>S in themselves and create a space for I>E>S for the employees, Piper saw a profound shift. When evaluating the incentive part of the program, employees actually provided positive feedback for once and said they finally felt the program met their unique needs. Many also showed appreciation for the company providing them access to their coach and not having to talk about their HRA results. And the feedback employees provided in the reflection survey showed a great increase in self-awareness.

Over the course of the next three years, Piper backed off more and more from its traditional wellness offerings. Leaders made a point to communicate feedback regarding the culture survey and the coaching experiences while working to improve organizational wellbeing. Piper also slowly reduced the amount of the incentives. Guess what? Participation in coaching didn't drop; it actually increased. More importantly, survey feedback showed a continuous decrease in the importance people placed on the incentive for participating and an increase in people caring about their own wellbeing. Piper still has a way to go with integrating the acquired locations, but it is much further along on its organizational and employee wellbeing journey than the company was a few years ago — and they are spending less money on incentives and ineffective wellness vendor services, allowing resources for coaching and other programs and resources employees actually appreciate.

For companies looking to further reduce their reliance on incentives *(perhaps eventually doing away with them altogether)*, as well as diminish the negative outcomes that often occur with their use, the following steps, pulled from reviews of the literature, can also be taken:

- Reward varying levels of accomplishment
- Reward a broad range of behaviors/balance
- Use smaller rather than larger rewards
- Use non-contingent *(now-that rather than if-then)* rewards[27]

Fostering Autonomy — A Path with Heart

This chapter was intended to frame a different path for creating and supporting change for humans and organizations, a path more in line with the latest understandings of the nature of physical reality and the complexities of the human experience. As we move from a control-oriented, biomedical, scientific management approach to change, our focus becomes less on manipulating behavior and more on nurturing autonomy. In his groundbreaking work, "A New Ethic for Health Promotion: Reflections on a Philosophy of Health Education for the 21st Century," Dr. David R. Buchanan sums up the pressing need for this alternative:

> *Instead of devoting all of our time and energy to creating the technologies of behavior control, I think that we should be moving in precisely the opposite direction: We should be doing everything in our*

power to increase human autonomy. Instead of seeking to develop programs that are more effective in altering people's behavior, we should focus on aiding people to make their own choices about how they want to live in light of their best understanding of the good life for themselves.[28]

It is within this framework that we next discuss the programs and resources that can best bring about the wellbeing of organizations and the employees who work within them.

Summary of Transformation Point #5
Wire the House: Rethink Change

Old Paradigm	New Paradigm
Theories/Models of Change	
• Skinner – Behavior Modification	• Intentional Change Theory *(ICT)*
• Transtheoretical Model *(TTM)*	• Theory U
	• Adaptive Solution Dynamic *(ASD)*
Fostering Engagement & Productivity	
• Give Feedback	• Foster Autonomy
• Manage Performance	• Enable Mastery
• Provide Rewards/Punishments	• Support Purpose
Health / Wellbeing Coaching	
• "Motivate" employees	• Engage employees
• S>E>I	• I>E>S

CHAPTER 13

Transformation Point #6:
Decorate the House
(Deploy QUALITY, Evidence-Based Programs and Resources)

> 66 *Most research suggests that the best way to reduce medical spending and absenteeism is to establish a culture that makes people want to go to work.*[1] 99

Tom Emerick, "Cracking Health Costs"

Now that the house is standing on a firm foundation and is structurally sound, it is time to start decorating by deploying programs and resources to support a thriving workplace culture. Although most of these programs will likely focus on employee wellbeing, when properly implemented, these programs can help both employee and organizational wellbeing to thrive. Unfortunately, deploying programs is too often where employee wellness initiatives start; organizations want to "do stuff." However, we have shown how essential it is to first implement *Transformation Points #1-5* if you want any program or resource to be integrated into your organizational culture and have lasting results. We cannot emphasize this enough: deploying programs and resources on a faulty foundation will NOT work!

> **We cannot emphasize this enough: deploying programs and resources on a faulty foundation will NOT work!**

In this chapter, we explore the quality, evidence-based programs and resources that support creating a culture in which organizational and employee wellbeing can thrive. Most strategies to improve and support a thriving workplace culture will likely include a variety of these, tailored of course, to meet the unique needs of your employees and organization. Which programs and resources you deploy and how you implement them is of critical importance. Here are some questions you might want to ask yourself before deciding to offer programs or resources:

- Are the programs and resources evidence-based?
- Will they support and foster both organizational and employee wellbeing?

- Might they negatively impact one or the other?
- Do they include support for all areas of wellbeing?
- Do they especially support the areas of wellbeing that matter most to our employees?
- Did we ask employees which areas of wellbeing matter most to them?
- Are we being fiscally responsible with resources in selecting the programs and resources that will make the greatest impact in creating a thriving workplace culture?

Because what organizations typically do in the name of supporting employee wellbeing does not allow a "yes" response to many of these questions, we begin our discussion of programs and resources by exploring the limitations and pitfalls of the traditional 4P *(pry, prod, poke and punish)* approach to wellness and then move ahead to what can be done instead.

Background: The Affordable Care Act Wellness Provisions

Employee wellness programs are now largely being driven by the wellness provisions of the Affordable Care Act (ACA). Before going further in our discussion about programs and resources to consider and those to avoid, we want to address motivation, incentives and change within the context of the ACA. Here, we provide a brief summary of the provision details. *(More detailed descriptions can be found elsewhere.)* There are two main types of programs described:[2]

1) Participatory Wellness Programs. Participatory *(or "participation-only")* wellness programs are programs that either do not provide a reward, or do not include any conditions for obtaining a reward based on satisfying a standard related to a health factor. Examples of participatory wellness programs include: gym membership reimbursements, diagnostic testing that rewards participation but does not base any part of the reward on the outcome, and rewards for attending no-cost health education seminars. These programs cannot adjust benefits or health insurance premiums based on a health factor, only on participating or completing a program.

2) Health-Contingent Wellness Programs. In contrast to participatory wellness programs, "health-contingent" wellness programs require an individual to satisfy a standard related to a health factor to obtain a reward or avoid a penalty. A health-contingent wellness program may involve performing or completing an activity related to a health factor or attaining or maintaining a specific health outcome. Health-contingent wellness programs are further divided into two types: "activity-only" and "outcome-based" wellness programs.

> • In an **activity-only wellness program**, an individual must perform or complete an activity related to a health factor to obtain a reward or avoid a penalty. An activity-only wellness program does not require the participant to attain or maintain a specific health outcome. Examples include completing a walking, diet, exercise or stress management program.

> • In an **outcome-based wellness program**, an individual must attain or maintain a specific behavior change or health outcome, such as not smoking, losing weight or receiving certain results on a biometric screening to obtain a reward or avoid a penalty. These programs usually have two parts: **1)** a measurement, test or screening as part of the initial standard; and **2)** an intervention that targets individuals who do not meet the initial standard with wellness activities. Examples of outcome-based wellness programs include tests for specific medical conditions or risk factors *(e.g, high cholesterol, high blood pressure, "abnormal" BMI, tobacco use or high glucose)*. These programs provide a reward to employees who are within a normal or healthy range but require individuals outside the normal or healthy range to take additional steps to obtain the reward or avoid the penalty. Such additional steps can include, but are not limited to, meeting with a health coach, taking a health or fitness course, participating in a tobacco cessation program, adhering to a health improvement action plan or complying with a healthcare provider's care plan.

The ACA wellness provisions increased the amount of reward/penalty permissible for health-contingent wellness programs. The maximum reward/penalty is now 30% of the total cost of health coverage, including both employer and employee premium contributions for the benefit option in which the employee is enrolled. In the case of smoking cessation, the maximum was increased to 50%. For health-contingent wellness programs, this includes both incentives *(such as discounts or rebates on premiums, waivers of cost-sharing, additional benefits and any financial or other incentive)*, as well as penalties *(such as surcharges or other financial or nonfinancial disincentives)*. Individuals must be given the opportunity to qualify for the reward at least once each year.

The workplace wellness industry has embraced the ACA wellness provisions as a "huge win" for employee wellness programs. And without understanding or questioning the evidence behind these wellness provisions, employers, vendors and benefits brokers are jumping on the bandwagon of providing reward/penalty programs in an attempt to control healthcare costs. Given our contention that we are at a crossroads of *Belief vs. Evidence*, we now examine the evidence regarding these wellness programs and healthcare savings.

The Safeway Amendment: Just Because You *Can* Doesn't Mean You *Should*

Clearly, employee wellness programs got a huge shot in the arm from the ACA, particularly when it comes to using penalties to punish employees who refuse to participate in them. In fact, according to the 2013 Staying @Work Report from Towers Watson & Company, by 2016, the percentage of employers who plan to punish their employees for not participating in their workplace wellness program is expected to triple. The report concluded:

- 22% of employers already incorporate penalties into their incentive structures
- 36% say they are planning to do so by the end of the year
- 61% plan to do so by 2016[3]

The research over the past three decades on the use of extrinsic motivation to "get" people to do things is quite clear; it doesn't work and can cause many unwanted side effects. And if you add just a pinch of common sense, it is difficult to comprehend why anyone would buy into these approaches to improve employee wellbeing. In his 2009 book, "Zero Trends," Dr. Dee Edington states the problem clearly:

Between the 1970s and 2000s wellness professionals made another mistake... They believed that people's behaviors were causing high healthcare costs... The solution was to sentence them to behavior change programs. As stand-alone programs such as smoking cessation or weight loss these efforts proved relatively ineffective.[4]

A quick look at how these wellness provisions made their way into the ACA in the first place may give us a clue to the answer to this dilemma. The inclusion of this provision *(aptly entitled the "Safeway Amendment")* came about primarily as a result of the testimony of Steven A. Burd, then CEO of Safeway Supermarket, who claimed that tying employees' behaviors and health outcomes to their insurance premiums was the answer to the employer's spiraling healthcare costs. In a 2009 article in "The Wall Street Journal" he stated:

Safeway designed just such a plan in 2005 and has made continuous improvements each year. The results have been remarkable. During this four-year period, we have kept our per capita health-care costs flat (that includes both the employee and the employer portion), while most American companies' costs have increased 38% over the same four years.[5]

What ensued next was nothing short of a well-staged, Hollywood, red-carpet production. Politicians on both sides of the aisle *(that's right, you heard us, both sides)* embraced Burd as some sort of celebrity, if not savior. Democratic Senator and Senate Finance Committee member Thomas R. Carper, Democrat of Delaware, proclaimed:

Safeway figured out how to incentivize people to take better care of themselves, and they have flat-lined their health care costs for 200,000 employees in the last four years.[6]

Senator John McCain, Republican of Arizona, got into the act, telling listeners at a town hall meeting in August 2009:

You know, there's a guy who has become pretty famous lately, and he's the CEO of Safeway... Safeway's health-care costs have gone down. Why can't we adopt that on a national scale?[7]

Even President Barack Obama jumped on the bandwagon in a speech to the American Medical Association, saying:

It's a program that has helped Safeway cut health-care spending by 13% and workers save over 20% on their premiums… And we're open to help employers adopt and expand programs like these.[8]

Not surprisingly, the leaders of the health promotion community embraced the bipartisan drinking of the Kool-Aid and headed to Washington to lobby intensely to get the amendment passed. And the rest, as the saying goes, is history. Thanks to the Safeway Amendment, incentive-driven employee wellness programs are now more popular than ever.

Unfortunately, as another well-known saying goes, it turns out there was a rather large "fly in the ointment" with respect to the reality as opposed to the rhetoric regarding the Safeway claims. Although it is undeniably true that Safeway's health insurance costs declined by 12.5% in 2006, it is also undeniably true that their employee wellness program did not launch until 2009 — some three years later![9] That is correct, three years after the claims were made. This means, of course, that the cost savings in 2006 had nothing whatsoever to do with the wellness program. Additionally, when the program did finally launch, only 28,000 of the 200,000 employees were eligible to participate! Furthermore, in the first year of the program, expenses rose *(not fell)* steeply. Responding to a question from a journalist about why, a Safeway senior vice president answered by saying, "We frankly did not have as much control over that as we should have."[10]

Wellness or Else!

Because almost everyone is running to jump on the Safeway bandwagon *(and since their data were essentially made up)*, a reasonable question might be: Is there actually scientific research regarding the practice of tying employees' health insurance premiums to health behaviors and health outcomes? It turns out that there is. Writing in "The New England Journal of Medicine" in 2011, a group of behavioral economists put it this way:

Although it may seem obvious that charging higher premiums for smoking (or high body mass index, cholesterol or blood pressure) would encourage people to modify their habits to lower their premiums, evidence that differential premiums change health-related behavior is scant. Indeed, we're unaware of any insurance data that have convincingly demonstrated such effects.[11]

Please remember that behavioral scientists make their living by trying to figure out ways to get people to do things that they don't necessarily want to do. But there is more to this story. Not only is there no evidence that this is an effective strategy for lowering healthcare costs, it turns out that there is a good likelihood of negative unintended consequences. In a 2013 article entitled "Workplace wellness regulations: First, do no harm," the Prevention Institute concurred with the conclusions of the behavioral economists, saying:

> *We also have a pretty good idea of what doesn't work,*
> *and heading the list are strategies that tie individual employees' share*
> *of health insurance premiums to health-related behaviors*
> *and/or meeting benchmarks.*[12]

However, they took matters just a bit further. Again, please keep in mind that the only thing the Prevention Institute does is prevention. Why then are they so opposed to the strategy epitomized by the Safeway Amendment? We encourage you to read the article to find this out, but here, in bullet form, are the main points regarding these punitive measures:

- They have not been linked to improved health outcomes.
- They may instill resentment in employees.
- They are likely to shift health costs to the least healthy.
- They are likely to have the most damaging effect on people of color and low-income workers.

Pretty difficult to add anything to that list! By the way, some other rather obscure health-related organizations were opposed to this approach for some of the same reasons. In a recent publication, the American Cancer Society, American Diabetes Association, and American Heart Association *(to name just three)* put it this way:

> *Based on the evidence to date regarding the impact of financial*
> *incentives on behavior, we believe the potential to discriminate against*
> *persons with chronic conditions — like heart disease, cancer and*
> *diabetes — far outweigh any potential benefits to improving wellness.*[13]

But what do they know about health anyway?

Trying to control employee lifestyle behaviors by manipulating health insurance premiums is clearly a misguided *(at best)* strategy. Such a strategy is not evidence-based, ignores the complexities of human behavior, and does not support all areas of wellbeing. It is a throwback to the 17th-century mechanistic, reductionist, control-obsessed, worldview. It does not work, and it engenders the likelihood of a variety of unwanted, negative consequences, both personal and organizational. As Al Lewis is fond of saying:

> *If you're a general, would you rather have troops with high morale or low cholesterol? Should wellness be something you do TO your employees or FOR your employees?*[14]

Perhaps most ironically *(and sadly)*, this punitive approach is very likely to penalize the people who are least able — for a whole host of reasons — to meet the biometric and behavioral benchmarks demanded of them to not be charged more for their insurance premiums, which these individuals are also less likely to be able to afford. It is important here to note that we are talking about a considerable sum of money. Assuming an average cost of an employer health plan for a family of approximately $16,000, about $4,800 of that *(30%)* would be at risk for failure to meet such benchmarks ($8,000 for smoking). With the median annual income in the United States being about $50,500 per year, this would account for almost 10% of annual income *(more for smoking)*. In a "Health Affairs" review of randomized trials of health-contingent programs at the workplace *(programs aimed at smoking, hypertension, obesity and high cholesterol)*, two lawyers and a professor of economics put it this way:

> *We found little evidence that such programs can easily save costs through health improvement without being discriminatory. Our evidence suggests that savings to employers may come from cost shifting, with the most vulnerable employees — those from lower socioeconomic strata with the most health risks — probably bearing greater costs that in effect subsidize their healthier colleagues.*[15]

This is, of course, the complete antithesis of everything that the ACA is supposed to be about. Our advice to everyone involved in workplace health is, please step away from the Safeway Kool-Aid!

Perhaps the one positive outcome from the Safeway debacle is that the research on the effectiveness of employee wellness programs has come under increasingly intense scrutiny. Because of the ACA wellness provisions, the RAND Corporation was commissioned to conduct a large study including some 600,000 employees at seven employers on the effectiveness of employee wellness programs.[16] They concluded the following:

- Participation in wellness programs was not associated with significant reductions in weight, blood pressure, blood sugar or cholesterol levels.
- The risk of unintended consequences is real.
- Any healthcare cost savings were not statistically significant.

Not surprisingly, with few exceptions *(aside from articles published in trade journals by researchers actually involved in delivering employee wellness programs)*, other research has reached similar conclusions. Here are the findings from just a few recent ones:

- **"A Systematic Review of the Evidence Concerning the Economic Impact of Employee-Focused Health Promotion and Wellness Programs":** "Evidence regarding economic impact is limited and inconsistent. Higher-quality research is needed to demonstrate the value of specific programs."[17]

- **"Managing Manifest Diseases, But Not Health Risks, Saved PepsiCo Money Over Seven Years":** "We found that seven years of continuous participation in one or both components was associated with an average reduction of $30 in health care cost per member per month. When we looked at each component individually, we found that the disease management component was associated with lower costs and that the lifestyle management component was not."[18]

- **"The Effectiveness of a Health Promotion Program after Three Years: Evidence from the University of Minnesota":** "No evidence that lifestyle management lowers health care costs."[19]

- **"The Relationship Between Return on Investment and Quality of Study Methodology in Workplace Health Promotion Programs":** "We found that as methodological quality improved, return on investment decreased, and we found a negative ROI in randomized controlled trials." [20]

In fact, even the claim from what is likely the sole piece of recent published research outside of the profession supporting savings from wellness programs *(ROI 3.27)* has now been recanted by none other than its lead author. Harvard health economics professor, Katherine Baicker, stated in a recent interview with "Marketplace" that it was actually "too early to tell" whether these programs save money:

We'll find out the answer better as more employers experiment with these programs, and we see what happens to the participants' weight [and] blood pressure.[21]

The concept of "experimenting" on employees is worrisome at best. And the fact that it is "too early to tell" whether programs work does not bode well at all for employee health and wellness professionals, especially considering that the wellness profession has been attempting to improve health and health risks in this manner for decades. As Dr. Dee Edington recently commented:

The field has been riding the behavior change horse for 40 years with little to show for it.[22]

The gap between what wellness program promoters and independent researchers claim concerning the ability of these programs to save money is likely based on the way the research is conducted and evaluated. The many serious pitfalls of the industry-conducted research have been examined in great detail elsewhere. We strongly recommend that any organizations considering implementing traditional 4P *(pry, poke, prod and punish)* wellness programs at the very least read these materials.[23]

Iatrogenesis — The Elephant In the Room

Even these multiple, serious pitfalls may actually be overshadowed by another factor which is rarely, if ever, discussed or included in this research. The elephant in the room in this case is iatrogenesis, which Wikipedia defines as "preventable harm resulting from medical treatment or advice to patients." Professionals who may sometimes cause harm to patients include physicians, pharmacists, nurses, dentists, psychiatrists, psychologists and therapists as well as alternative and complementary medicine practitioners. It also makes perfect sense to include wellness vendors, coaches, managers, CEOs and other business leaders as well — in fact, anyone involved in promoting change on an organizational or individual level. In these cases, of course, the individuals suffering as a result are the employees. Iatrogenesis is most often a consequence of the negative side of the Law of Unintended Consequences, which tells us that almost any initiative is likely to have "outcomes that are not the ones intended by a purposeful action." Any action, from smallest to largest, in any context can have unforeseen results. For instance, you might decide to sit down with your kids to watch a movie. You may be unaware of the possibility of negative consequences occurring from watching the film and your 5-year-old might get badly frightened by something that you would view as innocent.

Iatrogenesis in Action: The Penn State Fiasco

A "fiasco" is defined as "a thing that is a complete failure, especially in a ludicrous or humiliating way." Although the Safeway experience certainly fits the bill, recent events at Penn State likely qualify it as the poster child of fiascos for workplace wellness. Perhaps the best way to get the feeling for the real disaster that this supposed wellness program was is to get it directly from Dr. Brian Curran, the Penn State professor who started the revolt that eventually got it terminated. In his own words:

> *Penn State's new Health Care policies, which have been rolled out quietly in the middle of the summer, include an excessively invasive 'Take Care of Your Health' plan that forces employees, by imposing a massive, $1,200 a year surcharge, to submit to poorly and unprofessionally mass-organized blood tests and 'biometric screenings.' Included in this mandate is an additional mandate, requiring all employees and their spouses/SSDPs to fill out an incredibly invasive 'Wellness Profile' that, if taken, immediately shares ALL of the person's private medical information with WebMD, a third-party agency with a far from comforting record in the area of privacy. Not long after this 'initiative' was initiated, two new surcharges were announced: One directed at employees who self-identify as smokers, the other to employees with spouses covered by the plan who are presently eligible for coverage by their own employer. Each and every one of these policies raises serious questions related to patient privacy and medical ethics. But perhaps most importantly, their punitive character raises fundamental concerns regarding the relationship between Penn State as an employer and its employees, who might have expected better after enduring the challenges of the last two years.*
> *In light of these concerns, not to mention the almost complete lack of appropriate consultation with representative bodies across the university, we ask, indeed, we demand, that implementation be IMMEDIATELY stopped, or at the very least delayed, so that further consultation with the employees and their representatives can begin.*[24]

To make a long story short, the revolt went viral — reaching the national news, the newspapers and social media. After faculty petitions, the administration finally backed off from the $1,200 *(cough, cough)* incentive. As one writer commented:

> *Instead of creating a culture of health, Penn State has created a culture of resentment.*[25]

Of course, for those of us who have followed the research on the consequences of rewards and punishments for the last three or four decades, there is really nothing surprising about the reactions employees had to this fiasco.

Rethinking Four Common Elements of Employee Wellness Initiatives

So, if we don't want to fall victim to these pitfalls, what is the alternative? Let us briefly examine four of the most common components of employee wellness programs — biometric screenings, HRAs, weight loss programs and incentives — the typically associated iatrogenesis and what can be done instead.

Biometric Screenings:

Knowing your blood pressure, cholesterol, glucose and triglyceride levels certainly has value on an individual level. However, mass screenings, particularly when done at the workplace, are fraught with the potential for increasing costs due to overdiagnosis and overtreatment, frequently resulting in employees seeking further medical tests and treatment that can be both costly and sometimes dangerous, even if there is no real evidence of illness.[26] Although population screens of this type have generally fallen out of favor with governments and most of the health establishment, they have become one of the foundations of employee wellness initiatives *(can you guess why that might be?)*.[27] Adding to the problem, such workplace screenings often recommend tests for employees that are either:

> **1)** not recommended by preventive medicine specialists at all, and/or
>
> **2)** implemented at different frequencies *(usually more often for obvious reasons)* than recommended by the preventive medical establishment.

Health Risk Assessments (HRAs):

As we discussed in chapter 8, most HRA data will tell you that your employees need to lose weight, eat more fruits and vegetables, exercise more, quit smoking and perhaps reduce stress. HRAs are highly unlikely to save money *(as we mentioned before, because they are taken anonymously, there is no way to tell whether they do)* and more often may actually be a waste of money because:

1) They regularly recommend preventative actions *(including both type and frequency)* that are not medically valued.

2) They often result in having employees seek additional and often unnecessary medical help, which can be costly.

3) They often ask highly personal questions that employees may not want their employer to know about, so they promote lying and giving false information.

4) They are available for free online for anyone who wants to take them.[28]

What to Do Instead of Biometric Screenings and HRAs

Instead of squandering scarce resources on these interventions, we recommend you take those resources and use them to help employees become wiser healthcare consumers, and provide programs and resources that support ALL areas of wellbeing.

Healthcare Consumerism

We all know that our healthcare system is complicated. Equipping employees with the skills and resources to better navigate the system and partner with healthcare providers is the focus of developing and implementing an effective healthcare consumerism strategy. Consider the following figures:

• Approximately 80% of health problems are handled at home without seeking medical care.[29]

• Nearly 25% of doctor's visits are unnecessary and could have been handled with self-care.[30]

• More than 70% of emergency room visits are unnecessary.[31]

Employers can benefit by providing skill-building workshops and resources to support employees in becoming wiser healthcare consumers. When people learn to make better healthcare decisions, not only do they reduce unnecessary visits to physicians and emergency rooms, they also benefit from:[32]

- Reduced healthcare costs
- Improved quality of care
- Improved satisfaction with patient care
- Increased patient empowerment in taking an active role in care
- Saving time

We advocate for a three-pronged approach to healthcare consumerism:

1) *Making Better Decisions Regarding Seeking Care.* The goal behind this prong is to help employees make educated decisions regarding seeking care rather than guessing — which frequently leads to unnecessary care or avoiding care. The process involves providing employees with a quality self-care guide and implementing training where they are given scenarios to practice making informed decisions about whether to seek care. We prefer the "Healthwise® Handbook."[33] Even in our app-crazy world, people still like having the ability to quickly look in a book to help them make a care decision. And we have found that, even in companies struggling with organizational wellbeing and morale, something as simple as providing the self-care guide and training sends a message to employees that they are valued and that the company cares. The worst response we've ever received from an employee participating in this training is "Well, that wasn't as bad as I thought it would be. Thanks for the book." And many people express thanks and actually ask for duplicate self-care guides. In addition to providing a quality self-care guide, it is also important to teach employees how to identify a good quality website for making healthcare decisions and how to effectively prepare for a healthcare visit. We also recommend building reinforcement communication regarding self-care and healthcare consumerism decisions into your overall wellbeing communication plan. Our clients have found benefit in just focusing on this first prong. When we examine their medical claims the year prior to and the year after implementing self-care guides and training for making better healthcare decisions, we consistently see a significant reduction in questionable emergency room visits.

2) *Being an Advocate for Your Own Quality Care.* What do you call someone who squeaked by medical school with a "C" average? Doctor! Our point is that quality of care varies greatly. And it is estimated that doctors interrupt their patients within 18 seconds of the start of their conversation.[34] It is becoming increasingly important to equip people to get into the driver's seat and take an active role in their care. This includes coming prepared to make the most of a healthcare visit. However, many people forget to share important information or do not ask questions because they don't know what to ask or where to begin. The goal of this prong of a consumerism strategy is to provide training, tools and resources so employees know what to ask their healthcare provider, how to advocate for better care, and how they can play a role in reducing their risk of being a victim of medical error or poor quality care.

3) *Leveraging Available Resources.* One of the biggest frustrations we hear from companies is that they provide benefits and resources that hardly any employees use. Again, as we discussed in chapter 11, communication is critical. Including regular, consistent communication to reinforce any benefits and resources that can help employees make better healthcare decisions is an important part of a consumerism strategy. This includes reinforcing nurse lines, EAP resources, health plan programs and website resources, and any health advocacy services you may provide.

If you're looking for resources to help you create skill-building workshops for employees, two books we have found useful are:

- "The Empowered Patient" by Elizabeth Cohen. She provides tips for partnering with providers, avoiding misdiagnosis, quality trusted websites, saving money and dealing with insurance companies.[35]

- "YOU: The Smart Patient: An Insider's Handbook for Getting the Best Treatment" by Michael Roizen and Mehmet Oz.[36] They provide quizzes, resources for doing research on doctors, information on drug interactions and more *(Although both authors operate in the Old Paradigm in many respects, this book still has useful resources for developing healthcare consumerism training workshops).*

Programs and Resources that Support Thriving Employee Wellbeing

In addition to supporting employees in becoming wiser healthcare consumers, support their total wellbeing. The programs and resources you provide to support all areas of wellbeing should meet the needs of your employees *(based on data you hopefully collected)* and be perceived as valuable. As we mentioned in chapter 11, the more you can make wellbeing a platform for your workplace culture — part of who you are as a company and how you value the employee experience — the easier it will be to *create the conditions* for employees to see the programs and resources as aligning with the culture and the wellbeing strategy. The following are some common programs and resources our clients have used to support employee wellbeing while also supporting organizational wellbeing:

- **Career Wellbeing / Purpose:** Whatever programs and resources you provide in this area should best reflect if people like what they do at work each day and if they have a sense of purpose. What you provide for employees will vary based on your current state of both organizational and employee wellbeing. For organizations with poor organizational wellbeing, we advise spending more effort in this area of wellbeing than any other, because career wellbeing not only trumps every other area of wellbeing, but working to improve career wellbeing inherently can also improve organizational wellbeing. Some examples include:
  - Mentoring programs
  - Career paths
  - Comprehensive development *(detailed in chapter 10)*
  - Tuition reimbursement
  - Life purpose workshops

- **Social Wellbeing:** The programs and resources you provide in this area should help enhance the quality of relationships people have in their lives — their entire lives. Here are some examples that might be useful:
  - Workshops and coaching to increase self-awareness and improve communication skills
  - Flexible work arrangements and both maternity and paternity leave
  - Adoption assistance
  - Parenting and eldercare classes
  - Employee Assistance Programs
  - Health Advocate™

- **Financial Wellbeing:** What programs and resources you provide in this area should support employees in enhancing their sense of financial security. Here are some examples of ways you can support financial wellbeing:
  - Partner with local resources to provide one-on-one sessions with a financial planner
  - Emergency loan programs *(company provides emergency interest-free loans for employees who are in a financial pinch; employee makes payments via payroll deductions over a spread-out time period)*
  - Cost-sharing or reimbursing employees for completing quality, evidence-based programs to enhance their wellbeing

- **Physical Wellbeing:** The programs and resources provided should contribute to good physical health and having enough physical energy to get things done each day that are important. Again, what is provided needs to reflect what will matter most to your employees. Some examples include:
  - Health for Every Body® *(mentioned in the next section and detailed in chapter 15)*
  - Reducing or eliminating deductibles and copays for preventive care services *(e.g., age-recommended cancer screenings and physicals)*
  - Supporting regular movement *(e.g., sit-to-stand workstations, taking movement breaks, etc.)*
  - Wider variety of healthful food options available
  - Programs on intuitive eating and positive body image
  - Self-management programs for chronic conditions *(detailed later in this chapter)*
  - Policies and practices that support and encourage employees to stay home when they are sick

- **Emotional Wellbeing:** The programs and resources provided to enhance emotional wellbeing should promote resiliency and work-life balance and having enough mental energy to get important things done each day. Here are some examples:
  - Resilience-Building and Life Purpose workshops
  - Access to Certified Intrinsic Coach® coaches
  - Employee Assistance Programs *(that include three to five in-person visits; this becomes even more important when employees are struggling with financial wellbeing and your health insurance has a high deductible)*

— Time and space to pause and reflect during the day

— Mindfulness-Based Stress Reduction workshops *(provided the organization is also addressing workplace causes of stress)*

- **Community Wellbeing:** Programs and resources to enhance community wellbeing would ideally promote giving back to others. Some examples include:
    — Paid time-off benefit for volunteering

    — Company-sponsored volunteer events *(during work hours)*

    — Charitable giving programs

Weight Loss Programs, Competitions, Contests:

There is not a shred of evidence over the last three or four decades that any weight loss intervention results in long-term weight loss for all but a small handful of people. Studies of worksite weight loss programs *(even those including significant financial incentives)* have, without exception, reached the same conclusion.[37] Therefore, most participants end up losing and gaining substantial amounts of weight over and over again, an occurrence which may have significant negative health consequences.[38] The ongoing claims of weight loss promoters regarding the success of their programs financially *(and health-wise for that matter)* are always based on short-term results, which mean very little in either case. As a result of this built-in recidivism *(which, of course plays into the hands and wallets of those providing weight loss services)*, the typical dieter participates in these programs, on average, four times a year.[39] So, the next time a workplace claims to have saved X dollars as a result of X number of pounds that were lost in their year-long program, the workplace should be challenged to follow-up and see what happens a year or two after the program ends if we are to take their claims seriously.

What to Do Instead of a Weight Loss Program

As we have discussed previously, without exception, these programs invariably lead to weight cycling for all but a tiny minority *(5% or less)* of participants with all kinds of potential negative psychological and physiological consequences. As we mentioned earlier, Dr. Dee Edington commented that "weight loss money is money down the toilet."[40] Imagine going into your CEO's office and explaining to her that you have an initiative that you believe she should invest in that is guaranteed to fail 95% of the time? It probably doesn't take much imagination to guess what the response would be. Again, instead of wasting valuable resources on programs that attempt to make people smaller, or prescriptive nutrition and physical activity programs that end up appealing to few of the folks who could most benefit from them, we recommend investing in initiatives that help people to find peace with their bodies, their food and their movement. We will talk in greater detail about such a program, Health for Every Body,® in chapter 15.

Incentive Programs:

Finally, with respect to the ubiquitous use of rewards and punishments for producing change, promoted now with ever more intensity by the ACA wellness provisions, again, there is simply no published evidence that these result in anything but short-term compliance. In fact, scores of studies clearly demonstrate the lack of efficacy of these approaches. It is quite telling, and a testimony to the power of belief to trump evidence, that when I *(Jon)* present this evidence at health promotion conferences — usually listing 10 to 15 articles all reaching this same conclusion, I am frequently accused of "cherry-picking" the data — even though no one has ever provided a single article that refutes this conclusion. Sadly, we are clearly *stuck* in outdated beliefs. The costs of incentives being used to pressure and punish employees more than doubled from $260 to $521 per employee in just the last five years, and are projected to increase another 15% to almost $600 per employee in 2014.[41]

What to Do Instead of Incentives

If you remember back to chapter 12, we talked about the futility of trying to motivate *(pressure, coerce, incentivize)* people to behave differently and the decades of conclusive research that points to the real desired goal: *creating the conditions* within which people will motivate themselves. Because many companies have taken the advice of vendors, brokers and consultants who are not familiar with this literature *(or have chosen to ignore it)*, it may be difficult for these companies to completely discard their incentive structures all at once. We provided some examples in chapter 12 and will provide additional case studies in chapter 15 to detail ways that organizations can "correct" for the use of incentives and minimize the damage they can cause. Of course, as organizations wean themselves from the obsession with extrinsic motivation, they can begin to reallocate the considerable and ever-increasing amounts of money being wasted to more efficacious initiatives.

These four major components of typical employee wellness programs are consistently presented as "best practices" with many claims of ROI that have now been thoroughly refuted by the evidence. As Dr. Soeren Mattke, the senior scientist who led the much heralded RAND report and PepsiCo study, stated in a recent interview:

> *The industry went in with promises of 3-to-1 and 6-to-1 based on health care savings alone. Then research came out that said that's not true. Then they said 'okay; we are cost neutral.' And now as research says maybe not even cost neutral they say 'but it's really about productivity which we can't really measure but it's an enormous return'... What irks me are these aggressive sales tactics that make it a standard benefit based on unrealistic promises and then turning around and saying, 'but you shouldn't look at savings in the first place.'*[42]

When you combine the potential costs of iatrogenesis with the dismal likelihood of saving money from traditional 4P, *(pry, poke, prod and punish)* wellness programs, the appropriate conclusions seem fairly obvious. If the employer's role is to *create the conditions* within which people can thrive in their wellbeing, medicalizing the workplace makes little economic sense. Instead of wasting money playing doctor, employers can apply those monies towards providing quality tools and resources to help employees better partner with their healthcare providers for quality, cost-effective prevention and to meet their specific health needs.

> If the employer's role is to *create the conditions* within which people can thrive in their wellbeing, medicalizing the workplace makes little economic sense.

What DOES Save Money for Sure?

As you can see, there is considerable money to be saved by eliminating traditional 4P wellness approaches. The good news is that there are many additional initiatives and resources that organizations can incorporate into a comprehensive wellbeing strategy that actually do save money, while also positively impacting both organizational and employee wellbeing. The details of a number of these initiatives are covered in "Cracking Health Costs: How to Cut Your Company's Costs and Provide Employees Better Care."[43] One of the authors, Tom Emerick, has a wealth of experience in these matters, as he spent 15 years designing and managing benefits for more than 1.6 million employees at Walmart. One of the first recommendations we make to companies that we work with is to obtain and carefully read this book. Most of these interventions are relatively simple, cost very little to implement, and can save considerable amounts of money. Here are just a few examples:

- **Company-Sponsored Centers of Excellence *(CSCOE)* Model.** This is a best-practice for inpatient care, particularly designed to assist a company's "outlier population," defined as individuals who typically have multiple, serious illnesses; are often seeing a number of specialists; and may be in the middle of an episode of acute care. Employees who are facing illnesses of this nature, where expensive surgeries have been recommended, are given the opportunity to visit a CSCOE for a second opinion and then possibly for the surgery as well. Frequently all expenses, including travel and the assistance of a companion caregiver, are paid for by the company.

Even if this does not save the company money *(which it inevitably does, both because these centers are set up to deliver more coordinated and efficient care and because their second opinions often end up not recommending the expensive treatments recommended by the first opinion)*, the message it sends to employees is clear — the company is going to take care of you through these difficult times. This is certainly a far cry from the "Wellness or Else!" approach of 4P wellness programs.

- **Leapfrog Hospital Safety Scores.** This model does what CSCOEs do, but for the much more numerous hospital admissions that don't necessitate flying employees to other parts of the country for a second opinion. According to research from the nonprofit healthcare think tank Altarum Institute entitled "Steering Employees Toward Safer Care: Employer Strategies for Attaining Safer, Higher-Quality Hospital Care for Employees and Their Families":

Unsafe hospital practices may be one of the least publicized yet most modifiable aspects of healthcare quality.[44]

And since hospitalizations can account for 50% of an organization's overall healthcare spend, the potential savings are quite significant. Leapfrog was founded in 2000 by some frustrated large purchasers, including Boeing,

General Motors and General Electric. Employer members pressure hospitals to release data on their rates of errors, infections, mortality from key procedures and maternity-care quality. Leapfrog publishes these results annually along with a Hospital Safety Score *(a letter grade reflecting overall patient safety)* and makes them available to the public and purchasers on their website.[45] The bottom line is that, with very little effort or expense, utilizing Leapfrog can nudge your employees towards using safer and thus better hospitals, and this can save the organization money and protect employees from injury.

> • **Coordinated Care Model.** This model is focused on helping keep people out of hospitals whenever possible. It incorporates a horizontal, cross-functional team approach to benefits management in which all of the common functions are melded into one cohesive process instead of relying on multiple vendors with often little communication or coordination. Although more carriers and vendors are now claiming they provide coordinated care, such is not always the case. Research suggests a 2 to 4% savings, mostly from reduced hospitalizations after about the first year of implementation of a Coordinated Care Model.[46]

Chronic Disease Self-Management Programs:
In addition to the initiatives we just mentioned that are detailed in "Cracking Health Costs," there is encouraging evidence for a program that supports people with chronic conditions.

> • Chronic diseases account for 75% of the money our nation spends on healthcare.
>
> • Four chronic conditions *(heart disease, cancer, stroke and diabetes)* cause almost two-thirds of all deaths in the United States each year.
>
> • Nearly 92% of older adults have at least one chronic condition, and 77% have at least two.[47]

Stanford University partnered with the National Council on Aging to create the Chronic Disease Self-Management Program *(CDSMP)* in the early 1990s. CDSMP is a low-cost program designed to help people with chronic conditions learn how to manage and improve their own health while reducing healthcare costs. The program focuses on problems common among people dealing with any chronic condition *(e.g., pain management, nutrition, exercise, medication use, difficult emotions, communicating with doctors).* The program is designed to increase people's self-confidence in their ability to control their symptoms and thereby better manage how their health problems affect their lives.

The program is delivered in small-group, highly interactive workshops that meet once per week for two hours for six weeks. Each week engages participants to problem-solve, create action plans, make better decisions and create social support for change so they can better manage their condition. The sessions are peer-led; they are facilitated by a pair of leaders who are non-health professionals who also have a chronic disease. If one of the leaders happens to be a health professional, she/he is not acting in that role while leading the group and either discusses a personal chronic condition or how having a loved one with a chronic condition impacts her/him on a personal level.

The CDSMP is evidence-based and has been shown to have significant benefits.[48] A randomized control trial was conducted with over 1,000 people with heart disease, lung disease, stroke or arthritis who were followed for up to three years. Those who participated in the CDSMP had significant improvements in exercise, managing cognitive symptoms, communication with physicians, fatigue, disability, health distress, self-reported general health and limitations with social/role activities compared to those who did not participate. Additionally, CDSMP participants:

- Spent fewer days in the hospital
- Had fewer hospitalizations
- Had fewer outpatient visits

These results indicated a cost savings of $714 per person in emergency-room visits and hospital use.[49]

Stanford regularly offers training for people to become leaders of their CDSMP program; they advise organizations to send people in pairs to the training *(because two people lead the program)*. The training to become a CDSMP leader takes four full days; people can travel to Stanford, or Stanford can come to them. Additionally, many state health departments are offering the CDSMP leadership training for little to no cost via various grant funding projects. So, instead of punishing people with chronic conditions, why not equip people with an evidence-based program proven to help them have better health outcomes and improved wellbeing?

Embracing the New Paradigm to Support Employee Wellbeing

Hopefully, after reading this chapter, you can see the importance of embracing the New Paradigm to deploy programs and resources to support employee wellbeing, and ultimately organizational wellbeing. Rather than making faulty attempts to control healthcare costs with outdated wellness initiatives, focus on implementing programs and resources that support all employees in all areas of wellbeing that will also support organizational wellbeing.

With that in mind, we want to make one more important recommendation. We advise you to run quickly and far, far away from any wellness vendor, insurance carrier or broker who is trying to sell you a "simple" or "turnkey" wellness program. The complexities of human beings and organizations cannot be effectively supported with a reductionist turnkey platform of services that are not tailored to your organizational culture. However, with the right fit of programs and resources, you can use meaningful measures to guide your organizational and employee wellbeing efforts. We examine how to approach ongoing evaluation in the next chapter.

Summary of Transformation Point #6
Deploy QUALITY, Evidence-Based Programs and Resources

Questions you may want to ask when evaluating any program or resources to determine if they make sense for your organization:

- Are the programs and resources evidence-based?
- Will they support and foster both organizational and employee wellbeing?
- Might they negatively impact organizational or employee wellbeing?
- Do they include support for all areas of wellbeing?
- Do they especially support the areas of wellbeing that matter most to your employees?
- Did you ask employees which areas of wellbeing matter most to them?
- Are you being fiscally responsible in selecting the programs and resources that will make the greatest impact in creating a thriving workplace culture?

Instead of:	Do This:
• Biometric Screenings • Health Risk Assessments (HRAs)	• Healthcare Consumerism Skill-Building • Support ALL Areas of Wellbeing
• Weight Loss Challenges and Competitions	• Health for Every Body® • Intuitive Eating Programs
• Incentives	• Focus on Creating Thriving Organizational Wellbeing • Engage Better Thinking

CHAPTER 14
Transformation Point #7: Maintain the House
(Continuous Quality Improvement)

The dynamics of emotional tension exist at all levels of human activity. They are the dynamics of compromise, the path of mediocrity. As Somerset Maugham said, 'Only mediocre people are always at their best.'[1]

Peter Senge, "The Fifth Discipline"

The final step in transforming your workplace culture is maintenance. Because culture change is a journey, not a destination, how do you know if you're going in the right direction or if you need to course correct? We suggest that approaching organizational and employee wellbeing in a manner similar to that espoused by the concept of Continuous Quality Improvement *(CQI)* will help to guide efforts and provide course corrections over time to most effectively meet a moving target. CQI is a process used in organizations where everyone collectively strives to constantly improve quality. It encourages people to regularly ask the questions, "How are we doing?" and "Can we do things better?" CQI is a long-term approach focused on culture change that is guided by quality leadership, teamwork and input from all levels within the company. CQI is widely used in healthcare organizations to improve healthcare delivery.[2]

Keeping this in mind, you will always need to make adjustments to align your current reality with your future vision and desired culture. Realize that change, on both an organizational and individual level, takes time. However, because we are inherently impatient, this can lead to frustration and emotional tension. Yet, mastering this creative tension between current and future state elicits a tremendous capacity for perseverance and patience — and belief that change is possible.[3] Successful organizations use the gap between their vision and their current reality to generate energy for change; and the vision becomes an active force. As Peter Senge says:

It's not what the vision is, it's what the vision does.[4]

The Power of a Clear Vision

In his book, "The Power of Habit," Charles Duhigg described the story of Tony Dungy and the rise of the Indianapolis Colts to finally win the Super Bowl in 2007.[5] Tony Dungy served as an assistant coach for the University of Minnesota football team, and then the Pittsburgh Steelers, the Kansas City Chiefs, and the Minnesota Vikings. He eventually got a job as the head coach of the Tampa Bay Buccaneers in 1996 *(one of the worst teams in the NFL at the time)* and ended his coaching career with the Indianapolis Colts from 2002 until 2008. Tony is known for his unique coaching style. He knew that, most of the time, errors in the game are not physical; they're mental. So he focused on taking the thinking out of the game. He didn't want his players memorizing complicated plays because he knew when the stakes were high, they would think too much and second-guess themselves. Tony's approach was to teach his players to recognize visual cues that would tell them what the opposing team was going to do. He then had them drill the same responses to those actions over and over until they became automatic habits. When Tony first started applying this coaching approach with the Buccaneers, it took almost a year for the players' new habits to take hold. But, over time, the Buccaneers slowly started to improve, and they went to the playoffs for the first time in 15 years, winning the division championship in 1999. But in 1999, 2000 and 2001, the team got to be one game away from making it to the Super Bowl and blew it; despite the training, they cracked under pressure. Tony Dungy was fired. He went to the Indianapolis Colts and began the same process with them, and the Colts saw the same gradual improvement. So what was different with the Colts that they finally made it to the Super Bowl and won? They had belief in a greater purpose; they had a larger vision to guide them, something beyond just winning the coveted Super Bowl Champion title.

Tony described belief *(feeling aligned with a greater purpose and knowing they could do things differently in a way that would matter)* as a critical part of winning. However, although the Colts wanted to believe and sense that alignment, they would still slip back into their comfort zones and habits when things got really tense. Then, tragedy struck after the 2005 record season; Tony's son, Jamie, committed suicide three days before Christmas. Tony returned to his team a few days after the funeral only to have the Colts lose the first playoff game. Watching Tony during this tragedy changed something in the players; they finally started to believe, and they gave into Tony's vision for how football should be played in a way they hadn't before. The players had previously described being interested only in themselves, their contracts and their endorsements. After Jamie's death, their focus shifted to the collective vision, and to giving themselves to the team and to the potential for realizing Tony's vision. This time, the players truly believed the vision was possible and became a true team. That belief made everything stick — even at the most stressful moments — leading to the Colts finally taking home the trophy in 2007.

We aren't suggesting there has to be a tragedy like what happened to Tony Dungy's son to pull people together in your organization, to create change and to become the organization you want to be. In fact, too often organizations think there has to be a crisis to change, and they view change as fixing a problem. Certainly, if your organization is struggling, or even toxic, you may have a greater sense of urgency to change. But, as Jim Collins says in his best-selling book,[6] what it takes to move from "Good to Great" is change for the purpose of creating something new. So there needs to be a strong, shared belief that change is necessary, is good[7] and is possible. This becomes really important, because it will not always be a smooth ride; you will likely find you have taken some missteps and need to make course corrections along the way. That is what this final *Point of Transformation* is all about — embracing the fluidity of change and using your core values and the vision of your desired, thriving workplace culture to guide your journey.

Using Quality and Timely Evaluation to Navigate Your Journey

Quality and timely evaluation is a critical, yet often overlooked, step. If you don't know what you're trying to accomplish, what story you want to tell and what data you're going to use to guide your efforts, it becomes difficult to evaluate your progress. Both culture and wellbeing can be difficult to measure; they are moving targets because the world and life are ever-changing. It is critical to articulate where you've been, where you are currently and where you're going in terms of organizational and employee wellbeing. So, once you know how you want to tell your wellbeing story, it becomes easier to collect data on an ongoing basis and look for trends that will tell you if you're headed in the right direction.

There are many ways to go about ongoing evaluation. Whatever method you decide makes the most sense for your organizational and employee wellbeing journey, we suggest creating some sort of data repository that includes a simple evaluation plan so you know what data you want to review and how frequently you plan to review it. The organizational and employee wellbeing data we described in chapter 8 for understanding your baseline, current state and the additional metrics we described in chapter 9 for telling your wellbeing story comprise the metrics you will want to examine on an ongoing basis.

Some organizations take a more formalized approach to ongoing evaluation and integrate organizational and employee wellbeing metrics into their existing Balanced Scorecard, a formal organizational performance management system that helps leaders manage strategy implementation.[8] Typically, a Balanced Scorecard:

- Focuses on the strategic agenda of the organization
- Monitors a small number of metrics
- Includes both financial and non-financial metrics

Each measurement on a Balanced Scorecard is compared against its ideal target to assess if performance is meeting expectations. If this method is used, it is important not to take a 17th-century reductionist approach to reviewing and using the data. For example, you want to avoid looking at performance metrics in isolation *(whole = sum of its parts)* to plan for changes. Instead, examine everything in relation to everything else and within the context of the larger vision of a thriving workplace culture *(whole > sum of its parts)*.

For many organizations, it works just as well to simply use an Excel spreadsheet to house the data and create a Wellbeing Dashboard. Because much of the data we described in chapters 8 and 9 are likely already collected and housed elsewhere in the organization, creating an overall Wellbeing Dashboard may be as simple as copying and pasting the data into a new spreadsheet. Although it may initially seem redundant to copy existing data into a new spreadsheet, we have found it to be extremely helpful to have all of the organizational and employee wellbeing metrics in one spot for ease of evaluation. Additionally, because some data may have more information than is useful for assessing wellbeing, creating a separate dashboard allows for pulling out the relevant data and avoiding the addiction to metrics we described in chapter 8. Typically, there will be several worksheets included in the overall dashboard, each devoted to a particular category of data you want to track. Then, you can create worksheets to run analyses and provide overall summary data of trends. The summary data worksheets can assist you in determining how to best communicate your journey. The following are some examples of various worksheets you might want to create.

Organizational Wellbeing

Current Perceived Norms	Positive		2012-2014 Improvement	Neutral		2012-2014 Improvement	Negative		2012-2014 Improvement
	2012	2014		2012	2014		2012	2014	
Executive team is cohesive	66%	77%	+16.7%	24%	18%	-25%	9%	5%	-44.4%
Leaders value employees	71%	77%	+7.8%	15%	16%	+6.7%	15%	7%	-53.3%
The company has a clearly stated purpose	80%	91%	+13.8%	12%	8%	-33.3%	7%	1%	-85.7%
The climate fosters meaningful work	71%	75%	+5.6%	15%	7%	-53.3%	14%	11%	-21.4%
Employees are happy & proud to work here	83%	86%	+3.6%	10%	9%	-10%	7%	0%	-100.0%

The above example shows some of the items from the Thriving Workplace Culture Survey *(TWCS)* and compares current perceived norms over time. When positive ratings of norms increase and negative ratings decrease, it indicates things are moving in the right direction in terms of organizational wellbeing. Changes in the neutral ratings by themselves may not be as meaningful; it depends on what changes have occurred in both the positive and negative ratings.

Disconnect Between Current/Preferred Norms	2012	2014	Overall Improvement
Executive team is cohesive	1.3	0.6	-50.0%
Leaders value employees	1.6	0.9	-43.8%
The company has a clearly stated purpose	0.9	0.3	-66.7%
The climate fosters meaningful work	2.3	1.1	-52.2%
Employees are happy & proud to work here	1.7	0.7	-58.8%

This example uses the same norms from the TWCS and summarizes the degree of disconnect between current and preferred norms. As organizations improve and are living their desired culture, the disconnect between norms will decrease and be minimal. A greater disconnect between norms warrants concern and indicates that the organization is not living its desired culture.

Organizational Wellbeing

Wellbeing Satisfaction *(Satisfied or Very Satisfied)*	2012	2013	2014	Overall Improvement
Career	68%	70%	81%	**+19%**
Social	82%	82%	83%	**+1.2%**
Financial	70%	70%	69%	**-1.4%**
Physical	75%	75%	81%	**+8%**
Emotional	77%	80%	87%	**+13%**
Community	58%	75%	71%	**+22.4%**

Satisfaction with each area of wellbeing can be tracked over time. If the organization is effectively *creating the conditions* to support employee wellbeing, satisfaction with each area should improve or be maintained if it is already very high. For areas where satisfaction is lower, also look at whether employees actually want programs and resources to support them to determine what support will be meaningful.

Compliance vs. Engagement in Wellbeing	2012	2013	2014	Overall Improvement
Primary reason for participating in Wellbeing Perks: personally interested in wellbeing	15%	28%	42%	**+180%**
Primary reason for participating in Wellbeing Perks: wanted the incentive	85%	72%	58%	**-31.8%**
Importance of incentive in Wellbeing Perks participation: wouldn't participate without it	90%	82%	71%	**-21.1%**
Importance of incentive in Wellbeing Perks participation: neutral	8%	13%	13%	**+62.5**
Importance of incentive in Wellbeing Perks participation: would participate regardless	2%	5%	16%	**+7%**

For organizations who have already been *stuck* in Motivation 2.0 using incentive-based programs, this is a sample summary that indicates whether the company's efforts to improve organizational wellbeing and foster autonomous motivation are effective over time in reducing the importance of and dependence on incentives and increasing employees' engagement in their own personal wellbeing. In this example, it is evident the company's efforts are working to move away from compliance and support engagement.

Once you have a structure for housing your ongoing data collection, it's important to determine at what frequency you want to examine the data to determine if a change in direction is needed and what to look for that will tell you if you're headed in the right direction or not. So, once again, we want to revisit our conceptualization of Thriving Organizational Wellbeing to use as a guide as you evaluate your efforts.

Thriving Organizational Wellbeing

- The executive leadership team is truly a cohesive one.

- The mission, vision and values are clearly articulated, and every employee knows how he/she fits within them.

- Employees are empowered and enabled to leverage their strengths.

- Leaders and the work climate provide employees with autonomous support *(versus using incentives to drive behaviors)*.

- Clear, timely and meaningful communication is provided for employees, and employees share feedback and ideas that are actually used.

- Clear, timely and meaningful feedback is provided for employees in the spirit of ongoing growth and development *(versus simply measuring performance)*.

- The climate fosters innovation, creativity and meaningful work.

- Leaders truly value employees — and employees feel valued.

- Employees are encouraged and supported to be authentic and be themselves.

- People within the organization respect, support and care about one another as people, not just as employees there to complete certain job tasks.

- Accountability is embraced; the rules are clear and apply to everyone.

- Employees are provided the tools and resources they need to work safely and productively.

- Resources, programs, policies and the environment support employees' ability to thrive in all areas of wellbeing.

- Employees are happy and proud to work there!

Keeping this conceptualization of Thriving Organizational Wellbeing in mind, here are some key themes we suggest looking for as you examine your data to determine if you're headed in the direction of a thriving workplace culture:

- Do more employees feel valued?
- Is the overall disconnect between current and preferred norms decreasing?
- Is there an increase in positive ratings of current perceived norms and a decrease in negative ratings?
- Is the number of employees who view their role as a calling increasing?
- Are people's satisfaction with each area of wellbeing improving?
- Are people truly engaged in their own wellbeing *(versus participating in programs due to an incentive or penalty)*?

If your organizational and employee wellbeing efforts are moving in the right direction, you will see a positive trend in the above metrics. If not, course-corrections are likely needed. What you learn from holistically examining the data will ideally feed into *Transformation Point #2* with annual planning. Again, we suggest including input from as many employees as possible as you make tweaks and course corrections to the plan.

Communicating Your Culture and Wellbeing Journey

Once you've evaluated how you're doing, communicate the information on your wellbeing journey to employees, board members and any other stake-holders. It works best when you can align how you communicate your wellbeing journey with your overall communication strategy *(as described in chapter 11)*. Many of our clients create an annual "State of Wellbeing Report" that they provide to employees and stakeholders to keep the journey progress visible. These clients use the wellbeing metrics they determined were meaningful in *Transformation Point #2* and then use their Wellbeing Dashboard to tell their wellbeing story. Some organizations keep their reports simple by providing an overview of their organizational and wellbeing vision along with a few graphs and charts of the metrics to show how they're doing. Others create more colorful, elaborate reports. The point is that wellbeing becomes an integrated, formal part of communication. Just think of the message this sends about the importance of organizational and employee wellbeing!

Embracing the Journey

When you find your current state of organizational and employee wellbeing is not aligned with where you want to be, it is helpful to view this not as a failure but as an opportunity for learning and growth. In our S>E>I world, we tend to look at data as a finite measurement. Consequently, it's very common to be impatient and expect perfection. If things don't look the way we think they should, we tend to be dismissive. However, we have learned that organizations are complex systems made of complex human beings. When we can view data as ongoing feedback *(and can view it more in terms of I>E>S)*, we can use that feedback to inform and make subtle adjustments to strategic thinking and planning.[9]

We have now spent seven chapters reviewing in depth each of *The 7 Points of Transformation*. Although we've provided examples of how organizations have *created the conditions* to support thriving organizational and employee wellbeing, we want to help pull everything together so you can see how this blueprint and the New Paradigm interact in various organizations. Our next chapter is devoted to highlighting lessons learned from organizations putting both into action.

Summary of Transformation Point #7
Using a Wellbeing Dashboard for Continuous Quality Improvement

Metrics to Evaluate	Key Themes to Look For
Organizational Wellbeing Metrics	
Current perceived norms *(from culture survey)*	Are positive ratings of current perceived norms increasing? Are negative ratings decreasing?
Disconnect between current and preferred norms *(from culture survey)*	Is the disconnect between current and preferred norms increasing or decreasing?
Other organizational wellbeing metrics *(i.e., turnover, engagement, etc.)*	Does the data indicate things are moving in the right direction or warranting attention to course correct?
Number of employees who perceive their role as a calling	Is this increasing or decreasing?
Employee Wellbeing Metrics	
Satisfaction with each area of wellbeing	Is overall wellbeing satisfaction improving or not? Are there specific areas of wellbeing improving or worsening?
Importance of incentive in participating in Wellbeing Perks programs	Is the importance of the incentive increasing or decreasing? Are more people personally interested in their wellbeing?
Other employee wellbeing metrics determined in *Transformation Point #2*	Are the metrics indicating things are improving or worsening overall or in any specific area of wellbeing?

CHAPTER 15
The Finishing Touches: Applying the Principles
(The 7 Points of Transformation in Action)

> ❝*Our mental model of the way the world works must shift from images of a clockwork, machinelike universe that is fixed and determined, to the model of a universe that is open, dynamic, interconnected, and full of living qualities.*[1]❞

Joseph Jaworski, "Synchronicity: The Inner Path of Leadership"

The first questions we typically get asked when we present the blueprint of *The 7 Points of Transformation* are:

- *"How long does this take?"*
- *"Can you give us an example of a company that is doing ALL of those things and is successful?"*

We often chuckle and then remind the people asking the question that how long it will take to create a thriving workplace culture depends on where they are starting from — the more dysfunctional the culture, the longer it will likely take. The time it takes also depends on how serious the organization's leaders are about transforming their culture. If they skip steps and ignore the importance of shifting to the New Paradigm, it can take even longer. Because transforming workplace culture is a JOURNEY, not a destination, a better question might be: "How quickly can we get started on our journey, and how will we know we're going in the right direction?"

We also can't provide the name of one company that is doing everything well, because each company we work with is on its own journey — doing better in some of *The 7 Points of Transformation* than others. What we can say is that those organizations deliberately shifting from the Old Paradigm to the New Paradigm and following the blueprint are seeing improvements in both organizational and employee wellbeing. The Old Paradigm is based on outdated sciences and worldviews; it is prescriptive and looks for a cookie-cutter plan. The Old Paradigm embraces and values perfection and control. The New Paradigm is based on the new sciences. It is fluid, recognizes the uniqueness and complexities of both organizations and people, and embraces and values ongoing learning, growth and development from the inside out. With that in mind, in this chapter we explore examples of the various aspects of *The 7 Points of Transformation* in action, including:

1) **Examples of organizations** that have broken free of the Old Paradigm when it comes to employee wellbeing;

2) **A case study of an organization** that is succeeding in applying the New Paradigm to improve organizational and employee wellbeing;

3) **An effective, New Paradigm approach** for helping people who are struggling with weight- and eating-related issues that also supports total wellbeing; and

4) **A professional** who describes her own transformation journey from the Old to New Paradigm and how she leveraged the paradigm shift to support a thriving workplace culture.

Breaking Free from the Old Paradigm

Throughout this book, we have referenced organizations that are doing things differently and slowly breaking free from Old Paradigm thinking and approaches. We want to take a moment here to acknowledge some bold ways in which well-known organizations are doing just that — ways that align powerfully with supporting thriving workplace cultures.

- *Parkland Hospital* — located in Dallas, TX, is one of the country's largest safety-net hospitals *(hospitals that provide a disproportionate amount of care to vulnerable populations)*. Parkland recently raised the minimum wage it pays its workers. According to Jim Dunn, executive vice president and chief talent officer:

  We really want, in any way possible, to break down any gaps or anything between the top leaders and those who are closest to our patients... We feel like it's the right thing to do.[2]

  It's not hard to imagine the impact this action is likely to have on employee engagement, with all its attendant benefits for both organizational and employee wellbeing.

- *Starbucks* — has long been known for taking really good care of its employees. But its recent announcement took almost everybody by surprise. In the headline in "The New York Times" on June 16, 2014,

Howard D. Schultz, the company's chairman and chief executive announced: *Starbucks to Provide Free College Education to Thousands of Workers.*[3]

You read that correctly — a free college education. Plus, after graduating, employees are free to leave whenever they feel inclined to do so without penalty and with the company's blessing. Why on earth would a CEO of such a successful company make this offer? In Schultz's own words:

> *I believe it will lower attrition, it'll increase performance, it'll attract and retain better people.*

We've already established the importance of supporting ongoing growth and development. And we give kudos to Starbucks and consider the potentially amazing benefits of this bold business move — quite a far cry from the pitfalls of 4P wellness programs and, particularly, the fiascos at Penn State and Nebraska.

- *Patagonia* — is a world-renowned sports equipment and apparel company. In his book, "Let My People Go Surfing," CEO Yvon Chouinard describes Patagonia's philosophy of "breaking the rules of business" by taking care of its employees while also caring for the environment. Chouinard breaks all of the Old Paradigm rules when it comes to running the business. He truly keeps the customers' and employees' best interests in mind, and *creates the conditions* to ensure that work is enjoyable on a daily basis and to blur the lines between work, play and family. For example, people can dress however they want *(many even go barefoot)* and are given flex time so they can surf the waves when the conditions are good or tend to whatever they need for their personal lives. As long as the work gets done, leadership doesn't care when employees work. If employees want to bring their children to work, they can. Chouinard also makes great effort to care for the environment. Patagonia donates 1% of sales to groups working to save or restore habitat. The company also pioneered the use of recycled, reused and less toxic materials in its construction and remodeling projects, and cautions about overnight shipping due to the strain it puts on the environment.[4] Not only is Patagonia finding tremendous financial success, but Chouinard reported during an October 2013 talk at UCLA that the company receives around 900 applicants for every open position.[5] People are literally knocking down the doors to work there — talk about a thriving culture at work!

- ***The Conscious Capitalism Movement*** — Whole Foods Market's co-founder and co-CEO John Mackey has collaborated with professor Raj Sisodia to create the concept of Conscious Capitalism.[6] In their book by the same name, they detail a truly compassionate, holistic approach to business — one in which the underlying foundational goal is to maximize purpose, not profits. This movement aligns with the New Paradigm *(and new sciences)* understanding that when people feel part of something bigger than themselves, and when they are given the autonomy to find meaning and purpose in their work, the inevitable result will be success for all stakeholders *(customers, employees, suppliers, investors, society and the environment)*, including financial success. Many companies are beginning to understand the power of this approach. You can read more details about these companies, including Southwest Airlines, UPS, Tata, Costco, Panera, Google, The Container Store, and others in this revolutionary work.

In fact, it is hard to imagine a more insightful summary of the need for this new business paradigm than that expressed in CEO Mackey's own words:

To tap this deep wellspring of human motivation, companies need to shift from profit maximization to purpose maximization. By recognizing and responding to the hunger for meaning that is quintessential to the human condition, companies can unlock vast sources of passion, commitment, creativity, and energy that lie largely dormant in their team members and other stakeholders. Purpose-driven motivation is intrinsic motivation and is far more effective and powerful than extrinsic financial incentives.[7]

The common denominator in these pioneering, innovative organizations is that they are all intentionally breaking away from "old school business" practices and going out on a limb to live their core values and create a thriving workplace culture. But what about smaller companies whose operating margins are tight compared to larger companies? We now explore a case study of one of our clients who is not as large, "flashy" or well-known as the examples we just provided. But the company has been finding success in applying the New Paradigm to improve its organizational and employee wellbeing.

"Freemont Marketing": The New Paradigm and *The 7 Points of Transformation* in Action

It was hard to pick just one of our clients to highlight here. We have so many clients with amazing stories that include successes, challenges *(even some epic failures)*, and lessons learned as they apply the New Paradigm and *The 7 Points of Transformation* to build a thriving workplace culture. Each one has its own unique experiences that could bring valuable insight and learning. One of our clients, that we'll call "Freemont Marketing," particularly illustrates the dynamics involved with changing organizational and employee wellbeing. We choose to share Freemont's journey because it's similar to many companies that are straddling paradigms. Transitioning to the New Paradigm is not about perfection; it's about ongoing transformation. As is the case with Freemont, transformation can be messy but still have positive results.

Freemont is a smaller employer with about 70 employees. Its main functional areas include: sales, project management, order fulfillment, creative/design and production. Freemont's workforce is 76% male with an average age of 46. The company started down the path of implementing a traditional Old Paradigm wellness program and had it in place for about two years when we began working with them. We started at *Transformation Point #1* by reviewing data, which was quite minimal. So, we implemented our Thriving Workplace Culture Survey *(TWCS)*. We learned that Freemont's overall culture wasn't bad, but it wasn't thriving. Some specific areas identified that were getting in the way of thriving organizational wellbeing included:

- There was no clear company vision.

- There weren't comprehensive development opportunities for employees.

- Employees didn't perceive the executive team as all being on the same page.

- Inconsistencies existed between departments with regards to the quality of managers and the employee experience.

- There was not enough communication about the state of the organization.

- The company did not celebrate successes enough.

Once they knew their baseline, they moved to *Transformation Point #2* and started planning for their new future. Freemont was already two years into a five-year strategic plan, so company leaders began planning for wellbeing separately. The CEO presented the culture survey results at an all-employee meeting, shared his vision for creating a thriving workplace culture, and invited employees to participate in the planning process. Freemont had many long-tenured employees who were skeptical, so they were not enthusiastic about participating. In spite of our suggestions to the contrary, the CEO decided to jump to *Transformation Point #4*, hoping to create some momentum by creating a supportive climate and structure for employee wellbeing and then back-fill later. They formed a Culture and Wellbeing Team to create an initial three-year wellbeing plan along with operational objectives for the next 12 months. The team brainstormed ideas for rebranding the wellness program and had the employees vote to name the new wellbeing benefit. From there, the team created a list of all of the resources and programs the company had available to support each area of employee wellbeing and then created an Employee Wellbeing Overview. The team also developed an annual wellbeing communication plan and launched a marketing and communication strategy using wellbeing language and color-coding messages by area of wellbeing *(similar to examples we provided in chapter 11)*.

Once some of the structure was in place to help create a supportive climate, the CEO was anxious to "get going" and, again ignoring our gentle recommendations, moved directly to *Transformation Point #6*. We encouraged company leaders, and they agreed, to at least take a New Paradigm approach by implementing quality, evidence-based programs and resources. Freemont began by supporting employees with building the skills to be wiser healthcare consumers; and over the course of the next three years, we implemented the full healthcare consumerism strategy *(outlined in chapter 13)*. The CEO also started doing monthly summary letters to all employees reviewing the state of the business and highlighting employee wellbeing. And the company provided various programs and resources that supported all areas of wellbeing and emphasized developing better thinking.

Despite our guidance and warning, the CEO also insisted on keeping the "Healthy Living Rewards Program" that required employees to participate in a biometric screening, complete an HRA and earn points doing various other activities to receive an incentive. So we worked with the Culture and Wellbeing Team to modify the program to minimize the likely unintended, negative consequences of the incentives. The following changes were made:

- The program name was changed to "Wellbeing Perks Program," and regular, consistent communication was provided to ensure employees knew this program was NOT the same as the Employee Wellbeing Benefit, but rather one small component of the larger, holistic and comprehensive platform for supporting total wellbeing.

- The incentive was expanded to include health insurance premium discounts or additional wellbeing time off from work; employees could choose which reward they wanted to receive.

- The biometric screening and HRA requirement was replaced with a requirement to have a form signed by an employee's doctor indicating that person was current on all age-appropriate preventive exams and screenings, and program participants had to complete the healthcare consumerism workshops.

- The activities provided for earning points were tweaked to support all areas of wellbeing.

- The points were heavily weighted to encourage people to make the program personal and meet their unique needs by intentionally working on their own wellbeing and engaging in five coaching sessions with a Certified Intrinsic Coach®. Of the additional 300 points employees had to earn in this program, they could earn 250 points by completing this activity.

By taking this more holistic approach, employees reported an increase each year in their positive perception of the wellbeing benefit and provided examples of how their wellbeing and their family members' wellbeing had improved.

After two years, we implemented a repeat Thriving Workplace Culture Survey *(TWCS)* to determine what norms had changed. Although the results were somewhat improved from the initial TWCS, there were still issues with clarity of vision and leadership effectiveness. Once the CEO and executive team saw the results, they started to rethink their resistance to working on organizational wellbeing. They also realized they didn't have a strong succession plan and had several key leaders who would be retiring within the next four to five years *(including the CEO)*.

So we partnered with the executive team to revisit *Transformation Points #2, 3, and 5* to fill in the culture gaps. Over the next two years, Freemont implemented the following:

- Actively managed a small handful of employees who were toxic to the thriving culture that company leadership wanted to build and guided these employees out of the organization.

- Involved each department in creating a mission and vision to align with the company vision and added "vision/values alignment" to individual employee development plans.

- Developed a comprehensive leadership development strategy following the four-step framework we outlined in chapter 10; this included all leaders completing Intrinsic Coaching® development and having access to their own coaches to work on their adaptive challenges and personal wellbeing.

- Embedded wellbeing into all levels of employee development and provided all employees with access to a Certified Intrinsic Coach® to support them in adaptive change work.

Freemont leaders also decided to take steps to ensure the physical environment was supporting the company's culture transformation journey *(Transformation Point #4)*. Freemont provided all employees who wanted them sit-stand workstations, incorporated more family-friendly social events so employees didn't have to choose between work and family when events were offered, redesigned their office space to better support collaboration, and created "goof-off spaces" for people to blow off steam and reenergize during the day.

The Results of Freemont's Efforts

After the additional two years Freemont spent filling in the gaps and tending to its organizational wellbeing, company leaders saw profound results — much greater than the previous years when they only focused on employee wellbeing. Here are just some highlights:

- Perceived cultural norms improved dramatically with regards to the executive team, direct supervisors, work climate, clarity of company vision and overall engagement and happiness.

- The perception of employees feeling valued improved dramatically.

- The number of employees reporting that they view what they do as a calling increased.

- 82% of employees reported feeling the company positively impacted their overall wellbeing, and 57% felt the employee wellbeing benefit improved their job satisfaction *(a 29% increase over the previous two years)*.

- 86% of employees believed the wellbeing benefit was effective in engaging and supporting their overall wellbeing *(a 14% increase over the past two years)*.

- 34% of employees reported the wellbeing benefit had a positive influence on family members *(a 44% increase over the past two years)*.

- Employees' satisfaction with each area of wellbeing improved.

- For the Wellbeing Perks Program, there was a 29% decrease in people participating primarily for the incentive and a 32% increase in people participating because they were personally interested in their wellbeing; this shows they have been effective in "correcting" for the incentive and truly engaging employees.

- Overall sales increased 67% and their market share increased 23%.

When we asked the CEO to describe Freemont's organizational and employee wellbeing journey, here is what he said:

"We got off to a bumpy start and didn't appreciate the value of following ***The 7 Points of Transformation*** *in order. I think I thought we could ignore the organizational wellbeing stuff and just deal with employee well-being. But I finally learned that was faulty thinking; things were okay, but nothing really started gelling until we truly addressed our culture. They [Jon and Rosie] kept encouraging us to redirect our efforts and resources to leadership development and aligning employees with the vision, and we kept ignoring them. I'm pretty sure our own stubbornness cost us more pain, time and money in the long run; but perhaps we needed to feel the pain to finally address our organizational wellbeing and culture issues. Six years later, we are*

definitely still a work in progress — and probably always will be. But I feel much better about where our company is today, where we're headed, and the legacy we [the leaders] will be leaving behind. That's what I hope to be remembered for here."

As was clearly the case with Freemont, the journey to transform workplace culture takes considerable persistence and patience. We get that many people feel compelled to do something that will provide more immediate results. Unfortunately, from an employee wellbeing perspective, many times the go-to approach is to fall back on traditional ineffective and iatrogenic initiatives like weight loss challenges and programs. With that in mind, we now turn our attention to a quality, evidence-based program we mentioned in chapter 13 that embraces the New Paradigm to provide an effective alternative to weight management and also supports total wellbeing.

Shifting the Paradigm of Weight Management: Health for Every Body®

A focus on approaches that can produce health benefits independently of weight loss may be the best way to improve the physical and psychological health of Americans seeking to lose weight.[8]

National Institutes of Health

According to a recent review by the National Business Group on Health, weight management initiatives remain among the top three most popular lifestyle management programs at the workplace.[9] This is extremely discouraging for the following reasons:[10]

- **Lack of efficacy.** Trying to lose weight through exercise, food restriction and behavior modification is associated with a 90% to 95% failure rate. Despite these near impossible odds, more individuals are dieting than ever before. This begs the question: In what world is a failure rate of 90% to 95% considered an acceptable outcome? Given the current emphasis on "evidence-based" practices in healthcare, scientific validation is clearly lacking for continuing traditional weight management strategies.

- **Poor investment.** Most workplace wellness initiatives do not suffer from overfunding. Given these often dire budgetary challenges, it is critical that all programs and services be evaluated based on their financial efficacy. Is a health-promotion program for which the likely outcome is that one-third to half of the participants will drop out and 90% to 95% will be unsuccessful a wise financial investment for anyone other than the people providing the programs?

- **Iatrogenic effects.** There is compelling evidence that promoting weight loss is not just ineffective; it can be unintentionally, yet seriously, harmful. Our culture's obsession with weight and thinness has been linked to **1)** dramatic increases in eating disorders in the past decades; **2)** an estimated 80% prevalence of dysfunctional eating behaviors such as chronic dieting, undereating, overeating, good food – bad food thinking and fear of food;[11] and **3)** significant and increasing size prejudice and discrimination.[12] In addition, there is growing evidence of significant negative psychological and physiological consequences from the ongoing weight cycling that more often than not results from participation in these programs.[13]

We suggested in chapter 13 that, instead of wasting valuable resources on programs that attempt to make people smaller, or prescriptive-nutrition and physical activity initiatives that end up appealing to few folks who might really benefit from them, organizations can instead invest in approaches and programs that help people to find peace with their bodies, their food and their movement. We turn our attention now to such an approach and such a program — Health for Every Body®.

Health for Every Body® — Beyond Weight Management

Our Health for Every Body® *(HFEB®)* employee program *(to be discussed in more detail shortly)* is based on the Health At Every Size® *(HAES®)** philosophy, approach and movement with which I *(Jon)* have been intimately involved as a national leader for almost two decades. The HAES® approach helps people who are struggling with weight-related concerns to attain a more peaceful relationship with their bodies and their food by honoring and caring for the bodies that they presently have. It is an evidence-based approach that helps people to improve the quality of

their lives without the frustration, high dropout and iatrogenic consequences that often accompany traditional weight loss interventions.[14]

The basic conceptual framework of the HAES® philosophy includes belief
in and support for:

- The naturally existing diversity in body shapes and sizes.
- The ineffectiveness and dangers of dieting for weight loss.
- The importance of relaxed eating in response to internal
  body cues.
- The critical contribution of social, emotional, spiritual
  and physical factors, and their interdependence with health
  and happiness.

Although traditional strategies have a decidedly weight-centered focus —
with the primary goal of making people smaller — the HAES® approach
has a health-centered focus, supporting a holistic view of health that promotes "feeling good about oneself, eating in a natural, relaxed way and
being comfortably active." A comparison of the underlying assumptions of
the two approaches is shown below:

Comparison of the Traditional Weight Loss Paradigm With Health At Every Size®

Traditional Weight Loss Paradigm	Health At Every Size® Approach
Everyone needs to be thin for good health and happiness.	Thin is not intrinsically healthy and beautiful, nor is fat intrinsically unhealthy and unappealing.
Individuals who are not thin are "overweight" because they have no willpower, eat too much and do not move enough.	Individuals naturally have different body shapes and sizes, and different preferences for food and physical activity.
Everyone can be thin, happy and healthy by dieting.	Dieting usually leads to weight gain, decreased self-esteem and increased risk for disordered eating. Health and happiness involve a dynamic interaction among mental, social, spiritual and physical considerations.[15]

The three major components of the Health At Every Size® approach are:

1) **Size and Self-Acceptance.** The foundational cornerstone of the HAES® philosophy is self-acceptance. Self-acceptance is not a denial of the importance of self-care, but rather an affirmation that, just as human worth is not based on race, color or creed; it also is not dependent on body weight, shape or size. Our obsession with thinness has spawned a culturally accepted prejudice against individuals who do not live up to our unrealistic and constantly shrinking societal standards. Like racism, sexism, anti-Semitism and homophobia, this weightism:

is based on visible cues, i.e., the fat person is discriminated against primarily because of the way she looks… defines an entire group of people numbering in the millions within a narrow range of negative characteristics and behaviors… elevates the status of one group of people at the expense of another… and serves as a vehicle for the bigot's own anxieties, frustrations and resentments.[16]

The result of this prejudice is rampant social, economic and educational discrimination against larger individuals.[17] In fact, the latest research suggests weight discrimination is now more prevalent than discrimination based on sexual orientation, nationality/ethnicity, physical disability and religious beliefs. Indeed, for women, weight discrimination is even more prevalent than racial discrimination.[18] As the cornerstone of HAES®, self-acceptance involves honoring the natural diversity in the human form and challenging cultural weight prejudice.

2) **Physical Activity.** Physical activity is widely recognized as a critical element in human health, yet the majority of Americans of all sizes remain largely sedentary. Part of the problem may lie in traditional Old Paradigm approaches used to encourage people to become more active. As Thomas Moore writes in "Care of the Soul":

Usually we are told how much time to spend at a certain exercise, what heart rate to aim for, and which muscle to focus on for toning… If we could loosen our grip on the mechanical view of our own bodies and the body of the world, many other possibilities might come to light.[19]

HAES® focuses on promoting movement that is social, playful and pleasurable, and includes not just jogging, cycling and exercise classes, but also activities connected with everyday living, such as walking and gardening. Movement is encouraged for enjoyment, camaraderie and improved quality of life, not calorie burning and weight loss. Much accumulated research supports that physical activity can positively affect health and longevity regardless of weight status.[20]

In addition, this alternative paradigm acknowledges the prevalence of sedentary living in our society as largely a cultural phenomenon that can be significantly impacted only by addressing cultural barriers. This is especially true for larger individuals, many of whom are deterred from engaging in physical activity by fear of the ridicule and humiliation they have endured as a regular, ongoing part of their lives. For many such individuals, discovering movement in a size-friendly environment can be a means of beginning to rediscover and reconnect to the bodies they have been taught to hate and ignore.[21]

3) **Normal** *(intuitive, mindful, attuned)* **Eating.** Healthy eating is also clearly an important component of a healthy lifestyle. However, the externally focused, restrictive methods used by diet programs rarely succeed in helping people to become healthy eaters. There is strong evidence that human beings are capable of regulating caloric intake according to internal hunger, satiety and appetite signals, and that chronic food restriction such as dieting interferes with this process and actually increases the likelihood of overeating.[22] HAES® approaches refute the concept of "good" and "bad" foods and discourage the use of externally focused eating strategies. Instead, all foods are legalized, and the focus is placed on reducing anxiety about eating by relearning how to eat in response to internal signals: hunger, appetite and satiety. This innate ability to regulate our eating is referred to as "normal," "intuitive," "mindful" or "attuned" eating and fits clearly into the intrinsic, New Paradigm focus that we have been promoting throughout this book.[23]

As a result of being more aware of internal signals, individuals may or may not decrease their weight. However, regardless of their weight status, they are likely to improve their health by reducing the anxiety, guilt, preoccupation with food, bingeing, weight cycling and weight gain commonly associated with restricted eating *(dieting)*.[24]

Health Issues and Medical Treatment for Larger Individuals

The HAES® approach does not suggest that health professionals ignore effective healthcare for larger people. When larger individuals present with medical problems, health professionals can consider and offer the same approaches that they would for a thin person presenting with similar problems.[25] In the case of a thin person with essential hypertension, for example, conventional medicine suggests dietary changes, increases in aerobic physical activity and stress management followed by medication, if necessary. Yet, a larger individual presenting with the same diagnosis is told to lose weight, despite all that is known about the likely unhealthy consequences of this prescription. In fact, the HAES® approach can be followed regardless of the individuals presenting health-related problems. Even with individuals experiencing serious conditions, such as Type 2 diabetes and coronary artery disease, where weight is commonly seen as an important risk factor, substantial research shows that health status can be improved without changes in weight, and even in individuals who remain markedly obese by traditional medical standards.[26]

HAES® approaches also recognize that when people are struggling with food- and weight-related issues, it may be symptomatic of underlying distress that cannot be solved merely by delivering nutrition information and advice. Trying to help people with these kinds of issues and being sure to do no harm in the process necessitates a compassionate, weight-neutral, intrinsic, truly holistic approach.

Health for Every Body® at the Workplace

Health for Every Body® is an on-site, 10-week program based on the principles of Health At Every Size® that offers employees a unique, evidence-based approach for making peace with their food and their bodies. It was developed originally from a successful randomized controlled trial and retested and validated at a real-life quasi-experimental venue at a hospital in Mason City, Iowa.[27] We have overseen the implementation of this program in 15 cities over the past two years and have been delighted with the feedback from participants:

❝ *If it were offered tomorrow, I would sign up again for it exactly as is. It was really an amazing experience to go to week after week. I really think the fantastic part was the focus of doing things based on what feels good and right to you, and the lack of focus on expectations. I feel like the company really offered something innovative and outstanding, and I am never going to sit through another program that tells me that I must lose weight and how. I'm going to look for programs that focus on health as a happy, exciting thing."*

❝ *I feel empowered to make healthy choices for my own sake, not to fulfill others' expectations. A lot of that weight (pun intended) was lifted off me, and with it removed, I was really able to examine what I wanted from life. It turns out that I do not care so much about my weight, but I fervently care about being active and healthy. The series shifted my focus from unhealthy weight-obsessed practices to pleasurable movement and mindful eating. I would whole-heartedly recommend it."*

❝*The Health for Every Body® workshop was fantastic and we each left today, the last meeting, feeling better than we did when we started on the nonjudgmental journey of self-acceptance. It is a daily struggle, but we are now more equipped and aware, which is half the battle."*

It is really powerful for us to hear that people valued the program so highly, not because they reached some arbitrary short-term behavioral goal, won some award or avoided some punishment, but because: **1)** they learned to think differently about their body and their food, **2)** they felt good about the company offering them something free, voluntary and innovative, and **3)** they began the journey *(and understood it as a journey)* of nonjudgmental self-acceptance, a journey that can only happen from the inside out.

Incorporating the HAES® philosophy we have just explored, the HFEB® program is built around the six tenets listed below:

- **Education** — provide the latest scientific research on the relationship between weight and health.

- **Self-acceptance** — encourage participants to work on issues of body hatred from the inside out.

- **Normal *(healthy)* eating** — teach participants how to **1)** eat in response to internal *(intrinsic)*, rather than external *(extrinsic)*, cues; **2)** refrain from dieting *(restricting foods)*; and **3)** avoid "dieter's mentality," which includes good food – bad food thinking, fear of food, chronic dieting and starving – bingeing cycles.

- **Pleasurable movement** — de-emphasize weight loss and body sculpting as the primary goals of physical activity and emphasize pleasure, feeling good, improved health and increased energy.

- **Social support** — help participants recognize the critical role of relationships in addressing issues of weight and health *(as well as all other issues),* and begin to create and support a network of HFEB®-friendly health professionals in the community.

- **Size tolerance** — advocate for the fair and equal treatment of individuals of all shapes and sizes.[28]

HFEB® is more than a health education class, but it is not meant to be therapy. The group facilitator presents the week's lesson in the beginning of each hour, and participants spend the bulk of the time processing the information with exercises, small group work and discussion. Typically, the 10-week program runs for an hour each session with the following weekly topics:

1) Review current research on dieting, weight and health
2) Examine social and cultural pressures to be thin
3) Discuss the health consequences of body dissatisfaction/ hatred
4) Improve body acceptance and self-esteem
5) Explore pleasurable movement: fitter at any size
6) Reduce disordered eating: teach mindful, intuitive eating
7) Overview the health benefits of relationships and social support
8) Manage stress, develop mindfulness and focus on meaning and purpose
9) Improve and better manage health in the presence of a chronic illness
10) Solidify and protect improvements

We believe that employees have taken so strongly to HFEB® for a variety of reasons — reasons that reflect many of the New Paradigm concepts we have explored with regards to rethinking how we go about promoting organizational and employee wellbeing.

- **Everything about the program aligns with I>E>S.** There are no incentives or other throwbacks to outdated, control-oriented strategies; participants are encouraged to contribute as much or as little as they want without the lure of rewards or the fear of punishment.

- **It is all about relationships.** Rather than the usual obsessive focus on personal responsibility and individual behavior change, participants begin to envision health and the human experience as an ongoing process revolving around the important relationships in their lives.

- **Social Support.** The group members are encouraged to provide support for one another — not for some arbitrary weight loss or behavioral goal, but for the growth of each toward a more peaceful relationship with food and their bodies.

- **Inclusive.** This is not a program specifically for "overweight" or "obese" people, "couch potatoes," only women, or people who eat too much "junk food." It is a program for anybody *(Every Body)* who wants to feel better about who he or she is — from the inside out.

- **Evidence-based.** Finally, unlike programs that focus on weight loss *(for which there is both a complete lack of evidence of efficacy and decades of evidence of lack of efficacy)*, the HAES® approach has been documented to help people live a better quality of life, without the substantial dropout and iatrogenesis associated with traditional weight management programs.

We recognize that many of you reading this book may be struggling with how you can overcome Old Paradigm thinking about weight, culture and wellbeing and translate the New Paradigm and *The 7 Points of Transformation* into action at your own organization. So, we wrap up this chapter not in our words, but in the words of someone who has been working to shift from the Old to New Paradigm, apply the HAES® principles, and align organizational and employee wellbeing by activating and applying I>E>S in herself and in the employees she supports. We originally contacted Stephanie Downs to ask her if she would write about the great work she has been doing. Instead, she wanted to tell her story in a different way. We are honored and humbled by how she describes her own transformational journey.

A Transformational Journey to the New Paradigm, by Stephanie Downs, MS, CIC® *(in her own words)*

More than 15 years ago, I heard Dr. Jon Robison speak at the National Wellness Institute conference in Stevens Point, WI. What I learned altered my career path and started my journey in changing the way I work with people. At the time, I was working in a large school district in central Iowa providing programs and services for the employees of the district. What changed after hearing Jon speak about the fallacies of weight loss studies and HAES®? I decided from that day forward to never offer a diet or weight loss program again and excluded any measure of weight in outcomes and reports.

But that wasn't all. Jon didn't just share the other side of the weight loss industry; he shared this new perspective and historic look at what scientists were learning in fields like neuroscience and quantum physics. He shared this expansive base of research that explained WHY the "whole > the sum of the parts" and WHY we *(health and wellness professionals)* needed to rethink how we were working with and valuing people. It made so much sense and provided me with a new understanding of the challenges I had been facing; however, I wasn't sure what that meant in application. At the time, our field was moving from activity-based programs to outcome-based programming; practically every other continuing education workshop offered was on ROI and reducing healthcare costs — much of what we are still hearing today. So I did what most coordinators were doing at the time. I continued to operate in the Old Paradigm, not knowing what else to do and not having support to do things differently; I offered programs *(with the exception of weight loss)* and tracked healthcare costs.

Over the course of the next five years, I continued to explore the "other side" that Jon had exposed, and I completed two major life-changing programs. First, I earned my Masters of Science by completing my thesis work on "non-diet programs." The review of the literature confirmed much of what Jon had shared and was then ingrained in my philosophy forever. Never again would I offer or incorporate any program or measure related to a person's weight! In addition, I completed development in Intrinsic Coaching® that aligned with my New Paradigm of wanting to value people, not processes and outcomes. Not only did my own intrinsic capacity grow from this development, but I gained the skills to support I>E>S thinking in others. This was a missing link that now allowed me to think, plan and program from a New Paradigm that valued people more than expertise and systems. However, it wasn't until 2005, when I took a new job with the City of Ames, Iowa, that I was given the opportunity to bridge the transition from a traditional approach *(Old Paradigm)* to the New Paradigm.

Bridging the Gap Between Paradigms

The City of Ames already had a comprehensive wellness program. The City offered all of the traditional programs, including flu vaccines; biometric health screenings; a personal wellness questionnaire *(Health Risk Assessment)*; incentive programs on fitness, nutrition and stress management; luncheon sessions; a biennial health fair; and even an online wellness portal, to name a few. But all of these were still grounded in the Old Paradigm. I decided to create something that blended the Old and New Paradigms; it was called "Healthy4Life." It included traditional measures such as waist measure, smoking status, participation, biometrics *(blood pressure, LDL, triglycerides and glucose)* and a financial incentive linked to health insurance premiums. It also included a few cutting-edge programs. The program included two required criteria: the first was participating in a newly created, comprehensive healthcare consumerism training designed to educate our employees on benefits design and the healthcare system; the second was completing an annual preventive exam and age/gender-specific health screenings. Both criteria aligned with our prevention focus and wanting to equip people to work collaboratively with their healthcare teams. But the key component, and paradigm-shifting factor, was the Intrinsic Coaching®. It changed the way we worked with, valued and supported employees. Because Intrinsic Coaching® works with the thinking patterns of the individual *(not the problem or topic)* and builds his or her ability to activate I>E>S, the people we supported were able to see more and value their own uniqueness. And, the structure of Intrinsic Coaching® allowed for the flexibility that employees need; they decided when, where, how much and what. My expertise and advice still had value, but only in the context of their thinking and what they were wanting.

Did the program work? You bet it did! The pilot group went from 60% to 80% being at low-risk *(based on the biometric screening and HRA)* in the first two years and maintained at that level every year thereafter; and the percentage of high-risk participants decreased. The cornerstone of the program was Intrinsic Coaching® sessions. Because of this core component of integrating I>E>S, even within program constructs based in the Old Paradigm, people talked about "accountability" and "feeling valued," and they kept coming back. We had a 95% retention the first three years and more than 70% over the full seven years of the program. The program grew from the initial 48 participants to 125 participants in the last year. The only limiting factors in the program growth were the retirement of

300

participants and the availability of Certified Intrinsic Coach® coaches. "Healthy4Life" wasn't the only program feeling the shift to I>E>S. All trainings and workshops started integrating Intrinsic Coaching® principles and were centered on what the participants wanted to learn and experience — not just the content.

As I became more self-aware and skilled in activating I>E>S in my own thinking, I started seeing people in a whole new way — complete and whole, and fully capable of living well. I changed the way I developed programs and started with the person first, allowing for uniqueness and individuality. There was mutual trust and respect, and a growing sense of connection among the participants.

I'd wanted to think I had made the final leap to the "other side," a complete paradigm shift, but the reality was I was still holding onto the edge and hanging somewhere in between — straddling the Old and New Paradigm. The truth is that I didn't know for sure what the "other side" was and/or exactly how to get there. But, as life would have it, the student *(me)* was ready, and the teacher appeared. Into the wellness field emerged a new thought leader, Dr. Rosie Ward. Her groundbreaking *(and paradigm shattering)* announcement, "Wellness programs don't work and never will without thriving cultures and engaged employees," made me take a step back. All I could think was, "Are you kidding me? All this work and I still don't have it right?" Honestly, I was beginning to feel that I never would. But then I realized this was the missing piece. The fog was lifting around the New Paradigm; I could see the "other side" as clear as day, but this final leap was going to change everything. I wasn't sure I could let go of the safety of the Old Paradigm, and I wasn't sure the City was ready. I had questions I'm sure many people have when thinking about fully integrating organizational and employee wellbeing and operating from the New Paradigm:

- Could my organization actually embrace a new approach to leadership development?
- Do they have the time and resources to build a thriving workplace culture?
- Where would we start?

Fully Embracing the New Paradigm

I didn't get to have those questions answered with the City because I moved on to a new opportunity. In 2014, I started a new position with a large university in the state. The opportunity before me is to build wellbeing from scratch. I finally have the opportunity to step fully into the New Paradigm, so we have decided to start with workplace culture and organizational wellbeing. The University wants to do it right, and we want to do it well! We are having amazing conversations around wellbeing with employees that include all aspects of creating thriving organizational and employee wellbeing. We are embracing the complexities of being human and being a university, and are learning together as we stretch ourselves and take a team approach to building a foundation from which we can work and learn. We are educating our leadership and employees about the importance of both organizational and employee wellbeing so we all have a common framework on which to build our collective desired culture. We are at the very beginning of our wellbeing and culture transformation journey, but we have fully made the leap to the New Paradigm. We are finally on the "other side," moving forward and forging a whole new path. I do know there is no going back. We have to embrace the New Paradigm if we are going to make a difference in the future.

It may have taken 20 years for me to bring Dr. Jon Robison's work to fruition, but it is finally happening. I heard Jon speak again this summer at the same conference that started my paradigm transformation journey all those years ago. He was sharing the same information with updated research, exposing the challenges in the traditional research, asking us to be critical thinkers, and continuing to ignite passion and change for the wellbeing of others and our profession. This time he wasn't alone; Dr. Rosie Ward was there too, shining a light through a foggy night, guiding us out to a whole new frontier. I hope we will listen — to them, to the research, to our employees and to ourselves. I hope we will learn as we shift away from the practices that no longer make any sense and fully embrace the New Paradigm. I hope we will change. We don't have another 20 years to keep doing the same thing!

* Health At Every Size and HAES are registered trademarks of the Association for Size Diversity and Health and used with permission.

CHAPTER 16
Beginning the Journey

❝We are in one of those great historical periods that occur every 200 or 300 years when people don't understand the world anymore, and the past is not sufficient to explain the future.[1]❞

Peter Drucker

Hockey great Wayne Gretzky was famous for saying, "I skate to where the puck is going to be, not where it is." Because we have been so *stuck* in the 17th-century worldview when it comes to organizational and employee wellbeing, we recognize that we are asking businesses and professionals to venture into uncharted territory. However, our world is constantly changing, and if we don't chart a new path and skate to where the puck is going to be, we will remain *stuck*.

The scientific advances of the 20th and 21st centuries paint a dramatically different picture of reality from that proposed by the scientific assumptions of 400 years ago. It is a picture not of a giant machine-like universe in which everything can be understood by taking it apart and analyzing it piece by piece; but instead a living, breathing, evolving universe in which understanding the relationship of the parts to the whole is primary, and considering the context of issues and the unseen connections is vital for both organizations and employees to be able to thrive.

Imagine comparing a house built in 1920 to a modern, energy-efficient house under construction right now. The modern house has the advantage of scientific discoveries, technologies and know-how that simply did not exist in 1920. *The 7 Points of Transformation* provide a blueprint for organizational and employee wellbeing using a house metaphor; a house built to be in harmony with its surroundings; a house that is built in stages, yet always operates as an interconnected, holistic structure; a house that is at the same time a physical entity and also a home — a place that supports and nurtures its inhabitants. It takes time to do this correctly, assuming you're interested in building something more sustainable than a tree fort.

When we speak to groups about shifting paradigms and using *The 7 Points of Transformation* to create a thriving workplace culture, we inevitably get some version of this question: "Which of the seven steps should be tackled first when changing traditional paradigm thinking?" Our answer is always the same: You can't start decorating a house when you haven't even surveyed

The 7 Points of Transformation provide a blueprint for organizational and employee wellbeing using a house metaphor; a house built to be in harmony with its surroundings; a house that is built in stages, yet always operates as an interconnected, holistic structure; a house that is at the same time a physical entity and also a home — a place that supports and nurtures its inhabitants.

the land to know if you can build there; it makes no sense. If you want sustainability and a thriving workplace culture, start at the beginning and know what you're dealing with so you can use the feedback from each of *The 7 Points of Transformation* to inform your culture change journey. If you first need to gain the support of others in your organization and create a *burning platform* for the need to change your current approach to organizational and employee wellbeing, then hopefully the first six chapters of this book detailing why we are *stuck* will help you begin those discussions. Remember, transforming workplace culture is not a solo project. You will be most successful if you use the information in this book to help guide you to form alliances and partnerships to begin the necessary discussions to create the support for shifting to the New Paradigm and embarking on an adventurous culture change journey.

Feeling Overwhelmed?

We also frequently hear people say that they can see how the New Paradigm is more effective and that ultimately, their organization needs to focus on transforming culture. However, they feel overwhelmed at the thought of going there right now. They want to do something, so what will make the most sense? The step-by-step blueprint we have provided is designed to guide you on a long-term journey. Some organizations are ready to jump in head first in the deep end and begin the journey, while others are more comfortable with dipping their toe in the water first. We can't pretend to tell you in a book what is right for your organization. *The 7 Points of Transformation* is a blueprint; it is not rigid or prescriptive. If it were, we would be no further along than the Old Paradigm and Newtonian worldview.

That said, if your organization has what we describe as a 4P wellness program *(pry, poke, prod and punish)*, a great starting point would be to use our suggestions in chapter 13 for what to do instead to start showing employees they are valued as people, not viewed as machines, cattle or rodents. Additionally, starting at *Transformation Point #1* doesn't take too many resources and will at least give you a good basic understanding of the current state of your culture. From there, you can determine what makes sense for your organization as a starting point and fill in the gaps later. It's not perfect, but this isn't about perfection; it's about sustainability. Many of our clients have engaged us when they have some of *The 7 Points of Transformation* in place but not all, and they need support to fill in the gaps and start to better align organizational and employee wellbeing efforts.

The Dangers of Paradigm Straddling

"If you are not a part of the solution, you are a part of the problem."
Eldridge Cleaver

We warned in chapter 13 about the dangers of being seduced by cookie-cutter, turnkey approaches to organizational or employee wellbeing. We suggest raising a similar red flag for approaches and initiatives that attempt to straddle the Old and New Paradigms. It is not that everything in the universe should be viewed as black and white. That would certainly not follow from much of what we have learned from the new sciences. However, regardless of the strength of our beliefs, the sun does not revolve around the earth; the earth is not flat, and people and organizations are not predictable, controllable machines. So we suggest considerable diligence when examining proposals you may entertain from vendors, consultants, brokers, etc. We have already discussed many of these, but just by way of summary and emphasis, we suggest you may be paradigm straddling if:

1) You claim that your extrinsic motivation techniques for organizational and/or employee wellbeing will somehow lead to intrinsic motivation *(chapters 6 & 10)*.

2) You claim your goal is creating "healthy cultures" or "a culture of health" when the overwhelming focus remains on traditional *(and usually biomedical)* risk factors and health behaviors *(chapters 4, 5, & 13)*.

3) You believe you can transform your workplace culture by focusing only on climate and without fundamentally shifting how you develop leaders *(chapters 4, 10, 11, & 12)*.

4) You claim your organization truly values employees but still refer to them as "human capital" or "human resources" *(chapter 7)*.

5) You claim positive ROIs and cost savings from employee well-

being initiatives based on faulty research designs that give results that are highly improbable or mathematically impossible *(chapters 5 & 13).*

6) You say that your company cares about its employees and then conduct business in a top-down, authoritarian fashion *(chapters 4, 10, 11, & 12).*

7) You say your employee wellbeing efforts are made "for the employees" while you are implementing 4P "Wellness or Else!" programs *(chapters 5, 6, & 13).*

8) You say it is all about engagement, then force employees to participate and comply *(chapters 6, 10, & 13).*

9) You say it is all about better thinking, then talk about and treat employees as if they were rodents or cattle *(chapters 6, 10, & 13).*

10) You say it's not about the weight, then reward people for losing it in the short term *(chapters 13 & 15).*

The Dangers of Paradigm Straddling

Old Paradigm

New Paradigm

The Need for Effectively Fusing Organizational and Employee Wellbeing

If you are a business or organizational development professional, we hope you now have a better understanding of the critical importance of employee wellbeing and how closely it relates to organizational wellbeing, and ultimately organizational performance. We also hope the New Paradigm has better equipped you to:

1) Re-examine how you're fostering your desired culture;

2) Challenge consultants and vendors wanting to deploy Old Paradigm wellness programs and/or employee engagement initiatives; and

3) *Create the conditions* in which organizational and employee wellbeing can thrive.

If you are a health and wellness professional reading this book, we hope you now better understand critical aspects of organizational wellbeing that are imperative for any employee wellbeing initiative to succeed. We also hope you are better equipped to challenge the Old Paradigm and move away from autocratic, ineffective, 4P "Wellness or Else!" programs. In fact, we believe that this shift is likely the only way that workplace wellness can remain viable as a profession. We also hope you are equipped to effectively partner with people who are critical to organizational wellbeing, so, collectively, you can *create the conditions* in which employee wellbeing can also thrive.

It takes tremendous courage and commitment to face a complex adaptive challenge like transforming your workplace culture. After all, if people don't change, you won't make progress. All you will have are some nicely worded plans and intentions, but there will be no real change or solutions until the change journey is embraced by people. As Ronald Heifetz, founder of the Center for Public Leadership at Harvard University says:

> *It's not a solution until it's lived in people's lives.*
> *Unless people begin to take responsibility for reinventing*
> *the adaptation that's going to work where they're operating,*
> *there is no solution. There are only proposals.*[2]

Creating the conditions for working through adaptive change takes profound leadership. If you can't lead people through change, you won't make progress. However, mustering the courage and energy, and investing the time to address the adaptive changes required to promote and sustain a thriving workplace culture is the only way for organizations to prosper — and perhaps even survive — in our rapidly evolving work environment. Perhaps it is time for your organization to shed its cocoon and emerge into the New Paradigm. Are you ready to be a paradigm pioneer? Although the prospects may seem daunting, we suggest that the potential benefits are far too wide-reaching to ignore. Please join us in this critical revolution, spurred on by the words of the legendary Margaret Mead:

> *Never doubt that a small group of thoughtful, committed citizens can*
> *change the world; indeed, it's the only thing that ever has.*

With that, we leave you with our final, overarching, take-home recommendations for getting started.

Our Take-Home Recommendations

1) Read Outside Your Profession.

Fusing the worlds of Organizational Development and Employee Wellbeing is no small task; but it's necessary to create a truly thriving workplace culture. However, it's impossible to understand how to partner with people and how to guide the culture change journey if you're only reading within the narrow scope of your profession. Our reference list for this book is lengthy, and we also have a list of suggested readings broken down by key themes in this book at our home at **salveopartners.com**.

2) Make Sure What You're Doing is Evidence-Based.

Throughout this book, we've addressed the clash of *Belief vs. Evidence* and have used evidence to support why the Old Paradigm simply makes no sense in today's organization. You can't really ensure what you are doing is evidence-based if you haven't spent a considerable amount of time reading outside of your profession. Our general recommendation for consideration of programs, initiatives and resources is:

• If there is a lack of evidence of efficacy,
  proceed with great caution.

• If there is evidence of lack of efficacy,
  don't proceed at all.

3) And, Finally, Please Keep This in Mind:

The only way to achieve the goal of having employees act like creative, thinking, responsible, autonomous adults is to treat them like that is exactly what they are!

Notes

Introduction

1 **Tom Rath and Jim Harter.** *"Wellbeing: The Five Essential Elements."* New York: Gallup Press, 2010.

2 **Towers Watson.** *Global Workforce Study.* 2012. http://towerswatson.com/assets/pdf/2012-Towers-Watson-Global-Workforce-Study.pdf.

3 **The Centers for Disease Control and Prevention (CDC) and the National Institute for Occupational Safety and Health (NIOSH).** *Total Worker Health™.* http://www.cdc.gov/niosh/twh/

4 **The Energy Audit.** http://theenergyproject.com.

5 **E.H. Schein.** *"Organizational culture."* American Psychologist. 45.2 (1990). 109-119.

6 **Patrick Lencioni.** *"The Advantage: Why Organizational Health Trumps Everything Else in Business."* San Francisco, CA: Jossey-Bass, 2012.

7 **E.L. Deci and R. Flaste.** *"Why We Do What We Do: Understanding Self-Motivation."* New York: Penguin Books, 1996.

8 **David S. Hilzenrath.** *"Misleading claims about Safeway wellness incentives shape health-care bill."* The Washington Post. January 17, 2010.

9 **Charles S. Jacobs.** *"Management Rewired."* New York: Penguin Group, 2009.; Daniel H. Pink. *"Drive: The Surprising Truth About What Motivates Us."* New York: Riverhead Books, 2009.; Alfie Kohn. *"Punished by Rewards."* Boston: Houghton Mifflin, 1999.; E.L. Deci and R. Flaste. *"Why We Do What We Do: Understanding Self-Motivation."* New York: Penguin Books, 1996.; T.M. Amabile. *"Motivating Creativity in Organizations: On Doing What You Love and Loving What You Do."* California Management Review. 40.1 (1997). 39-58.; Paul L. Marciano. *"Carrots and Sticks Don't Work: Build a Culture of Employee Engagement with the Principles of RESPECT™."* New York: McGraw-Hill, 2010.

10 **Jacobs,** *"Management."*; C.C. Manz and C.P. Neck. *"Inner leadership: Creating Productive Thought Patterns."* The Executive. 5.3 (1991). 87-95.; D. Rock and J. Schwartz. *"The Neuroscience of Leadership."* Strategy+Business, 43 (Summer 2006). 1-10.; R.E. Boyatzis. *"An Overview of Intentional Change from a Complexity Perspective."* Journal of Management Development. 25.7 (2006). 607-623.; C. Otto Scharmer. *"Theory U: Learning From the Future as it Emerges."* San Francisco: Berrett-Koehler, 2009.

11 **Carla Saporta and Jeremy Cantor.** *"Workplace Wellness Regulations: First Do No Harm."* The Prevention Institute. The Greenlining Institute. Congress Blog. 18 January 2013. http://thehill.com/blogs/congress-blog/labor/278079-workplace-wellness-regulations-first-do-no-harm#ixzz2yEm5FLbq.

Chapter One

1 **Thomas S. Kuhn.** *"The Structure of Scientific Revolutions."* Chicago: University of Chicago Press, 1996.

2 **Stephen R. Covey.** *"The 7 Habits of Highly Effective People."* New York: Simon and Schuster, 1989.

3 **Joel A. Barker.** *"Discovering the Future: The Business of Paradigms."* St. Paul, MN: ILI Press, 1989.

4 **Covey,** *"7 Habits."*

5 **Barker,** *"Discovering."*

6 *Ibid.*

7 **Upton Sinclair.** *"I, Candidate for Governor: And How I Got Licked."* Oakland: University of California Press, 1994.

8 **Willis W. Harmon.** *"Global Mind Change: The Promise of the 21st Century."* San Francisco, CA: Berrett-Koehler Publishers, 1998.

9 **William Morris (ed.).** *American Heritage Dictionary of the English Language.* Boston: Houghton Mifflin, 1978.

10 **Kuhn,** *"Structure."*

11 **James S. Goodwin and Jean M. Goodwin.** *"The Tomato Effect: Rejection of Highly Efficacious Therapies."* JAMA. 251.18 (1984). 2387-2390.

12 **Kuhn,** *"Structure."*

13 **Barker,** *"Discovering."*

Chapter Two

1 **Fritjof Capra.** *"The Turning Point: Science, Society, and the Rising Culture."* Toronto: Bantam, 1983.

2 *Ibid.*

3 **Carolyn Merchant.** *"The Death of Nature: Women, Ecology and the Scientific Revolution."* San Francisco, CA: Harper, 1980.

4 **R.D. Laing.** *"The Voice of Experience."* New York: Pantheon, 1982.

5 **Capra,** *"Turning Point."*

6 **Merchant,** *"Death of Nature."*

7 **Charles Darwin.** *"The Origin of Species."* Toronto: Bantam, 1999.

8 **Sheryl Sandberg.** *"Lean In: Women, Work, and the Will to Lead."* New York: Knopf, 2013.

Chapter Three

1 **Fritjof Capra.** *"The Web of Life: A New Scientific Understanding of Living Systems."* New York: Doubleday, 1996.

2 **Brian Greene.** *"The Elegant Universe: Superstrings, Hidden Dimensions, and the Quest for the Ultimate Theory."* New York: W.W. Norton & Company, 1999.

3 **Richard Feynman.** *"QED: The Strange Theory of Light and Matter."*
Princeton, NJ: Princeton University Press, 1985.

4 **Fritjof Capra.** *"The Turning Point: Science, Society, and the Rising Culture."*
Toronto: Bantam, 1983.

5 **Greene,** *"Elegant Universe."*

6 **Danah Zohar.** *"The Quantum Self: Human Nature and Consciousness Defined by the New Physics."* New York: Quill/William Morrow, 1991.

7 **Greene,** *"Elegant Universe."*

8 *Ibid.*

9 **H.P. Stapp.** *"Quantum Physics and the Physicist's View of Nature: Philosophical Implications of Bell's Theorem."* In *"The World View of Contemporary Physics."* Ed. R.E. Kitchener. Albany, NY: SUNY Press, 1988.

10 **Capra,** *"Turning Point."*

11 **Margaret Wheatley.** *"Leadership and the New Science: Discovering Order in a Chaotic World."* San Francisco, CA: Berrett-Koehler, 2006.

12 **John Briggs and David Peat.** *"Turbulent Mirror: An Illustrated Guide to Chaos Theory and the Science of Wholeness."* New York: Harper & Row, 1989.;
James Gleick. *"Chaos: Making a New Science."* New York: Penguin Books, 1987.

13 **Wheatley,** *"Leadership."*

14 **C. Stephen Byrum.** *"From the Neck Up: The Recovery and Sustaining of the Human Element in Modern Organizations."* Littleton, MA: Tapestry Press, 2006.

15 **Ken Resnicow and Roger Vaughan.** *"A Chaotic View of Behavior Change: A Quantum Leap for Health Promotion."* International Journal of Behavioral Nutrition and Physical Activity." 3.25 (2006).

16 *Ibid.*

Chapter Four

1 **Charles S. Jacobs.** *"Management Rewired."* New York: Penguin Group, 2009.

2 *Ibid.*

3 **C. Stephen Byrum.** *"From the Neck Up: The Recovery and Sustaining of the Human Element in Modern Organizations."* Littleton, MA: Tapestry Press, 2006.

4 **Peter Drucker.** *"Managing Oneself."* Boston: Harvard Business Press, 2007.

5 **R. Fairlie and J. Marion.** *"Affirmative Action Programs and Business Ownership Among Minorities and Women."* Small Business Economics. 39 (2012). 319-339.

6 **A.W. Brooks, L. Huang, S.W. Kearney, and F.E. Murray.** *"Investors Prefer Entrepreneurial Ventures Pitched by Attractive Men."* PNAS Early Edition. 2014.

7 *Ibid.*

8 **Sheryl Sandberg.** *"Lean In: Women, Work, and the Will to Lead."*
New York: Knopf, 2013.

9 **Arianna Huffington.** *"Thrive."* New York: Harmony, 2014.

10 **Bureau of Labor Statistics.** *Employment Outlook 2010-2020.*
http://www.bls.gov/opub/mlr/2012/01/art4full.pdf

11 **Bentley University.** *"An In-depth Look at Millennial Preparedness for Today's Workforce."* Jan. 2014. http://www.slideshare.net/BentleyU/prepared-u-project-on-millennial-preparedness

12 **PricewaterhouseCoopers International Limited.** *"Millennials at Work: Reshaping the Workplace."* 2012. http://www.pwc.com/en_M1/m1/services/consulting/documents/millennials-at-work.pdf

13 *Ibid.*

14 **Jacobs,** *"Management."*

15 **Margaret J. Wheatley.** *"Leadership and the New Science: Discovering Order in a Chaotic World."* San Francisco: Berrett-Koehler, 1999.

16 *Ibid.*

17 *Ibid.*

18 **Margaret J. Wheatley.** *"Finding Our Way: Leadership for an Uncertain Time."* San Francisco: Berrett-Koehler, 2005.

19 **Peter M. Senge.** *"The Fifth Discipline: The Art & Practice of the Learning Organization."* New York: Doubleday, 2006.

20 *Ibid.*

21 **Wheatley,** *"Leadership."*

22 **Wheatley,** *"Finding."*

23 **C. Stephen Byrum.** *"The Right Question: Critical Conclusions from Yale's Institute for Excellence."* 2012. http://tnshrm.shrm.org/files/Steve%20%20Byrum%20Yale%20Excellence.pdf

24 **C. Stephen Byrum.** *"Personal Communications."* 2010. Additional information at http://www.judgmentindex.com/case_studies/

25 *Ibid.*; **Byrum,** *"Right Question."*

26 **The Energy Project.** www.theenergyproject.com

27 **The Energy Project.** *"The X Factor in Engagement, Productivity & Performance."* 2011.

28 **Energy Project**

29 **American Psychological Association.** *"Stress in America: Our Health at Risk."* February, 2013.

30 **Energy Project,** *"X Factor."*

31 **J.M. Torpy, C. Lynm, and R.M. Glass.** *"Chronic Stress and the Heart."* JAMA. 298.14 (2007).

32 *Ibid.*

33 **Paul J. Rosch.** *"Job Stress: America's Leading Adult Health Problem."* USA Magazine. May, 1991. ; *"American Academy of Family Physicians Survey, 1988."* U.S. News & World Report. December 11, 1995.

34 Wheatley, *"Finding."*

35 **Paul L. Marciano, PhD.** *"Carrots and Sticks Don't Work: Build a Culture of Employee Engagement with the Principles of RESPECT™."* New York: McGraw-Hill, 2010.

36 **J.K. Harter, F.L. Schmidt, and C.L.M. Keyes.** *"Well-being in the Workplace and its Relationship to Business Outcomes: A Review of the Gallup Studies."* In *"Flourishing: The Positive Person and the Good Life."* Eds. C.L.M. Keyes & J. Haidt. Washington, DC: American Psychological Association, 2003. 205-224.

37 **Towers Perrin.** *"Building a More Engaged Health Care Workforce."* White Paper, August, 2008.

38 **Dale Carnegie & Associates.** *"What Drives Employee Engagement and Why it Matters."* 2012. http://www.dalecarnegie.com/engaging-employees/

39 **Watson Wyatt.** *"Driving business results through continuous engagement."* White Paper, 2009.

40 **J.K. Harter, J. Canedy, and A. Stone.** *"A Longitudinal Study of Engagement at Work and Physiologic Indicators of Health."* Presented at the 2008 Work, Stress, and Health Conference, Washington, D.C.

41 **S. Crabtree.** *"Engagement Keeps the Doctor Away."* Gallup Management Journal Online, 1-5. 2005. http://gmj.gallup.com/content/14500/Engagement-Keeps-Doctor-Away.aspx

42 *Ibid.*

43 **S. Agrawal and J.K. Harter.** *"Engagement at Work Predicts Change in Depression and Anxiety Status in the Next Year."* Omaha, NE: Gallup, 2009.

44 *Ibid.*

45 http://strengths.gallup.com/private/Resources/Q12Meta-Analysis_Flyer_GEN_08%2008_BP.pdf.

46 **G.R. Stephenson.** *"Cultural Acquisition of a Specific Learned Response Among Rhesus Monkeys."* In *"Progress in Primatology."* Eds. D. Starek, R. Schneider, and H.J. Kuhn. Stuttgart: Fischer, 1967. 279-288.

47 **E.H. Schein.** *"Organizational Culture."* American Psychologist. 45.2 (1990). 109-119.; E.H. Schein. *"Organizational Culture and Leadership."* San Francisco: Jossey-Bass, 1985.

48 **S. Crabtree.** *"Worldwide, 13% of Employees Are Engaged at Work."* Gallup Poll. October 8. 2013.

49 **Towers Watson.** *Global Workforce Study.* 2012. http://towerswatson.com/assets/pdf/2012-Towers-Watson-Global-Workforce-Study.pdf

50 *"Unhealthy, Stressed Employees Are Hurting Your Business."* Gallup Business Journal. May 22, 2012.

51 **Adrian Gostick and Chester Elton.** *"All In: How the Best Managers Create a Culture of Belief and Drive Big Results."* New York: Free Press, 2012.

52 **Schein,** *"Culture."*

53 **Schein,** *"Culture and Leadership."*

54 **C.D. Morgan.** *"Culture Change/Culture Shock."* Management Review. 87.10 (1998). 13.

55 **W.M. Juechter, C. Fisher, and R.J. Alford.** *"Five Conditions for High-Performance Cultures."* Training & Development. 52.5 (1998). 63-67.

56 **Patrick Lencioni.** *The Advantage: Why Organizational Health Trumps Everything Else In Business.* San Francisco: Jossey-Bass, 2012.

57 **Dee Edington, PhD.** *"The Art of Health Promotion."* Sept./Oct. (2012).

58 **Rob Goffee and Gareth Jones.** *"Creating the Best Workplace on Earth."* Harvard Business Review. May, 2013.

59 **Deloitte Consulting.** *"Deloitte Human Capital Trends 2014."* http://marketing.bersin.com/deloitte-global-human-capital-trends-2014.html.

60 **Senge,** *"Fifth."*

61 **Michael Giardina.** *"Toxic Workplaces Override Wellness Efforts: Stanford Professor."* Employee Benefit News. April 7, 2014.

Chapter Five

1 **D.B. Morris.** *"Illness and Culture in the Postmodern Age."* Berkeley: University of California Press, 1998.

2 **Fritjof Capra.** *"The Turning Point: Science, Society, and the Rising Culture."* Toronto: Bantam, 1983.

3 **C.B. Inlander, L.S. Levin, and E. Weiner.** *"Medicine on Trial: The Appalling Story of Ineptitude, Malfeasance, Neglect and Arrogance."* New York: Prentice-Hall, 1988.

4 **Capra,** *"Turning Point."*

5 **Ray H. Rosenman.** *"The Questionable Role of the Diet and Serum Cholesterol in the Incidence of Ischemic Heart Disease and Its 20th Century Changes."* Homeostasis. 34.1 (1993). 1-44.

6 **Pooling Project Research Group.** *"Relationship of Blood Pressure, Serum Cholesterol, Smoking Habit, Relative Weight, and ECG Abnormalities to Incidence of Major Coronary Events: Final Report on the Pooling Project."* Journal of Chronic Disease (Special Issue). 31 (1978). 201-306.

7 **C.B. Thomas and E.A. Murphy.** *"Further Studies on Cholesterol Levels in the Johns Hopkins Medical Students: The Effect of Stress at Examinations."* Journal of Chronic Diseases. 8 (1958). 661-668.

8 **Harlan M. Krumholz, MD; Teresa E. Seeman, PhD; Susan S. Merrill, PhD; Carlos F. Mendes de Leon, PhD, et. al.** *"Lack of Association Between Cholesterol and Coronary Heart Disease Mortality and Morbidity and All-Cause Mortality in Persons Older Than 70 Years."* JAMA. 272.17 (1994). 1335-1340.

9 **J.M. Hoeg.** *"Evaluating Coronary Heart Disease Risk: Tiles in the Mosaic."* JAMA. 277 (1997). 1387-1390.

10 **Candace B. Pert.** *"Molecules Of Emotion: Why You Feel The Way You Feel."* New York: Scribner, 1997.

11 **Damien G. Finniss, Ted J. Kaptchuk, Franklin Miller, and Fabrizio Benedetti.** *"Biological, Clinical, and Ethical Advances of Placebo Effects."* Lancet. 375 (2010). 686–695. ; H. Brody. *"The Placebo Response: How You Can Release the Body's Inner Pharmacy for Better Health."* New York: Cliff Street Books, 2000.; T.J. Kaptchuk, E. Friedlander, J.M. Kelley, M.N. Sanchez, and E. Kokkotou, et al. *"Placebos without Deception: A Randomized Controlled Trial in Irritable Bowel Syndrome."* PLoS ONE 5.12 (2010).

12 **R. Hahn.** *"The Nocebo Phenomenon: Concept, Evidence, and Implications for Public Health."* Preventive Medicine. 26 (1997). 607-611.

13 **J.M. Mossey and E. Shapiro.** *"Self-rated Health: A Predictor of Mortality Among the Elderly."* American Journal of Public Health. 72 (1982). 800-807. ; E. Idler and S. Kasl. *"Health Perceptions and Survival: Do Global Evaluations of Health Status Really Predict Mortality?"* Journal of Gerontology. 46.2 (1991). 555-565. ; G.A. Kaplan and T. Camacho. *"Perceived Health and Mortality: A Nine-Year Follow-Up of the Human Population Laboratory Cohort."* American Journal Epidemiology. 117.3 (1983). 292-304.

14 **C. Peterson, G. Vaillant, and M. Seligman.** *"Pessimistic Explanatory Style is a Risk Factor for Physical Illness: A Thirty-five Year Longitudinal Study."* Journal of Personality and Social Psychology. 55.1 (1988). 23-27.

15 **C. Peterson.** *"Explanatory Style as a Risk Factor for Illness."* Cognitive Therapy and Research 12.2 (1988). 119-132. ; T. Maruta, R. Colligan, M. Malinchoc, and K. Offord. *"Optimists vs. Pessimists: Survival Rate among Medical Patients over a 30-Year Period."* Mayo Clinic Proceedings. 75 (2000). 140-143. ; S. Segerstrom, S. Taylor, M. Kemeny, and J. Fahey. *"Optimism is Associated with Mood, Coping, and Immune Change in Response to Stress."* Journal of Personality and Social Psychology. 74.6 (1998). 1646-1655.

16 **S. Cohen, D. Tyrrell, and A. Smith.** *"Psychological Stress and Susceptibility to the Common Cold."* The New England Journal of Medicine. 325 (1991). 606-612. ; J. Kiecolt-Glaser and P. Marucha, et al. *"Slowing of Wound Healing by Psychological Stress."* The Lancet. 346 (1995). 1194-1196.

17 **D. McClelland and C. Kirshnit.** *"The Effect of Motivational Arousal Through Films on Salivary Immunoglobulin A."* Psychology and Health. 2 (1988). 31-52. ; K. Olness, T. Culbert, and D. Uden. *"Self-Regulation of Salivary Immunoglobulin A by Children."* Pediatrics. 83.1 (1989). 66-71. ; B. Hewson-Bower and P. Drummond. *"Secretory Immunoglobulin A Increases During Relaxation in Children With and Without Recurrent Upper Respiratory Tract Infections."* Developmental and Behavioral Pediatrics. 17.5 (1996). 311-316. ; H. Lefcourt, K. Davidson-Katz, and K. Kueneman. *"Humor and immune-system functioning."* Humor. 3.3 (1990). 305-321. ; J. Kiecolt-Glaser, R. Glaser, D. Williger, J. Stout, et. al. *"Psychosocial Enhancement of Immunocompetence in a Geriatric Population."* Health Psychology. 4.1 (1985). 25-41.

18 **J. Kabat-Zinn, A. Massion, J. Kristeller, L. Peterson, K. Fletcher, L. Pbert, W. Lenderking, and S. Santorelli.** *"Effectiveness of a Meditation-Based Stress Reduction Program in the Treatment of Anxiety Disorders."* American Journal of Psychiatry. 149.7 (1992). 936-943. ; C.R. Amparo, R.H. Schneider, C.N. Alexander, R. Cook, and H. Myers, et. al. *"Effects of Stress Reduction on Carotid Atherosclerosis in Hypertensive African Americans."* Stroke. 31 (2000). 568-573.

19 **R.S. Miller.** *"As Above So Below: Paths to Spiritual Renewal in Daily Life."* New York: G.P. Putnam's Sons, 1992.

20 **Accident Compensation Corporation.** *"New Zealand Acute Low Back Pain Guide."* 2004. http://www.acc.co.nz/PRD_EXT_CSMP/groups/external_ip/documents/internet/wcm002131.pdf

21 **N.M. Hadler.** *"Occupational Musculoskeletal Disorders."* Philadelphia: Lippincott, Williams & Wilkins, 1999.

22 **http://www.who.int/genomics/public/geneticdiseases/en/index3.html**

23 **http://www.webmd.com/depression/news/20090309/heart-disease-tied-to-depression-anger**

24 **http://www.ncbi.nlm.nih.gov/pmc/articles/PMC2464619/**

25 **Sheldon Cohen.** *"Social Relationships and Health."* American Psychologist. 59.8 (2004). 676-684.

26 **Harold G. Koenig and Harvey J. Cohen.** *"The Link between Religion and Health: Psychoneuroimmunology and the Faith Factor."* Oxford: Oxford University Press, 2001.

27 **Harold G. Koenig.** *"Spirituality and Health Research: Methods, Measurements, Statistics, and Resources."* West Conshohocken, PA: Templeton, 2011.

28 **Jon Robison and Karen Carrier.** *"The Spirit and Science of Holistic Health: More than Broccoli, Jogging, and Bottled Water; More Than Yoga, Herbs, and Meditation."* Bloomington, IN: Authorhouse, 2004.

29 **V. Felitti.** *"Relationship of Childhood Abuse and Household Dysfunction to Many of the Leading Causes of Deaths in Adults."* American Journal Of Preventive Medicine. 14.4 (1998). 245-258.

30 **Michael Marmot,** *"The Status Syndrome: How Social Standing Affects our Health and Longevity."* New York: Henry Holt, 2004.

31 **World Health Organization Commission on Social Determinants of Health.** 2008. http://www.who.int/social_ determinants/thecommission/finalreport/en/

32 **Marmot,** *"Status."*

33 **Morris,** *"Illness and Culture."*

34 **Ivan Illich.** *"Medical Nemesis: The Expropriation of Health."* New York: Pantheon, 1982.

35 **T. Rath and J. Harter.** *"Wellbeing: The Five Essential Elements."* New York: Gallup Press, 2010.

36 **Laura McKibbin, MSW, LICSW.** *"Food for Thought Pyramid."* http://www.food-for-thought-pyramid.com/

37 **R. Ornstein and D. Sobel.** *"Healthy Pleasures."* Reading, MA: Addison-Wesley, 1989.

Chapter Six

1 **Alfie Kohn.** *"Punished by Rewards."* Boston: Houghton Mifflin, 1999.

2 **S. Lahiry.** *"Building Commitment through Organizational Culture."* Training and Development. 48.4 (1994). 50-52. ; C.P. Neck and C.C. Manz. *"Thought Self-leadership: The Influence of Self-talk and Mental Imagery on Performance."* Journal of Organizational Behavior. 13.7 (1992). 681-699.

3 **Margaret Wheatley.** *"Finding Our Way: Leadership for an Uncertain Time."* San Francisco: Berrett-Koehler, 2005.

4 *Ibid.*

5 *Ibid.*; Charles S. Jacobs. *"Management Rewired."* New York: Penguin Group, 2009

6 **Jacobs,** *"Management."*; Pink, *"Drive."*; Kohn, *"Punished."*; Deci and Flaste, *"Why We Do What We Do."*; Amabile, *"Motivating Creativity."*; Marciano, *"Carrots and Sticks."*

7 **Ken Resnicow and Roger Vaughan**. *"A Chaotic View of Behavior Change: A Quantum Leap for Health Promotion."* International Journal of Behavioral Nutrition and Physical Activity. 3.25 (2006).

8 **Wheatley,** *"Finding."*

9 **Marciano,** *"Carrots and Sticks."*

10 **B.F. Skinner.** *"Can psychology be a science of mind?"* American Psychologist. 45 (1990).

11 **B.F. Skinner.** *"Walden Two."* New York: Macmillan, 1948.

12 **H. Petri.** *"Motivation: Theory, Research and Application"* (3rd ed.). Belmont, CA: Wadsworth, 1991.

13 **M. Gagne and E.L. Deci.** *"Self-determination Theory and Work Motivation."* Journal of Organizational Behavior. (2005). 331-362.

14 **Jacobs,** *"Management."* ; Pink, *"Drive."* ; Kohn, *"Punished."* ; Deci and Flaste, *"Why We Do What We Do."*; Amabile, *"Motivating Creativity."*; Marciano, *"Carrots and Sticks."*

15 **Marciano,** *"Carrots and Sticks."*

16 **Pink,** *"Drive."*; Kohn, *"Punished."*

17 **Wheatley,** *"Finding."*

18 *Ibid.*

19 **D. Ornish.** *"Keynote."* Art and Science of Health Promotion Conference. San Francisco, CA. March, 2005.

20 **Jean-Jacques Laffont and David Martimort.** *"The Theory of Incentives: The Principal-Agent Model."* Princeton, NJ: Princeton University Press, 2002.

21 **Deci and Flaste,** *"Why We Do What We Do."*

22 **Kevin Volpp, David A. Asch, Robert Galvin and George Loewenstein.** *"Redesigning Employee Health Incentives."* NEJM. 365 (2011). 388-390

23 **Jeffrey T. Kullgren, MD, MS, MPH; Andrea B. Troxel, ScD; George Loewenstein, PhD; David A. Asch, MD, et. al.** *"Individual- Versus Group-Based Financial Incentives for Weight Loss: A Randomized, Controlled Trial."* Annals of Internal Medicine. 158.7 (2013). 505-514.

24 *Ibid.*

25 *Ibid.*

26 **Deci and Flaste,** *"Why We Do What We Do."*

27 **Jacobs,** *"Management."*

28 *Ibid.*

29 **Marciano,** *"Carrots and Sticks."*

30 **Neck and Manz,** *"Thought Self-leadership."*; Manz, *"Self-leadership."*

31 **Neck and Manz,** *"Thought Self-leadership."*

32 **Manz and Neck,** *"Inner Leadership."*

33 **Ray Williams.** *"How to Motivate Employees: What Managers Need to Know."* Wired for Success. 13 February 2010. http://www.psychologytoday.com/blog/wired-success/201002/how-motivate-employees-what-managers-need-know-0.

34 **Charles Duhigg.** *"The Power of Habit: Why We Do What We Do in Life and Business."* New York: Random House, 2014.

35 **Rock and Schwartz,** *"Neuroscience."*

36 **Jacobs,** *"Management."*

37 **R.S. Hartman.** *"The Structure of Value."* Carbondale, IL: Southern Illinois University Press, 1967.

38 **L. Pomeroy.** *"The New Science of Axiological Psychology."* New York: Rodopi, 2005

39 **C.S. Byrum.** *"From the Neck Up: The Recovery and Sustaining of the Human Element in Modern Organizations."* Toronto: Tapestry Press, 2006.

40 **Christina Marshall.** Intrinsic Solutions, International, www.isintl.com.

41 **Hartman,** *"Structure."*; Marshall, *"Intrinsic."*

42 **Hartman,** *"Structure."*

43 **Pomeroy,** *"New Science."*

44 **Jacobs,** *"Management."*

45 *Ibid.*

46 *Ibid.*

47 **R. Ward.** *"The Relationship of Individual Intrinsic Capacity with Job Satisfaction, Organizational Commitment, and Perceived Life Balance: An Exploratory Study of the Intrinsic Coaching®"* Doctoral dissertation. Capella University, 2008. ProQuest Digital Dissertations. (UMI No. 3329852).

48 **Kohn,** *"Punished."*

Chapter Seven

1 **Daniel H. Pink.** *"Drive: The Surprising Truth About What Motivates Us."* New York: Riverhead Books, 2009.

2   **Charles S. Jacobs.** *"Management Rewired."* New York: Penguin Group, 2009.

3   **Senn Delaney.** *"Why Culture Matters: Lessons from an Executive Panel Discussion."* 2008. www.senndelaney.com.

4   **C.D. Morgan.** *"Culture Change/Culture Shock."* Management Review. 87.10 (1998). 13.

5   **Tony Hsieh.** *"Delivering Happiness: A Path to Profits, Passion, and Purpose."* New York: Business Plus, 2010.

6   **Margaret J. Wheatley.** *"Leadership and the New Science: Discovering Order in a Chaotic World."* San Francisco: Berrett-Koehler, 1999.

7   **Jacobs,** *"Management."*

8   **E.H. Schein.** *"Organizational Culture and Leadership."* San Francisco: Jossey-Bass, 1985.

9   **W.A. Schiemann.** *"Organizational Change: Lessons from a Turnaround."* Management Review. 81.4 (1992). 34-37.

10 **J.P. Kotter.** *"Leading Change: Why Transformation Efforts Fail."* Harvard Business Review. (March-April 1995). 59-67.

11 **Wheatley,** *"Leadeship."*

12 *Ibid.*

13 **Schein,** *"Organizational Culture and Leadership."*

14 **Schiemann,** *"Organizational Change."*

15 **E.H. Schein.** *"Organizational Culture."* American Psychologist. 45.2 (1990). 109-119.

16 **Jim Hart.** http://sdtv.senndelaney.com/senn-delaney-ceo-jim-hart-discusses-why-organizational-culture-can-and-should-be-intentionally-shaped.

17 **Jacobs,** *"Management."*

18 **Wheatley,** *"Leadership."*

19 **Rudyard Kipling.** *"A Book of Words."* http://ebooks.adelaide.edu.au/k/kipling/rudyard/words/chapter23.html.

20 **Pink,** *"Drive."*

21 **Al H. Ringleb and David Rock.** *"NeuroLeadership in 2009."* NeuroLeadership Journal. 2 (2009).

22 **Robert J. Grossman.** *"Countering a Weight Crisis."* HR Magazine. 49.3 (March 2004).

23 **Hsieh,** *"Delivering."*

Chapter Eight

1   **William Bruce Cameron.** NEA (National Education Association) Journal. (1958).

2   **Paul. R. Niven.** *"Balanced Scorecard."* Second ed. Hoboken, NJ: John Wiley & Sons, 2006.

3   **Peter M. Senge.** *"The Fifth Discipline: The Art & Practice of the Learning Organization."* New York: Doubleday, 2006.

4 **Margaret J. Wheatley.** *"Finding Our Way: Leadership for an Uncertain Time."* San Francisco: Berrett-Koehler, 2005.

5 **Donald O. Clifton and Paula Nelson.** *"Soar with Your Strengths."* New York: Dell, 1992. ; Tom Rath. *"StrengthsFinder 2.0."* New York: Gallup Press, 2007. ; Tom Rath and Barry Conchie. *"Strengths Based Leadership."* New York: Gallup Press, 2008.

6 **Peter M. Senge.** *"The Fifth Discipline: The Art & Practice of the Learning Organization."* New York: Doubleday, 2006.

7 **Wheatley,** *"Finding."*

8 **Senge,** *"Fifth Discipline."*

9 **Wheatley,** *"Finding."*

10 **Margaret J. Wheatley.** *"Leadership and the New Science: Discovering Order in a Chaotic World."* San Francisco: Berrett-Koehler, 1999.

11 **Kim S. Cameron and Robert E. Quinn.** *"Diagnosing and Changing Organizational Culture."* San Francisco: Jossey-Bass, 2006.

12 **E.H. Schein.** *"Organizational Culture."* American Psychologist. 45.2 (1990). 109-119.

13 **Tony Hsieh.** *"Delivering Happiness: A Path To Profits, Passion and Purpose."* New York: Business Plus, 2010.

14 **Cameron and Quinn,** *"Diagnosing."*

15 **BlessingWhite.** *"Employee Engagement Report."* 2011. www.blessingwhite.com.

16 **Deloitte Consulting.** *"Deloitte Human Capital Trends 2014."* http://marketing.bersin.com/deloitte-global-human-capital-trends-2014.html.

17 **Josh Bersin.** *"It's Time to Rethink the 'Employee Engagement' Issue."* Forbes. April 10, 2014. http://www.forbes.com/sites/joshbersin/2014/04/10/its-time-to-rethink-the-employee-engagement-issue/.

18 **Josh Bersin.** *"Why Companies Fail to Engage Today's Workforce: The Overwhelmed Employee."* Forbes. March 15, 2014. http://www.forbes.com/sites/joshbersin/2014/03/15/why-companies-fail-to-engage-todays-workforce-the-overwhelmed-employee/.

19 **Bersin,** *"Employee Engagement."*

20 **Gretchen Spreitzer and Christine Porath.** *"Creating Sustainable Performance."* Harvard Business Review. (Jan. – Feb. 2012), p. 93-99.

21 *Ibid.*

22 **Mark Graham Brown.** *"Forget Employee Engagement – Are They Happy?"* Business Finance Magazine. November 30, 2011.

23 **Roger Connors and Tom Smith.** *"Change the Culture, Change the Game: The Breakthrough Strategy for Energizing Your Organization and Creating Accountability for Results."* New York: Penguin Group, 2012.

24 **Agency for Healthcare Research and Quality.** https://cahps.ahrq.gov/.

25 **Jennifer Robison.** *"Leading the Way to Better Patient Care."* Gallup Management Journal. November 20, 2012. http://www.gallup.com/businessjournal/158840/leading-better-patient-care.aspx.

26 **Terese Corey Blanck and Judy Anderson.** *"Emerging Advantage Research."* http://www.emergingadvantage.com.

27 *"Deloitte Human Capital"*

28 **The Energy Project.** *"The X Factor in Engagement, Productivity & Performance."* 2011.

29 **Monster Worldwide.** *"Dangerously Stressful Work Environments Force Workers to Seek New Employment."* 2014. http://www.about-monster.com/content/dangerously-stressful-work-environments-force-workers-seek-new-employment.

30 **C. Stephen Byrum.** *"The Right Question: Critical Conclusions from Yale's Institute for Excellence."* 2012. http://tnshrm.shrm.org/files/Steve%20%20Byrum%20Yale%20Excellence.pdf.; C. Stephen Byrum. Personal communications. 2010. Additional information at http://www.judgmentindex.com/case_studies/.

31 **National Safety Council.** *"Injury Statistics, 2010 Edition."* www.nsc.org.

32 **Chana Joffe-Walt.** *"Unfit for Work: The Startling Rise of Disability in America."* 2013. http://apps.npr.org/unfit-for-work.

33 **Peter M. Senge.** *"The Fifth Discipline: The Art & Practice of the Learning Organization."* New York: Doubleday, 2006.

34 *Ibid.*

35 **Wheatley,** *"Leadership."*

36 **Wheatley,** *"Finding."*

37 **J.P. Kotter.** *"Leading Change: Why Transformation Efforts Fail."* Harvard Business Review. (March – April, 1995)., 59-67.

38 **W.M. Juechter, C. Fisher, and R.J. Alford (1998).** *"Five Conditions for High-Performance Cultures."* Training & Development., 52.5 (1985). 63-67.

39 **Tony Hsieh.** *"Delivering Happiness: A Path to Profits, Passion and Purpose."* New York: Business Plus, 2010.

Chapter Nine

1 **Stephen R. Covey.** *"The 7 Habits of Highly Effective People."* New York: Simon & Schuster, 1989.

2 **Michel Robert.** *"The New Strategic Thinking Pure & Simple."* New York: McGraw-Hill, 2006.

3 **Margaret J. Wheatley.** *"Leadership and the New Science: Discovering Order in a Chaotic World."* San Francisco: Berrett-Koehler, 1999.

4 **W. Chan Kim and Renee Mauborgne.** *"Blue Ocean Strategy."* Boston: Harvard Business School Press, 2005.

5 **Peter M. Senge.** *"The Fifth Discipline: The Art & Practice of the Learning Organization."* New York: Doubleday, 2006.

6 **Kim and Mauborgne,** *"Blue."*

7 **Wheatley,** *"Leadership."*

8 *Ibid.*

9 **A.A. Thompson, A.J. Strickland, and J.E. Gamble.** *"Crafting and Executing Strategy."* 14th ed. Boston: McGraw-Hill/Irwin, 2005.

10 **Wheatley,** *"Leadership."*

11 **Kim and Mauborgne,** *"Blue."*

12 *Ibid.*

13 **Patrick Lencioni.** *"The Advantage: Why Organizational Health Trumps Everything Else In Business."* San Francisco: Jossey-Bass, 2012.

14 *Ibid.*

15 *Ibid.*

16 *Ibid.*

17 *Ibid.*

18 **Tony Hsieh.** *"Delivering Happiness: A Path To Profits, Passion and Purpose."* New York: Business Plus, 2010.

19 **Wheatley,** *"Leadership."*

20 **Patrick Lencioni.** *"The Five Dysfunctions of a Team."* San Francisco: Jossey-Bass, 2002.

21 **Wheatley,** *"Leadership."*

22 **Charles S. Jacobs.** *"Management Rewired."* New York: Penguin Group, 2009.

23 **Margaret J. Wheatley.** *"Finding Our Way: Leadership for an Uncertain Time."* San Francisco: Berrett-Koehler, 2005.

24 **Jacobs,** *"Management."*

25 **Wheatley,** *"Leadership."*

26 **Jacobs,** *"Management."*

27 **L.D. Ordonez, M.E. Schweitzer, A.D. Galinsky, and M.H. Bazerman.** *"Goals Gone Wild: The Systematic Side-effects of Over-prescribing Goal-setting."* Academy of Management Perspectives. 23.1 (2009). 6-16.

28 *Ibid.*

29 **Robert Kegan, Lisa Lahey, Andy Fleming, and Matthew Miller.** *"Making Business Personal."* Harvard Business Review. (April, 2014).

30 **Jacobs,** *"Management."*

31 *Ibid.*

Chapter Ten

1 **Edgar H. Schein.** *"Organizational Culture."* American Psychologist, 45.2 (1990). 109-119.

2 **Ronald A. Heifetz and Donald L. Laurie.** *"The Work of Leadership."* Harvard Business Review. (December 2001). 131-141

3 *Ibid.*

4 **Ellen Van Velsor.** *"Learning New Ways: A Conversation with Ronald A. Heifetz."* LIA. 23.1 (2003). 19-22.

5 *Ibid.*

6 **Margaret Wheatley and Debbie Frieze.** *"Leadership in the Age of Complexity: From Hero to Host."* Resurgence Magazine. (Winter 2011).

7 **Heifetz and Laurie,** *"Work."*

8 *Ibid.*

9 **Wheatley and Frieze,** *"Leadership."*

10 *Ibid.*

11 **J.P. Kotter.** *"What Leaders Really Do."* Harvard Business Review on Leadership. Boston: Harvard Business School Press, 1998. 37-60.

12 **J.P. Kotter.** *"Leading Change: Why Transformation Efforts Fail."* Harvard Business Review. (March-April 1995). 59-67.

13 **Robert K. Greenleaf.** *"Servant Leadership: A Journey into the Nature of Legitimate Power and Greatness."* Mahwah, NJ: Paulist Press, 2002.

14 **Christine Jacobs, Holger Pfaff, Birgit Lehner, Elke Driller, Anika Nitzsche, Brigitte Stieler-Lorenz, Jürgen Wasem, and Julia Jung.** *"The Influence of Transformational Leadership on Employee Well-Being: Results from a Survey of Companies in the Information and Communication Technology Sector in Germany."* Journal of Occupational and Environmental Medicine. 55.7 (July 2013). 772-778.

15 **P. Godin.** *"Achieving Vision: Managers vs. Leaders."* Manage. 50.1 (1998). 10-12.

16 **M. Maccoby.** *"Understanding the Difference Between Management and Leadership."* Research Technology Management. 43.1 (2000). 57-59.

17 **Peter M. Senge.** *"The Fifth Discipline: The Art & Practice of the Learning Organization."* New York: Doubleday, 2006.

18 **Kevin Cashman.** *"Leadership from the Inside Out."* Minneapolis, MN: TCLG, 1998.

19 **Kevin Cashman.** *"The Pause Principle."* San Francisco: Berrett-Koehler, 2012.

20 *Ibid.*

21 **Joseph Jaworski.** *"Synchronicity: The Inner Path of Leadership."* San Francisco: Berrett-Koehler, 1998.

22 **Josh Bersin.** *"The Five Elements of a 'Simply Irresistible' Organization."* Forbes. (April 4, 2014). http://www.bersin.com/blog/post/The-Five-Elements-Of-A-Simply-Irresistible-Organization.aspx.

23 **Tony Schwartz.** *"Why Don't We Act in Our Own Best Interest?"* Harvard Business Review Blog. (January 31, 2012). http://blogs.hbr.org/2012/01/why-dont-we-act-in-our-own-bes/.

24 **Charles S. Jacobs.** *"Management Rewired."* New York: Penguin Group, 2009.

25 **Jaworski,** *"Synchronicity."*

26 **Senn Delaney.** *"Why State of Mind Matters in Times of Great Challenge."* Results from Thriving Global Leadership Survey. 2008. www.senndelaney.com.

27 *Ibid.*

28 **Senn Delaney.** *"Creating Superior Business Results through a Thriving State of Mind."* Research Report. 2008. www.senndelaney.com.

29 **Delaney,** *"State of Mind."*

30 **Intrinsic Solutions, International.** http://www.isintl.com/history-and-today.shtml.

31 **L. Pomeroy.** *"The New Science of Axiological Psychology."* New York: Rodopi, 2005.

32 **Rosie Ward.** *"The Relationship of Individual Intrinsic Capacity with Job Satisfaction, Organizational Commitment, and Perceived Life Balance: An Exploratory Study of the Intrinsic Coaching®."* Doctoral dissertation. Capella University. 2008. ProQuest Digital Dissertations. (UMI No. 3329852).

33 *Ibid.*

34 **Intrinsic Solutions, International.**

35 **Charles Duhigg.** *"The Power of Habit: Why We Do What We Do in Life and Business."* New York: Random House, 2012.

36 **The Arbinger Institute.** *"Leadership and Self-Deception: Getting Out of the Box."* San Francisco: Berrett-Koehler, 2010.

37 **Simon Sinek.** *"Leaders Eat Last."* New York: Penguin Group, 2014.

38 **Sandee Tisdale and Marcie Pitt-Catsouphes.** *"The Importance of an After-Work Smile."* Harvard Business Review, the Magazine. (October, 2012). http://hbr.org/2011/10/the-importance-of-an-after-work-smile/ar/1.

39 **Charles S. Jacobs.** *"Management Rewired."* New York: Penguin Group, 2009.

40 **Tony Hsieh.** *"Delivering Happiness: A Path to Profits, Passion and Purpose."* New York: Business Plus, 2010.

41 **Cashman,** *"Pause."*

42 **Bersin,** *"Five Elements."*

43 **Margaret J. Wheatley.** *"Leadership and the New Science: Discovering Order in a Chaotic World."* San Francisco: Berrett-Koehler, 1999.

44 **T. Rath and J. Harter.** *"Wellbeing: The Five Essential Elements."* New York: Gallup Press, 2010.

45 **Wheatley,** *"Leadership."*

46 **Wheatley and Frieze,** *"Leadership."*

47 **Leslie Kwoh.** *"When the CEO Burns Out."* The Wall Street Journal. (May 7, 2013). http://online.wsj.com/articles/SB10001424127887323687604578469124008524696.

48 **Patrick Lencioni.** *"The Advantage: Why Organizational Health Trumps Everything Else In Business."* San Francisco: Jossey-Bass, 2012.

49 *Ibid.*

50 **Cashman,** *"Pause."*

51 **C. Otto Scharmer.** *"Theory U: Learning from the Future as it Emerges."* San Francisco: Berrett-Koehler, 2009.

52 **Bersin,** *"Five Elements."*

53 **Jason McPherson.** *"With Development Opportunities, Having a Good Manager Matters."* (April 8, 2014). http://blog.cultureamp.com/its-about-development-opportunities/.

54 **Bersin,** *"Five Elements."*

55 **Senge,** *"Fifth Discipline."*

56 **Arianna Huffington.** *"Thrive."* New York: Harmony, 2014.

Chapter Eleven

1 **Tony Hsieh.** *"Delivering Happiness: A Path to Profits, Passion and Purpose."* New York: Business Plus, 2010.

2 *Ibid.*

3 **Rodd Wagner and James K. Harter.** *"12: The Elements of Great Managing."* New York: Gallup Press, 2006.; Tom Rath. *"StrengthsFinder 2.0."* New York: Gallup Press, 2007.

4 **Hsieh,** *"Delivering."*

5 **Matthew Kelly.** *"The Dream Manager."* New York: Hyperion, 2007.

6 **Robert Kegan and Lisa Laskow Lahey.** *"Immunity to Change: How to Overcome It and Unlock the Potential in Yourself and Your Organization."* Boston: Harvard Business Press, 2009.

7 *Ibid.*

8 *Ibid.*

9 **Robert Kegan, Lisa Lahey, Andy Fleming, and Matthew Miller.** "Making Business Personal." Harvard Business Review. (April, 2004).

10 **Robert Kegan, Lisa Lahey, and Andy Fleming.** "Does Your Company Make you a Better Person?" HBR Blog. (January 22, 2014). http://blogs.hbr.org/2014/01/does-your-company-make-you-a-better-person/

11 **Kegan, et. al.,** *"Making Business Personal."*

12 **Kegan, Lahey, and Fleming,** *"Does Your Company."*

13 **Robert Kegan, Lisa Lahey, Andy Fleming, Matthew Miller, and Inna Markus.** *"The Deliberately Developmental Organization."* White Paper from Way to Grow Inc., LLC. 2014.

14 *Ibid.*

15 **Kegan, Lahey, and Fleming,** *"Does Your Company."*

16 **Kegan, et. al.,** *"Making Business Personal."*

17 **Kegan, et. al.,** *"The Deliberately Developmental."*

18 **Kegan, et. al.,** *"Making Business Personal."*

19 **Margaret J. Wheatley.** *"Leadership and the New Science: Discovering Order in a Chaotic World."* San Francisco: Berrett-Koehler, 1999.

20 **Senn Delaney.** *"Communicating to Drive Culture Change."* 2008. www.senndelaney.com

21 **Patrick Lencioni.** *"The Advantage: Why Organizational Health Trumps Everything Else In Business."* San Francisco: Jossey-Bass, 2012.

Chapter Twelve

1 **Margaret Wheatley.** *"Finding Our Way: Leadership for an Uncertain Time."* San Francisco: Berrett-Koehler, 2005.

2 **Ronald A. Heifetz and Donald L. Laurie.** *"The Work of Leadership."* Harvard Business Review. (December 2001). 131-141

3 *Ibid.*

4 **D. Rock and J. Schwartz.** *"The Neuroscience of Leadership."* Strategy+Business. 43 (Summer 2006). 1-10.

5 *Ibid.*

6 **Rosie Ward.** *"The Relationship of Individual Intrinsic Capacity with Job Satisfaction, Organizational Commitment, and Perceived Life Balance: An Exploratory Study of the Intrinsic Coaching®."* (Doctoral dissertation, Capella University, 2008). ProQuest Digital Dissertations. (UMI No. 3329852).

7 **J.O. Prochaska, J.C. Norcross, and C.C. DiClemente.** *"Changing for Good: The Revolutionary Program that Explains the Six Stages of Change and Teaches you How to Free Yourself From Bad Habits."* New York: William Morrow, 1994.

8 **J. Adams and M. White.** *"Why Don't Stage-based Activity Promotion Interventions Work?"* Health Education Research. 20.2 (2005). 237-243.

9 **J.H. Littell and H. Girvin.** *"Stages of Change: A Critique."* Behavioral Modification. 26.2 (April, 2002). 223-73.; Johannes Brug, Mark Conner, Niki Harre, Stef Kremers, Susan McKellar, and Sandy Whitelaw. *"The Transtheoretical Model and Stages of Change: A Critique."* Health Education Research: Theory and Practice. 20.2 (2005). 244-258.

10 **R.E. Boyatzis.** *"An Overview of Intentional Change from a Complexity Perspective."* Journal of Management Development. 25.7 (2006). 607-623.

11 **R.E. Boyatzis and K. Akrivou.** *"The ideal self as the driver of intentional change."* Journal of Management Development, 25.7 (2006). 624-642.

12 **S.N. Taylor.** *"Why the Real Self is Fundamental to Intentional Change."* Journal of Management Development. 25.7 (2006). 643-656.

13 **Boyatzis,** *"Overview."*

14 **C. Otto Scharmer.** *"Theory U: Learning from the future as it emerges."* San Francisco: Berrett-Koehler, 2009.

15 *Ibid.*

16 **Tony Hsieh.** *"Delivering Happiness: A Path To Profits, Passion and Purpose."* New York: Business Plus, 2010.

17 **Charles S. Jacobs.** *"Management Rewired."* New York: Penguin Group, 2009.

18 **Daniel H. Pink.** *"Drive: The Surprising Truth about What Motivates Us."* New York: Riverhead Books, 2009.

19 **Tony Hsieh.** *"Delivering Happiness: A Path to Profits, Passion and Purpose."* New York: Business Plus, 2010.

20 *Ibid.*

21 **Jacobs,** *"Management."*

22 *Ibid.*

23 **Josh Bersin.** *"The Five Elements of a 'Simply Irresistible' Organization."* Forbes. (April 4, 2014). http://www.bersin.com/blog/post/The-Five-Elements-Of-A-Simply-Ir-resistible-Organization.aspx/.

24 **Jacobs,** *"Management."*

25 **W.R. Miller and S. Rollnick.** *"Ten Things that Motivational Interviewing is Not."* Behavioral and Cognitive Psychotherapy. 37 (2009). 129-140.

26 **S.B. Gingerich, D.R. Anderson, and H. Koland.** *"Impact of Financial Incentives on Behavior Change Program Participation and Risk Reduction in Worksite Health Promotion."* American Journal of Health Promotion. 27.2 (2012). 119-122.

27 **Alfie Kohn.** *"Punished by Rewards."* Boston: Houghton Mifflin, 1999.

28 **David R. Buchanan.** *"A New Ethic for Health Promotion: Reflections on a Philosophy of Health Education for the 21st Century."* Health Education & Behavior. 33.3 (June, 2006). 290-304.

Chapter Thirteen

1 **Tom Emerick and Al Lewis.** *"Cracking Health Costs: How To Cut Your Company's Health Costs and Provide Employees Better Care."* New York: John Wiley & Sons, 2013.

2 **Wellness Programs After the Affordable Care Act (Part One).** http://www.nixonpeabody.com/files/158014_Benefits_Alert_Wellness_Plans_8AUG2013.pdf.

3 **Towers Watson and Company.** *"2013 Staying @Work Report."* http://www.towerswatson.com/en-US/Insights/IC-Types/Survey-Research-Results/2013/12/staying atwork-survey-report-2013-2014-us.

4 **Dee W. Edington.** *"Zero Trends: Health as a Serious Economic Strategy."* University of Michigan Health Management Research Center. 2009.

5   **online.**wsj.com/news/articles/SB124476804026308603?mg=reno64-wsj&url=
http%3A%2F%2Fonline.wsj.com%2Farticle%2FSB124476804026308603.html

6   **http://www.washingtonpost.com**/wp-dyn/content/article/2010/01/15/AR
2010011503319_2.html.

7   **realclearpolitics.com/**articles/2009/08/25/senator_mccains_townhall_meeting_
98028.html

8   *Ibid.*

9   **David S. Hilzenrath.** *"Misleading Claims about Safeway Wellness Incentives Shape
Health-Care Bill."* The Washington Post. (January 17, 2010).

10 *Ibid.*

11 **nejm.org/**doi/full/10.1056/NEJMp1105966.

12 **Carla Saporta and Jeremy Cantor.** *"Workplace Wellness Regulations:
First Do No Harm."* The Prevention Institute. The Greenlining Institute. Congress Blog.
(January 18, 2013). http://thehill.com/blogs/congress-blog/labor/278079-workplace-
wellness-regulations-first-do-no-harm.

13 ***"Financial Incentives to Encourage Healthy Behaviors: A Joint Issue Brief
from the American Cancer Society Cancer Action Network, the American Diabetes
Association, and the American Heart Association."*** http://pulse.ncpolicywatch.org/
wp-content/uploads/2009/11/PolicyStatement-AHA-ACS-ADA2.pdf.

14 **blogs.hbr.org/**2013/08/attention-human-resources-exec/

15 **"Health Affairs"** 32. 3 (2013). 468-476.

16 **S. Mattke, H. Liu, J.P. Caloyeras, C.Y. Huang, et al.** *"Workplace Wellness Programs
Study."* Santa Monica, CA: RAND Corporation, 2013. (Pub. No. RR-254-DOL).

17 **"Journal of Occupational & Environmental Medicine."** 55.2 (February 2013).
209-222.

18 **"Health Affairs."** 33.1 (2014). 1124-1131.

19 **J.A. Nyman, J.M. Abraham, M.M. Jeffery, and N.A. Barleen.** *"The Effectiveness
of a Health Promotion Program after Three Years: Evidence from the University of
Minnesota."* Med Care. 50.9 (2012). 772–778.

20 **Siyan Baxter, Kristy Sanderson, Alison J. Venn, C. Leigh Blizzard, and
Andrew J. Palmer.** *"The Relationship between Return on Investment and Quality of
Study Methodology in Workplace Health Promotion Programs."* American Journal of
Health Promotion. 28.6 (July/August 2014). 347-363.

21 **http://www.marketplace.org/**topics/business/health-care/can-your-boss-fine-you-not-
disclosing-your-weight.

22 **http://edingtonassociates.wordpress.com/**2013/08/21/dee-edingtons-thoughts-on-the-
penn-state-employee-revolution/.

23 **http://healthaffairs.org/**blog/2013/01/16/is-it-time-to-re-examine-workplace-wellness-
get-well-quick-schemes/. ; http://healthaffairs.org/blog/2013/07/01/toward-a-scientific-
approach-to-workplace-wellness-a-response-to-ron-goetzel/. ; Al Lewis and Vik
Khanna. *"Surviving Workplace Wellness... With Your Dignity, Finances, and Major
Organs Intact."* 2014.

24 **http://www.change.org**/p/penn-state-president-rodney-a-erickson-benefits-office-and-trustees-stop-the-new-penn-state-wellness-program-and-its-surcharges.

25 **blogs.hbr.org**/2013/08/attention-human-resources-exec/.

26 **Alan Cassels and H. Gilbert Welch.** *"Seeking Sickness: Medical Screening and the Misguided Hunt for Disease."* Vancouver: Greystone Books, 2012. ; H. Gilbert Welch. *"Overdiagnosed: Making People Sick in the Pursuit of Health."* Boston: Beacon Press, 2012.; Otis Webb Brawley. *"How We Do Harm."* New York: St. Martin's Griffin, 2012.

27 **National Heart, Lung and Blood Institute.** *"Third Report of the Expert Panel on Detection, Evaluation, and Treatment of the High Blood Cholesterol in Adults (Adult Treatment Panel III): Executive Summary."* item 01-3670. http://www.nhlbi.nih.gov/health-pro/guidelines/current/cholesterol-guidelines/index.htm.; *"Have We Entered a Period Where People Are Screening Too Much for Disease?"* Wall Street Journal Reports. (February 20, 2013). http://online.wsj.com/articles/ SB10001424127887323949 404578314423256694276.; *"Choosing Wisely, an Initiative of the American Board of Internal Medicine Foundation."* choosingwisely.org.; *"CV Screening Fails to Prevent Disease Over Long Term."* MedPage Today. (April 19, 2013). medpagetoday.com/MeetingCoverage/ EuroPRevent/38585?utm.content=&utm_medium=email&utm_campaign=DailyHeadlin es&utm_ source=WC&xid=NL_DHE_20130420&eun=g511423d0r&userid=511423&email=vik.khanna.health@gmail.com&mu_id=5634735.

28 **Al Lewis and Vik Khanna.** *"Surviving Workplace Wellness... With Your Dignity, Finances, and Major Organs Intact."* 2014.

29 **Healthwise.** www.healthwise.org.

30 **U.S. Department of Health and Human Services.** *"National Hospital and Ambulatory Medical Care Survey."* 2006.

31 **http://www.fiercehealthcare.com**/story/70-er-visits-patients-employer-sponsored-insurance-deemed-unnecessary/2013-04-29.

32 **healthylife.com**/documents/AIPM%20White%20Paper-Medical%20Self-Care%20Savings.pdf.

33 **http://www.healthwise.org**/products/printguides/handbook.aspx.

34 **Jerome Groopman.** *"How Doctors Think."* New York: Mariner Books, 2008.

35 **Elizabeth Cohen.** *"The Empowered Patient."* New York: Ballantine, 2010.

36 **Michael Roizen and Mehmet Oz.** *"YOU: The Smart Patient: An Insider's Handbook for Getting the Best Treatment."* New York: Scribner, 2006.

37 **K. Volpp, L. John, A.B. Troxel, L. Norton, et al.** *"Financial Incentive-Based Approaches for Weight Loss."* JAMA. 300.22 (2008). 2261-2267. ; L. John, G. Loewenstein, A.B. Troxel, L. Norton, et al. *"Financial Incentives for Extended Weight Loss: A Randomized Controlled Trial."* Journal of General Internal Medicine. 26.6 (2011). 621-626.

38 **D.M. Bhammar and G.A. Gaesser.** *"Health Risks Associated with Weight Cycling."* Wellness, Not Weight: Health at Every Size and Motivational Interviewing. Ed. Ellen R. Glovsky. San Diego: Cognella, 2014.

39 **"The U.S. Weight Loss and Diet Control Market."** Marketdata Enterprises, Inc. (March 9, 2011).

40 **Dee Edington,** *"Countering a Weight Crisis."* HR Magazine. (March 1, 2004).

41 **shrm.org**/hrdisciplines/benefits/articles/pages/wellness-spending-up.aspx.

42 **blogtalkradio.com**/cohealth-checkup/2014/01/29/rands-soeren-mattke-discusses-do-wellness-programs-produce-a-roi.

43 **Emerick and Lewis,** *"Cracking."*

44 **altrum.org.**

45 **leapfrog.org.**

46 **Emerick and Lewis,** *"Cracking."*

47 **ncoa.org**/press-room/fact-sheets/chronic-disease.html#sthash.JQUTSuZF.dpuf.

48 **K.R. Lorig, D.S. Sobel, A.L. Stewart, B.W. Brown, A. Bandura, et. al.** *"Evidence Suggesting That a Chronic Disease Self-Management Program Can Improve Health Status While Reducing Hospitalization: A Randomized Trial."* Medical Care. 37.1 (January 1999). 5-14. http://www.ncbi.nlm.nih.gov/pubmed/10413387; K.R. Lorig, D.S. Sobel, P.L. Ritter, D. Laurent, et al. *"Effect of a Self-management Program on Patients with Chronic Disease."* Effective Clinical Practice. 4.6 (November-December 2001). 256-62. http://www.ncbi.nlm.nih.gov/pubmed/11769298; K.R. Lorig, P. Ritter, A.L. Stewart, D.S. Sobel, et al. *"Chronic Disease Self-management Program: 2-year Health Status and Health Care Utilization Outcomes."* Med Care. 39.11 (November 2001). 1217-1223. ncbi.nlm.nih.gov/pubmed/ 11606875? dopt=Abstract.

49 *Ibid.*

Chapter Fourteen

1 **Peter M. Senge.** *"The Fifth Discipline: The Art and Practice of the Learning Organization."* New York: Doubleday, 2006.

2 **R. Grol.** *"Improving the Quality of Medical Care: Building Bridges among Professional Pride, Payer Profit, and Patient Satisfaction."* JAMA. 286 (2001). 2578-2585. doi:10. 1001/jama.286.20.2578 ; D.C. Leach. *"Evaluation of Competency: An ACGME Perspective."* Accreditation Council for Graduate Medical Education. American Journal of Physical and Medical Rehabilitation. 79 (2000). 487-489. doi:10.1097/00002060-200009000-00020.; P.L. Dyne, R.W. Strauss, and S. Rinnert. *"Systems-based Practice: The Sixth Core Competency."* Academy of Emerging Medicine. 9 (2002). 1270-1277 doi:10.1111/j.1553-2712.2002.tb01587.x.

3 **Senge,** *"Fifth."*

4 *Ibid.*

5 **Charles Duhigg.** *"The Power of Habit: Why We Do What We Do in Life and Business."* New York: Random House, 2012.

6 **Jim Collins.** *"Good to Great: Why Some Companies Make the Leap… and Others Don't."* New York: Harper Collins, 2001.

7 **Senge,** *"Fifth."*

8 **Paul R. Niven.** *"Balanced Scorecard."* 2nd ed. Hoboken, NJ: John Wiley & Sons, 2006.

9 **Margaret J. Wheatley.** *"Leadership and the New Science: Discovering Order in a Chaotic World."* San Francisco: Berrett-Koehler, 1999.

Chapter Fifteen

1 **Joseph Jaworski.** *"Synchronicity: The Inner Path of Leadership."* San Francisco: Berrett-Koehler, 1996.

2 **Bob Herman.** *"Parkland Health to Boost its Minimum Wage, Funded by Exec Bonus Pool."* Modern Healthcare. (June 12, 2014). http://www.modernhealthcare.com/article/20140614/MAGAZINE/306149794.

3 **Richard Pérez Peña.** *"Starbucks to Provide Free College Education to Thousands of Workers."* The New York Times. (June 16, 2014). http://www.nytimes.com/2014/06/16/us/starbucks-to-provide-free-college-education-to-thousands-ofworkers.html?_r=0.

4 **Yvon Chouinard.** *"Let My People Go Surfing: The Education of a Reluctant Businessman."* New York: The Penguin Group, 2006.

5 **https://www.youtube.com**/watch?v=EHS2X-KoN_w

6 **John Mackey and Rajendra Sisodia.** *"Conscious Capitalism Liberating the Heroic Spirit of Business."* Boston: Harvard Business Review Press, 2014.

7 *Ibid.*

8 **National Institutes of Health.** *"Annals of Internal Medicine."* (1992). http://consensus.nih.gov/1992/1992WeightLossta010html.htm

9 **National Business Group on Health.** http://www.shrm.org/hrdisciplines/benefits/articles/pages/wellness-spending-up.aspx

10 **J. Robison, K. Putnam, and L. McKibbin.** *"Health at Every Size: A Compassionate, Effective Approach for Helping Individuals With Weight-Related Concerns—Part II."* AAOHN Journal. 55.5 (2007). 185-192.

11 **Frances Berg.** *"Women Afraid to Eat: Breaking Free in Today's Weight-Obsessed World."* Hettinger, ND: Healthy Weight Network, 2001.

12 **Rebecca M. Puhl and Chelsea A. Heuer.** *"The Stigma of Obesity: A Review and Update."* New Haven: Nature Publishing Group, 2009. http://www.yaleruddcenter.org/resources/upload/docs/what/bias/weightbiasstudy.pdf

13 **Dharini M. Bhammar and Glenn A. Gaesser.** *"Health Risks Associated with Weight Cycling."* in *"Wellness not Weight: Health at Every Size and Emotional Interviewing."* Ed. Ellen R. Glovsky. San Diego, CA: Cognella, 2014.

14 **Linda Bacon, Judith S. Stern, Marta D. Van Loan, and Nancy L. Keim.** *"Size Acceptance and Intuitive Eating Improve Health for Obese, Female Chronic Dieters."* Journal of the American Dietetics Association. 105 (2005). 929-936.; Julie T. Schaefer and Amy B. Magnuson. *"A Review of Interventions that Promote Eating by Internal Cues."* Journal of the Academy of Nutrition and Dietetics. 114 (2014). 734-760.

15 **Jon Robison.** *"Weight, Health & Culture: Exposing the Myths, Exploring the Realities."* in *"Wellness not Weight: Health at Every Size and Motivational Interviewing."* Ed. Ellen R. Glovsky. San Diego, CA: Cognella, 2014.

16 **W.C. Goodman.** *"The Invisible Woman, Confronting Weight Prejudice in America."* Carlsbad, CA: Gurze, 1995.

17 **S. Solovay.** *"Tipping the Scales of Justice: Fighting Weight-Based Discrimination."* New York: Prometheus, 2008.

18 **R.M. Puhl,** *"Perceptions of Weight Discrimination."* International Journal of Obesity. 32 (2008). 992-1000.

19 **T. Moore.** *"Care of the Soul: A Guide for Cultivating Depth and Sacredness in Everyday Life."* New York: Harper-Perennial, 1994.

20 **Glenn Gaesser.** *"Fatness, Fitness & Health: A Closer Look at the Evidence."* WELCOA. Absolute Advantage, 2006. ; S. Blair, P. McAuley. "Obesity Paradoxes." Journal of Sports Sciences. 29.8 (2001). 773-782.

21 **P. Lyons.** *"Weight and Health: A New Approach for the New Year."* Wellness Management: Newsletter of the National Wellness Association. 11.4 (1995). 5-7.

22 **A.E. Field, S.B. Austin, C.B. Taylor, and S. Malspeis.** *"Relation Between Dieting and Weight Change among Preadolescents and Adolescents."* Pediatrics. 112 (2003). 900-906.; D. Neumark-Sztainer, M. Wall, J. Guo, M. Story, et. al. *"Obesity, Disordered Eating and Eating Disorders in a Longitudinal Study of Adolescents."* Journal of the American Dietetic Association. 106 (2006). 559-568

23 **J.R. Hirschmann and C.H. Munter.** *"When Women Stop Hating Their Bodies: Freeing Yourself From Food and Weight Obsession."* 1st edn. New York: Fawcett Columbine, 1995.; J. Matz and E. Frankel. *"Beyond a Shadow of a Diet: The Comprehensive Guide to Treating Binge Eating Disorder, Compulsive Eating, and Emotional Overeating."* New York: Routledge, 2014.; E. Satter. *"Secrets of Feeding a Healthy Family: How to Eat, How to Raise Good Eaters and How to Cook."* Madison, WI: Kelcy Press, 2008.; E. Tribole and E. Resch. *"Intuitive Eating: A Revolutionary Program That Works."* 2nd edn. New York: St. Martin's Griffin, 2010.

24 **Schaefer and Magnuson,** *"Interventions."*

25 **D. Burgard and P. Lyons.** *"Alternatives in Obesity Treatment: Focusing on Health for Fat Women."* in Feminist Perspectives on Eating Disorders. Eds. P. Fallon, M. Katzman, and S. Wooley. New York: Guilford, 1994.

26 **Linda Bacon and Lucy Aphramor.** *"Weight Science: Evaluating the Evidence for a Paradigm Shift."* Nutrition Journal. 10.9 (2011).

27 **Robison, et. al.,** *"Health."*; Bacon, et. al., *"Size Acceptance."*

28 **Robison, et. al.,** *"Health."*

Chapter Sixteen

1 **John R. Childress and Larry E. Senn.** *"In the Eye of the Storm."* Los Angeles: Leadership Press, 1995.

2 **Ellen Van Velsor.** *"Learning New Ways: A Conversation with Ronald A. Heifetz."* LIA. 23.1 (March/April 2003). 19-22.

Acknowledgments

We want to honor the many, many friends and colleagues who have been so supportive of our challenging the status quo over the years and who enthusiastically encouraged us to lay out those challenges and create the blueprint for change that resulted in the creation of this book.

We also want to thank all of our clients for letting us tell their stories *(even though we changed many of their names to protect confidentiality)*. We hope that eventually more of them will let their identities be known; to inspire others to learn from their journeys.

The entire team at our publishing company, IHAC, Inc., has been amazing throughout this process. We are extremely grateful to them for turning this book idea into a reality. From the very beginning the team has had only one answer to all of our requests *(most of which have initially gone through senior vice president Wendy Haan)*: "We are on it and will make it happen." What a pleasure! And we especially want to give a huge, warm shout-out to Shawn Connors, president, for believing in us and in the cause, and for being willing to challenge the status quo and bump heads with the health promotion and business establishments right along with us.

Additionally, we want to acknowledge those who have gone before us for their persistence in challenging the *stuckness* we describe in the first section of this book through their own work — for not being satisfied with "business as usual" — especially when it isn't working. In particular, we want to recognize:

- *Organizational Wellbeing* — Peter Senge, Margaret Wheatley, Edgar Schein, Patrick Lencioni, Charles Jacobs, The Arbinger Institute, Mihaly Csikszentmihalyi, Tom Rath and Jim Harter. They have revolutionized how we look at business and firmly established the importance of culture, ongoing learning and leadership development, and how the complexities of humanity inform the way we frame the employee experience.

- *Employee Wellbeing* — Wendy Lynch, Al Lewis, Vik Khanna and Tom Emerick. Their work has awakened many people in both business and the health professions to the pitfalls and dangers of current approaches to workplace wellbeing. They are exceptionally bright and caring folks who want to see wellbeing done FOR and WITH, not TO employees.

- *Rethinking Change* — Edward Deci, Daniel Pink, Alfie Kohn, C. Otto Scharmer, Robert Kegan, and Christina Marshall. Their work has exposed outdated paradigms regarding human behavior and change and provided us with a rich perspective for how to better support people's desire to thrive.

These pioneers *(and many others we certainly missed here)* have been pivotal in helping pave the way for us to provide this fusion of organizational and employee wellbeing and create *The 7 Points of Transformation*.

We also want to acknowledge current business leaders who are essentially defying the conventional wisdom regarding what it means to run a successful organization by demonstrating the profound benefits of caring for more than just profits. We highlighted many of them in this book, and we hope there are many more out there like Tony Hsieh, John Mackey, Yvon Chouinard, and Howard Schultz.

Translating decades of consulting, speaking and teaching content to a book was no small task and required a great deal of patience from our families and friends when we were absent and chained to our computers for so many months. To Dave, Jerilyn, Peyton and Joshua — we thank you for your understanding, love and support!

Finally, we want to acknowledge each other. We have been on parallel paths challenging the status quo for decades, passionate about making a difference for workplace culture and employee wellbeing. It has been invigorating and an absolute joy for us to create this unique work together. As one enlightened leader put it, he wants his employees to view their time at work not as a job or even a career, but as a calling. This book, from beginning to end, has for us felt like a calling — a labor of love. We sincerely hope you feel the same way about it and that it makes it easier for you to facilitate moving organizational and employee wellbeing more quickly and effectively into the 21st century.

Sincerely, Rosie and Jon

Index

4P (pry, poke, prod, punish), xv, 254, 264

7 Points of Transformation. *See* transformation

A

adaptive change. *See* leadership

Adaptive Solution Dynamic, 234–235. *See also* behavior change

Affordable Care Act as related to incentives, ix, 91, 96; health-contingent and participatory wellness programs, 246–248; Safeway, ix, 248–252; wellness provisions, 245–248

Ames, city of, 299–300

annual planning, 166–169

B

back pain, back claims, 71, 142–143

Bacon, Sir Francis, 14, 15

Baicker, Katherine, on ROI, 253–254

Balanced Scorecard, 274; Wellness Dashboard, 274

Barker, Joel, on paradigms, 2

behavior change, 33; Adaptive Solution Dynamic, 234–235; carrots and sticks, 90–91; health coaching, 239–241; Intentional Change Theory, 230–231; Motivational Interviewing (MI), 238–241; prescensing, 232–234; Theory U, 231–234; Transtheoretical Model of Behavior Change, 228–230, 239. *See also* change; motivation; Motivational Interviewing (MI)

behavior modification. *See* behavior change

Bersin, Josh, on engagement, 136

biomedical model, biomedicine, 65–66, 87, 145–146. *See also* mechanistic model

biometric screening, 145, 165, 256–258

bosses. *See* leadership

brain, electrical and chemical, 69–70; neuroscience and motivation, 101–103

Buchanan, David R., on autonomy, 243–244

Burd, Steven, Safeway, 249

burnout. *See* stress

Butterfly Effect, 30

Byrum, C. Stephen, on Taylorism, 38, 43–44

C

Cameron, Kim and Robert Quinn, on organizational culture, 130

Capra, Fritjof, 9, 10, 19, 24

carrots and sticks. *See* motivation

Cartesian. *See* Descartes

Cashman, Kevin, on leadership, 177

Centers for Disease Control and Prevention (CDC), Total Worker Health, ii

Certified Intrinsic Coach. *See* Intrinsic Coaching

change, rethinking, 225–244; Adaptive Solution Dynamic, 234–235; Intentional Change Theory (ICT), 230–231; models, 228–235; Transtheoretical Model of Behavior Change (TTM), 228–230; Theory U, 231–234. *See also* behavior change

chaos theory, x, 30–35, 74

Chopra, Deepak, 70–71

Chouinard, Yvon, Patagonia, 283–284

Chronic Disease Self-Management Program (CDSMP), 266–267

claims data, 140–143

Collins, Jim, on change, 273

communication, 208–212, 278–279; annual plan, 217; branding, 218–221; leaders' guide, 221–222; MSU Syndrome, 210; strategy, 215–218

Company-Sponsored Centers of Excellence (CSCOE), 265

complementarity, 22–23

Conscious Capitalism, 284

Consumer Assessment of Healthcare Providers and Systems, 138

Continuous Quality Improvement (CQI), 271–279; Balanced Scorecard, 274; Wellness Dashboard, 274

Coordinated Care Model, 266

core values, 154–156, 166, 201; example of alignment, 156–158; Permission-to-Play, 155

Coronary Pooling Project, 66–68

corporate culture, vi; blueprint for transforming, 151–171; Continuous Quality Improvement, 271–279; inside out approach, 118–119, 177; supportive climate, 201–223; Thriving Workplace Culture Survey (TWCS), 130–150; transformation, 118–119; workplace culture, 116–119; Zappos Culture Book, 147–148

Health At Every Size. *See* Health for Every Body

health coaching, 238–241

Health for Every Body, 263, 290–298

Health Risk Assessments (HRA), 12, 145, 165; alternative use for, 256–258

healthcare consumerism, 257–259

healthy work culture. *See* corporate culture

heart disease, 66-68; Ornish, Dean, 94

Heifetz, Ronald, on leadership, 174

Hsieh, Tony, 116, 123, 147–148, 201. *See also* Zappos

Huffington, Ariana, 39–40, 47

I

iatrogenesis, related to wellness programs, 254–264

Illich, Ivan, definition of health, 82

incentives, 91, 241–243, 248–249; alternatives to, 263–264; hospital weight loss campaign, 96–97. *See also* behavior change; motivation

Indianapolis Colts, 272

Institute of Noetic Sciences, 2

Intentional Change Theory, 230–231

Intrinsic Coaching, 181–184, 191, 195–198; in practice, 225–226, 287, 299

intrinsic motivation, ix, 93, 95–111; coaching, 181–184; power of intrinsic thinking, 109–110. *See also* extrinsic motivation; motivation

J

Jacobs, Charles, brain rewards, 103; culture change, 99, 159–161; management and performance evaluation, 236–237

Jaworski, Joseph, on leadership, 177, 180

Jones Corp., case study, 58–60

K

Kegan, Robert and Lisa Laskow Lahey, employee development, 206; Deliberately Developmental Organization (DDO), 207–208

Kelly, Matthew, on employee personal development, 205–206

Kim, W. Chan and Renee Mauborgne, on strategic planning, 154

Kuhn, T.S., on paradigms, 4, 7–8

L

M

MSU Syndrome, 210

N

National Business Group on Health, 290

National Health Observances, 216. *See also* communication

National Institute for Occupational Safety and Health (NIOSH), Total Worker Health, ii

new science, 19–25; in action 281–302; summary of key components, 35. *See also* paradigms; physics; quantum physics

Newtonian thinking, 26, 32

Niven, Paul, on performance measures, 125–126

Non-locality, 27–28

O

organic worldview, 10

organizational culture, 50–53; and heath, 53; measuring, 130–150; supportive climate, 201–223; survey considerations, 129–137; workplace culture surveys, 130–150. *See also* corporate culture

Organizational Culture Assessment Instrument (OCAI), 130

organizational development, vi

Organizational Performance Study, 180–181

organizational wellbeing, viii, 37–61, 235–237; applying new science, 41–42; Continuous Quality Improvement, 271–279; crisis of capacity, 43–44; data, use of, 128–150, 274–279; evaluation worksheets, 275–276; fusing with employee wellbeing, 306–308; Jones Corp., case study, 58–60; measuring happiness, 136–137; programs, evidence-based, 245–269; summary of data to collect, 150; summary of paradigm shift, 61; thriving, definition, 54–55, 128. *See also* employee engagement; employee wellbeing; stuckness; Thriving Organizational Wellbeing

Ornish, Dean, on behavior change, 94. *See also* heart disease

P

paradigms, 8, 17, 303–308; belief vs. evidence, 1–8; new paradigm in action, 111, 281–302; old paradigm of sickness and disease, 64–65, 87, 282; paradigm pioneer, 7–8; summary, shift in employee wellbeing, 85

Pasteur, Louis, on germ theory, 65

Patagonia, 283–284

patriarchy, 14–17, 38–40

Six Sigma, 12

size acceptance. *See* Health for Every Body; weight loss/management programs

Skinner, B.F., 33, 230, 240; behavior modification, 91–95

stages of change model. *See* behavior change; Transtheoretical Model of Behavior Change

Starbucks, 282–283

Status Syndrome, 78

strategic planning, 151–171, 303–308; burning platform, 169–171, 304; long-term, 158–161; whom to include, 153

stress, measuring on surveys, 139-150. *See also* employee wellbeing; psychoneuroimmunology

stuckness, 2, 32, 37–61, 233–234; and employee wellbeing, 63–85; definition, iii, viii; getting people to change, 87–111; in mechanistic universe, 9–17

supportive climate, 201–223. *See also* culture change

surveys, considerations in doing, 131–134; workplace culture, 130–150

systemic thinking. *See* extrinsic motivation; Intrinsic Coaching; intrinsic motivation

T

Taylor, Frederick W. (Taylorism), 37–38, 91, 237. *See also* incentives

terms, outdated, 120–121

Theory U, 231–234. *See also* behavior change

Thriving Organizational Wellbeing, conception of, 128; definition, vii–viii; evaluation, 277–279. *See also* organizational wellbeing

Thriving Workplace Culture Survey (TWCS), 130–150, 285, 287

tomato effect, 6

Towers Watson, Global Workforce Study, ii, 51–52; Staying @ Work Report 2013, 248

transformation, 7 points of, blueprint for transforming workplace culture, 151–171; Continuous Quality Improvement, xvi; create a supportive climate, xiv; data collection and analysis, xii; deploy quality, evidence-based programs and resources, xv; develop quality leaders, xiii, 173–199; in action, 281–302; outline, xiii–xvi; overview, 115–123; rethink change, xiv; strategic and annual planning, xii (*See also* annual planning; strategic planning); summaries of transformation points, 150; summary of Continuous Quality Improvement, 279; summary on creating a supportive climate, 223; summary for developing quality leaders, 199; summary of evidence-based programs and resources, 269; summary of rethinking change, 244; summary of strategic and annual planning, 171

About the Authors

Recognizing a gap, Rosie and Jon formed Salveo Partners, LLC to help organizations build thriving workplace cultures through a fusion of organizational development and employee wellbeing. To learn more about Rosie, Jon and Salveo Partners, please visit: **salveopartners.com**.

Rosie Ward, PhD, MPH, MCHES, BCC, CIC®

Rosie Ward is an accomplished speaker, writer, coach and consultant. She has spent more than 20 years in worksite health promotion and organizational development, blending the disciplines to work with executive and leadership teams to enhance effectiveness by shifting thinking patterns. She uses her extensive knowledge to help organizations develop and implement strategies to create a thriving workplace culture that values and supports wellbeing and the unique, intrinsic needs of employees.

Rosie has degrees in kinesiology, public health and a PhD in Organization and Management where her research focused on organizational culture, intrinsic motivation and coaching. She is regularly interviewed for business publications and is a contributing author to the book "Organization Development in Healthcare: High Impact Practices for a Complex and Changing Environment."

Additionally, Rosie is a Board-Certified Coach, a Certified Intrinsic Coach® and a Certified Intrinsic Coach® Mentor, leading the Intrinsic Coach® Development Series; she leverages this coaching methodology as a cornerstone for leadership development with her clients and for developing providers in clinics and hospitals to improve patient experience and outcomes.

Rosie lives in the Minneapolis area with her husband and their son.

Jon Robison, PhD, MS, MA

Jon Robison is an accomplished speaker, teacher, writer and consultant. He advocates shifting health promotion away from its traditional, biomedical, control-oriented focus; with a particular interest in why people do what they do and don't do what they don't do.

Along with numerous scientific articles and book chapters, Jon is co-author of "The Spirit and Science of Holistic Health, More than Broccoli, Jogging & Bottled Water, More than Yoga Herbs & Meditation," a textbook for students and a guidebook for practitioners who wish to incorporate holistic principles and approaches into their work. This work formed the foundation for Kailo, one of the first truly holistic employee wellness programs. Kailo earned prestigious awards in both Canada and the United States, and the creators lovingly claim Jon as its father.

Jon has also been a national leader in the Health At Every Size® movement for almost two decades and served as co-editor of the journal "Health At Every Size.™" He is one of the featured health professionals in the powerful Documentary "America the Beautiful II — The Thin Commandments."

Jon lives in Michigan with his wife, their son, two cats and Lady, their 7-pound watch dog.